TRAINING RESEARCH
CONSULTANTS
A Guide for Academic Libraries

For Mom

EDITED BY
JENNIFER TORREANO AND
MARY O'KELLY

Mary O'Kelly

Association of College and Research Libraries
A division of the American Library Association

Chicago, Illinois 2021

TABLE OF CONTENTS

PART I: INTRODUCTION TO THEORY AND PRACTICE

PART II: LIBRARY CASE STUDIES

273   Case Study 12. Peer Research Consultants at the University of Minnesota-Twin Cities: Student-Driven Success
Kate Peterson, Jody Gray, & Andrew Palahniuk

299   Case Study 13. Research Mentor Program at UNH Manchester: Peer Learning Partnerships
Carolyn White Gamtso, Annie Donahue, & Kimberly Donovan

321   Case Study 14. On Not Reinventing the Wheel: Borrowing from the Writing Center Peer Consultant Model
Kate Hinnant & Jill Markgraf

PART III: PERSPECTIVES FROM CAMPUS COLLABORATORS

337   Collaborators 1. Nothing is Permanent Except Change: The Adaptive Writing Center Training Model
Patrick Johnson & Melanie Rabine

PART IV: PERSPECTIVES FROM THE CONSULTANTS

ACKNOWLEDGEMENTS

First, the editors would like to thank our families for their support and endless confidence in us. We wish to specifically thank each of the chapter contributors for sharing their professional expertise with all of us and staying with such a long, complex, and important project. We also deeply appreciate ACRL's long-running commitment to our vision; without their encouragement and enthusiasm—particularly from Erin Nevius and Kathryn Deiss—this project would not have been possible. Finally, we both are privileged to enjoy working with immensely collegial and smart colleagues who have cheered us on from the very beginning, offering insightful advice and patient listening. We appreciate all of it and dedicate this to them, a nation-wide network of supportive and dedicated colleagues, representing the best in collaborative library creativity.

INTRODUCTION

Jennifer Torreano

Hello, readers! I am so glad you picked up this book filled with case studies, theories, and reflections from colleagues across the country. The insights shared by contributing authors have sparked new ideas and enriched my own thinking, and I am sure the book will do the same for you. Each chapter contains valuable perspectives from program managers, campus partners, or research consultants themselves. This book represents a community of colleagues who are immersed in the world of research consultants.

For me, this community has been transformative. I have worked with research consultants at Grand Valley State University for the last nine years, and my work never fit squarely in any scholarly communities. Finding wisdom and inspiration from library services, writing centers, communication centers, and student affairs has been gratifying and expanded my understanding of my work tremendously. However, I have always longed for a conversation that is directly applicable to what I think about every day: research consultants. As research consultant programs become more common in academic libraries, I am delighted to find myself in the company of the authors of this book, a community of practitioners and scholars who believe in the value of peer learning in research conversations.

HOW I SEE RESEARCH CONSULTANTS AND THEIR TRAINING

Research consultants build exploratory environments for students, encouraging creativity and the testing of new ideas. Consultants do this by demonstrating empathy for the challenge of developing a new skill, framing exploration as a part of learning, and encouraging bravery. These courageous conversations remind students that they are capable of success, no matter how challenging the tasks.

I believe that training for research consultants should use the same framework. For research consultants to be effective, they need to believe that they are *capable* of being effective. Working with students is a challenging task, and the quality of each consultation is affected by the consultants' self-efficacy. We want our research consultants to be calm and nimble during consultations, trying new methods when faced with obstacles and sometimes rethinking their whole strategy, all without getting flustered. Consultants need to be able to show students that researching is rarely a linear process and challenges are to be expected. By focusing training on building the consultants' self-efficacy—their belief in their own abilities[1]—we give them the resilience they need to support students and model successful approaches to learning. Building research consultants' self-efficacy is a central goal of training at Grand Valley State University.

MY CONTEXT AND APPROACH TO TRAINING

The training program that Mary O'Kelly and I designed together at GVSU takes a multi-pronged approach to research consultant training, using orientation, training sessions, mentor groups, peer observations, and supervisor evaluations to encourage consultants' growth and learning. Each component of training is designed to address the four sources of self-efficacy described by Albert Bandura:[2]

1. Mastery experiences—training must be challenging, yet ultimately successful for each consultant.
2. Vicarious experiences—watching their peers succeed increases consultants' belief in their own capabilities.
3. Social persuasion—build in positive feedback after moments of success.
4. Interpretation of stress—frame adrenaline as increased energy that improves consultant performance.

We designed the research consultant training program to be a rigorous growth experience with support built in to every component. We build consultant confidence by including experienced consultants to model success, create a supportive community, and provide feedback during the critical phases of training. This method fosters self-efficacy before new consultants begin their work with students and as they experience inevitable challenges and victories along the way.

TRAINING COMPONENTS AT GVSU
Orientation

An intensive two-day orientation before the semester starts provides an opportunity to teach the basics of both research and consulting work, and to address self-efficacy before it begins to influence the work of research consultants. Beginning the semester with training in a cooperative learning environment creates a social support network among the consultants so they can build positive efficacy beliefs together. We group consultants together to work on tasks such as brainstorming research topics and finding sources to promote collaborative learning. Orientation is carefully designed to ensure individual successes for all research consultants.

Bandura offers suggestions to reduce anxiety[3] that we use during orientation. Though his suggestions are for therapists working with people harboring more extreme fears, the methods are applicable to new consultants who are nervous about working with students. We start with short pieces of consultations, building to a full consultation over time. People avoid extended stress but will endure it for short episodes, so allowing consultants to gain mastery over one part before moving onto the next keeps them from becoming overwhelmed or overly anxious.[4] We use this method:

1. Model a research consultation with experienced consultants.
2. Break down the structure of a consultation into a series of manageable steps.
3. Ask new consultants to practice with more experienced consultants.

Beginning by modeling a consultation allows consultants to vicariously experience a research consultation for the first time. It is a low-pressure introduction to the structure of a consultation, and research consultants have the opportunity to see what success looks like. Highlighting that experienced consultants were recently new consultants at their own orientations emphasizes the similarities between the models and the observers, encouraging consultants to imagine their own future successes.

Breaking down the individual steps of a consultation gives new consultants time to become comfortable with each piece before practicing with more experienced consultants. Preparing new consultants for how they might feel during the consultation, along with strategies to push through the anxiety, frames their interpretation of the physiological stress response and reassures them that such a response is normal. This helps consultants to see adrenaline as an energizing response that sharpens focus instead of a sign of incompetence or inadequacy.

All new and experienced consultants are paired to practice what they've learned. With each successful mock consultation, new consultants build self-efficacy. Honest but supportive conversations continue throughout the academic year in a variety of formats, including mentor groups.

Mentor Groups

Mentor group meetings provide an ongoing opportunity for research consultants to build workplace social support in an environment free from evaluation. In mentor groups, a number of consultants meet to discuss their work—successes, failures, questions—with no supervisor present. Facilitated by an experienced consultant, mentor meetings are dedicated times for consultants to learn from each other and build supportive relationships.

Mirroring the peer learning that happens in a research consultation, mentor meetings function as a safe space for consultants to share stories, building self-efficacy through vicarious experiences and social persuasion. Consultants discuss missteps and strategies to prevent them in future consultations, recognizing that others experience similar struggles. These conversations also build confidence by giving consultants the opportunity to provide feedback to their colleagues. Mentor group meetings work well with an agenda that dedicates a portion of the time for conversations about recent consultations and the rest dedicated to professional development that supports different needs throughout the semester. For example, a mentor meeting close to final exams focuses on working with stressed-out students, while the first mentor meeting of the fall semester is a reflection on their first real consultations with strangers. Mentor group meeting topics are often timed to coincide with specific training sessions, as well.

Training Sessions

Training sessions throughout the academic year provide ongoing support and professional development for research consultants. Training is an opportunity to model strategies for researching difficult topics and, when taught by liaison librarians, sessions can reassure consultants that even experienced professionals stumble or don't know where to start sometimes. These stories help consultants understand that their apprehension is a common experience and not a reflection of their own capabilities. Consultants will inevitably feel some anxiety when presented with new material, and training sessions provide a structured forum for overcoming heightened stress and ultimately succeeding.

Peer Observations

After new consultants have been working with students for a few weeks, peer observations provide an opportunity to receive feedback and learn new strategies from each other. This training method is most effective when each consultant observes and is observed by another consultant during real research consultations. Being on both sides of the observation may expose consultants to strategies they have never used before while also ensuring they receive feedback on their own work. Watching other consultants successfully use new strategies promotes self-efficacy through vicarious experience.

While being observed by peers can be scary for new consultants, confronting their anxiety head-on and receiving encouragement supports self-efficacy. New consultants are inevitably much better at their jobs than they believe, and the dread they feel has proved to be unfounded every time we have done peer observations at Grand Valley. Every observation has included significant positive feedback in addition to suggestions for improvement. When being observed, new consultants are persuaded that they have potential to be or are already good consultants. This feeling of success fosters self-efficacy.[5]

Consultant Evaluations

During consultant evaluations, I emphasize that consulting is a skill that can be improved, not an innate ability. Focusing on what consultants are doing well and strategies they could use to improve performance is more helpful for consultants when they are reminded that suggestions are not a reflection of their capabilities.

Evaluation meetings are also a good time for consultants to create goals for themselves. There is significant evidence that motivation can be increased by setting clear, challenging goals.[6] I focus on helping consultants imagine realistic goals that promote growth while also providing support to achieve the goals through additional training. Parts of the training program—mentor groups and training sessions—are adjusted as the semester goes on to be responsive to consultant needs. Social persuasion is a source of self-efficacy, and supervisor encouragement during goal setting can help consultants believe they are capable of achieving the goals they set.

TRAINING DESIGN DEPENDS ON CONTEXT

The research consultant program at GVSU emphasizes building consultant confidence, and that is a reflection of my professional philosophy and our institutional culture. Other consultant programs lean on different theories and institutional needs, and their programs look very different. Every case study described in this book represents a program designed to best serve the needs of students at that particular institution. The variety of approaches is a testament to the creativity and student focus of each contributor.

HOW TO USE THIS BOOK

This book is designed as a collection of perspectives and training materials that you can adapt for your own context. The book is organized in four parts:

1. Introduction to theory and practice
2. Library case studies
3. Perspectives from campus partners
4. Consultant perspectives

The theory section is made up of two chapters, the first focusing on using learning theories and the second describing the role of research consultants in encouraging student intellectual development. The next two sections—library case studies and perspectives from campus partners—make up most of the book. Each of these chapters includes information about program administration, hiring practices, training, and assessment. Perhaps most importantly, nearly all of these chapters include training materials as appendices. Creative Commons licenses are noted for each chapter so you can easily see how to use and modify materials for your own institutions. Finally, the book ends with two reflections from research consultants, reminding us of the impact of these programs on the consultants themselves.

Your library's culture, structure, and student body will impact what works for you and your institutions. I encourage you to use this book as a source of inspiration, adapting ideas and training materials to best serve your own students. Peruse, gather ideas, and join this wonderful community.

Jennifer Torreano
Knowledge Market Manager, Grand Valley State University Libraries

NOTES
1. Albert Bandura, *Self-Efficacy: The Exercise of Control* (New York: W. H. Freeman and Co., 1997).
2. Albert Bandura, "Self-Efficacy," in *Encyclopedia of Human Behavior Vol. 4*, ed. V. S. Ramachaudran (New York: Academic Press, 1994).
3. Bandura, "Self-Efficacy," in *Encyclopedia of Human Behavior.*
4. Ibid.
5. Ibid.
6. Ibid.

BIBLIOGRAPHY
Bandura, Albert. "Self-Efficacy." In *Encyclopedia of Human Behavior Vol. 4*, edited by V. S. Ramachaudran, 71–81. New York: Academic Press, 1994.
———. *Self-Efficacy: The Exercise of Control.* New York: W. H. Freeman and Co., 1997.

Part I

INTRODUCTION TO THEORY AND PRACTICE

Chapter 1

THE LIBRARY:
A New Project-Based Learning Classroom

Amy Benton

OVERVIEW

> *The whole is greater than the sum of its parts.*
>
> — Aristotle

Informal learning and peer learning occur in higher education more often than faculty might realize. When working with adult learners, the approach to teaching and training may vary slightly from a classroom that is facilitated by direct instruction. However, being mindful of different approaches and incorporating sound learning theories into peer learning can result in a very successful outcome for both the instructors as well as the learners. Learning theory can be described as the context in which many feel that learning occurs, such as behaviorism, constructivism, multiple intelligences, and transformative learning. Although these constructs remain the same regardless of the age group, the approach to adult learners is slightly different when it comes to instruction and training. This chapter discusses the best practices of using learning theory with adult learners as well as the implications for working with these learners.

As a new generation begins to enroll on campus, the style of students also changes.[1] This group of students has a short attention span, needs stimulation, and has a tendency to hide behind technology. This becomes an issue when instructors continue to teach in a traditional format such as direct instruction. To meet this challenge, instructors are trying to create learning environments in which students drive the process rather than the instructors. Peer-to-peer teaching provides this specific opportunity. Research[2,3] has shown that students who work in groups to solve problems or who simply work with their peers on a project are more likely to reach a sophisticated outcome than a student working alone.

TRAINING
Learning Theory

How is learning defined in the library? How does the librarian define it? According to Pritchard,[4] learning is the process in which an individual gains additional knowledge. It is important to acknowledge that there are many theoretical perspectives on learning theory. These include behaviorism, constructivism, cognitivism, humanism, social-cognitive and social-learning theory, as well as brain-based learning. In short, behaviorism is driven by rewards and gratification and by what is "seen" happening. Constructivism is focused more on the premise that individuals construct their own knowledge and, as we learn, what is already known influences what is to be learned. Social learning theories tend to focus on the environment and how individuals might learn from watching others. Brain-based learning focuses on the premise that individuals are only able to learn once their brains are equipped to handle the information. Each of these theories tends to operate on the premise that knowledge is something that is acquired when given from one individual to another—for example, a teacher to a student. As these many philosophical influences unfolded, educators and mentors had to take into consideration learning styles. Learning styles suggest that the way information is presented to any individual can impact the ability for the learner to grasp the information. The styles that are often considered are visual, auditory, and tactile, or multiple intelligences that were established by Gardner.[5] The intelligence that we are most associated with will come into play in how we might approach problems and understand the new ideas that are being introduced. As individuals mature and complete a K-12 education, oftentimes they are able to identify exactly what type of learners they are. This is a concept that many adult learners already have the capability of understanding.

ADULT LEARNERS
Theory

Given that the demographic of the first-year student is changing and transfer students come to institutions with a variety of skills, libraries need to position themselves within the institution as a valuable partner. One way to do this is to show how the instructional capability of libraries aligns nicely with that of faculty expectations as well as student needs. Rather than simply being a service that is on-hand for students, libraries can become an important ally in helping students with their research and assisting faculty in student success. In one aspect, the library is considered a resource for finding information, perhaps where a book might lie, or even assisting with media files. However, when it comes to conducting research, oftentimes learners go to the faculty as a resource for conducting research rather than simply reaching out to the individuals who work within the library. It is important to recognize that as individuals become older, the ways they learn and process information is different from the traditional PK-12 environment. This delivery of instruction to adults is called andragogy. There are four principles that need to be considered when working with adults.[6] Adult learners tend to be self-directed and resist having information imposed upon them; they have life experience, and this helps the foundation of who they are and what they already know; they are present and ready to learn and would like to be actively engaged; last, they tend to be task-motivated.[7] This indicates that these learners desire more cooperation between their peers as well as their instructors.

Learning Behaviors of Adult Learners

When assigned a task, adult learners seek information first by consulting with faculty.[8] The next place adult students go to find information is the internet. Although the internet has been a key component of conducting research, Martin[9] noted that it is replacing information provided by libraries for common assignments such as literature reviews and for ready reference. Bypassing the tools available in the library and reference services can prove detrimental to the student who does not have the ability to distinguish between reliable and unreliable information.[10] When adult learners were asked about their use of the library and how they may have utilized library services, Maughan[11] found that more than half did not have substantive knowledge about the library services, resources, and instruction.

PEER-TO-PEER LEARNING

As noted by Boud,[12] peer learning encompasses a variety of activities. These activities range from a mentor/mentee model or problem/project-based learning to a simple buddy system. The key to this style of learning is that it is reciprocal; rather than the one-way communication model of direct instruction, it is a two-way interaction that involves the sharing of knowledge, ideas, and experiences.

The figure below models closely to the constructivist theory that is commonly discussed in PK-12 education, one in which the learning is done collectively by sharing what each individual already knows. Peer learning often happens outside the classroom, but the students themselves may not be aware it's happening. Without effective implementation, this experience could potentially become confusing for the students. Without any type of instructor present to resolve any misconceptions that are created, the newly acquired knowledge would be incorrect.

Figure 1.1. Direct instruction and peer-to-peer interaction and learning

One speaking, many listening   **Many speaking, many listening**

Table 1 displays a side-by-side comparison of traditional direct instruction to a potential peer-to-peer instruction model.

Table 1.1. Comparison model		
	Learning Teaching Sample 1	**Learning Teaching Sample 2**
Learning Modes	Passive, Individual	Active, Social, Collaborative
Content Organization	Hierarchy, Top Down	Heterarchy, Bottom Up
Content Experts	Instructor	Peers
Theory	Behaviorism	Constructivism

HOW DOES PEER-TO-PEER TEACHING WORK?

While peer-to-peer teaching isn't new, it is important to recognize that it is different from peer interaction loosely based on conversation. Peer-to-peer teaching is when one student instructs another and one is an expert and one is a beginner. These peer-to-peer interactions can be invaluable because they allow students to share collective knowledge. Below is one example that might be utilized in a library context and fulfills not only the peer-to-peer interaction but also addresses pedagogical and andragogical learning theories. Table 2 displays how students retain information, and the proportions address how peer-to-peer interactions are more beneficial to the student than direct instruction alone. These interactions provide active learning and reinforce knowledge that already exists.

Table 1.2. Proportions of what learners remember and retain from delivery style
90% of what we say and do (teaching others)
70% of what we say (participation in a discussion or present)
50% of what we see and hear (discussions, demonstrations, movies)
30% of what we see (looking at pictures)
20% of what we hear (listening)
10% of what we read (reading)

As this table presents, one model of learning suggests that more learning happens when students practice and teach than when they passively sit and listen to a lecture or read. If we combine this model with best practices in andragogy, training might look more like this: (1) use changing contexts; (2) peers provide feedback; and (3) learning is nonlinear and distributed across many participants to help discover new information or potentially solve the problem. For example, trainees learning how to evaluate a source for credibility might present their own findings and information and wait for feedback from others, both verbally and visually. When this type of academic discourse and discussion occurs, the learners are better able to retain information and apply at a later date.

Working in the library as a student is the one place where self-directed learning or informal learning seems paramount to direct learning or more formal instruction. When libraries and adult learners converge, this environment provides an exemplar for peer-to-peer teaching to occur. If librarians and trainers can understand learning theory and andragogy, a transformative learning process can be created for student success.

ASSESSMENT

In the problem-solving heuristics suggested by Minsky,[13] an independent adult student might go through the process below on their own prior to ever entering a peer-to-peer teaching experience. At the point they have reached the final decision, their frustration and anxiety might be quite high. This frustration might be alleviated had peer-to-peer teaching been in place prior to taking an independent path.

- If a problem is similar to one you've encountered in the past, apply what happened before and adjust accordingly.
- If a problem still presents a challenge, divide and conquer. It may be easier to solve tackling one part at a time.

- If you've not encountered this type of problem before, adjust how you are thinking about it. Try to describe it in a different way.
- If too many ideas present themselves, make the problem more specific; if too few, make the problem more general.
- If a problem is too hard, try to simplify; once simplified, apply the same solution to the full problem.
- Focus on what is making the problem too difficult. Time spent doing this is time spent wisely.
- When your ideas do not seem to work, most likely there is an expert at this. Ask yourself what they might do.
- If none of the above work, you can always ask another person for help.

As noted in Sedivy-Benton and O'Kelly,[14] "Tapping into the up-to-date knowledge of a subject specialist librarian broadens the exposure students have to the full range of research support systems." Once this relationship has been established and the librarians and their instruction become valued, they become a natural part of the team and the students feel comfortable going to both the faculty member as well as the librarians. One potential problem that might arise is that the faculty member might not hold the same skills as librarians do and, therefore, the student may be underserved, especially if only relying on the faculty member.[15] However, implementing a peer-to-peer learning program, with the assistance of a group leader and facilitator, a greater knowledge base and expertise for up-to-date knowledge both within the classroom as well as the library can be established. Consider all of the experts that might already exist in the group!

One place to start might be the reference desk. As Soria, Fransen, & Nakerud[16] suggest, rather than focusing on the question of the student, perhaps focus on the identity of the student and establish a personal relationship. Students who did indeed interact with reference services found that they had come to actually rely on them for conducting research.[17] An additional way would be to integrate information literacy into existing courses rather than having a stand-alone workshop. One caveat to consider is the connection to the learner. When it comes to using the information literacy strategies to benefit them in the library, experience in creating and utilizing techniques for the internets persisted, but the classroom instruction (direct instruction) was forgotten. One student noted that she remembered the advanced search techniques for Google but could not recall how to use the advanced techniques for the university search engine. Library information is usually covered in these sessions may be new to these students and the brevity of the sessions can inhibit long-term recall. All aspects of information literacy just can't be covered in a two-hour workshop.[18] Provide training that is real-time in order to address the use of databases, and focus on the use of these databases to address an issue or a problem. This may reach those students who do not like the shift from print to electronic as well as those students who want the information immediately without having to put effort into learning.[19]

Figure 1.2. Exemplar for project-based visual

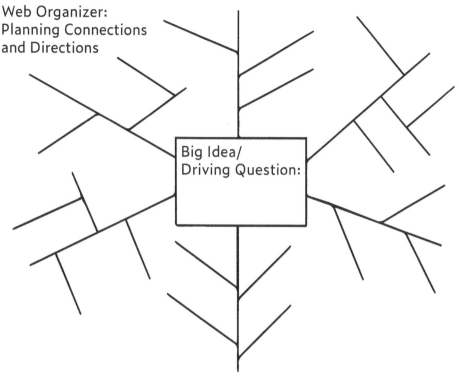

Web Organizer:
Planning Connections
and Directions

Big Idea/
Driving Question:

Here is one way to apply this model to training: Start the training program with an icebreaker in which the participants take turns sharing their own strengths. Then take those comments and group them into areas such as technology, communication, or social-ization. The training would then take that peer-to-peer teaching a step further and have them work together in their groups to solve the problem. The librarian can serve as a facilitator as the peers work together to address the problem and come up with possible solutions. For example, a group of students might need to figure out how to solve access to library resources for students who are not on campus. Using peer-to-peer interaction, they could potentially come up with a variety of possible solutions using the above-refer-enced web organizer. One additional possible option would be to post the web organizer by the reference desk where a variety of students could walk by and populate the web with possible solutions, and then the student group could reconvene to evaluate the options. The results of these options could be twofold: a potential problem in the library has been addressed and the students have created collaborative relationships with one another.[20]

REFLECTION

In 2005, Lippincott's[21] recommendations seemed advanced, but time has proved that these recommendations for library reference services still hold true today. Below are a few things to consider when creating academic support for faculty and students:

- Incorporate visual cues. This can be accomplished by incorporating local library information into popular access portals such as Google. Perhaps this could unfold by placing a dry erase board at the main library desk so students can write issues they are having.
- Deliver service with style. While this new demographic of students enjoys the option of presenting their work in a multimedia format, they still need guidance on how to represent this knowledge. This could be represented through a network that allows for additional peer-to-peer teaching, connecting students with peer experts.
- Provide reference services. Provide services to faculty and students in a real-time delivery format, such as instant messenger or chat, which allows them to have responses in minutes rather than waiting for an email to be answered. Another option is to refer students to a peer-consulting service.
- Offer interactive and portable services. Consult with students and faculty in the development of mobile library services. This would allow students to become part of the process and establish a stronger peer-to-peer network.
- Integrate physical and virtual environments. Provide equitable access to those students and faculty who are away from campus. This allows the users to see the instruction and resources as a whole unit rather than only an on-campus physical space.

These guidelines fit nicely with the term embedded librarianship. Like journalists are embedded in a news story, librarians would embed themselves within the courses that are being taught and would be available when additional instruction is needed.[22] This idea takes the librarian out of the traditional library and fosters collaboration with faculty, with the two working side-by-side and assisting the students in the creation of knowledge, whether by connecting students or providing informal mentoring. This may foster ongoing, scaffolded development of information literacy rather than a one-time exposure. By embedding themselves within the course online and in classrooms face-to-face, librarians have the potential to influence and impact students outside of the confines of the library. Therefore, when the students come to the library, the knowledge that has already been shared in their courses can then be employed in any type of peer-to-peer interaction that might occur.

Libraries must structure themselves in ways that are responsive to their populations, from creating relevant search engines to fostering collaborative relationships with faculty and students. This means gaining an overall knowingness of how individuals learn and implementing these practices into training at the library. If libraries are to remain relevant and a key component in the academic lives of faculty and students, they must become key partners in the instruction of undergraduate students, graduate students, and faculty. It is important for libraries to understand how to utilize a constructivist approach to training. And if they have a population of andragogous learners, it is important to consider how that training should be approached. A key component of this is understanding what the student needs to accomplish and their perspective in pursuing it.

These theories can inform instruction and lead to student engagement and learning. The learners' needs to be considered include social, cognitive, and stylistic. It is crucial that librarians provide instruction and emphasize that all of the services are available to faculty and students. And becoming embedded in the university setting will only further the relationships with faculty and students.

NOTES

1. Lorna Edwards, "Gen Y @ 30: charmed, tech savvy and ready to take over," The Age, January 9, 2010, accessed December 17, 2015, http://www.theage.com.au/national/gen-y--30-charmed-tech-savvy-and-ready-to-take-over-20100108-lyy6.html#ixzz1dxiE3vxY.
2. Paul Wilson, "Mutual Gains from Team Learning: A Guided Classroom Exercise," *Review of Agricultural Economics* 27, no. 2 (2005): 288–96.
3. Elsie S.K. Chan, "An Innovative Learning Approach: Integrate Peer-to-Peer Learning into Blended Learning," *International Journal of Global Education* 1, no. 1 (2012): 19–25.
4. Alan Pritchard, *Ways of Learning: Learning Theories and Learning Styles in the Classroom* (Oxfordshire, UK: Routledge, 2013).
5. Howard Gardner, *Frames of Mind: The Theory of Multiple Intelligences* (New York: Basic Books, 2011).
6. Malcolm S. Knowles, *Andragogy in Action: Applying Modern Principles of Adult Learning* (San Francisco: Josey-Bass, 1984).
7. Cari Kenner and Jason Weinerman, "Adult Learning Theory: Applications to Non-traditional College Students," *Journal of College Reading and Learning* 41, no. 2 (2011): 87–96.
8. Amy Jo Catalano, "Using ACRL Standards to Assess the Information Literacy of Graduate Students in an Education Program," *Evidence Based Library and Information Practice*, 5, no. 4 (2010), accessed 2015, http://ejournals.library.ualberta.ca/index.php/EBLIP/article/view/8878.
9. Jason Martin, "The Information-Seeking Behavior of Undergraduate Education Majors: Does Library Instruction Play a Role?," *Evidence Based Library and Information Practice* 3, no. 4 (2008): 4–17.
10. Stella Korobili, Aphrodite Malliari, and Sofia Zapounidou, "Factors that Influence Information-Seeking Behavior: The Case of Greek Graduate Students," *The Journal of Academic Librarianship* (2011): 155–65.
11. Patricia Davitt Maughan, "Library Resources and Services: A Cross-Disciplinary Survey of Faculty and Graduate Student Use and Satisfaction," *Journal of Academic Librarianship* (1999): 354–66.
12. David Boud, "Making the Move to Peer Learning," in *Peer Learning in Higher Education: Learning From & With Each Other*, eds. David Boud, Ruth Cohen, and Jane Sampson (Oxfordshire, UK: Routledge, 2014).
13. Marvin Minsky, *Michigan Institute of Technology* (January 22, 2009), accessed December 17, 2015, http://web.media.mit.edu/~minsky/OLPC-4.html.
14. Amy Sedivy-Benton and Mary O'Kelly, "Connecting Theory to Practice: Making Research Real for Graduate Students," in *Handbook of Research on Scholarly Publishing and Research Methods*, ed. C. V. Wang (Hershey, PA: IGI Global, 2015), 54.
15. Catalano, "Using ACRL Standards."
16. Krista Soria, Jan Fransen, and Shane Nackerud, "Library Use and Undergraduate Student Outcomes: New Evidence for Students' Retention and Academic Success," *Libraries and the Academy* (2013): 147–64.
17. Jack Mezirow, *Learning as Transformation: Critical Perspectives on a Theory in Progress* (San Francisco: Jossey-Bass, 2000).
18. William Badke, "How We Failed the Net Generation," *Online* (2009): 47–49.

19. Rosemary Green and Peter McCauley, "Doctoral Students' Engagement with Information: An American-Australian Perspective," *Libraries and the Academy* 7, no. 3 (2007): 317–32.
20. Darla Myers, "How I Plan and Implement Project/Inquiry Based Learning In My Class," Inquiring Minds: Mrs. Myers' Kindergarten (blog), October 25, 2014, accessed December 17, 2015, http://mrsmyerskindergarten.blogspot.com/2014/10/how-i-plan-and-implement-projectinquiry.html.
21. Joan Lippincott, "Net Generation Students and Libraries," *Educause Review* (2005): 56–66.
22. Jake Carlson and Ruth Kneale, "Embedded Librarianship in the Research Context: Navigating New Waters," *College & Research Libraries News* (2011): 167–70.

Chapter 2

HOW RESEARCH CONSULTANTS CAN ENCOURAGE STUDENT INTELLECTUAL DEVELOPMENT

Jennifer Torreano

INTRODUCTION

Students frequently enter research consultations expecting to find information that supports what they believe, only to find information that contradicts or complicates their understanding. Experiencing this kind of psychological discomfort, called cognitive dissonance, is an essential part of intellectual development in college students. Cognitive dissonance is the catalyst that prompts students to move along the spectrum from believing there is one right answer to a research question to eventually weighing contradictory ideas with evidence.[1] However, cognitive dissonance can also result in confirmation bias[2] and retreating to earlier ways of understanding under some conditions.[3] Worse yet, some students experience library anxiety, a form of shame that inhibits learning, instead of cognitive dissonance in these situations.[4] How can research consultants effectively support students who struggle to reconcile information that contradicts their current worldviews?

11

Because of their peer relationship with students and the conversational nature of their work, research consultants are in a unique position to create environments that encourage student intellectual development. This chapter takes an interdisciplinary approach in exploring research on intellectual development, library anxiety, and cognitive dissonance in order to describe strategies for creating developmentally supportive research consultations.

PERRY'S THEORY OF INTELLECTUAL AND ETHICAL DEVELOPMENT

Originally published in 1970, William Perry's theory of intellectual and ethical development, commonly referred to as the Perry scheme, describes how college students grow in their understanding of the nature of knowledge. The scheme was developed by analyzing data from a longitudinal study involving interviews of Harvard College students in the 1960s. Interviews revealed patterns in the ways that students characterized their interpretations of the world, following a similar trajectory during their time in college.[5] There are nine developmental positions identified by Perry's scheme which fit into four overarching categories: Dualism, Multiplicity, Relativism, and Commitment in Relativism.[6] Broadly, students develop more complex understandings of knowledge as they progress through the scheme.

In Dualism, students see the world in binary: good versus bad, right versus wrong. There is always one answer to a given question, and Authority is absolute.[7] As students' progress within Dualism, they begin to see that several opinions may exist on a given topic, but the variance is rationalized as others being misinformed or as strategic confusion by Authorities so students learn to overcome such obstacles to find the "correct" answer. Students in Dualism are often frustrated by their courses, perceiving their professors as falsely complicating questions and refusing to give them the right answers.[8]

Students next move into Multiplicity, a series of developmental positions that recognize the existence of uncertainty. However, all uncertainty is considered temporary, as information not yet known. Students in Late Multiplicity can go in two directions: believing all opinions are equally valid or learning to use relativistic thinking in order to please Authority figures.[9]

Students begin to see that some interpretations have more value than others in Relativism. Authority with a capital "A" becomes authority: a status contextually conferred on those with expertise on a given topic. Students in Relativism begin demonstrating source evaluation skills, weighing various opinions and interpretations with evidence in context to determine their own beliefs.[10]

The final developmental sequence in Perry's theory involves making Commitments to their own beliefs and identity within a relativistic view of the world. Students tentatively decide what they believe, live through the consequences, and begin to commit more confidently in other aspects of their lives.[11]

Though Perry's theory outlines developmental positions that describe students' current knowledge paradigms, his findings emphasize the importance of movement: "Perhaps development is all transition and 'stages' only resting points along the way."[12] Students develop through cognitive dissonance: as their understandings of the nature of knowledge and authority are challenged, students are compelled to modify their worldview to make sense of the new information.

During interviews, students acknowledged the innate urge to progress toward more complex knowledge paradigms.[13] Growth comes with difficulties for students, however, including questions about the world and their place in it, uncertainty about the accuracy of their own perceptions, and a possible new distance between students and their hometown communities if the beliefs they grew up with have been challenged. Sometimes the implications for students' identities cause them to pause in development, become detached from their learning, or even retreat to earlier dualistic positions, which Perry calls "alternatives to growth."[14]

Understanding how students view the nature of knowledge throughout their development in college is essential for teaching information literacy: If we reach too far beyond where they currently are, they will not hear us. Many of the frames described in the *Framework for Information Literacy in Higher Education*[15] require Multiplicity or Relativism to understand. Teaching research consultants to pay special attention to conversations involving these frames can make the difference between students beginning to see the world in a new way and feeling alienated.

THRESHOLD CONCEPTS AND THE FRAMEWORK

The Framework uses threshold concepts, which are based partially on Perry's theory (Perkins, 2008). Threshold concepts are ideas that, when grasped, help learners understand disciplines in a new way.[16] Meyer and Land derived the notion of threshold concepts from interviews with educators in various disciplines about the ideas that change students' understanding of those disciplines.[17] As Parker Palmer notes, "Every discipline has a gestalt, an internal logic, a patterned way of relating to the great thing at its core. [...] Every academic discipline has such 'grains of sand' through which the world can be seen."[18] Meyer and Land found that these irreversible paradigm shifts also change the conversations that students participate in and the language they use, bringing students closer to seeing themselves as participants in scholarly communities.[19] In short, threshold concepts teach students to think like scholars.

Threshold concepts can be difficult to grasp, sometimes causing students to get stuck in a transitional state called *liminality*. Meyer, Land, and Smith explain:

> Insights gained by learners as they cross thresholds can be exhilarating but might also be unsettling, requiring an uncomfortable shift in identity. Paradoxically this may be experienced as a sense of loss as an earlier, more secure stance of familiar knowing has to be abandoned as new and unfamiliar knowledge is encountered.[20]

This tendency toward growth combined with fears of changing identity mirrors Perry's theory of intellectual development. Like Perry, researchers studying threshold concepts have found that students sometimes find temporary alternatives to growth—including long pauses in a current paradigm—and retreat to earlier ways of understanding.[21]

The Framework identifies six threshold concepts for information literacy: authority is constructed and contextual, information creation as a process, information has value, research as inquiry, scholarship as conversation, and searching as strategic exploration.[22] Two of these concepts, *scholarship as conversation* and *authority is constructed and contextual*, require advanced knowledge paradigms to fully grasp.

The threshold concept of *scholarship as conversation* is an understanding that all research and learning is an ongoing building and renegotiation of knowledge. This frame also recognizes disagreement: "Instead of seeking discrete answers to complex problems, experts understand that a given issue may be characterized by several competing perspectives as part of an ongoing conversation in which information users and creators come together and negotiate meaning."[23] The Framework describes students who understand the concept of *scholarship as conversation* as being disposed to understand the continually evolving nature of discourse and having the ability to place a particular conversation within a larger disciplinary context when determining a work's value.[24] These skills are only possible with advanced knowledge paradigms, the latter requiring Relativism.

The frame of *authority is constructed and contextual* also requires advanced developmental positions within Perry's scheme. The Framework describes this threshold concept as:

> Information resources reflect their creators' expertise and credibility, and are evaluated based on the information need and the context in which the information will be used. Authority is constructed in that various communities may recognize different types of authority. It is contextual in that the information need may help to determine the level of authority required.[25]

The Framework describes students who understand *authority is constructed and contextual* as having many dispositions including the urge to question authority and consider a wide range of views regardless of their place in the academic canon.[26] These dispositions represent an advanced understanding of the nature of knowledge and authority which require at least Multiplicity and often Relativism.

The complexity of the threshold concepts described in the Framework require advanced knowledge paradigms, but simply challenging student beliefs is not enough. Students' emotions and self-perceptions can impact their ability to explore seeing the world in new ways. If students experience library anxiety during research consultations, learning will be impeded.

LIBRARY ANXIETY

One of the most common forms of academic anxiety, library anxiety is estimated to impact 75-85% of undergraduate students.[27] Library anxiety has a number of characteristics, described by Mellon: "1. Students generally feel that their own library-use skills are inadequate while the skills of other students are adequate. 2. The inadequacy is shameful and should be hidden. 3. The inadequacy would be revealed by asking questions."[28] Onwuegbuzie and Jiao found that low self-efficacy is a hallmark trait of library anxiety, leading to procrastination, which is predictive of low performance in research courses.[29]

Both Mellon and McAfee have categorized library anxiety as an experience of shame.[30] All of the emotions associated with library anxiety are emotions experienced in shame, which can have a paralyzing effect that blocks student learning.[31] Mellon's study concluded that students experiencing library anxiety frequently believe that their peers understand research processes, and that asking questions of librarians would reveal their own ignorance. Students fearing exposure makes the reaction of library employees, including research consultants, particularly important: "Staff can unknowingly respond to shame with shame by showing confusion, disapproval, indifference, irritation, or disrespect. […] Library anxiety cannot exist without library staff being the imagined 'other' of the negative evaluation."[32] How libraries respond to students experiencing library anxiety impacts student success. To understand how research consultants can reduce library anxiety, we must first understand shame.

SHAME

Shame is the core of library anxiety. A social emotion, shame is connected to fears of abandonment and ostracism. Brown explains that shame is commonly conflated with guilt, though the two emotions are different:

> The vast majority of shame researchers agree that the difference between shame and guilt is best understood as the difference between "I am bad" (shame) and "I did something bad" (guilt). Shame is about who we are and guilt is about behaviors.[33]

Fearing exposure of their flaws, people experiencing shame react in a variety of predictable ways to protect themselves.

Responses to Shame

Because connection to others is essential for survival, shame is processed in the limbic system which reacts with fight, flight, or freeze.[34] Shame bypasses the neocortex, which is responsible for reasoning and learning, and causes feelings of anger, the urge to run away, or even temporary paralysis. The cognition required to recognize safety and think through the problem at hand is not possible when a person feels shame. As a result, Brown found that people often react to unexpected shaming events without understanding the reason for their own response.[35]

Students experiencing or anticipating shame/library anxiety in research consultations may try to protect themselves in the following ways:

- evading by procrastinating, remaining silent, and avoiding topics with which they struggle.
- flattery toward the consultant.
- anger at the assignment, professor, or even the consultant.

Concealing shame is instinctual. Discussing it would necessitate revealing the perceived flaws at the root of the shame experience and acknowledging the belief that such flaws make an individual unworthy of connection with others.[36] Instead, people pretend the behaviors or characteristics that they are ashamed of do not exist and use defense mechanisms to deflect when they feel exposed.[37] Students keep their shame a secret, believing that doing so protects them from disconnection, when in reality the secrets isolate the people keeping them.[38]

Impact of Shame in Education

Shame is commonly experienced by students. Starting at a young age, shaming events become common in school: 80% of the participants interviewed in one study by Brown saw themselves and their learning abilities differently after experiencing shame in elementary and middle school.[39] Because people instinctually hide their shame, it may manifest as other problems. Shame may be the culprit when students seem exhausted and disengaged, when they quickly become overwhelmed in class, or when they seem scattered and disorganized.[40] In conversation, students may seem defensive, uncertain, angry, or distant.[41] Johnson's study concluded that students who are shame-prone attribute poor grades and difficulty learning new concepts to a lack of ability, rather than study strategies or learning environments, making the students less resilient and less likely to persist.[42]

Shame does not only impact students' emotions; it also impedes cognition. Walker notes that because shame attacks the sense of self, students "revert to concerns at the lowest levels of Maslow's hierarchy of needs; there is no luxury of being able to learn in such a state."[43] In this self-protective mode, students turn inward and become incapable of learning and connecting with others.[44] Any changes become impossible because students are focused on self-preservation.[45]

Learning environments frequently exacerbate shame by making students feel isolated. Because asking questions would reveal ignorance, students often hide their confusion from professors and classmates:

> Social-community pressure to appear *learned* has become more important than actually *learning*. When we spend our time and energy building and protecting our image of 'knowing,' it is highly unlikely that we will risk admitting we don't understand or asking questions—both of which are essential to real knowledge building."[46]

Shame isolates individuals and then builds upon itself: Students who perform poorly in class because they don't ask questions feel even more shame, blaming their own abilities rather than the learning environment or their study strategies. This low self-efficacy creates the sense that they do not belong.[47]

A sense of community is necessary for moving onto more advanced knowledge paradigms. Learning requires vulnerability: What often prompts students to reach out to new ways of understanding is the sense that other students are growing alongside them.[48] Feelings of community and belonging create an environment of safety, where taking risks is understood to be part of the college experience.[49] Shame gets in the way of this growth, isolating students from their learning communities and hindering cognition.

Overcoming Shame

Though shame cannot be completely avoided, people can overcome shame and become more resilient to shaming experiences. Brown's 2006 study concluded that people with shame resilience have four important characteristics: the capacity to be vulnerable and to respect the vulnerability of others; relationship-building skills; an awareness of cultural shame triggers and the ways in which societal expectations can be unrealistic; and the ability to talk about shame with others, which requires emotional awareness and vocabulary. "Speaking shame," as Brown calls it, is particularly useful in research consultations because discussing shame feelings with others curtails isolation and builds community.[50] Discussing academic struggles or fears of failure, a common feature in research consultations, diminishes shame and begins to build the sense of belonging necessary for development.

COGNITIVE DISSONANCE

Shame impedes development, but a related phenomenon called *cognitive dissonance* can encourage intellectual growth. In 1957, Leon Festinger completed a series of research studies that led to the theory of cognitive dissonance. Cognitive dissonance is the psychological discomfort caused by inconsistencies, and it is often induced by exposure to new information or conversation with others who hold differing opinions.[51] A catalyst for growth in Perry's theory of intellectual and ethical development, cognitive dissonance prompts students to reconcile the discrepancies between their current worldview and the new knowledge paradigms with which they are confronted in college.[52]

Cognitive dissonance is similar to guilt, an emotion that occurs when a person's actions or beliefs are at odds with their perception of themselves.[53] Two people experiencing the same event may feel two different emotions, one cognitive dissonance/guilt and the other shame, depending on how they attribute the cause of the event, the amount of safety they feel in being vulnerable, and whether the experience reflects their own perceived weaknesses.[54] When confronted with a new idea at odds with their current understanding in a classroom, one student may have the sense that everyone in the class is growing together and that learning to see things differently is part of the process (cognitive dissonance) while another may see the new information as a criticism of their current understanding or values (shame). Researchers have found that cognitive dissonance and guilt prompt self-reflection, while shame has the opposite effect, making people less likely to reflect on their beliefs or actions.[55] Cognitive dissonance is helpful; shame is not.

Causes of Cognitive Dissonance

Festinger's research studies concluded that exposure to different perspectives or new information can cause cognitive dissonance. Cognitive dissonance frequently occurs in conversations between people who share differing opinions. Because beliefs and behavior are central to identity, topics that are central to a person's self-concept will create more dissonance than topics a person cares less about.[56] For example, if a student believes authority figures have the right answers but disagrees with a professor's interpretation of a topic, the student will experience cognitive dissonance. The dissonance will be magnified if the topic is important to the student. Cognitive dissonance also occurs when people are presented with contradictory information, especially by two perceived authorities.[57]

In disagreements with others, Festinger found that two factors affect the magnitude of dissonance a person experiences. The first is whether contradictory information is visible to the individual in real life; if so, the amount of dissonance will increase.[58] For example, a student may initially believe that the money earned from a minimum wage job could cover students' tuition. That student would experience an increase in dissonance by watching friends in this circumstance struggle financially or by failing to earn enough to pay their own tuition. The second factor is the number of people who agree or disagree and how much their perspectives are valued by the person experiencing the dissonance.[59] This factor explains a common occurrence in research consultations: A student who sees their home community as an authority experiences cognitive dissonance when the views of that community are revealed to be at odds with an academic community, another perceived authority.

Festinger's studies also revealed that the complexity of opinions can impact dissonance, with dichotomous stances leading to more dissonance: "If one person says 'black' and another says 'white,' the disagreement, and the dissonance in the cognition of each, will be greater than if the disagreement is between 'black' and 'dark gray.'"[60] As students develop a more complex understanding of the nature of knowledge and authority, they move away from the "black and white" view of dualism and see these "shades of gray."[61] With increased cognitive development comes less cognitive dissonance, or a higher tolerance for it.[62]

Dissonance Reduction

Festinger's study concluded that people instinctively try to resolve cognitive dissonance when it occurs. Typically, enough dissonance creates a tipping point that causes the person to change their mind, but they may first try to change their environment or add additional information to outweigh the uncomfortable information.[63]

Festinger identified many barriers to dissonance reduction, one of which is particularly relevant for research consultations: social ramifications. When a community shares a worldview, an individual would need to find a new community to support their new beliefs if they were to change.[64]

The entanglement of beliefs presents additional complications. Beliefs are rarely isolated: they are linked to other beliefs which may be increasingly tied to a person's identity and view of the world. In the example of the person who believes that a minimum wage job can pay for tuition, reconsidering that view may threaten the person's understanding of capitalism, wealth inequality, and America as a meritocracy. Changing one belief creates a domino effect of cognitive dissonance that can feel overwhelming.

Because cognitive dissonance is so uncomfortable, people often avoid it with confirmation bias, seeking out information that reflects their current understanding. Confirmation bias allows a person to minimize cognitive dissonance by mentally changing the nature of the information or the credibility of its source before the information causes psychological discomfort.[65] Interestingly, even this distorted information is stored in the brain as fact. The more the information is called upon, the more the person relies on it, making the belief more central to their worldview and identity.[66]

Cognitive dissonance is necessary to evolve, despite the discomfort. As students' beliefs are challenged, they see that new ways of thinking are possible. With time and a sense of safety, students feel brave enough to try on more complex ways of understanding the nature of knowledge. In conversations that feel exploratory and free from evaluation, students are more likely to consider competing perspectives and test the idea that knowledge is socially constructed—a live, ongoing conversation that evolves as more people contribute. Research consultations are the perfect environment for this exploration.

PEER LEARNING

Students are able to have more exploratory conversations with peer consultants because they are not authority figures. Peer consultants are simply there to help, and students are far more likely to ask questions that they fear are "stupid" and try on new ideas when speaking with peer consultants versus their professors, whose work includes judging student competence. In these peer conversations, students are more likely to actively engage and leave with a sense of relief and confidence.[67]

Community

Peer learning conversations provide a sense of connection that is critical to learning. As Parker Palmer notes:

> Learning demands community—a dialogical exchange in which our ignorance can be aired, our ideas tested, our biases challenged, and our knowledge expended, an exchange in which we are not simply left alone to think our thoughts.[68]

The common thread in literature about intellectual development, library anxiety, shame, and cognitive dissonance is the importance of community for growing and learning. Community support is essential for cognitive development,[69] working through shame[70] and library anxiety,[71] and experiencing cognitive dissonance as a catalyst for growth.[72] Though research consultations cannot serve as a replacement for a supportive community of friends and family, these conversations can provide a sense of connection and belonging to college students being asked to rapidly develop their understanding of the nature of the world.

The natural exploration that takes place in research consultations encourages students' intellectual development. Kenneth Bruffee identifies the major goal of peer learning to be helping students understand the nature of knowledge, authority, and scholarship within academic communities. Peer consultants are able to help students learn "normal discourse"—the way people think and talk within a community—by providing a space to try, fail, and learn together in conversation. When students learn the normal discourse central to a community, they are able to join that community and contribute to its perpetually evolving conversation.[73] This outcome reflects Relativism within Perry's scheme—the ability to interpret and evaluate arguments in context—and the threshold concepts of *scholarship as conversation* and *authority is constructed and contextual* in the Framework.

Vulnerability

Research in education,[74] library science,[75] and psychology[76] identifies vulnerability as being essential for learning. Vulnerability cultivates creativity and the ability to learn from feedback, and sharing it with others diminishes feelings of shame.[77]

Peer learning consultations provide an opportunity to practice vulnerability in a space free from evaluation. Baxter Magolda found that students are often reluctant to admit their confusion to their professors, staying quiet in class rather than asking questions.[78] However, during peer consultations, students frequently exercise more vulnerability because they are working alongside a non-expert who is not assessing their work.[79]

Empathy

To create a space that encourages vulnerability, peer consultants must exercise empathy. Wiseman defines empathy as: "(1) to be able to see the world as others see it; (2) to be nonjudgmental; (3) to understand another person's feelings; and (4) to communicate your understanding of that person's feelings."[80] Empathy is a skill that can be learned, not an innate characteristic. Though displaying empathy can be difficult, Brown's 2006 study has determined that simply acknowledging and validating another person's feelings can relieve the other person's sense of shame.[81] Peer consultants can do this through sharing their own vulnerabilities when appropriate or simply listening without judgment.[82]

DEVELOPMENTALLY SUPPORTIVE RESEARCH CONSULTATIONS

Several themes are present in the research on supportive learning environments: collaborative learning, encouraging vulnerability, acknowledging growth and loss, asking questions, and balancing challenge and support. We can apply these strategies to encourage intellectual development.

Collaborative Learning

Collaborative learning creates a sense of community that is critical to student development.[83] Mellon found that students often feel isolated, certain that their peers and instructors all learn more easily than them,[84] a finding supported by Onwuegbuzie and Jiao's 2004 study.[85] Recognizing that learning is a challenging process for everyone creates the sense that all learners—including students' instructors—are growing together, building student resilience. This feeling of community is heightened when others recognize individual students as part of the community, as learners who are developing alongside everyone else.[86] By discussing their own evolutions as students and framing consultations as a time to learn together, research consultants can foster a sense of belonging.

Encouraging Vulnerability

Learning requires vulnerability, so research consultants must practice empathy in their interactions with students. Recognizing that students' emotions are central to their learning, and working to create environments where vulnerability and courage are understood as important components of education diminishes shame[87] and encourages cognitive development.[88] In practice, this often means simply pausing the agenda of the consultation in order to talk with a stressed out or upset student about how they are feeling. Referrals to campus counseling and other resources may be appropriate, but often simply letting students express their academic concerns without judgment offers a sense of relief.

Acknowledging Growth and Loss

Demonstrating empathy is necessary for encouraging vulnerability, and it is also needed to support students as they develop. Learning from cognitive dissonance and moving on to more complex knowledge paradigms involves letting go of old ways of thinking.[89] Progress comes with grief for old worldviews and the people that students used to be. Perry implores us to recognize the courage it takes to see the world differently and the inevitable loss that follows.

Along with grief, a more complex view of the nature of knowledge and authority brings more responsibility for individuals. When students are active creators of knowledge and participants in an eternal dialogue, rather than passive recipients of absolute truth, they must determine what they believe and how they will contribute to the conversation. Perry recommends acknowledging the bravery such a step takes by simply listening with full attention.[90] As students are challenged to be vulnerable and shift their knowledge paradigms, research consultants can provide support by recognizing the students' courage and acknowledging the sense of loss that comes with moving onto more complex understandings of the world.

Asking Questions

Posing thoughtful questions that induce cognitive dissonance can encourage student development. Students in earlier developmental positions frequently state ideas as fact, and using Socratic method to prompt evaluation of their opinions and the evidence they use to support them introduces relativism and may create cognitive dissonance.[91] For example, questions about bias and contradictory views are needed to understand the threshold concept of *authority is constructed and contextual*. Gentle questioning can expand students' perspectives.

Research consultants need to be patient and respectful during these conversations. Silence can be uncomfortable, and consultants, feeling the pressure, often further prompt students or fill the quiet with their own thoughts. A better response is letting the silence hang so students have time to think and summon the courage to speak their thoughts aloud, then mirroring students' words back to them to check for understanding.[92] Perry found that, if prompted too much, students feel pressure to deliver the answer the questioner is looking for, even if it means pretending to hold a more advanced knowledge paradigm.[93] Instead, research consultants should provide space, listen to students, and meet them where they are developmentally.

Balancing Challenge and Support

Experiencing cognitive dissonance is uncomfortable, and students need additional support to tolerate the discomfort without isolating themselves from the experience or regressing to earlier developmental positions.[94] Nevitt Sanford's Theory of Challenge and Support explains that students become overwhelmed with too much challenge, and too much support inhibits learning.[95] Palmer describes this balance that must be achieved to create a supportive learning environment:

> A learning space must have features that help students deal with the dangers of an educational expedition: places to rest, places to find nourishment, even places to seek shelter when one feels overexposed. But if that expedition is to take us somewhere, the space must also be charged. If students are to learn at the deepest levels, they must not feel so safe that they fall asleep: they need to feel the risks inherent in pursuing the deep things of the world or of the soul. No special effects are required to create this charge—it comes with the territory. We only need fence the space, fill it with topics of significance, and refuse to let anyone evade or trivialize them.[96]

The challenges and supports that students require shift as they grow, so research consultants must remain attentive and continually adjust their approach to support student needs.

How much support or challenge students need depends on their security in their current developmental positions. Perry found that students can choose whether to move on to new knowledge paradigms or retreat in alternatives to growth. The more support students experience, the safer they feel in trying out more complex worldviews, and the more likely they are to grow intellectually. If students have just reached a new developmental position, they are unlikely to be ready to move on, so it is important to determine students' receptivity to new knowledge paradigms before inducing cognitive dissonance.[97] For example, if a student has just moved from seeing the world in black and white to recognizing a variety of legitimate perspectives, prodding too much about who is considered an authority in a particular discipline may overwhelm the student. That conversation would be more appropriate for a student who seems comfortable with contradicting ideas. Research consultants are skilled at understanding tone and body language, and the same principles apply to these determinations.

CONCLUSION

Helping students learn to navigate the overwhelming amount of information they are confronted with in college is a central goal of research consultant programs and academic libraries more broadly. Determining what has value, considering whose voices are being promoted and whose are missing, and understanding scholarship as a conversation require an advanced understanding of the nature of knowledge, learned in the hard-won late stages of intellectual development. To get there, such development needs careful tending so it is not halted by shame. By creating safe and exploratory learning environments, research consultants can encourage students to be brave and try on new ways of seeing the world.

Teaching these strategies to research consultants is a worthwhile endeavor. Perry found that "the Position at which a student was rated as a freshman was not predictive of the Position at which he would be rated in his senior year," indicating that supportive learning environments may have tremendous impact on student intellectual development.[98] With empathy, curiosity, and a balance of challenge and support, research consultants can create the conditions that students need to grow.

NOTES

1. William Perry, *Forms of Intellectual and Ethical Development in the College Years: A Scheme* (San Francisco: Jossey-Bass, 1999).
2. Leon Festinger, *A Theory of Cognitive Dissonance* (Stanford: Stanford University Press, 1957).
3. Perry, *Development in the College Years*.
4. Constance A. Mellon, "Library Anxiety: A Grounded Theory and its Development" *College and Research Libraries* 47, no. 2 (1986): 160-165.
5. William Perry, "Cognitive and Ethical Growth: The Making of Meaning." In *The Modern American College* (6th ed.), ed. Arthur Chickering (San Francisco: Jossey-Bass, 1990), 76-116.
6. Perry, *Development in the College Years*.
7. Ibid.
8. Ibid.
9. Ibid.
10. Ibid.
11. Ibid.
12. Ibid., 78.
13. Perry, *Development in the College Years*.
14. Ibid.

15. Association of College & Research Libraries, *Framework for Information Literacy in Higher Education*, 2016. http://www.ala.org/acrl/standards/ilframework.

16. Ray Land, Jan H.F. Meyer, and Jan Smith, *Threshold Concepts Within the Disciplines* (Rotterdam, Sense Publishers, 2008).

17. Jan H.F. Meyer and Ray Land, "Threshold Concepts and Troublesome Knowledge: Linkages to Find Ways of Thinking and Practising Within the Disciplines," in *Improving Student Learning—Theory and Practice Ten Years On*, ed. C. Rust (Oxford: OCSLD, 2003).

18. Parker Palmer, *The Courage to Teach: Exploring the Inner Landscape of a Teacher's Life* (20th anniversary ed.) (San Francisco: Wiley, 2017), 125.

19. Jan H.F. Meyer and Ray Land, "Threshold Concepts and Troublesome Knowledge: Epistemological Considerations and a Conceptual Framework for Teaching and Learning," *Higher Education* 49 (2005): 373-388.

20. Land, Meyer, and Smith, *Threshold Concepts*, x-xi.

21. Ibid.

22. Association of College & Research Libraries, *Framework for Information Literacy*.

23. Ibid., 18.

24. Association of College & Research Libraries, *Framework for Information Literacy*.

25. Ibid., 4.

26. Association of College & Research Libraries, *Framework for Information Literacy*.

27. Mellon, *College and Research Libraries*.

28. Ibid., 160.

29. Anthony J. Onwuegbuzie and Qun G. Jiao, "Information Search Performance and Research Achievement: An Empirical Test of the Anxiety Expectation Model of Library Anxiety," *Journal of the American Society for Information Science and Technology* 55, no.1 (2004): 41-54.

30. Erin McAfee, "Shame: The emotional basis of library anxiety," *College and Research Libraries* 79, no. 2 (2018): 237-256; Mellon, *College and Research Libraries*.

31. Ibid.

32. Ibid., 247.

33. Brené Brown, *I Thought it was Just Me (But it Isn't): Making the Journey from "What Will People Think?" to "I Am Enough"* (New York: Avery, 2007), 13.

34. Brené Brown, *Daring Greatly: How the Courage to be Vulnerable Transforms the Way we Live, Love, Parent, and Lead* (New York: Avery, 2012); Diane Elizabeth Johnson, "Considering Shame and its Implications for Student Learning," *College Student Journal*, 46, no. 1 (2012): 3-17.

35. Brené Brown, "Shame Resilience Theory: A Grounded Theory Study on Women and Shame," *Families in Society* 87, no. 1 (2006): 43-52.

36. Brown, *Daring Greatly: How the Courage to be Vulnerable Transforms the Way we Live, Love, Parent, and Lead*.

37. Jude Walker, "Shame and Transformation in the Theory and Practice of Adult Learning and Education," *Journal of Transformative Education* 15, no. 4 (2017): 357-374.

38. Brown, *I Thought it was Just Me*.

39. Ibid.

40. Johnson, *College Student Journal*.

41. Walker, *Journal of Transformative Education*.

42. Johnson, *College Student Journal*.

43. Walker, *Journal of Transformative Education*, 365.

44. Walker, *Journal of Transformative Education*.

45. Johnson, *College Student Journal*.

46. Brown, *I Thought it was Just Me*, 275.

47. Johnson, *College Student Journal*.

48. Perry, *Development in the College Years*.

49. Ibid.

50. Brown, *Families in Society*.

51. Festinger, *A Theory of Cognitive Dissonance*.

52. Lori D. Patton, Kristen A. Renn, Florence M. Guido, and Stephen John Quaye, *Student Development in College: Theory, Research, and Practice* (San Francisco: Jossey-Bass, 2016).

53. Eric Stice, "The Similarities Between Cognitive Dissonance and Guilt: Confession as a Relief of Disso-nance," *Current Psychology: Research and Reviews* 11, no. 1 (1992): 69-77.
54. Brown, *Daring Greatly.*
55. April McGrath, "Dealing with Dissonance: A Review of Cognitive Dissonance Reduction," *Social and Personality Psychology Compass* 11, no. 12 (2017): 1-17.
56. Festinger, *A Theory of Cognitive Dissonance.*
57. Ibid.
58. Ibid.
59. Ibid.
60. Ibid., 181.
61. Perry, *Development in the College Years.*
62. Festinger, *A Theory of Cognitive Dissonance.*
63. Ibid.
64. Ibid.
65. Cornelia Mothes, "Confirmation Bias." In *The SAGE Encyclopedia of Political Behavior.* (Thousand Oaks, CA: SAGE, 2017).
66. James H. Kuklinski, Paul J. Quirk, Jennifer Jerit, David Schwieder, and Robert F. Rich, "Misinforma-tion and the state of democratic citizenship," *The Journal of Politics* 62, no. 3 (2000): 790-816.
67. Muriel Harris, "Talking in the Middle: Why Writers Need Writing Tutors," *College English* 57, no. 1 (1995): 27-42.
68. Palmer, *The Courage to Teach*, 79.
69. Perry, *Development in the College Years.*
70. Brown, *Daring Greatly.*
71. McAfee, *College and Research Libraries.*
72. Festinger, *A Theory of Cognitive Dissonance.*
73. Kenneth Bruffee, "Collaborative Learning and the 'Conversation of Mankind,'" *College English* 46, no. 7 (1984): 635-652.
74. Marcia Baxter Magolda, *Knowing and Reasoning in College: Gender-Related Patterns in Students' Intellectual Development* (San Francisco: Jossey-Bass, 1992); Perry, *Development in the College Years*; Walker, *Journal of Transformative Education.*
75. McAfee, *College and Research Libraries.*
76. Festinger, *A Theory of Cognitive Dissonance.*
77. Brown, *Daring Greatly.*
78. Baxter Magolda, *Knowing and Reasoning in College.*
79. Harris, *College English.*
80. Quoted in Brown, *I Thought it was Just Me*, 37.
81. Brown, *Families in Society.*
82. Walker, *Journal of Transformative Education.*
83. Perry, *Development in the College Years.*
84. Mellon, *College and Research Libraries.*
85. Onwuegbuzie and Jiao, *Journal of the American Society for Information Science and Technology.*
86. Perry, *Development in the College Years.*
87. Walker, *Journal of Transformative Education.*
88. Baxter Magolda, *Knowing and Reasoning in College*; Perry, *Development in the College Years.*
89. Perry, "Cognitive and Ethical Growth" in *The Modern American College.*
90. Ibid.
91. Perry, *Development in the College Years.*
92. Palmer, *The Courage to Teach.*
93. Perry, "Cognitive and Ethical Growth" in *The Modern American College.*
94. Perry, *Development in the College Years.*
95. Patton et al., *Student Development in College: Theory, Research, and Practice.*
96. Palmer, *The Courage to Teach*, 77-78.
97. Perry, *Development in the College Years.*
98. Ibid, 241.

BIBLIOGRAPHY

Association of College & Research Libraries, *Framework for Information Literacy in Higher Education*, American Library Association, 2016. http://www.ala.org/acrl/standards/ilframework.

Baxter Magolda, Marcia. *Knowing and Reasoning in College: Gender-Related Patterns in Students' Intellectual Development*. San Francisco: Jossey-Bass, 1992.

Brown, Brené. *Daring Greatly: How the Courage to be Vulnerable Transforms the Way we Live, Love, Parent, and Lead*. New York: Avery, 2012.

———. *I Thought it was Just Me (But it Isn't): Making the Journey from "What Will People Think?" to "I Am Enough."* New York: Avery, 2007.

———. "Shame Resilience Theory: A Grounded Theory Study on Women and Shame," *Families in Society* 87, no. 1 (2006): 43-52.

Bruffee, Kenneth. "Collaborative Learning and the 'Conversation of Mankind.'" *College English*, 46, no. 7 (1984): 635-652.

Festinger, Leon. *A Theory of Cognitive Dissonance*. Stanford: Stanford University Press, 1957.

Harris, Muriel. "Talking in the Middle: Why Writers Need Writing Tutors." *College English* 57, no. 1 (1995): 27-42.

Johnson, Diane Elizabeth. "Considering Shame and its Implications for Student Learning." *College Student Journal* 46, no. 1 (2012): 3-17.

Kuklinski, James H. Paul J. Quirk, Jennifer Jerit, David Schwieder, and Robert F. Rich. "Misinformation and the state of democratic citizenship," *The Journal of Politics* 62, no. 3 (2000): 790-816.

Land, Ray, Jan H.F. Meyer, and Jan Smith. *Threshold Concepts Within the Disciplines*. Rotterdam: Sense Publishers, 2008.

McAfee, Erin. "Shame: The emotional basis of library anxiety." *College and Research Libraries* 79, no. 2 (2018): 237-256.

McGrath, April. "Dealing with Dissonance: A Review of Cognitive Dissonance Reduction." *Social and Personality Psychology Compass* 11, no. 12 (2017): 1-17.

Mellon, Constance A. "Library Anxiety: A Grounded Theory and its Development." *College and Research Libraries* 47, no. 2 (1986): 160-165.

Meyer, Jan H.F., and Ray Land. "Threshold Concepts and Troublesome Knowledge: Linkages to Find Ways of Thinking and Practising Within the Disciplines," in *Improving Student Learning—Theory and Practice Ten Years On*, edited by C. Rust. Oxford: OCSLD, 2003.

———. "Threshold Concepts and Troublesome Knowledge: Epistemological Considerations and a Conceptual Framework for Teaching and Learning." *Higher Education* 49 (2005): 373-388.

Mothes, Cornelia. "Confirmation Bias." In *The SAGE Encyclopedia of Political Behavior*. Thousand Oaks, CA: SAGE, 2017.

Onwuegbuzie, Anthony J. and Qun G. Jiao. "Information Search Performance and Research Achievement: An Empirical Test of the Anxiety Expectation Model of Library Anxiety." *Journal of the American Society for Information Science and Technology* 55, no.1 (2004): 41-54.

Parker Palmer. *The Courage to Teach: Exploring the Inner Landscape of a Teacher's Life* (20th anniversary ed.) San Francisco: Wiley, 2017.

Patton, Lori D., Kristen A. Renn, Florence M. Guido, and Stephen John Quaye. *Student Development in College: Theory, Research, and Practice*. San Francisco: Jossey-Bass, 2016.

Perry, William. "Cognitive and Ethical Growth: The Making of Meaning." In *The Modern American College* (6th ed.), edited by Arthur Chickering , 76-116. San Francisco: Jossey-Bass, 1990.

———. *Forms of Intellectual and Ethical Development in the College Years: A Scheme*. San Francisco: Jossey-Bass, 1999.

Stice, Eric. "The Similarities Between Cognitive Dissonance and Guilt: Confession as a Relief of Dissonance." *Current Psychology: Research and Reviews* 11, no. 1 (1992): 69-77.

Walker, Jude. "Shame and Transformation in the Theory and Practice of Adult Learning and Education." *Journal of Transformative Education* 15, no. 4 (2017): 357-374.

Part II

LIBRARY CASE STUDIES

Case Study 1

RESEARCH AND WRITING CENTER AT BRIGHAM YOUNG UNIVERSITY:
Developing Leadership and Collaboration

Elise Silva and Suzanne Julian

OVERVIEW

Brigham Young University's (BYU) Research and Writing Center (RWC) is a joint effort between information literacy librarians and BYU's University Writing Program. The RWC piloted in September 2013, responding to the need for a more rounded approach to research and writing help. The program recognized that writing and research are recursive, created a place where students could get help with both, and provided holistic help to patrons.

In the past, the Research Center and the Writing Center were separate—both in hard-to-reach places and both in different buildings. In 2009, the Writing Center moved a satellite program into the Harold B. Lee Library but still was separate from the Research Center. When the Writing Center's organizational structure changed a few years later, the University Writing Program, housed in the English department, and the Information Literacy Program, housed in the library, recognized that the time was right to change their service models and combine the two centers by proposing a joint initiative. The RWC's unique model is built on respect for subject expertise (thus, training writing tutors and research consultants differently) and prioritizing collaboration in the research and writing process.

Initially, there was some concern from the library that the service would be redundant because the Harold B. Lee Library already ran many helpdesks throughout the building where student workers were well trained to help patrons with research questions. The Information Literacy Coordinator co-wrote a proposal with writing faculty that suggested the center be advertised heavily for freshmen students taking first-year writing while the helpdesks tended to be more discipline-specific. The proposal outlined that the RWC would provide a place for extended research help while helpdesks offered a standing service where consultations generally lasted only a few minutes.

The project proposal was accepted and the center moved to the ground floor near the main circulation desk where a popular reading sampler collection had been. Though the center was given no funding for remodeling, it was given a modest budget for furniture and student wage increases. The pilot was approved for two years.

Both research consultants and writing tutors enjoyed the new center due to better visibility and heavier traffic. Research supervisors noticed a shift in the longevity of research

consultants due to a fixed schedule and higher pay. Some library departments were still wary of the center, worrying that the student research consultants were not trained as well as the helpdesk employees because they were generalists. However, the center soon proved to be great for referrals as RWC research consultants would escort a student to a helpdesk if the consultant was unable to answer discipline-specific research questions. The pilot ended in April 2015 and the center was approved to continue running as a fully functioning part of the library's main floor.

> Prior to working in the Research and Writing Center, I considered research to just be a supplement to my writing. I would write the majority of my paper before even considering research.... I have learned how to effectively research in a way that guides the rest of my writing process. I find my papers now have more substance, I learn more, and I can do it in less time.
>
> *Research Consultant, Brigham Young University*

In fall 2013, the first semester in the new location, 2,087 students received tutoring services. One year later, in fall 2014, 3,248 students received help—an increase of 56 percent. The majority of the tutoring sessions continue to be for writing help, though research numbers continue to increase, particularly for freshman students.

Philosophy and Goals

The mission of BYU's research consultant program is to provide research and writing help through peer tutoring for the general student body. To accomplish this, our research consultants must understand the requirements and research needs for GE classes and are able to ask questions to help clarify informational needs. Furthermore, through a collaborative approach, our research consultants are aware of what help writing tutors can give and feel comfortable referring students with writing questions to other RWC staff better trained in that area.

Our philosophy and goals are intertwined. We want to provide a welcoming customer service-oriented experience to help patrons

- fulfill an immediate research need and
- have some take-away skills that will help them in future research situations.

The RWC actively advertises library services. We also practice carefully assessing the student's research maturity so as not to overwhelm a patron with unnecessary information or research paths. This aligns very closely with the Harold B. Lee Library's mission to "advance scholarship" and "nurture lifelong… growth"[1] and Brigham Young University's aim to foster "lifelong learning and service."[2] In the Research and Writing Center, we believe that the ability to efficiently and effectively navigate complicated research situations is an integral component to becoming an effective citizen, thinker, and lifelong learner. Therefore, the importance of developing the ability to find reliable, timely, and authoritative information and assessing information for relevance is paramount to a student researcher's experience within the center.

Organization

As a collaborative effort, the organizational structure is cooperative but separate, maintaining subject expertise while also allowing for teamwork and innovation. The instruction program includes three full-time faculty, an RWC Specialist, and fifteen student employees. Student employees are first hired as teaching assistants (TAs), then are promoted to research consultants, and of those, one is picked to be the student lead supervisor.

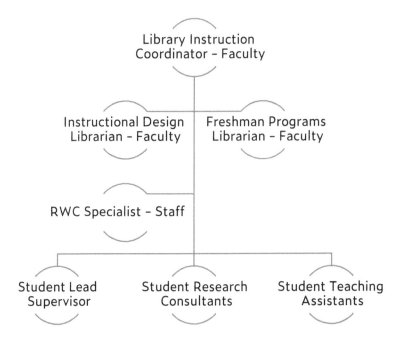

The Writing Center director manages a separate Writing Center on campus and co-manages the RWC with the library instruction coordinator. The director has two part-time staff members who manage the daily operations of both the Writing Center and the Research and Writing Center. The twenty writing tutors assigned to the RWC are hired, trained, and supervised by the Writing Center, and the research consultants are supervised by the library. Both entities cross-train receptionists to run the RWC's front desk.

Promoting the Program

Promotions for the Research and Writing Center include outreach to new students during orientation and educational efforts in GE writing classes. The library has a twenty-minute introduction during New Student Orientation and the RWC features prominently. During a calendar year, the library's Information Literacy Program typically reaches 21,391 students during 1,241 library instruction sessions. Of that number, 530 sessions are for GE first-year writing sessions, 360 are for GE advanced writing sessions, and 350 are discipline-specific instruction. The services of the Research and Writing Center are promoted most heavily in the first-year writing instruction sessions.

Library Instruction Sessions

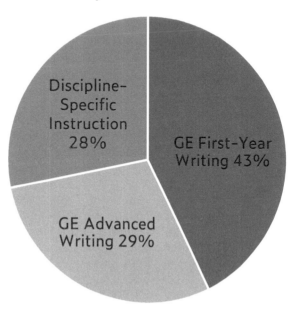

Discipline-Specific Instruction 28%

GE First-Year Writing 43%

GE Advanced Writing 29%

The library promotions team has been extremely helpful in providing social media, flyers, and news articles on the services of the RWC. The Writing Center contributes to the RWC promotions by providing RWC-branded pencils for students and making presentations to campus writing classes.

In our promotion efforts, we have realized that what rings true for real estate sales is also true for selling our service: location is a major factor. The best advertisement for our services is the student traffic that passes in front of our center each day.

Communication

Since so many parties help with the maintenance of the RWC, it is vital that communication is effective and efficient. Email between the coordinators and directors is the primary communication method. It serves as a record of decisions and a way of communicating information to departments that are collaborating but still separate in their management. However, student employees are not as responsive to email as the faculty and staff are. We believe this may be a reflection of changing communication methods among younger students. As such, we text student employees to remind them of meetings and to check on their progress with projects, etc. We also find that face-to-face meetings can be a valuable method of communication, and we hold these regularly on a weekly-to-monthly basis depending on the attendees and purpose.

> I've learned how to gauge a student's understanding and how to recognize areas they struggle with. I have learned how to teach rather than lecture and how to inspire confidence within a student and their quest to research.
>
> *Research Consultant, Brigham Young University*

HIRING

On the library side, our hiring practices are done with significant input from our current research consultants, specifically the student lead supervisor who is in charge of much of the day-to-day scheduling of the RWC and the TA hours in our instruction classrooms. We find the input of the students invaluable in the process as they can assess a potential candidate's character from a perspective that faculty and administrators lack and can get a sense of how well the student would fit into a wider group dynamic within the RWC—a dynamic we prefer to keep fun, friendly, and light. This places great trust in our student employees, but we feel that trust is well-placed as it allows them to practice important leadership skills.

> This job has helped me recognize my career aspirations. Thanks to this job, I am applying to graduate school to get my masters in library science. From working here, I have learned how much I love working with students and helping build their understanding. This job has given me the opportunity to act as a library instructor, which has allowed me to collaborate with professors at a professional level and has given me the confidence to aid others in their academic research.
>
> *Research Consultant, Brigham Young University*

In terms of our initial TA hire, we have minimum requirements that a potential candidate possess, but we look mostly for personality and critical-thinking skills. (See Appendix A. Library Instruction Teacher's Assistant Job Posting.) We find that research skills are easier to teach than congeniality, solid interpersonal behavior, and the ability to think through problems in a productive way. Therefore, much of our interviewing process tries to pinpoint such personality and thinking traits that we have found (through experience) lead to successful research consultants. Our training is then meant to fill in the gaps when it comes to research methodology and tools that our students must know for their jobs.

Hiring Timeline and Application Process

We hire on a semesterly basis, generally posting the job description two to three weeks prior to the semester, conducting interviews the first week of the semester, and hiring by the second week of the semester. Though we have been tempted to hire and train before the semester starts, we find that with holiday breaks and summers off, many of our best students aren't available to interview until the semester has begun; so, to increase our applicant pool, we wait. We also tend to hire quickly, within a few days of interviewing, so that the student does not interview for or accept another job on campus. A small interview and hiring window works best for us to get the work done and get students hired so that we can start training as soon as possible.

To apply, all candidates must file an online application along with a cover letter, résumé, and availability chart. In a typical fall semester, we receive around one hundred applicants for four or five open TA spots. We first look at the cover letters. Since interpersonal communication skills are so important to us, we believe that a badly written cover letter does not show much potential in a candidate. Poorly written, sparse, or generic cover letters generally weed out about half of our applicant pool, and we send a generic form letter via email to students who do not make the initial cut. Next, we evaluate résumés for communication skills and customer service/research background. Finally, we call around twenty students to interview.

Conducting Interviews

We choose to include several interviewers, including one student employee, on each interview conducted. Asking questions is also important for us, as it allows a potential employee to showcase both strengths and weaknesses and give a variety of modes through which a candidate can showcase personality, expertise, and future potential. At the end of select interviews, we run a role-play simulation with promising candidates.

After the questioning part of the interview concludes, the interviewers will have an agreed-upon signal (e.g., a word they use or the way they hold their pen), which tells the other interviewers that they think this candidate has good potential and would like to see how they react in a hypothetical situation simulation. We do this because sometimes there is disagreement on a candidate's potential, so this signal allows any interviewer who thinks the candidate would role-play well to indicate that to the rest of the group in a way that isn't awkward in front of the candidate. Those who are not invited to role-play are out of the running at this point and receive a call within a day or two from one of the interviewers explaining such.

> Some of the highlights of working as a research consultant are the side jobs. These projects given by the department are a great way to practice project management skills, teamwork, and timeliness. The best projects are the ones that require collaboration from you and your coworkers.
>
> *Research Consultant, Brigham Young University*

Those asked to role-play do so on the spot. The role-play includes an interviewer posing as a freshman writing student who needs help narrowing his or her research topic. Successful role-playing interviews tend to involve the research consultant giving the hypothetical student time to talk, asking the student about his or her interests, and asking increasingly complex questions throughout the process so the student comes up with the topic him or herself. An interview with the questions and the role-play tend to take fifteen minutes.

TRAINING
Training Philosophy

Our training approach is team-based. Team and mentored learning opportunities exist in every level of employee engagement within our program. If our employees are invested in the program and in one another, it becomes a place where we help each other succeed. We foster a team-player environment where our employees are integral in training one another, and administrators rely on our veteran research consultants to impart knowledge to newer employees. An easier approach might be a highly standardized, rigid, top-down training program in which a single supervisor would be in charge of uber-organized instruction. This would assure consistency, to be sure. But because we value the personal interactions that the research consultants develop among themselves, we relinquish some of this power in service of active learning opportunities, leadership chances for student employees, and innovative training strategies that are consistently being developed from the ground up.

Training Overview

We employ four levels of training which give our student employees a well-rounded introduction to their work and continued learning experiences throughout their time with us.
The training tiers are as follows:

- mentored training
- team training
- cross training
- library-wide training

Mentored training. We start with the individual mentor/mentee pairings that begin from
the first semester a student is employed. A new employee (at a TA level) is paired with a
more experienced research consultant who works in the RWC. Through a semester-long
partnership, the new employee will be required to shadow and work with their mentor
as they complete different training exercises both in the library instruction classrooms
and in research consultations in the RWC. (See Appendix B. HBLL TA Training Packet.)

> One of the best parts about being a research consultant is helping
> people discover library resources. Sometimes, people come in and
> have no idea how to use the databases or find library materials.
> As we go through the tutorial, they get so happy with each new
> discovery! I love helping people that are excited to learn and utilize
> the different resources that the library has.
>
> *Research Consultant, Brigham Young University*

New TAs are expected to complete classroom observations in our library instruction
classrooms in the first two to three weeks of the semester. They can sign up to shadow
their mentor or another experienced TA for these and must get them signed off in their
training packet. We expect them to shadow a variety of courses—from our advanced
writing sessions conducted by different subject librarians to our freshman writing sessions
conducted by information literacy librarians. Since our freshmen come in a sequence of
three visits to the library, the trainee must watch an entire succession. We also ask new
employees to log several hours of shadowing in the RWC with their assigned mentor.
While shadowing, the students are taught how to run the front desk and how to record
consulting data; they also observe one-on-one consultations.

Team training. A second level of training is our weekly team training, which is coordinated by our student lead supervisor and the RWC specialist. Weekly training meetings

are meant not only to meet the immediate needs of the program, including scheduling, but also to fill holes in knowledge that need to be addressed as soon as possible. This includes exercises in technology, programs, database assignments, and role-playing activities that go over productive research consulting practices. This is also where we remind students of work expectations, behaviors, and correct any problematic issues we've noticed in the previous week. Such meetings can also be a time for students to socialize, plan parties, and play games. Both research consultants and TAs attend these meetings. We generally try to keep the tone warm and inclusive, especially when we need to hold special training like those on safety, stress management, or FERPA regulations.

> I can't believe how much my own research has improved. An assignment that would have taken me several hours in the past can now be done in minutes. Not only is my research more focused and streamlined, but my search results are more relevant, succinct, and cohesive (my search results used to be all over the place!).
>
> *Research Consultant, Brigham Young University*

Cross training. A third level of training is the monthly program training which is held with the entire staff of the RWC, including both research consultants and writing tutors. This is coordinated by Writing Center and library administrators. This training tends to be formal in tone since there are more people present. Examples of past training include customer service skills, when to refer students between research and writing employees, and how to deal with difficult students/situations in the RWC.

Library-wide training. Finally, library-wide training occurs a few times a semester and includes all public services library student employees—from circulation staff, to help desk staff, to student secretaries, and beyond. This training varies widely but will familiarize students with the strategic vision of the library, make students aware of any physical changes happening in the building, and train with widely needed research methods and technologies. A reference librarian sets the agenda for these meetings.

Work Expectations

Employee work expectations are outlined in a formal document our HR department keeps on file for each student. The document is reviewed each semester both in training meetings (at the beginning of the semester) and in one-on-one evaluations (at the end of the semester). The document, and documentation of reviewing it, are signed both by employee and supervisor. The document in full is included at the end of this chapter as Appendix C. Student Employee Work Expectations, but it generally outlines the following:

- when a student is allowed to work
- protocol for clocking in and out
- how to handle absences
- when and where to take breaks
- the dress standard
- how to respond in emergency situations
- work ethic
- confidentiality

Such information is helpful to have on file for a few reasons: (1) so that students understand the expectations of their continued good standing as an employee, and (2) so that if ever the occasion arose to let a student employee go, substantiation of the work expectations would be readily available.

> One of the most effective parts of my training has been working with the subject librarians. When we are teaching assistants, we are also able to learn about different databases within a variety of subject areas. I have also enjoyed role-playing different topics because it helped me understand if a topic was narrow enough or too broad.
>
> *Research Consultant, Brigham Young University*

Student Leadership Opportunities, Incentives, and Increasing Challenges

Our students have many opportunities to become leaders in the program. The top position is the student lead supervisor who acts as a supervisor over both RWC employees and TAs (See Appendix D. Student Job Description for list and description of each position). The student lead supervisor's responsibilities include

- scheduling and staffing;
- day-to-day maintenance of the RWC (under supervision of RWC specialist);
- running weekly training meetings; and
- attending a weekly coordination meeting with the information literacy coordinator and RWC specialist.

Students do not apply for this position but instead are chosen by administrators after reviewing research consultants' seniority, initiative, leadership potential, interpersonal skills, and dependability.

As discussed, other veteran consultants are asked to mentor new TAs on a semesterly basis, and even our newest employees are given leadership opportunities as they help administrators plan and carry out new student orientation and volunteer to help administrators and librarians with projects. The incentive for moving from TA to research consultant is also monetary and is subject to the following:

- openings in the RWC for new consultants
- a student's timely completion of the training packet
- observations by mentors, supervisors, and administrators as to the student's intellectual and emotional maturity

In addition to the wage increase when a student moves up to a research consultant level, there is also more of a fixed schedule (whereas TAs are "on call" employees whose hours depend on when help is needed in the instruction classrooms). There is another wage increase for the student lead supervisor. We also have a discretionary wage increase budget to award students each semester depending on their performances. The student sets goals at the beginning of each semester that range from behavioral to knowledge-based, and these goals are reviewed at the end of each semester in the end-of-semester evaluation. (See Appendix E. Student Employee Evaluation.)

> It's great to have everyone involved in the writing process in one place. If the student I'm assisting has writing questions, I can have them sit down with a writing tutor almost immediately instead of having them pack up their work and referencing them to another section of the library. It makes helping the students easier for us (the library employees), and for the student themselves.
>
> *Research Consultant, Brigham Young University*

Observations

Qualitative employee observations are an integral part of how we assess an employee's progress, assign raises, and more job responsibilities. In our newest employees, we care about dependability, timeliness, and the ability to follow directions. In more seasoned employees, we look for problem-solving skills, well-rounded customer service skills, and initiative in developing deeper research understanding. Such learning outcomes are outlined in our on-file job description for our student employees.

Observations take place both informally and formally. Informally, library instructors are always welcome to report any problems they encounter with TAs to the freshman programs librarian. Formally, a survey is sent out once a semester to library instructors, who must rate the TA's helpfulness, dependability, and note anything else the TA could do to improve his or her service. Other formal observations are conducted in the RWC by the RWC specialist who monitors research consultations and fills out an observation form which will later be discussed with the student employee. (See Appendix F. Research Consultant Observation Form.)

Team Building

One of the greatest benefits of having so many opportunities for leadership within our program is the way it builds camaraderie among our research consultants and TAs. Mentoring allows students to get to know each other on a personal level, and our weekly training meetings, which are largely student-led, are another great place to work on workplace unity. Each meeting we start with "happy thoughts" in which our employees share something funny, exciting, or happy that has happened to them recently. This gives us a chance to share good news and congratulate one another on achievements.

> For my learning style, the most helpful training has been shadowing my coworkers and the subject librarians. I get to watch them handle real study topics ranging from easy topics to extremely difficult. I feel like this method of training continuously gives me new tricks up my sleeve when I face a difficult consultation. It also gives me new research ideas that I never would have come up with on my own.
>
> *Research Consultant, Brigham Young University*

Our employees also initiated a weekly award that is given out at each of our training meetings: The EBSCO Award. The award is a humorous trophy given from student to student to recognize exceptional effort or initiative in the week previous. This employee recognition has no monetary benefit, but because it gives students a chance to recognize each other, it builds a culture in which students are looking for the best in one another and are liberal in their praise.

Our largest difficulty so far has been to build camaraderie between the research consultants and writing tutors who work together in the RWC. Because the writing tutors are trained separately from the research consultants, there can be terminology-related or methodological differences that may create tension between workers. The monthly joint training meeting has helped smooth out some of those tensions and allowed research consultants to feel more integrated into the writing center culture, and joint parties have also helped. We are still working on ways to fully integrate and create a sense of trust and community within the center that will benefit employees and students alike.

ASSESSMENT

Assessment data is collected in a variety of typical ways, such as surveys, focus groups, and counting interactions. The data is divided into feedback from student employees and those using the services.

When students arrive for a session in the Research and Writing Center, they are asked to provide basic information on a client intake form (see Appendix G. Research and Writing Center Intake Form). The tutors complete the form after meeting with the students and that data is entered into an online program designed for "academic support, writing, and advising centers" called WCOnline.[3] In addition, we use the client intake form to ask students for permission to send them a survey following their tutoring session. Those who agree receive an email with a link to a satisfaction survey, the response rate being 69 percent. That data is collected and reviewed each semester to see what is going well and what needs to be addressed the following semester.

The completed client intake forms are entered into WCOnline for every tutoring and consulting session. That data is stored and reports are generated once a semester and compiled for an annual report. Data that is generally not collected by the library but is included in our reports includes the following:

- total number of research/writing sessions per semester
- average consult time
- most sought-after services
- referrals to other tutors
- referrals to subject librarians
- referrals to library services
- wait time

Student focus groups are also used to give more detailed feedback on the service provided in the RWC. These are generally held once a year with twenty to thirty student participants divided into four focus groups.

Student employee focus groups are also held once a year in a combined training meeting. The student employees are divided into smaller groups and the library assessment office provides discussion leaders so supervisors are not present during the sessions. Students are asked to describe the work being done in the RWC, what is going well, and what they wish would change. Identifying information is removed from the session transcripts to maintain confidentiality and to promote genuine feedback. The report is compiled by the Library Assessment Office before being given to the RWC supervisors and coordinators.

REFLECTION

As evidenced by discussions with our student employees, their time as research consultants helps them in various aspects of their scholarly and personal lives, from increased confidence and leadership skills to a more complex understanding of research methodology. They showcase exceptional growth in their time as TAs and consultants, which makes us proud to work with them.

We have learned many lessons in preparing a training program for our research consultants, and one of those lessons is that teaching itself is a powerful learning tool. By requiring our employees to teach (whether it be through individual consultations, through instructing small groups of students, or through teaching each other in training meetings or as mentors) we give them opportunities to grow in ways that no tutorial by itself ever could. Furthermore, though we use the term "training," we realize that good instruction of any kind is based on sound educational principles that jumpstart learning. This means that active participation rather than passive learning is paramount to our employees' success as TAs and as research consultants.

No program is perfect, however, and in reflecting on the current iteration of the RWC we have learned that though collaboration is highly productive, it can also be difficult to execute practically. Finding a balance between subject expertise (i.e., training writing tutors and research consultants separately) and collaborative effort (i.e., running a shared center in a shared space) requires flexibility and the ability to troubleshoot problems when they arise in a unified manner—a balance we are still seeking to achieve. For instance, service models may differ. While a writing expert might follow more of a "tutor" model, a research consultant might value a "customer service" model in interacting with patrons. Sharing a space, however, provides greater understanding and respect for the roles of both writing tutors and research consultants as well as a greater consideration of how intertwined the research and writing processes truly are.

Overall, our joint venture has been very successful, and it is a service that continues to grow due to robust advertising, institutional support, and most importantly, the superb quality of our student employees.

APPENDIX A

LIBRARY INSTRUCTION TEACHER'S ASSISTANT JOB POSTING

Description:

Responsibilities include assisting teachers with presentations and students with their individual research projects during scheduled library instruction classes, providing research help to small groups of students and working on assigned library projects. Training includes a weekly meeting, observing library instruction sessions, and observing consultations in the Research and Writing Center.

Qualifications:

- Be available to work a variety of hours (including day and evening). Hours are on call and will vary each week between 5–15 hours depending on the instruction loads.
- Be prompt and dependable.
- Be able to communicate clearly with students/teachers and collaborate with coworkers.
- Be able to learn technology and other research skills quickly.

Preferred Experience:

- Experience with research and library databases
- Tutoring or teaching experience

Application Instructions: Apply online. Include cover letter explaining why you are applying for this job, detailing your qualifications and showcasing your related experience. Include a résumé with relevant work experience. Include a class schedule. BYU is an equal opportunity employer.

APPENDIX B

Elise Silva and Suzanne Julian

HBLL TA Training Packet

The Harold B. Lee Library
Brigham Young University

Day One

_____ Y-Time (clocking in and out, correcting missed punches)
_____ Important areas (break rooms, emergency exits)

Initial Training

Opening and Closing the Rooms
- Lights
- Computers
- Projector
- Door
- Printer
- Lost and found

Instruction Rooms
- Touch screen
- Lights and spotlights
- Laser pointer
- Phones
- Markers
- Podium
- Microphone

Instruction Room Calendar
- Logging in
- Signing up
- Stats (color coding system)
- Color system

Advanced Writing System
- Taking roll
- Adding students

Technology Troubleshooting
- Printer paper
- Paper jams
- Computer troubleshooting
- Helpdesk tickets

☐ Complete the library audio tour that is required for all First-Year Writing Courses. Take the accompanying quiz and, upon completion, turn it in to your supervisor or their assistant to receive your score.

      I completed the Library Audio Tour on: ___/___/____ and received a score of: ____/____

      Signature: _____

Elise Silva and Suzanne Julian

☐ First, shadow 5 classes (either advanced writing or freshman writing). Then, assist in 5 classes that conduct one-on-ones. Have the student employee you shadow initial below the date:

5 classes you shadowed

Date: ___/___/___   ___/___/___   ___/___/___   ___/___/___   ___/___/___

TA initials: _____   _____   _____   _____   _____

5 classes you assisted with one-on-ones:

Date: ___/___/___   ___/___/___   ___/___/___   ___/___/___   ___/___/___

TA initials: _____   _____   _____   _____   _____

Basic Research Skills

As a TA, you will also have the opportunity to help students search for scholarly information. In order to become more familiar with the databases available at the library, please complete the following items:

☐ Follow this link to the iLearning Library Tutorials and click on the "Research Starter Guide" link that is toward the bottom of the page: (http://lib.byu.edu/sites/ilearning/library-tutorials/).

Academic Search Premier is one database that is owned by a company called EBSCO. EBSCO has many databases that you can search at the same time, and each one indexes different subject-specific materials. Below are some of the most commonly used EBSCO databases, but there are many more. Go to an EBSCO database and at the top next to the name of the database, click on the "Choose Databases" link.

☐ Fill in the following table by conducting searches in EBSCO databases. Use the keywords listed in the columns to run the same search in the different databases listed in the rows. Write the number of results found for each search:

Database	Social media AND advertis*	Myocardial infarction AND cholesterol	Anxiety disorders AND depression
Business Source Premier			
MEDLINE			
PsycINFO			

Elise Silva and Suzanne Julian

Research and Writing Center

As preparation to work in the RWC, please shadow your mentor in the two positions of the RWC: Receptionist and Consultant.

Name of RWC mentor: _____

☐ You will shadow your mentor for 5 receptionist hours and 5 consultant hours. Please list the dates that you completed these sessions:

Receptionist Hours:

___/___/___   ___/___/___   ___/___/___   ___/___/___   ___/___/___

Consultant Hours:

___/___/___   ___/___/___   ___/___/___   ___/___/___   ___/___/___

☐ Consultations are essential in the Research and Writing Center, and being personable and interested in the student and their goals is a key to success. You must observe 5 one-on-ones in the RWC and assist with 5 one-on-ones in the RWC. In the box below, please list 3 things you learned while observing and 3 things you learned while assisting (this could have to do with the best way to deal with students, how to start a consultation, how to deal with difficult situations, etc.).

5 hours you observed one-on-ones:

Date ___/___/___   ___/___/___   ___/___/___   ___/___/___   ___/___/___

Initials: _____   _____   _____   _____   _____

5 consultations and you assisted with one-on-ones:

Date ___/___/___   ___/___/___   ___/___/___   ___/___/___   ___/___/___

Initials: _____   _____   _____   _____   _____

Elise Silva and Suzanne Julian

In-Depth Research Skills

The following sections outline an in-depth training process to help you become familiar with the research process and the databases available to students.

PICK TOPIC

Select one of the listed questions as your research question for this project:

Business:

- How does employee appreciation relate to employee productivity?
- What is the role of ethics in international business?

Education:

- Should the arts be required courses in public education?
- How has the internet changed higher education?

Engineering and Technology:

- Is colonization on Mars technologically feasible?
- What is the most efficient source of renewable energy?

Family, Home, and Social Sciences:

- What is the influence of the European Union on world economic/political/cultural trends?
- What is the effect of China's one-child policy?

Fine Arts and Communications:

- What type of advertising brings in the most revenue?
- How does photography shape public opinion?

Humanities:

- What is the effect of wartime on artistic expression?
- What do pop culture icons of today suggest about our society?

Life Sciences:

- What causes obesity in young children?
- Are humans under threat of mass extinction?

Nursing:

- Can music be effectively used in therapy/medical treatment?
- What are effective preventative measures and recovery methods for addiction?

Elise Silva and Suzanne Julian

BACKGROUND RESEARCH

Open "Research Starter Guide" and use the databases under the heading "Finding and Narrowing Your Topic" to do background research on your topic. This will help you answer the next three questions.

Find 2 background sources and list them:

_____

_____

List 2-3 possible ways to narrow your research question into something you could sustain a discussion on for an 8-10 page paper:

_____

_____

_____

Answer this question in the space below: Is your research question/idea an "issue?" Why? (i.e., are there multiple sides or opinions on this issue? Is it an arguable topic?)

⭐ **At this point, make an appointment to discuss your work with RWC administrative assistant.** ⭐

SUPPORTING ARTICLES

Find at least 2 articles in an **EBSCO** database

List database:

_____

Cite the article in MLA format:

_____

_____

List database:

_____

Cite the article in MLA format:

_____

_____

Store articles in a bibliography generator like RefWorks, ProQuest Flow, EndNote, Zotero (or other).

Elise Silva and Suzanne Julian

Find at least one article in a **ProQuest** database

List database:

_____

Cite the article in MLA format:

_____

_____

Store article in a bibliography generator like RefWorks, ProQuest Flow, EndNote, Zotero (or other).

Use a **subject guide** to find a useful database and article.

List subject guide:

_____

List database:

_____

Cite the article in MLA format:

_____

_____

Store article in a bibliography generator like RefWorks, ProQuest Flow, EndNote, Zotero (or other).

Find **one other** database or website and useful article.

List database:

_____

Cite the article in MLA format:

_____

_____

Store article in a bibliography generator like RefWorks, ProQuest Flow, EndNote, Zotero (or other).

Elise Silva and Suzanne Julian

Pick 2 of the articles you've gathered above and answer the following questions:

Is this a "scholarly" article? Discuss:	Is this a "scholarly" article? Discuss:
Is this article authoritative and current? Discuss:	Is this article authoritative and current? Discuss:
Is this article relevant for your information needs and is its content accurate? Discuss:	Is this article relevant for your information needs and is its content accurate? Discuss:

 At this point, make an appointment to discuss your work with RWC administrative assistant.

Elise Silva and Suzanne Julian

PAPER AND THESIS DEVELOPMENT

Write a concise thesis for your paper. Remember, a good thesis responds to a scholarly conversation, so follow the "they say/I say" pattern (i.e., other scholars argue _____ while I argue _____). You can agree, disagree, or point out a gap in previous scholarly conversations regarding your topic.

To show you've read and understood the articles you've gathered, highlight key article sections that engage with your thesis. (You can print and attach these sections of the article, copy and paste them to a Word document, or re-type them.)

OPPOSING ARTICLES

Now, find at least 2 articles that support an <u>opposing</u> argument to your thesis:

List database:

_____

Cite the article in MLA format:

_____

_____

How does this article oppose your thesis?

_____

_____

_____

List database:

_____

Cite the article in MLA format:

_____

_____

How does this article oppose your thesis?

_____

_____

_____

 At this point, make an appointment to discuss your work with RWC administrative assistant.

APPENDIX C

STUDENT EMPLOYEE WORK EXPECTATIONS

LIBRARY INSTRUCTION TEACHER'S ASSISTANT OR RWC RESEARCH CONSULTANT

BYU Harold B. Lee Library

Student employees are a valued resource in the Harold B. Lee Library and are essential to helping the library fulfill its mission to provide information resources and services to our patrons. Though not all-inclusive, the following information contains various library student employee policies that will help you better understand and successfully fulfill your work responsibilities.

Work Hours

You are expected to adhere to a weekly work schedule established with your direct supervisor. Schedules should be within the hours of 8 AM to 10 PM, Monday through Friday.

While actual hours may vary, the ***maximum*** amount of hours an undergraduate student employee may work is:

- Fall/Winter Semesters—**20 hours per week*** (U.S. resident graduate students may work up to 28 hours per week)
- Spring/Summer Terms—**40 hours per week*** (international students must be on a University-approved break to work more than 20 hours per week)

Clocking In & Out

The only acceptable devices for clocking in or out are:

- the department phone
- the department's designated timeclock
- the computer workstation at which you are assigned to work

---

* The work week runs Saturday 12:00 AM–Friday 11:59 PM. Additional hours may be worked during approved breaks or holidays as approved by a student's supervisors. Students may ***not*** exceed an average of 28 hours per week during the Affordable Care Act (ACA) measurement period.

You should *not* clock in or out using personal wireless devices, which includes cell phones, tablets, laptops, etc., or other computers or devices outside your immediate work area. Any exceptions must be approved in advance by your supervisor. If you encounter any problems clocking in or out, you should immediately notify your supervisor.

If you miss a timeclock punch, the missing time may be submitted online via Y-time using one of the acceptable devices listed above. At the end of each pay period, you should be sure to review your timecard and report any necessary corrections you are unable to make yourself to your supervisor.

Dependability/Absences

Attendance for scheduled or assigned shifts is mandatory, and you should be punctual. If you anticipate being late for work due to an emergency, or in cases of illness, you should contact your supervisor as soon as possible. If an illness, injury, or emergency situation requires you to be absent more than one day, you must contact your supervisor each day to report that you will not be attending work. Other time off, for whatever reason, must be approved *in advance* by your supervisor. You are responsible for securing any needed substitute (from among the current department student employees).

You are encouraged to give your supervisor at least two weeks notice before ending your employment with the library or transferring to another library department.

Breaks & Food/Drink

For every four *consecutive* **hours** of work, you may take one, on-the-clock, **ten**-minute break. This time may not be taken at the beginning or end of the shift and break time may not be accumulated. Breaks include any personal time spent at work, including chatting, reading, checking personal communication or otherwise engaging activities unrelated to work. If you are scheduled for a shift of more than five consecutive hours, a meal break of at least 30 minutes should be taken. You must clock out and back in before and after these meal breaks.

Break rooms are located on the 2nd and 6th floors. Only library staff and student employees may use the break rooms. You may consume food and drink at work in a responsible manner out of the public eye. Intense odors spread easily throughout the library, so strong-smelling foods should only be consumed in the break rooms. Microwaving popcorn is *not* allowed anywhere in the library.

Dress Standards & Honor Code

Because you are dealing with the public, you are expected to have *a higher dress standard than the general public* and are not allowed to wear shorts, hats, flip-flops, exercise clothing, political buttons, or similar campaign items while at work. If any of these requirements are not met, you may be asked to clock out to remedy the issue and then return to work.

Nametags enhance security and are a public service tool. You are required to wear your library name tag when on duty (including while in the break rooms) in a proper way as directed by your supervisor.

Safety & Emergencies

In order to help keep the library safe for patrons and personnel, you are required to report any safety hazards or maintenance issues to your supervisor. Please use care and caution while performing your work duties. Any injury to you or a patron occurring at the library needs to be reported within 24 hours to your supervisor.

If you become aware of a crime or emergency happening while you are working, you should immediately call library security (801-422-1515). If you are made aware of a problem, but the situation no longer exists, you should inform your supervisor and let them take the proper steps to address the issue.

Work Ethic & Assignments

At all times when being paid by the university to work, you should demonstrate integrity and professionalism by: completing assigned duties and projects in a timely fashion; providing exceptional customer service; seeking additional tasks from supervisors as time permits; continually learning about library resources and tools; and investigating ways to improve library processes, procedures, and organization.

You should *not* engage in studying, doing homework, gaming, personal reading, browsing, or using social media, reading or writing personal emails, instant messaging, watching videos (non-work related), texting or talking on cell phones, internet browsing, etc. Social and other personal conversations should be kept to a minimum, as unnecessary and excessive conversation with other employees or acquaintances can delay work and disturb patrons. You are not allowed to study or just "hang out" in offices or work areas during non-work hours. Exceptions to these policies may be approved by your supervisor, especially as necessary for completion of work assignments.

Department meetings, including regular staff and training meetings, should be attended every week unless arranged beforehand.

You are not allowed to use departmental/office computers, printers, copiers, phones, or related equipment for personal or school-related activities. This also includes the use of the internet for anything other than work assignments.

Confidentiality

As a student employee, you are required to uphold the confidential nature of patron and personnel records maintained by the library and university, being careful to never disclose information in verbal, written, or electronic form to any unauthorized person. You should only access information to which you have a legitimate need that is directly related to your job duties.

As a matter of security, do not share door codes and passwords, full employee schedules, or personal contact info with anyone who does not work at the Research and Writing Center.

Out of respect to writers, tutoring sessions are kept confidential, with the exception of private or formal training discussions. Likewise, client report forms are confidential unless a writer requests faculty notification.

I have read and understand the student employee work expectations outlined in this document. Further, I understand that compliance to these expectations is a condition of my employment in the Harold B. Lee Library and will influence performance evaluations and possible wage increases.

_____

Signature of Student   Date

_____

Signature of Supervisor   Date

APPENDIX D

STUDENT JOB DESCRIPTION

Date: December 8
Department: Learning Commons
Title: Research and Writing Center Consultant (Student Position)

JOB SUMMARY

The Research and Writing Center Consultant assists individual students with their research projects and makes referrals to additional services that will help the student successfully complete their project.

Essential Functions

A consultant will

- tutor students with their research skills
- assist in the Research and Writing Center as a receptionist as well as a consultant
- provide assistance in library instruction classrooms
- complete library instruction-related projects as assigned
- attend training meeting and complete training assignments
- mentor new employees
- track interactions in the classroom and the RWC by recording statistics as required

Training and Employee Expectations

Teacher's Assistants

By the end of the first semester, TAs should be able to

1. interact with peers and patrons professionally
2. assess a patron's research needs accurately
3. ask appropriate questions during consultations
4. take care of the instruction classrooms
5. know how to aid teachers while instructing
6. have a basic knowledge of general databases, research guides, and citation managers

Research Consultants:

By the end of a year of working, research consultant should be able to

1. be proficient at the Teacher's Assistant (TA) responsibilities

2. manage the receptionist duties with accuracy
3. consult at a high professional level
4. take initiative in independent projects and as mentors
5. handle difficult patrons/situations well
6. develop critical-thinking skills with the ability to ask deep, penetrating questions
7. navigate subject-specific databases and understand the nuances of the library website
8. know about non-library services which may aid in research

Lead Student Supervisor:

By the time a student is invited to become a lead student supervisor, he or she should be able to

1. demonstrate strong leadership skills
2. be dependable and accurate in projects and work commitments
3. mentor new employees
4. assist the library instruction coordinator by being able to teach, conduct meetings, assist in the hiring process, and train.
5. meet weekly to coordinate the schedule and projects

APPENDIX E

STUDENT EMPLOYEE EVALUATION

BYU Harold B. Lee Library

Name:	BYU ID #:
Department:	Supervisor:

Based on the job's expectations and requirements, please evaluate your student employee:

Development Plan: (Please list goals and areas of improvement)

Current Wage:	Raise Amount:

Student Signature: _____Date:_____

Supervisor Signature: _____Date:_____

I have reviewed the employee work expectation document with employee (☐ yes ☐ no):

APPENDIX F

RESEARCH CONSULTANT OBSERVATION FORM

Introduction	Examples/Practices
☐ Consultant is open/friendly ☐ Assignment is reviewed and discussed ☐ Review student's research knowledge ☐ Sets objective and expectations	**Questions/Suggestions**
Consultation	**Examples/Practices**
☐ Listens actively ☐ Asks open-ended questions ☐ Student navigates computer ☐ Check for student's understanding ☐ Student contributes to conversation ☐ Gives student time to work	**Questions/Suggestions**
Conclusion	**Examples/Practices**
☐ Student leaves with a research plan and resources to complete assignment	**Questions/Suggestions**

APPENDIX G

RESEARCH AND WRITING CENTER INTAKE FORM

Welcome to the Research & Writing Center!

Help in all stages of the writing process

Name _____

Date _____

Instructor _____

Course _____

Name/Number _____

Assignment _____

Time Arrived _____

* Please write clearly & complete an individual client report form for ALL participants

Please Circle: First-Year Sophomore Junior Senior Graduate Faculty Community Member

When is your assignment due?

☐ Today   ☐ 3-4 days

☐ 1-2 days   ☐ 5+ days

☐ **Please notify my instructor that I came in.**

Instructor's Email Address: _____

☐ **I'm willing to complete a brief email survey about the RWC.**

Tutor/Consultant's Name _____   **Comments to Instructor:**

Session Start Time _____

Session End Time _____

Writing

☐ Understanding the Assignment
☐ Brainstorming/Prewriting
☐ Thesis/Argument
☐ Evidence/Support/Examples/Analysis
☐ Organization
☐ Introduction/Conclusion
☐ Topic Sentences/Transitions
☐ Sentence Structure
☐ Tone/Voice/Style
☐ Grammar/Usage/ Punctuation
☐ Citations/Formatting

Research

☐ Topic Development
☐ Background Research
☐ Scholarly Sources
☐ Evaluating Sources
☐ Citation Assistance
☐ Expanding or Narrowing Search Results
☐ Finding Library Materials
☐ Using Research Guides
☐ Using Interlibrary Loan
☐ Online Sources Used:

_____

Referred to ☐ Research Consultant ☐ Writing Tutor ☐ Librarian/Help Desk (specify) _____

NOTES

1. "Harold B. Lee Library Mission Statement," Harold B. Lee Library, accessed December 15, 2015, https://lib.byu.edu/about/library-administration/ <discontinued link>.
2. "Aims of a BYU Education," Brigham Young University, accessed December 15, 2015, https://aims.byu.edu/.
3. "WCOnline," WCOnline, accessed December 15, 2015, https://mywconline.com/index.php.

BIBLIOGRAPHY

Brigham Young University. "Aims of a BYU Education." Accessed December 15, 2015. https://aims.byu.edu/aims-of-a-byu-education <discontinued link>.

Harold B. Lee Library. "Harold B. Lee Library Mission Statement." Accessed December 15, 2015. https://lib.byu.edu/about/library-administration/.

WCOnline. "WCOnline." Accessed December 15, 2015. https://mywconline.com/index.php.

Case Study 2

INFORMATION COMMONS AT BUTLER UNIVERSITY:
Committed to Service and Student Development

Amanda Starkel

OVERVIEW

In 2009, Butler University Libraries were looking for a way to pull librarians away from the reference desk and give them more time to focus on liaison responsibilities such as instruction. In collaboration with the Center for Academic Technology, the Information Commons program was established. This student employment program cross-trained students in both research and academic technology assistance skills. Equipped with these skills, students provided quality service at both Information Commons locations: the reference desk in the main campus library and in the Center for Academic Technology.[1]

Evolution

From 2009 to 2014, the delineation of services between the circulation desk and the Information Commons reference desk caused frustration for both staff and patrons. Occasionally, we heard of patrons circling the fountain in the atrium as they were referred back and forth between the two desks. Information Commons students were responsible for answering reference questions, in person and via phone/email/chat. Their schedule covered six days a week and did not extend from open to close. There was a separate circulation desk located right next to the entrance of the library. This desk was staffed by a different group of student employees and library staff members at all hours when the library was open. They managed the circulation of all materials, including equipment, reserves, interlibrary loans, and media items.

Single Service Point in the Library

In the fall of 2014, Butler University Libraries merged the circulation desk and the Information Commons reference desk as a response to our patrons' frustrations. We believe the decision was supported by data and would allow us to offer better service to our patrons. The new single service point was placed in an entirely new location on the first floor of the main campus library so that it would be clear to patrons that a change occurred. Information Commons students assumed responsibility for staffing this new desk from open to close. After reviewing circulation and reference statistics, as well as gate count numbers, the libraries decided to double-staff the service point during the busiest times—from 9 a.m. to 9 p.m. on most days. Only the Information Commons students are present at the service point, but staff is available in nearby offices if help is requested. This works well, as students desire to work independently but "want to have professionals available for assistance when difficult questions arise or when they are confronted with the rare unpleasant customer."[2]

	BEFORE (Two Desks)	AFTER (Single Service Point)
Total Library Information Commons hours/week	59	170.5
Days of the week covered	6	7
Total number of Information Commons student employees	20–25	30–35
Information Commons' student responsibilities	• Answer face-to-face reference questions • Answer emails for the primary library email address • Answer phone calls to the reference line • Staff the library's chat service	• Answer face-to-face reference and directional questions • Answer email for the primary library email address • Answer phone calls to the main library line • Staff the library's chat service • Handle circulation of all material, including reserves and equipment • Open and close the building

Adapting to Changes

As our university continues to expand and develop, spaces and organizational structure evolve. In 2014, the Center for Academic Technology came under the libraries' umbrella and this staff began reporting to the dean of libraries, and shortly thereafter, the Center relocated on the third floor of the main campus library. This placed the two service locations of the Information Commons program within the same building. Changes of this nature led us to assess and be responsive to any opportunities that arise as a result of this relocation.

> After working here, I realize IC brings much more to me than just a convenient location. I enjoy working in such a professional environment that is more than just a desk job (though desks are often involved). I feel the experience I am gaining, through interactions with library patrons and professors, is very valuable in my life moving forward. I am also very aware of the skills that I am learning and their helpfulness as well.
>
> *Information Commons student employee, Butler University*

Goals of the Program

From its inception, the Information Commons program has been committed to providing service to the Butler community. However, the program was conceived as much more than student-run service points. The program provides student employees with valuable experiential learning and development opportunities. The strategic priorities of the program are described below:

- Information Commons' student employees will demonstrate initiative in providing exemplary customer service at our service points and with our projects and partners.
- The Information Commons program is committed to giving its student employees a "unique opportunity to grow professionally and gain practical, in-demand skills."[3] The specific learning outcomes include the following:

  o **Professional development and workforce preparation**. Student employees will develop the collaborative, problem-solving, and professional skills necessary to succeed in a multicultural workforce and global society.
  o **Leadership development and reflective practice**. Student employees will progress in their self-development through reflective practice and leadership opportunities.

- o **Information literacy and technology skill development**. Student employees will establish strategies to find, understand, evaluate, and use information, technology, and media ethically and legally.
- o **Connection and balance**. Student employees will enhance their liberal arts education by working across disciplines and promoting work-life balance and integration of their knowledge and skills within their academic, extracurricular, and professional lives.

As Perozzi, Kappes, and Santucci assert in their publication, *Learning Outcomes and Student Employment Programs,* "Infusing learning outcomes into the student employment process is not easy, yet it adds significantly to the students' experiences."[4]

Peer Learning

The program is also heavily invested in peer learning. Peer-to-peer teaching occurs at the service point between our employees and patrons, the majority of whom are undergraduate students. The majority of our shifts in both locations are staffed by multiple students at a time, so a lot of mentoring occurs informally as students "look over each others' shoulders to learn something new."[5] There is also a more formal mechanism for peer-to-peer teaching among the employees, and there are two tiers to the program. Students are hired at the assistant level and can be promoted to the associate level. Typically, we have eight associates in total. The associates are paired and then given a small team of assistants to manage. They model exceptional behavior and lead their assistants through the Information Commons process, starting with training. They gain valuable experience as a manager by handling disciplinary issues, taking part in the hiring process, and helping their supervisors strategize about the long-term success of the program.

ADMINISTRATION

Because the Information Commons program is a collaboration, it is overseen by professional staff in both the Center for Academic Technology and in the libraries. In 2013, the libraries retooled an existing librarian position to be the Information Commons and eLearning librarian. The Center for Academic Technology designated an academic technology specialist to manage their side of the program. These two individuals are equal partners in supervising students and making decisions for the program, such as hiring and strategic planning. However, there is some autonomy: the Information Commons and eLearning librarian crafts all of the library and research training and is responsible for making sure all library service outcomes are being met.

When the libraries moved to a merged service point staffed by Information Commons students, it greatly expanded the responsibility involved in managing the library side of the program. Library administration decided to repurpose two full-time staff positions to assist the Information Commons and eLearning librarian with the management of the Information Commons program and the library service point. The Information Commons staff associate works the opening shifts and the Information Commons staff assistant works closing shifts, Sundays through Thursdays. The Information Commons and eLearning librarian works more traditional Monday through Friday hours. Additionally, the newly appointed Information Commons academic technology specialist works a Saturday shift in the library. Between these four professional staff, nearly every hour that Information Commons students work is supported by a staff member directly connected to the program.

Trello: A Communication Tool

At times it has been a challenge to facilitate communication among a large, mostly remote team. One tool that has helped quite a bit is Trello, and we use it in several ways. (See Appendix A. Information Commons Trello Boards.) Each semester, we create a Project Board and a Board for each associate pair team. The first column of the Project Board is for announcements. This has been an effective way to share necessary information from shift to shift. The Project Board also helps us coordinate projects, in-class training sessions, discussions, and hands-on learning opportunities. The associate pair team boards have a column for each student assistant, where the students are expected to track progress through training and provide daily shift updates.

HIRING

Information Commons hires undergraduate student employees. Since the merge into one service point at the library, we have had a team of about thirty to thirty-five student employees, including a team of eight associates. We rarely hire freshmen during their first semester, since we hire at the end of the spring to staff the fall. We do not give preference to students of any major. The starting wage is $8/hour, which is above the state minimum wage. We give raises for each year of service and upon promotion to the role of associate. (See Appendix B. Information Commons Associate: Expectations for the Associate Role.) When students are hired, we assume continuing appointment and do not make them reapply each semester. We also have been flexible in allowing students to step back for a semester and return to the program later. A large number of Butler students study abroad or participate in internships, so we have found that this arrangement is necessary in order to retain quality employees.

> Through my time at Information Commons, I have really experienced efficient teamwork and good communication. This will not only help me through the rest of my time here at Butler but once I have a real-life internship or job I will know how to work in a team setting efficiently. I have also learned how to deal with people really well. Many different types of people come to the front desk so it has been important to accommodate each one in a way that is best for them.
>
> *Information Commons student employee, Butler University*

Schedule

We create a consistent schedule for an entire semester. Student assistants must work eight hours per week, and associates should work ten hours per week. Students are scheduled to work in both locations, and whenever possible, we attempt to spread out associate hours so that they overlap with the assistants on their team. Students are able to post and claim shifts from each other using a shared Google Calendar. The schedule runs from the first day of class to the last day of class; we create sign-up spreadsheets for hours over breaks and finals weeks. Whenever possible, we hire at the end of a semester to staff the following semester. This means we hire at the end of the spring semester for the fall, and we, unfortunately, are not typically hiring during the first weeks of school when many students are looking for employment. However, hiring in this way means we are typically fully staffed and getting acclimated to a regular schedule from day one of the semester.

Applications and Interviews

In the past, we have asked students to submit a résumé and cover letter; however, most of the cover letters we received were generic and gave little indication whether or not a candidate would be a good fit. More recently, we tried something new and replaced the cover letter with a more direct prompt to respond to: "Please write a brief paragraph or two about how your experiences, interests, or academic/professional/personal goals align with the Information Commons program." This method was more successful because it required students to reflect and compose an original answer. We create a rubric to score the applicants, and the location supervisors and the associates participate in an application review.

Rate the applicant:	Weak	Fair	Strong	NA
Technology skills/experiences				
Research skills/experiences				
Customer service skills/experiences				
Professionalism				
Interest in developing leadership skills				
Time management				
How did the applicant comport him/herself? Did they communicate well and use good examples?				
Do you think this candidate would be a good fit for the program? Why or why not?				

Associates also take part in the interview part of the process. These students attend interviews, if they are able, and we record the interviews so that those who can't be present can still participate in the decision process. We have created a set of questions focused on the values of the program, and most of these questions ask the candidate to share specific experiences or examples.

TRAINING
Handbook and Expectations

The Information Commons program clearly outlines expectations for attire and behavior in our *Student Handbook*. While on shift, students are expected to wear professional clothing and their individual nametags. This helps identify them as employees and prepares them for a professional work environment. Occasionally, we use a "jeans day pass" as a reward. Students are not permitted to work on homework, use their cell phones, or be on social media during their shifts. In order to fully benefit from the program and reach its goals, they should be engaged in training, projects, or service while on shift. Schedule, absence, and disciplinary policies are also outlined in the handbook. Each student signs and submits a page stating that they have read and understand the handbook.

We realize that we ask a lot of these student employees, considering that they often work only eight hours/week and split that time between two locations. Fortunately, Butler students have proved themselves to be exceptionally quick learners able to excel above our expectations. They are willing to invest in the training because they see the immediate and long-term returns for their academic and professional careers.

ONBOARDING AND FIRST SHIFTS

During their first shifts, students are led through a lengthy checklist by either a student associate or an Information Commons professional staff member. This process is meant to provide context and orient students to the spaces and circulation processes. It is made clear that students are not expected to retain all the information from day one; additional training is coming and many quick-reference resources exist as well.

> Skills that I have learned through IC have allowed me to become a more helpful person around my professors and peers. I am able to assist them with technological questions and issues, and I found myself more useful around campus. This allowed me to have more self-confidence with my studies, even though indirectly, as I became more aware of what I am capable of. It also helped me reduce my—and everyone's—fear of failure. I became more fearless in trying and applying new things in my academic life and studies.
>
> *Information Commons student employee, Butler University*

BUAnswers

One such reference resource is our version of the Springshare product, LibAnswers (BUAnswers). The libraries continue to expand use of this tool as an answers hub for campus; it includes all our contact information, a connection to our live chat, and more than 200 frequently asked questions and answers. Additionally, Information Commons has created a private group within this tool. It hosts more than 130 frequently asked questions and answers that are only visible to Information Commons students and staff when they are logged in. Our student employees can search both public and internal questions at the same time, by keyword. They also have the ability to add or edit existing questions within this system. This resource has influenced training in a few key ways. First, it alleviates the need for students to remember every detail of training covered since directions or answers are a quick search away. Second, it empowers our training activities to dig deeper and be more hands-on since they do not also have to serve double-duty as quick reference.

Core Training via Moodle

After a student has completely walked through the first shifts checklist, he/she logs into our course management system (Moodle). We have created a course for the Information Commons program and it houses all core training for both the library and Center for Academic Technology sides of the program. We have defined "core training" as the skills or knowledge that we expect all students within the program to possess. Training on the Center for Academic Technology side focuses on Butler-supported tools, including Moodle, Panopto, and Wordpress. The contents and objectives of the library training sections are detailed in the next section.

We work to ensure that training is self-directed, sustainable, and successful. The training is divided into sections and students are directed to tackle the sections in a certain order. Service in both locations is primary, so we limit audio/video training and make sure that the training can be interrupted or completed over multiple shifts. Students can work at their own pace, and their associates monitor their progress and offer support along the way. There are mandatory checkpoints built into the path so that we can make sure the training is accomplishing its goals. Several sections of library training focus not only on skill development but on understanding the philosophy behind our service and teaching. As Langan notes, "For this ambitious generation, [the why] helps them to connect the pieces, and satisfies their inherent needs for greater control. Rather than dictating a specific behavior, training should be based in theory so as to satisfy their need for great global understanding and need for learning."[6] There are things to read, view, explore, and practice within each section. Training focuses on specific procedures and philosophy as well as clearly communicating "standards of acceptable performance."[7]

LIBRARY TRAINING SECTIONS

- **The basics**. Introduce shared tools and expectations.
  - ○ Read and sign the *Information Commons Handbook*.
  - ○ Read information about our shared tools and how students are expected to use them (stats tracking form and Trello).
  - ○ Complete a Guide on the Side tutorial that introduces the public and staff sides of our FAQ tool (BUAnswers).
- **Library circulation**. Reinforce what students learn in the first shifts checklist and make sure students understand how to check items in and out using our circulation system.
  - ○ Watch a video to refresh your understanding of the circulation system (WMS).
  - ○ Complete a Guide on the Side tutorial about searching with WorldCat Discovery.
  - ○ Review information about circulation procedures. Then complete the circulation policy and procedure quiz.

Checkpoint: A face-to-face simulation between assistant and one of their associates. Associates work from a training certification guidelines document. (See Appendix C. Library Circulation.) Associates assume the patron role and ask assistants to accomplish certain tasks or answer questions to demonstrate mastery of certain skills (for example, checking out a laptop). Assistants get feedback and are deemed "certified" in circulation if they perform well. Assistants who do not perform well return to the training section on Moodle and receive some additional guidance from an associate or staff member.

- **Customer service**. Share our teaching philosophy and make sure students understand our expectation for exemplary customer service for various communication channels.
  - Review infographic about the library's customer service philosophy, the point of referral, and frequently asked questions about customer service in the library.
  - Review information about expectations for phone, email, and chat services. Then simulate chat and email questions to get a feel for answering questions in virtual environments.
  - Use Quizlet.com and Google Forms to learn and test your knowledge of subject liaisons within the library.
- **Research skills I**: Make sure students know how to employ basic research skills at the service point.
  - Go through the software LC Easy to learn about the Library of Congress.
  - Complete a Guide on the Side tutorial to learn about our Journals A–Z tool.
  - Review our eBooks LibGuide and complete an exploration activity to gets hands-on practice viewing, downloading, and printing ebooks from various collections.

Checkpoint: The checkpoint for customer service and research skills are combined into one patron simulation activity. Again, the associates work from a training certification guidelines document. (See Appendix D. Customer Service & Research Skills I.) Associates can perform this checkpoint in person or virtually. They ask assistants to assist with two basic research tasks (finding a book on the shelf and finding a few full-text articles). Associates help assistants navigate the research consultation and give feedback about customer service throughout the interaction.

- **Creative Commons and design**. Introduce Creative Commons and design concepts that students will need to integrate into their other training and projects.
  - Read and view materials to learn about Creative Commons and principles of design.
  - Explore and share resources about an aspect of design that interests you (topics selected so far include infographics in the classroom, book cover and college logo design, and PowerPoint presentation tips).

Checkpoint: Demonstrate the ability to search for and attribute Creative Commons works by adding three images and attributions to a shared LibGuide.

- **Information literacy**. Create a shared definition of information literacy and help students internalize these principles with their work with Information Commons and to the larger goals of the libraries and university.
  - Read and learn about the information literacy standards and the new framework

and how it connects to what we do at Information Commons.

- o View two videos from Project Information Literacy that summarize the habits of student researchers. Then utilize research skills and share information about our users' library or research habits.
- o Complete an information cycle tutorial to gain a better understanding of the ecosystem of scholarship.

Checkpoint: Write a reflection about how you will use information literacy to inform your service at Information Commons.

- **Library tools and advanced research**. Allow the students to get familiar with the tools and concepts that they can use to create and give back to the Information Commons program and libraries.
  - o Learn about our LibGuides tool. Then conduct hands-on research and create a LibGuides box about a particular database.
  - o View a Guide on the Side tutorial about creating a Guide on the Side.
  - o Create accounts and follow directions to get to know citation management systems.

> My personal growth—ability to greet customers, help them without reserve, have confidence in my skills—has definitely grown since I've been with IC. My professional skills, as well, have grown: I've gained experience in technical writing and working with different programs, as well as working with fellow ICers in a setting much different than a normal academic group project.
>
> *Information Commons student employee, Butler University*

Project Work

Training on Moodle is extensive and it does take students quite a while (at least two months) to work their way through all of the library sections.[8] However, students do eventually get to the point where they have completed training and are looking for other ways to stay engaged while on shift. The next phase in the Information Commons program lifecycle is project work.

Projects are defined as tasks, outside the scope of training or service, that take more than an hour of student time. They should keep students engaged during their shifts, serve as opportunities for students to continue to develop or practice their skills, and meet needs within the program, the library, the Center for Academic Technology, or for a campus partner. All student employees or library staff members are welcome to propose projects to the Information Commons and eLearning librarian. Often, projects stem naturally from conversations with campus partners or observations from students or staff. They require students to practice time management, utilize their information literacy skills, and think critically about ways to present information.

Flexibility in what projects can be allows us to meet the needs of not only our program and patrons but also our millennial student employees. Students enjoy projects: after working through a lot of individualized training, they relish being able to collaborate with each other and professionals within the library. They also appreciate that they can observe a problem, suggest a solution, and have the ability to work concretely toward a solution. This indulges the millennial inclination to be hands-on and heard within the workplace.[9] There have been some challenges with the project model, though, and these are detailed in the Reflections section.

Instructional Assistance

The libraries are committed to developing the information literacy skills of Butler students. This commitment was reflected in both the libraries' mission and as one of the priorities within its 2013–2016 Strategic Plan.[10] Information Commons students complete the Information Literacy section of training and learn not just why these concepts matter to the libraries but how they connect into larger campus goals and can be integrated into their daily service with Information Commons. Information Commons also works to support information literacy instructional efforts by working directly with liaison librarians.

Our liaison system matches a librarian with departments or even entire colleges on campus. The librarian is responsible for building relationships, maintaining the collection, and offering instruction to their liaison area(s). Information Commons students have been able to assist with this workload. Librarians have partnered with Information Commons students to create projects, such as testing activities before classes or creating new online instructional content. For example, the business librarian has had Information Commons students run through online tutorials and give feedback about the activities and how long they took to complete. Our performing and fine arts librarian worked with an Information Commons student to develop a virtual tour of the music areas of the library that could be embedded in her LibGuides. Several librarians have had students utilize their creative commons training to assist in adding images to their LibGuides.

Information Commons students also offer support within classroom sessions. Liaison librarians can bring these students into the class to provide additional technology or troubleshooting support. Several liaisons have even had the Information Commons students teach certain segments of their classes: the business librarian has business majors in the Information Commons program demonstrate search logs and share personal research testimony to first-year business experience classes. The Center for Academic Technology also sends students into classrooms on campus to teach technology tools, such as iMovie. This peer-to-peer teaching has been well-received by student audiences, and Information Commons students appreciate the opportunity to practice and share their skills in service to the campus.

Not only does this alleviate the workload of the liaison librarian, but it also provides valuable student insight that can improve our ability to reach our primary audience. It also is a good experience for the Information Commons students to work in collaboration with a librarian who demonstrates professionalism. We manage instruction projects and in-class sessions using Trello, and associates are instrumental in assigning students and facilitating progress.

> I knew to teach others you needed patience and to be specific, but never knew how patient and specific you had to be. When patrons come into CAT or the Library for help, I now listen to their problems fully, think of where to start, and what would be the easiest way for them to learn. Going through this process has allowed me to grow and see what I need to improve on.
>
> *Information Commons student employee, Butler University*

Professional Development Opportunities

We promote a number of voluntary professional development opportunities, and whenever possible, we incentivize students by allowing them to be paid for their efforts. We have partnered with the Internship and Career Services office to hold sessions where our students can get specific feedback about how to describe their work with Information Commons on a résumé or in an interview. Our business librarian has devised a popular Business Research Workshop. Students can attend the workshop and complete the out-of-class homework on the clock. We engage students in discussions geared toward their career goals, and one of the hands-on learning activities that students can do on shift is to create a LinkedIn profile and network.

ASSESSMENT

Butler University Libraries is committed to regular assessment, and the Information Commons program is a piece of the puzzle. In the spring of 2015, we completed a full assessment of the Information Commons program, which identified strengths and areas for improvement.

Assessment of Service Goals

Gate counters on the front doors of the library provide information about our traffic patterns. Our circulation system (WMS) tracks how many times we check items in or out. In order to understand the other activity of our service point, we ask students to record transactions on our custom form (hosted on Reference Analytics within LibAnswers). We've ensured that the form is flexible enough to intake data for both IC locations. This form provides information about the number and type of transactions as well as information about the types of patrons we serve. Additionally, the libraries conducted a LibQual survey in the spring of 2015. These data sources have provided us a baseline for assessing satisfaction with our service levels.

When students assist with in-class sessions, we gather the same types of information as library instruction sessions do: number of attendees, course type, topic covered, etc. We also track how many Information Commons students participated and how much of their time it took. Since a large amount of student time is spent on project work, we devised a way to quantify and track these efforts as well. Each project that is created is labeled by audience served and number of students and hours involved. At the completion of the semester or year, we can easily see where efforts were spent and share this information with administrators. For example, in one spring semester, Information Commons students worked on twenty-eight different projects.

Assessing Student Employee Development Goals

To know whether or not the program was meeting its other goals, we analyzed a number of quantitative data sources. At various points during the lifecycle of the Information Commons student, they are asked to reflect on personal and professional development in alignment with the program's goals. It was not efficient for us to extract this data from multiple places, so we asked students to begin a Reflection Portfolio. (See Appendix E Introducing the Reflection Portfolio.) These are public Wordpress blogs that serve as the place for students to reflect during their entire tenure within the program. In addition to helping to encourage reflective practice and show the student their growth, the portfolios serve as an easier platform for us to gather evidence of progress in accordance with the goals of the program. Another source of data is the mid-semester review. Students have completed the review for the past two fall semesters. Students are asked to rate their confidence levels and give feedback about their experience with the program.

REFLECTION

The Information Commons program is constantly evolving. As with other student employment programs, we deal with high student turnover. We also have experienced quite a bit of staffing and physical change. Developing policies and training that are effective and sustainable is an incredible time commitment, but we agree with Stanfield and Palmer: "The sacrifices of time and energy we invest in training time will be rewarded."[11] The LibQual data shows that our patrons are satisfied with the level of service we provide them. Librarians have commented that they not only enjoy working with the Information Commons students but feel that it has made a difference in their liaison areas and improved their teaching. Information Commons student employees themselves find tremendous benefit in the experiences the program provides. One student reflected that "I have gained skills that I would not have gained in college if it wasn't for working at Information Commons." It is reaffirming to know that our program aligns with those across higher education in "working toward a common goal of helping students become educated, contributing members of a global society."[12]

Lessons Learned: Sustainable Ways to Keep Students Engaged

Projects offer a lot of opportunities for growth and development, but they take a lot of time to generate and prepare. They don't often involve a large number of students or a long amount of time, and students typically require a lot of facilitation throughout the process. During certain points in the history of Information Commons, the majority of our workforce finished with training and looked for projects, and it has been nearly impossible to keep up with the demand. This led us to devise more sustainable options for ongoing training and engagement. One such option is something we call Hands-on Learning Activities. These activities are the equivalent of "electives" within a curriculum. They allow students more freedom than core training in Moodle; students can find ways to customize the activities to their areas of individual study or they can work collaboratively with others on the team. These activity prompts live on Trello and are designed so that they can be paused and revisited later if the student's shift gets busy or they are needed for an urgent project. Examples include exploring one of the top-ranked technologies of the year, creating an infographic about a topic of their choice and exploring government websites.

Hands-On Learning Activity Prompt: The Top 100 Tools for Learning has been compiled based upon international feedback. Pick a tool from the list. Explore it thoroughly and conduct a SWOT analysis for the tool, gathering info about cost, ease of use, permanence, competition, etc. Then create a LibGuide box (for a public audience) to summarize what you've learned and introduce the tool to others. Use proper attribution for text or images.

Areas of Improvement

There seem to be endless possibilities for growth in the program. We continue to reassess training and seek activities that better integrate library and technology training pieces. Specifically, we are exploring future competency-based training models. We always aim to engage more students in projects and in-class instructional training. One challenge on our campus is awareness and outreach; we are often grouped with information technology (IT instead of IC) or simplified into just a "circulation desk." The confusion with IT means that patrons often seek help from the wrong location or get frustrated when we are not able to assist with tasks outside of our expertise. It's important to work with IT to complement services, facilitate easy referral between our areas, and communicate with campus that we are separate but cooperative entities. Calling Information Commons a circulation desk oversimplifies the skills and services of our students and may prevent questions or collaborations from some patrons. The more we are able to get the campus to be aware of who we are and what we offer, the more we can contribute. Our next steps include updating our website, being more intentional with our social media and marketing efforts, and finding ways to tell our story and build an army of Information Commons advocates.

APPENDIX A

INFORMATION COMMONS TRELLO BOARDS

IC HAS THREE DIFFERENT ACTIVE TRELLO BOARDS

IC PROJECTS

Created new for each semester.

Includes important announcements, project management, classroom training events, and alternative training.

Check every day – and participate as appropriate.

More info on the following page.

IC TEAM BOARD

Created new for each semester.

Each IC team member gets his/her own column with cards that allow for easy tracking of progress through training.

Give a status update every day so your associate are aware and can support your work on training and projects.

ASSOCIATE TEAM BOARD

Accessible only to associate team and IC staff.

You'll find that you use Trello more and more as you progress through the IC Program. Make sure you feel comfortable with it!

CC BY – Amanda Starkel, Butler University

PROJECT BOARD

THE BASICS:
- Check the announcements column every shift.
- Drag new cards to the top so the newest stuff is what we see first.

	ANNOUNCEMENTS	NEW/PENDING ASSIGNMENT PROJECTS	ACTIVE PROJECTS	CLASSROOM TRAINING/ ASSISTANCE	DISCUSSIONS	HANDS-ON LEARNING ACTIVITIES
WHAT GOES IN THIS COLUMN?	Things that the rest of the team needs to be aware of. Announcements, events, issues, etc.	Open projects proposed by staff members or campus partners. If you have an idea for a project, bring it to your associate or IC staff!	Projects that are in progress.	Requests for training or assistance in a classroom or instruction session (technology or research).	Articles or snippets related to IC's work with questions to guide discussion among the group.	These are supplemental training opportunities. They allow for learning in a more collaborative, creative way.
WHO CAN POST / CLAIM THESE CARDS?	Everyone is encouraged to post to this column to share information! Reminder: What you are posting may need to be brought directly to the attention of a staff member or entered in BUAnswers for long-term access.	You should be through the core elements of training before being assigned to a project. Associates or IC staff can stick folks who seem like a good fit onto the cards. If you see a project that you want to be involved in, let your associate know.	Those who are working on the project should be actively posting status updates. It should be clear to anyone looking at the card who is doing what and where things are within the process.	The person coordinating training efforts will assign people to cards based on their training levels and availability. Those assigned to a training should use the card to communicate and ensure that they are prepared.	Everyone is welcome to respond to discussion posts when they have a little bit of downtime. Prompts will be posted by associates or IC staff. If you have an idea for a prompt, let your associate know.	Those who are through their core training can complete these activities. There is no order or urgency to these activities. These activities will be posted by associates or IC staff. If you have an idea for an activity, let your associate know.
WHAT HAPPENS TO THIS CARD?	Once a card is no longer relevant, it can be archived.	Once folks are on the card and they start to make progress, these cards move into the Active Projects column.	Once a project is completed, it should be moved to the Completed Projects column.	Once the training session is complete, the card should be moved to the Completed Training/Assistance column.	When discussion seems to have reached a conclusion, the card should be archived.	These cards will rarely be cleaned off.

APPENDIX B

INFORMATION COMMONS ASSOCIATE: EXPECTATIONS FOR THE ASSOCIATE ROLE

Develop

1. Continue to grow in areas related to the values of the IC program, specifically in regard to:
   o Research/technology skills
   o Communication and project management
   o Customer service
   o Professionalism
2. Develop your leadership skills through research, reflection, and practical experience with your team.
3. Demonstrate good goal setting, assessment, and change implementation.

Lead

1. Model handbook policies (dress code and work ethic) and ideal engagement with the values of the program.
2. Help maintain morale and service standards for entire IC team.
   o Be the "eyes and ears on the ground" for IC staff.
   o Advocate for your coworkers. Empower them to give constructive feedback, suggest projects, or find ways to make their work connect to their interests in meaningful ways. Take their comments and concerns to IC supervisors.
   o Monitor progress and performance in order to assess those deserving a "high-five."
3. Co-manage a team of assistants. This requires you to demonstrate good communication and teamwork with your associate partner. Good team management looks like this:
   o **Mentoring yours assistants through training.**
     ▪ Know your assistants and what they are working on. Assist if they have questions. Hold friendly and encouraging conversations with them (in person or virtually) about staying on track with their training and encourage them to openly communicate about questions, suggestions, etc.
     ▪ When assistants reach the end of a section, conduct or arrange training certification. Demonstrate that training goes more in depth and further than a checklist. Draw on personal experiences and real

scenarios to make sure they have necessary skills and the ability to think on their feet.

- ○ **Mentoring your assistants through projects and other tasks.**
  - Continue to know what your assistants are working on. When they are through their training, assign assistants to projects. Know your assistants' interests, preferences, and strengths, and delegate projects and tasks that are most likely to keep them engaged.
- ○ **Foster reflection and professional development of your assistants.**
  - Encourage your assistants to post to their reflection portfolios as prompted or as they experience "landmark" experiences (such as assisting with their first in class training, completing a big project,etc).
  - Read and respond to all reflection portfolio posts for your team. Provide support and accountability. Elevate issues that need the attention of the IC staff.
  - Encourage your assistants to take advantage of professional development tasks and opportunities through IC.
- ○ **Address disciplinary issues if they arise, under the guidance of IC staff.**

Invest

- Take responsibility for the program as it is now and continue to refine the IC structure according to the needs of the program, the faculty/staff, the University, and the Butler community.
  - ○ Help ensure that we are providing service at a satisfactory level. Troubleshoot when issues arise.
  - ○ Assist in the creation and maintenance of tasks, hands on learning topics, discussion topics and projects
  - ○ Assist in the assessment of the IC program.

APPENDIX C

LIBRARY CIRCULATION

Specific Skills Mastered/Knowledge Obtained:

- Must be able to check items and in and out using WMS.
  - o Should understand circulation of special items like equipment, room keys, etc.
- Must understand the processes related to reserves, ILL, holds, and PALShare.

How Can We Measure that this Skill Development/Knowledge Intake Has Happened?

- Policy quiz—should occur within first week of employment.
- Training Certification—in-person testing of skills and knowledge by associate or staff. Should happen within first week. Includes a mix of hands on practice, simulation, and questions.

Training Certification:

1. Review the results of the Circ policy quiz. Specifically, make sure they have answered the essay questions properly.
2. Do the circ simulations described below, including additional questions as appropriate.
3. Ask if they have any questions.
4. If they do everything correctly, mark them as "certified" on Trello.

Concept	Demonstration	Additional Questions
	Except for the normal check in/out, you can ask the ICer to simulate and describe the process in detail instead of actually physically having to do each one.	These can be asked as appropriate, along with other related "scenario-based" questions that help ICers think on their feet. The point of many of these is to encourage ICers to check their resources (BUAnswers, website, etc).
Normal check in/out and use of WMS	Have the ICer physically check out/in multiple items. For check out, make sure they offer/print a receipt and remove security. For check in, make sure they use WMS correctly, add security, and put it on the right book cart. Also, make sure they are checking that each item is displaying in WMS after being scanned.	• Are you allowed to check out to a person who doesn't have an ID on them? • How long do most books check out for? • Can a person pay their fines here? • Can a public patron check out books? • Which discs hold DVDs and which hold CDs?

Circ of laptop	Checking out a laptop: They should ask you about your preference—PC or Mac. Make sure they give you a charger, laptop, AND case. Also make sure they mention that you'd need to log in before taking it off campus.	• What do you have to do when a laptop is returned? • What do we do if someone is having trouble with a laptop? • What do you do if someone wants a laptop and we are out?
PALShare / ILL / Holds / Reserves	Checking in/out a PALShare item: Make sure they check the item out in WMS and write the due date on the cover sticker. When returning, make sure it checks in with WMS, the receipt is printed and placed inside, and the item is placed in the return bin on the PALShare shelf. ILL: Make sure students can explain how ILL works and understand that we don't have to do anything in WMS when checking out or in.	• What happens if someone wants to take out a 4-hour reserve 1 hour before close? Can they keep it overnight? • What do you do if a professor wants to drop off a reserve item? • When will we put items on hold? • If you see someone standing by the ILL shelf for a while, what should you do?

APPENDIX D

CUSTOMER SERVICE AND RESEARCH SKILLS I

Specific Skills Mastered/Knowledge Obtained:

- Must understand our teaching philosophy and demonstrate exemplary customer service
- Should understand expectations for various communication channels (chat, email,phone)
- Should have familiarity with subject librarians and understand the appropriate point of referral
- Should have necessary basic research **skills**, including understanding Library of Congress and how to track down specific items.

How Can We Measure that this Skill Development/Knowledge Intake Has Happened?

- Practice activities
  o Chat, email simulations
- Training Certification—in-person testing of skills and knowledge by associate or staff. Includes a mix of hands-on practice, simulation, and questions.

Training Certification:

1. Identify the book and articles that you are going to ask the ICer to lookup.
   o Articles—one that's available full-text online AND in print, and one that isn't available
2. Ask if they've had any questions doing these two sections of training.
3. Test their skills with the demonstration activities below. At least one should bed one face-to-face, but the others can be done via chat or phone. For the face-to-face demonstration, explain that you are going to simulate some interactions and ask them to treat you as a regular patron new to the library.
4. Give feedback. We want it to be known that this isn't something that you can completely master. Customer service and research skills will continue to grow and evolve. So we're looking for you to give the ICer some specific feedback or suggestions for continued development:
   o Suggest specific improvements, such as asking "Anything else?" at the end of an interaction or doing a better job narrating each step of a process.
   o Encourage them to practice more with the search tools.
   o Ask them to think of a specific patron interaction they've had and dissect it. What did they do really well? What would they do differently? Post to reflection portfolio if appropriate.

Concept	Demonstration	Additional Questions
	Except for the normal check in/out, you can ask the ICer to simulate and describe the process in detail instead of actually physically having to do each one.	These can be asked as appropriate, along with other related "scenario-based" questions that help ICers think on their feet. The point of many of these is to encourage ICers to check their resources (BUAnswers, website,etc).
Find book on shelf	Ask the ICer to help you locate a book in Irwin. Make sure they use good customer service, showing you the screen, explaining where they are searching,etc. Make sure they either take you up to the shelf or do an adequate job explaining how LoC works so you could feel confident in finding it on your own.	• What happens if the book isn't on the shelf where it's supposed to be? • How would you suggest that a patron consider using an ebook copy of a title? • If all we own is an ebook,can they still request print via ILL?
Find article full-text	Ask the ICers to locate two articles: 1. An article that they should be able to find full-text online AND in print 2. An article that isn't available For the online full-text,make sure they can link you to the actual text of the online article. For the print,check that they can actually find this on the shelf in the bound copy. For the article that isn't available, they should be promoting ILL services. For all processes, they need to use good customer service to show you each step and explain along the way what's happening.	• What do you do if the link doesn't work? • Can someone access these from off-campus? • Why are articles sometimes not immediately available (embargoed)? • If I wanted to find more articles on this topic,where could I search?

APPENDIX E

INTRODUCING THE REFLECTION PORTFOLIO

What Is It?

Your reflection portfolio will serve as documentation of your learning experiences within the Information Commons program. It will capture your growth and help you develop skills such as metacognition, reflection, self-evaluation, and goal-setting.

Writing a reflection post should inspire you to think deeply about your training and IC experiences. It should allow you to make connections between your Information Commons work and academics, extracurriculars, and professional experiences.

So Is this Replacing Individual Trello Cards?

Not at all. You still should post to your Trello card at the end of every shift. You will only post to the reflection portfolio occasionally, for the following reasons:

- You have reached a point in your training where you encounter a reflection prompt.
- A reflection prompt is distributed via email to the entire Information Commons listserv.
- You have an experience or epiphany that you want to document within your portfolio.

Who Will Read My Posts?

While this is a place for personal reflection, we also wanted your portfolio to be available to the rest of the Information Commons team. Therefore, your posts will feed into the larger Information Commons main page unless you specifically mark them as private. They may also be shared within the Libraries and the Center for Academic Technology.

Your associates will regularly read your reflections and offer guidance, support, and encouragement where necessary. However, when you write, we suggest that you write for yourself instead of thinking of them as your audience.

Guidelines for Posts:

- Take your time and really think about the prompt. Whenever possible, include specific details and examples to illustrate your thoughts.
- Use appropriate language.
- To the best of your ability, use proper spelling and grammar. This is not a formal graded writing assignment, but it is still good practice to use language correctly.
- Do not mention patrons or other ICers by name.

NOTES

1. "Information Commons," Butler University, accessed December 9, 2020, https://www.butler.edu/information-commons/.
2. Steven D. Zink, Ann Medaille, Madeline Mundt, Patrick T. Colegrove, and Duncan Aldrich, "The @ One Service Environment: Information Services for and by the Millennial Generation," *Reference Services Review* 31, accessed November 23, 2015, https://doi.org/10.1108/00907321011020761.
3. Amanda Starkel, "Investing in Student Employees: Training in Butler University's Information Commons Program," *Indiana Libraries* 33, no. 2 (2014): 83–86, accessed December 15, 2015, https://journals.iupui.edu/index.php/IndianaLibraries/article/view/16639/pdf_952.
4. Brett Perozzi, ed., *Enhancing Student Learning Through College Employment* (Bloomington, IN: Association of College Unions International, 2009), 83.
5. Zink, "The @One Service Environment," 108–24.
6. Kathleen Langan, "Training Millennials: A Practical and Theoretical Approach," *Reference Services Review* 40, no. 1 (2012): 24–48, accessed November 23, 2015, https://doi.org/10.1108/00907321211203612.
7. Jane M. Kathman and Michael D. Kathman, "Training Student Employees for Quality Service," *The Journal of Academic Librarianship* 26, no. 3 (2000): 176–82, accessed November 23, 2015, http://www.sciencedirect.com/science/article/pii/S0099133300000963.
8. Kathman and Kathman, "Training Student Employees."
9. Langan, "Training Millennials," 24–48.
10. "Butler Libraries," Butler University, accessed December 9, 2020, https://www.butler.edu/library.
11. Andrea G. Stanfield and Russell L. Palmer, "Peer-ing into the Information Commons: Making the Most of Student Assistants in New Library Spaces," *Reference Services Review*, 38, no. 4 (2010): 634–46, accessed November 23, 2015, https://doi.org/10.1108/00907321011090773.
12. Perozzi, *Enhancing Student Learning*, ix.

BIBLIOGRAPHY

Butler University. "Butler University Libraries." Accessed December 9, 2020. https://www.butler.edu/library.

———. "Information Commons." Accessed December 9, 2020. https://www.butler.edu/information-commons/.

Kathman, Jane M., and Michael D. Kathman. "Training Student Employees for Quality Service." *The Journal of Academic Librarianship* 26, no. 3 (2000): 176–82. Accessed November 23, 2015. http://www.sciencedirect.com/science/article/pii/S0099133300000963.

Langan, Kathleen. "Training Millennials: A Practical and Theoretical Approach." *Reference Services Review* 40, no. 1 (2012): 24–48. Accessed November 23, 2015. https://doi.org/10.1108/00907321211203612.

Perozzi, Brett, ed. *Enhancing Student Learning Through College Employment*. Bloomington, IN: Association of College Unions International, 2009.

Stanfield, Andrea G., and Russell L. Palmer. "Peer-ing into the Information Commons: Making the Most of Student Assistants in New Library Spaces." *Reference Services Review*, 38, no. 4 (2010): 634–46. Accessed November 23, 2015. https://doi.org/10.1108/00907321011090773.

Starkel, Amanda. "Investing in Student Employees: Training in Butler University's Information Commons Program." *Indiana Libraries* 33, no. 2 (2014): 83–86. Accessed December 15, 2015. https://journals.iupui.edu/index.php/IndianaLibraries/article/view/16639/pdf_952.

Zink, Steven D., Ann Medaille, Madeline Mundt, Patrick T. Colegrove, and Aldrich Duncan. "The @ One Service Environment: Information Services for and by the Millennial Generation." *Reference Services Review* 38, no. 1 (2010): 108–24. Accessed November 23, 2015. https://doi.org/10.1108/00907321011020761.

Case Study 3

THE LIBRAT PROGRAM AT CAL POLY:

Full Partners in Peer Learning

Brett Bodemer and Kaila Bussert

OVERVIEW

The LibRAT Program at California Polytechnic State University in San Luis Obispo was first piloted in 2010. Although the program has expanded in scope and depth, the key to its continued success has been a commitment to core principles discovered during its initial launch. To this day, the LibRATs (Library Reference Assistance Technicians) form a small cadre of intensively trained students who are treated with respect as adults and as undergraduates. Communication, learning, and responsibility are multidirectional, and the LibRATs are full partners in the success of the program.

The original design of the program was to post students in residence halls to provide research assistance, but this model failed to generate research questions. However, we discovered the LibRATs to be an untapped resource and we were determined to find ways to repurpose them. In 2011, unforeseen librarian leaves created a staffing shortfall, and we found a solution ready at hand: LibRATs. Within one year, the LibRATs were full partners in providing research assistance and in leading lower-division information literacy sessions. As research assistants, LibRATs now staff all Research Help Desk and local chat hours at the Robert E.

93

Kennedy Library. The LibRATs also now lead more than one hundred instructional sessions per year. The rapid and sustained growth of our instruction program made possible by the LibRATs' participation resoundingly justified the hiring of a foundational experiences librarian, who now coordinates the instructional component of the LibRAT program.

ADMINISTRATION

Our program may be unique in getting unqualified support from major stakeholders. The Kennedy Library administration nurtured the pilot and has provided continuous support through generous allocations of librarian time and payroll funds for the LibRATs. The administration also bolsters the program through the creation of high-quality videos promoting LibRAT services. These videos serve as outreach on many levels—to students, to the campus, and to potential donors. The LibRAT program has been recognized on our campus as an excellent example of "earn-by-doing," and a LibRAT became the first employee with wages supplied from a Library Student Assistant Endowment. The librarians at Cal Poly have been just as enthusiastic. They were the first to understand how LibRATs freed them up for providing more complex initiatives, instruction, and consultations. They have welcomed the LibRATs from day one as a key asset in helping our library fulfill its mission.

Two librarians hired and trained students for the original pilot, but for many years afterward, LibRAT research help and LibRAT instruction activities were coordinated by a single librarian. With the arrival of the foundational experiences librarian in 2014, two primary hemispheres of responsibility were established, one for reference and the other for instruction. Needless to say, the program remains intrinsically unified, and the two coordinators work closely together to ensure seamless execution. The benefits of this model of supervision are tremendous. It enables the two supervisors to coach the LibRATs with concentrated emphasis on either reference or instruction. The reference coordinator has the bandwidth to further LibRAT interviewing skills and information-seeking techniques, while the foundational experiences librarian can enrich LibRAT teaching competencies and collaborate with them on the design and delivery of new instructional modules.

HIRING

Whether you are just starting a program or replenishing your cohort of peer consultants, one of the most important considerations to keep in mind is devising a hiring timeline that allows peer consultants a sufficient window for training. If you are starting a new program, identify a target date for deployment and work backward through training, hiring, and interviewing in order to advertise the position at the right time. If you are replenishing your staff, scan the horizon to anticipate your attrition due to graduation, and again work backward to identify the number of necessary hires and to establish a complete timeline.

Cal Poly is on the quarter system, and we look at our needs approximately nine months in advance. We typically hire in early winter so new LibRATs can train throughout the winter quarter and receive more training and gain the full range of on-the-job experience through spring quarter. This way, by the fall of the next year, when reference and teaching are in high demand, they are fully equipped for both.

> It's really great to have this skill set and be able to teach others how to do what they need to do for a class. I also enjoy being able to look up something that I otherwise wouldn't know about. Why else would I ever look up articles on Chechnyan soil science?
>
> *First Generation LibRAT, Cal Poly SLO*

Below is a schematic of our hiring and training timeline:

- November: Determine the number of LibRATs needed by next September.
- December: Advertise the position on the campus job site.
- January: Interview and hire.
- Winter quarter: Begin intensive initial training.
- Spring quarter: Continue training.
- Fall quarter: Launch fully prepared LibRATs.

As you can see from the above timeline, each student represents a huge investment so it is crucial to get the right students. One way to do this is to advertise widely and attractively to the target audience. Our target audience consists of lower-division students, preferably first-years. The logic of hiring first-years is that they prove a better return on training investment if they stay until graduation. (As an aside, the fact that only three LibRATs have ever left before graduation is a sign of their thorough engagement!) For the first two generations, we used stanchions in the library and the Cal Poly student job website. Later, we limited advertising to the campus job website and to word of mouth via faculty, who have brought their classes to our lower-division instruction sessions. The job website allows us to specify that the position is open to first- and second-year students, and we make the job attractive to the kind of candidates we seek by "selling" the job for all the skill benefits it will bring—improved interpersonal skills, presentation skills, and research skills. (See Appendix A. Job Posting for LibRAT Position.)

We require applicants to post three items to the online job site: résumé, cover letter, and standard application. This demand for three components performs some initial weeding: if an applicant can't follow directions well enough to provide all three, there is no point in pursuing an interview. Cover letters speak (for better and worse) about communication skills, and résumés provide information relevant to the qualities we seek. We particularly look for work in the service industry on the reasoning that we can gauge their attitude toward service. We also look for traces of volunteer work as a clear indication of a helpful disposition. Out of a student population of nineteen thousand, we have received as many as sixty applications and as few as thirty. Even in years when we are filling only one or two anticipated vacancies, we still invite twelve to fifteen applicants to interview. The interviews last ten minutes, conducted either by a single librarian or, more optimally, by two librarians in tandem. Hiring is one facet of the program where we do *not* invite the LibRATs to participate. It could prove extremely awkward in cases when friends apply, but worse, if we failed to genuinely embrace their input on an equal basis, we would risk the social breach of devaluing their contribution. This is something in all aspects of this program that we strive to minimize.

TRAINING
Training Philosophy

While the content of training is, of course, important, it is not our first focus when we think about training. Our abiding focus is instead on the social dynamics and mutual learning experienced by all parties through personal contact *during* training. Our training deliberately involves librarians, seasoned LibRATs, and new LibRATs. The content is only the tip of the iceberg. *What* we learn is important, but *how* we learn, how we learn *together*, and what we learn *about each other* is crucial to the success of our program. Even as librarians share what we know (or think we know), we model and shape an environment in which the students freely share what they know (or think they know.) Librarians know librarian life far better than students, and students know student life far better than librarians, so we both have a great deal to gain by listening and sharing. Our training process establishes an open community of practice by setting expectations for responsibility, communicating authentically, and listening well. This social foundation supports our program by welcoming and helping our newest members and by sustaining the desire of all parties to continually learn. Not unsurprisingly, it contributes to the evolution of training itself.

Research Assistance

Anyone proposing to build a research consultant program from scratch should count on putting intensive time and work into the training of the initial cohort. Once the first cohort has been created, however, the students can share in the training of the next generations. You may also encounter a steep learning curve. With our first cohort, for example, we had a poor situational understanding and indulged in the librarian habit of being *too* thorough. Our concern to equip the first peer assistants for success was genuine and laudable, but in retrospect it was overkill. While our essential training content has not significantly changed (e.g., service attitude, the reference interview, search skills, procedures, and safety) we have deliberately dialed back our multiple and extended explorations of database after database. We have shifted our focus instead toward providing assistance for known local needs, questions, and assignments. An example of this shift is the LibRAT-devised proficiency test for trainees. This is based on frequently asked questions and is updated for each training cycle.

After establishing the first cohort of peer assistants, training becomes much easier. This is largely because seasoned mentors can actively participate in training. In contrast to our "launch" model of instruction, in which two librarians spent two hours per week for nine weeks training the first cohort, new students now train for ninety minutes per week with a librarian for nine weeks but also shadow at the desk two hours per week with either a seasoned LibRAT or a librarian. This hybrid model provides the program with the trifecta of pivotal social benefits, conceptual knowledge, and real-life experience in reference techniques.

> The small network of my co-workers at the Research Help Desk are something quite special. Each has a heart for working with other students, a passion for solving difficult problems, and a genuine desire to learn something new every day. This program is a quintessential element in what makes Cal Poly, Cal Poly—learn by doing.
>
> *Third Generation LibRAT, Cal Poly SLO*

Instruction

Our library instruction program for lower-division English and communication studies courses has evolved into a robust face-to-face delivery in which LibRATs lead over half of the 200 library research workshops each academic year. Perhaps even more so than for reference, we use an on-the-job training model for LibRAT instruction that befits Cal Poly's "learn-by-doing" ethos. Instructional training begins indirectly via their research help training, where general knowledge of library resources and services, searching skills, and conducting a reference interview are first taught and honed. This provides them with foundational knowledge and customer service dispositions to build on as instructional leaders. Our first experiments with LibRATs as session leaders took place in 2011. Originally, we were curious to see if they could do it and how they would respond to doing it, wondering if this might be one way to repurpose their talents after the crash and burn in the residence halls. Two LibRATs agreed to try, and the rest soon followed. To forestall anxiety, we made it clear that they should be genuinely themselves and allow ample space for their personalities, their status as students, and senses of humor. We pared the sessions to essentials, and for two years, while incorporating both assessment and LibRAT input, we introduced incremental changes to the instructional design.

Since the arrival of the foundational experiences librarian, the curriculum has been redesigned to incorporate more active learning methods into a new series of three fifty-minute workshops: Orientation, Research Workshop A, and Research Workshop B. Each workshop offers collaborative activities addressing one of the following learning outcomes: (1) searching the library's databases strategically; (2) identifying the best sources to use for research assignments; and (3) practicing the process of evaluating information sources for credibility and relevance. (See Appendix B. Library Research Workshops—LibRAT Lesson Plans.) Each quarter, faculty can select any combination of workshops they wish. While the new curriculum menu requires more training and practice for the LibRATs, it is designed to leverage their role as peer guides who "mentor in the center."

> I'd like to add that my experience as a LibRAT wasn't limited to just work; incredibly close relationships were built within our small team at Kennedy Library. We all helped each other, sharing encounters, tough questions to be resolved, better solutions for problems we were met with.
>
> *Third Generation LibRAT, Cal Poly SLO*

Aside from short training sessions at the start of each quarter to go over the workshop lesson plans, activities, and handouts, instruction training happens primarily in the classroom. We schedule as many "live" opportunities as possible for newly hired LibRATs to observe and co-teach workshops before they are ready to teach on their own. Instruction training follows the hiring and reference training timeline mentioned earlier:

- Winter quarter: newly hired LibRATs observe several workshops and attend weekly instruction training sessions with the lead librarian.
- Spring quarter: newly hired LibRATs co-teach at least two workshops with librarians and more experienced LibRATs before teaching one workshop on their own.
- Fall quarter: all LibRATs are prepared to teach workshops on their own.

Once everyone is up and running, the lead librarian observes each LibRAT facilitating a workshop and provides constructive feedback. LibRATs also are paired to co-teach workshops every quarter to continually learn from each other in the classroom. At present, we use a Moodle site to house our teaching materials, course syllabi, student participant evaluations, and communications about the workshop schedule.

Our foremost instructional training goal is for LibRATs to skillfully facilitate workshops from start to finish while relating to participants as authentic and trusted peers. We coach them on both content and pedagogical technique for each of the four different classroom activities. For example, one activity prompts participants to compare scholarly and popular sources. LibRATs must learn how to introduce the activity and learning goals, guide student participants through the activity, and provide explanations as groups report out their answers. With the change to an active learning curriculum, it is vitally important for LibRATs to engage student participants by asking questions. The librarian works with LibRATs individually on effective questioning strategies as part of classroom observation feedback. As we train students on the mechanics of the activities, we still pay keen attention to affective components, encouraging them to develop their personal style, humor, and confidence as peer guides. Although LibRATs are not librarians with a deep knowledge of information science, they are in a unique position to explain concepts from a student's point of view and connect with students who are at a novice level of understanding.

As LibRATs become more experienced, we have varied ways to challenge them. They can serve as peer-trainers and role models for the new and less-experienced consultants, lead library workshops that rely on discipline-specific knowledge or other skill sets, and create instructional content. LibRATs in STEM majors lead research workshops for technical writing classes, such as Writing for Engineers, which require some familiarity with the discipline. When LibRATs reveal their status as engineering majors to a class of other engineering students, instant rapport is established. LibRATs also assist librarians with three library workshops every summer for Cal Poly's Summer Institute, a program for first-generation and historically disadvantaged students. With the luxury of three sessions with each contingent of students, this program offers an annual chance to experiment with new activities and games. More than once we have collaborated with LibRATs on new activities for Summer Institute that have then been incorporated into the following year's lower-division instruction. One summer, a LibRAT created a new scavenger hunt using a web application, which we then used for the general orientation workshop in the fall. The LibRAT who made the game became the lead trainer for the other LibRATs in using it. To assist with the creation of instructional materials, including screencasts and videos, we have a dedicated budget enabling LibRATs to work on such projects if they have available hours in their schedule.

With an on-the-job peer teaching training model, you should expect to spend a considerable amount of time on scheduling. It is essential for a librarian to schedule student consultants in advance and proactively manage changes and additions week by week. The lead librarian assigns student consultants the workshops and peer observations based on their shared schedule with the Research Help Desk. This ensures that teaching duties are divided more or less equally each week and maximizes the hands-on practice our student consultants need to become more confident and successful instructional leaders. It is the responsibility of the LibRATs to trade hours with each other through their own preferred channels, which have included both a Facebook Group and Groupme text, and then enter changes to the shared calendar. We find that Google Calendar currently offers the best means to mutually share schedules with consultants. One issue that arises for us is not being able to cover both the Research Help Desk and all the workshops, many of which are requested for early evening or night hours. When necessary, LibRATs assigned to cover the Research Help Desk during these times will lead workshops instead of staffing their desk shift, on the view that it is preferable to help twenty-five students with a known and impending research assignment than to answer a handful of itinerant questions at the desk. Such repurposing of "desk" hours also helps to keep the budget within bounds.

ASSESSMENT
Research Assistance

To assess the LibRAT performance at the Research Help Desk in 2011, we implemented an online survey form to record all transactions. A single required prompt in this form remains simultaneously our most important assessment and ongoing training tool. Amazingly simple, it allows us to continually "close the loop" and improve our services. The prompt is an open text field for entering brief descriptions of all questions and answers provided at the Research Help Desk. Originally, we printed the entries and assigned seasoned LibRATs to "rank" the answers on a scale of 1 to 3 (poor, satisfactory, good) but quickly realized that the most important information was not this somewhat problematic ranking of the questions but the actual content of the questions and answers themselves. We now print, read, and annotate these weekly. We similarly review chat transcripts on a weekly basis. These procedures allow us to identify weaknesses, share knowledge, and devise improvements in service—and not solely for the LibRAT team. Often we suggest website and other improvements based on what we learn. For instance, drawing on raw data and LibRAT input, we created a "Top Twenty FAQ" web page. After placing prominent links to it on the library homepage, our directional and technical questions dropped by nearly 400 the following academic year. And this was not simply part of a general drop; the volume of basic and in-depth research questions remained comparable to the previous year. This deliberate recording, review, and repurposing of data is a great way to disperse knowledge across our entire team. To expand LibRAT exposure to more discipline-specific and complex answers, librarians also record questions and answers in the same online form and we include a variety of these in the weekly desk printouts. Both ongoing and elegantly simple, this formative assessment serves us well in identifying actionable areas for improvement.

Instruction

Formal online assessment of LibRAT instruction began immediately after the first experimental outings with teaching. It would be wonderful to say that this was done solely because it is a best practice, but that would be less than truthful. In fact, there were two other mitigating reasons. The first was that nobody actually had time to observe them teach, and the online form filled out by student participants at least provided some sense of what was happening. Of equal importance was the fact that it was the simplest way to get immediate feedback to the LibRATs for improvement and/or for building their confidence. The survey mirrored one used by a librarian and included five Likert-scale prompts and several open-text responses. As soon as possible after any LibRAT-led session, the coordinator emailed a report to the LibRAT, often with praise but now and again with a needful suggestion or two. As we learned in subsequent quarters, because the reports offered quantitative averages for the Likert-scale prompts, the students were often extremely eager to see the results. (In any program of this sort, one should never underestimate the allure of competition to students this age—not even competition against themselves!) We also began administering an annual online survey at the end of fall quarter to faculty who had brought their classes. This allowed us a glimpse into their perceptions and provided us opportunities to tweak session content and design.

For both these assessments, we shared results with the instructional faculty, as part of an effort to sustain their interest in the program and to demonstrate our seriousness about striving to meet their needs. And this was not merely lip service. In 2012, in response to input from the faculty survey, we tweaked our instructional design to focus more on the concept of "peer review" and that same year implemented a pre-test and post-test to look for improved understanding. While this assessment effort showed an impact on student learning in the aggregate, it remained "statistically" weak precisely because it was aggregate data and not individually tracked. Nonetheless, we shared the results with the instructors, it resonated well, and requests for sessions grew even stronger. (For full details of instruments and data, see Bodemer.)[1]

The Holy Grail, of course, was to implement an authentic assessment providing statistically solid evidence of student learning. In 2012, we designed a rigorous study and implemented it in 2013. The study established intervention groups who received instruction and control groups who did not, and at the end of the quarter, rubrics were applied to each source in each paper after viewing not only the citation but the source itself. The results did show a small statistical effect. Unfortunately, counter to our original design, and in order to reduce variables, the study necessitated that the same session leader deliver all the sessions, and the only individual available for all the sessions was one librarian, not a LibRAT. So, even for the small effect shown, it proved nothing in regard to LibRAT impact on student learning. Speaking from our experience, this study was labor-intensive, time-intensive, and although it was rewarding to collaborate with a statistician, the opportunity costs were huge. The time might have been better spent working with the LibRATs to further enhance their teaching or reference skills. The big takeaway from the small effect resulting from this rigorous study is that library instruction is just *one* epicycle in a number of epicycles that constitute information literacy and that there are doubtless more effective and meaningful ways to both improve delivery and demonstrate library impact.

With this in mind, we have again focused on providing LibRATs with immediate feedback, but with our added librarian resources, are now devoting more direct support for individualized training. Using a Google Form, our online survey responses now populate a live spreadsheet where LibRATs can access responses to questions on their own, including ones pertaining to the effectiveness of the workshop leader. We ask participants to respond to two prompts about the workshop leader:

- The workshop leader presented information in a way that I could understand.
- The workshop leader encouraged and responded to questions.

Perhaps not surprisingly, students respond positively to instruction from their peers, with LibRAT instruction receiving higher percentages than librarians for the evaluation question, "The workshop leader presented information in a way that I could understand." However, we would again need to design and implement a rigorous study to see whether— and to what extent—peer-led learning has an impact on student learning.

Classroom observations are also used as a means to evaluate and refine the skills of the LibRATs as instructional leaders. As noted previously, the lead librarian observes each LibRAT many times throughout the year, and LibRATs co-observe each other as teaching partners. Observations receive structure through a checklist designed for constructive evaluation of expected outcomes. The checklist is specific and organized by workshop and learning activity. (See Appendix C. LibRAT Teaching Observation Checklist.) The overall goal is to build an infrastructure of reflective practice. The LibRATs are praised for their strengths and encouraged to improve with each intervention. Yet, it is also important to note that the LibRATs are not simply passive objects of observation but are also enlisted as participant-observers. And, as with so many other aspects of our program, their input is solicited, taken seriously, and implemented when possible.

REFLECTION
Lessons Learned

At the start of our chapter, we mentioned that our program's sustained success stemmed from adherence to core principles discovered very early in the running. The most important of these principles is that our program is as much about relationships as it is about information, and not just peer to peer but LibRAT to librarian. We made this discovery when the pilot in the residence halls floundered. Shortly before our end-of-quarter debriefing and pizza meeting, we sent an email to the LibRATs prompting them to reply to several questions for discussion at the meeting. We asked them both specific and general questions. Specifically, we asked them for any theories they might have about why they had received so few questions. In response, they pointed out something that was obvious to them but not to us: we had stationed them in residence halls for first- and second-year students, but the curriculum for such students required very few research papers that would drive them to ask such questions. We also solicited responses about what they did and did not like about the program. On the negative side, they confessed to feeling like "creepers" sitting in the residence halls waiting for questions that did not come. On the positive side, they were nonetheless extremely excited by the potential of the program and were thrilled with all the skills they had gained through the training. In fact, they were the ones who first suggested the idea of spending time shadowing librarians at the Research Help Desk to gain more experience. When we took them up on this suggestion, it set the stage for their eventual migration to the desk. With this first generation, we learned that we were all rowing together and that they wanted the program to succeed as much as we did. The *esprit de corps* derived from the mutual respect of treating them as full partners from the very outset is something we have maintained through each succeeding generation. Current LibRATs may not even be aware of it, but the tenor and means of the program's continued success have been nurtured by predecessors they have never met.

> We provide excellent service to the students of Cal Poly. Students may find it hard to confront the unknown face of a librarian of any faculty. Students can relate with another student who has been in their shoes. We may not have the expert level of knowledge of a true librarian, but we do have the resources and training to help all types of patrons.
>
> *Fourth Generation LibRAT, Cal Poly SLO*

Challenges

One of the greatest challenges in coordinating a student team is identifying times when everyone can meet. Because such opportunities are so rare, in order to increase focus on instructional coaching during the annual "fall refresher" meeting, we migrated much of desk and reference content to asynchronous online formats. One LibRAT and a librarian created a lightweight JING screencast showing important changes on the library home page as well as an online Jeopardy game which provided a review of that information along with other procedural and database changes. These tools were highly popular with the LibRATs, so we will make more of these kinds of learning objects for future training.

Another challenge for such a program is right-sizing the student team. If you have too few consultants, it is hard to provide full coverage for desk hours and teaching assignments. On the other hand, if you have too many students, you run the risk of offering too few hours for the LibRATs. This dilutes their economic interest and psychological engagement and even diminishes their skills through lack of steady practice. From the LibRAT point of view, the sweet spot is six or seven consultants, which provides enough hours for everyone. From the librarian point of view, however, eight or nine LibRATs is preferable. This creates more flexibility in scheduling both the desk and instruction.

Long-Term Benefits to Consultants

Although lasting qualitative benefits are hard to gauge, we can certainly attest to significant career impacts for graduating LibRATs. A first-generation LibRAT successfully applied for a position at a law library in her first year of pursuing a JD degree, worked during her remaining time in law school as a research assistant for a professor, and obtained a position as a deputy city attorney. Another LibRAT pursued a PhD in animal science and included her online LibRAT teaching evaluations as part of her application. One LibRAT landed his first job working at NASA's Jet Propulsion Laboratory, working on the Mars Rover, and credits the presentation skills he developed as a LibRAT with giving him an edge over other applicants. Three other LibRATs have even obtained degrees in librarianship. Of these three, one has a tenure-track faculty position, another works as an information architect in the private sector, and the third recently graduated from UCLA.

Future Plans

In tandem with developing more asynchronous, online learning objects for reference training, we also plan to increase group sessions for enhancing instruction skills. This will include a professional training workshop at the beginning of the academic year, with mini-workshops offered at the start of winter and spring quarters. The ever-increasing demand for instructional sessions requires the librarians to collaborate with LibRATs on producing online learning solutions to complement face-to-face delivery.

In the last three years, the LibRAT repertoire has expanded to include visual and quantitative literacies. We are currently training the LibRATs to teach workshops about finding and using images and data in the research process. This is in response to shifts in campus curriculum and our emphasis on a metaliteracy model of information literacy within the polytechnic and "learn-by-doing" ethos of our campus. While this may sound difficult, this expansion will, in fact, reinforce what our consultants are experiencing in the classroom. We know they will be eager, as always, for the challenge of learning and expanding their skills, especially when they see its relevance to their lives outside the library. As the LibRAT program evolves, we expect it to continue flourishing. The key, no matter what the future holds, is to remain true to the principle of including the students as full partners.

APPENDIX A

JOB POSTING FOR LIBRAT POSITION

Job Title: LibRAT (Library Research Assistance Technician)

Location: Kennedy Library

Hours: Weekdays and some weekend hours. 8–15 hours per week. Will accommodate class schedule. Minimum commitment of one quarter

When: Hiring early winter quarter; paid training starts mid-winter quarter

Job Description

The Library Research Assistance Technician (LibRAT), after receiving initial training in Kennedy Library resources, will provide research assistance at the Research Help Desk and via online chat help. The LibRAT will receive ongoing training and will also lead lab sessions for GE courses. This service-oriented position offers the opportunity to develop advanced information, interpersonal, and presentation skills. The LibRAT will be responsible for a variety of tasks, including, but not limited to

- representing Kennedy Library and providing help with assignments and research tools and strategies at the Research Help Desk and via online chat;
- providing basic Kennedy Library information to patrons;
- performing searches for materials via catalogs and databases;
- providing informal tutorials on use of library resources;
- acquiring further expertise in research assistance skills;
- leading instruction sessions for GE courses;
- assisting in the design and delivery of training to future LibRATs;
- maintaining Research Help Desk documentation; and
- working with supervisors to maintain selected resources and support smooth functioning of the Research Help Desk.

Minimum Qualifications
- Superior interpersonal communication skills
- Team player
- Ability to work independently

Preferred Qualifications
- Previous employment in service-oriented positions
- First- and second-year class standing
- Knowledge of library catalogs and databases

APPENDIX B

LIBRARY RESEARCH WORKSHOPS— LIBRAT LESSON PLANS

Orientation Workshop: Kennedy Library Scavenger Hunt (OR)

- Students learn about Kennedy Library's books, technology, services, and study spaces using a fun team scavenger hunt game. Recommended for the Fall Quarter.
- **Activity 1: GooseChase Scavenger Hunt**

Research Workshop A: Searching Library Databases (RWA)

- Students learn how to search Kennedy Library's databases strategically and identify the best sources to use for their research assignments.
- **Activity 1: Name That Source**
- **Activity 2: Database Search Challenge**

Research Workshop B: Evaluating Information Sources (RWB)

- Students practice the process of evaluating the relevance and credibility of information sources with individual "lab" research time.
- **Activity 1: Evaluating an Information Source for Credibility**

APPENDIX C

LIBRAT TEACHING OBSERVATION CHECKLIST

LibRAT teacher: _____

Observer: _____

Date: _____

Type of Workshop: [RWA] [RWB]   Course: _____

Introduction

- ☐ Begins on time
- ☐ Introduces self and role as a LibRAT
- ☐ States the goals of the workshop and the "learning checklist"
- ☐ Leads class to the library website and the "Research 101" guide
- ☐ Explains the Research Help services

Feedback:
Please elaborate on what went well and what could be better with your ideas for improvement.

Research Workshop A, Activity 1: Name That Source
record start time: _____ end time: _____

- ☐ Introduces the "Types of Sources" handout
- ☐ Gives clear directions about the activity
- ☐ Encourages participation from students during the class debrief
- ☐ Explains the key characteristics of each type of source
- ☐ Answers questions clearly and checks to see answers are understood by the class
- ☐ Paces the activity well from beginning to end

Feedback:
Please elaborate on what went well and what could be better with your ideas for improvement.

Research Workshop A, Activity 2: Database Search Challenge
record start time: _____ end time: _____

- ☐ Demonstrates where to locate Library Research Databases
- ☐ Explains the purpose of "Search Everything" and "Academic Search Premier"
- ☐ Gives clear directions about the activity
- ☐ Encourages participation from students during the class debrief
- ☐ Answers questions clearly and checks to see answers are understood by the class
- ☐ Summarizes database search strategies:
  How to use keywords; refine results; get citations; save articles; use Find It.
- ☐ Paces the activity well from beginning to end

Feedback:
Please elaborate on what went well and what could be better with your ideas for improvement.

Research Workshop B, Activity 1: Evaluating an Information Source for Credibility
record start time: _____ end time: _____

- ☐ Directs class to read the list of evaluation criteria
- ☐ Gives clear directions about the activity
- ☐ Encourages participation from students during the class debrief
- ☐ Answers questions clearly and checks to see answers are understood by the class
- ☐ Guides class through their evaluation of the example source
- ☐ Paces the activity well from beginning to end

Feedback:
Please elaborate on what went well and what could be better with your ideas for improvement.

Closing and Evaluation
- ☐ Ends class on time
- ☐ Directs class to the Evaluation
- ☐ Reiterates that Research Help is available

Feedback:
Please elaborate on what went well and what could be better with your ideas for improvement.

Overall
- ☐ Is welcoming and friendly
- ☐ Speaks clearly and loudly
- ☐ Speaks: about right | too slow | too fast
- ☐ Has good eye contact
- ☐ Listens well
- ☐ Encourages participation and questions
- ☐ Walks around the room to help students during the activities
- ☐ Uses the classroom technology effectively (e.g., uses the dual screens; navigates the guide, website, and online worksheets)

What was successful?

What could be improved and how?

NOTES

1. Brett Bodemer, "They CAN and They Should: Undergraduates Providing Peer Reference and Instruction," *College & Research Libraries*, 75, no. 2 (2014): 162–78; see also Bodemer, "They Not Only CAN But They SHOULD: Why Undergraduates Should Provide Peer Reference and Instruction," *ACRL 2013 Conference Proceedings* (2013), available online at http://www.ala.org/acrl/sites/ala.org.acrl/files/content/conferences/confsandpreconfs/2013/papers/Bodemer_BasicILInstruction.pdf.

BIBLIOGRAPHY

Bodemer, Brett. "They CAN and They Should: Undergraduates Providing Peer Reference and Instruction." *College & Research Libraries*, 75, no. 2 (2014): 162–78.

———. "They Not Only CAN But They SHOULD: Why Undergraduates Should Provide Peer Reference and Instruction." *ACRL 2013 Conference Proceedings* (2013). Available online at http://www.ala.org/acrl/sites/ala.org.acrl/files/content/conferences/confsandpreconfs/2013/papers/Bodemer_BasicILInstruction.pdf.

Case Study 4

RESEARCH DESK ASSISTANTS AT THE COLLEGE OF WILLIAM AND MARY:

A Winning Collaboration

Lauren M. Manninen and Don Welsh

OVERVIEW

How is it possible for a small team of research librarians to increase their teaching load, double the number of independent consultations, ramp up campus outreach on scholarly communication issues, and continue to provide excellent service at a walk-up service point? They could hire more librarians or work double shifts, but when those are not options, they hire graduate student assistants. Which is exactly how the research team from the Earl Gregg Swem Library at the College of William and Mary chose to answer the demands of growing and changing needs for professional librarian's involvement on campus. The Research Desk Assistant (RDA) program enables the continued staffing of the popular stand-alone research service point while freeing professional librarian calendars for increased teaching loads and community engagement opportunities.

The College of William and Mary in Williamsburg, Virginia, is a residential, public, liberal arts institution, enrolling approximately 6,300 undergraduate and 2,100 graduate students. The Earl Gregg Swem Library is the college's primary academic library. Professional school and departmental libraries notwithstanding, Swem supports the bulk of the research needs of undergraduate and graduate students, faculty, and staff. The library is staffed by twenty-five professional and thirty operational staff, including nine research and instruction subject liaison librarians. In Swem, research services are provided through a stand-alone service point, virtually, and in one-on-one consultations. When classes are in session, the research desk is staffed Monday through Thursday, 9 a.m. to 9 p.m., Friday, 9 a.m. to 6 p.m., and Sunday, 1 p.m. to 9 p.m.; the research desk is not staffed on Saturday.

The development of a new undergraduate curriculum for the college provided new opportunities for librarian involvement in information literacy instruction. Librarians were integrated into many new courses. However, increased instruction coupled with library-wide initiatives to expand support and programing around scholarly communication issues required time and attention from liaison librarians. In the fall of 2014, the research team and library administration made a decision to implement changes in the staffing of the stand-alone research desk service point. The RDA program was the answer to increasing demands on profession librarians' working hours while continuing to provide excellent reference service to the university community. The first cohort of RDAs joined the research team in fall 2014.

With the exception of scheduling conflicts, the program provides graduate student staffing for the research desk in four-hour shifts for the majority of hours the desk is open. The main role of the RDAs is to support professional librarians through staffing the research desk service point, answering directional, technological, and basic research questions. RDAs are encouraged to triage difficult or involved inquiries to the research team; however, they are also trained and empowered to help patrons on their own as much as possible during the night and weekend hours.

The philosophy of the RDA program is to provide an employment opportunity for graduate students while fostering growth in their learning, knowledge, research, and public service skills. Unlike student workers at other library service points, RDAs must be graduate students. Research librarians felt strongly that a graduate student is more mature, experienced with academic research, and prepared for the important role of library public service. The research desk is heavily trafficked by undergraduate students, many of whom are residential as well as graduate students and faculty members. We felt that graduate students would also provide the best rapport with our patrons. The research team devotes time and effort to extensive training, which is then reflected in the work that RDAs do for the campus community.

ADMINISTRATION

The RDAs are members of the research team and report to the head of research. The science librarian, an early-career librarian and a past participant in a similar student program at Eastern Kentucky University Libraries, leads ongoing training, assessment, and hiring efforts. All professional librarians on the research team are empowered and encouraged to engage with RDAs, provide project work for RDAs, and to address questions or concerns as they arise.

For promotional efforts, the RDA program underwent a soft launch. The library never made a formal announcement that research librarians were "going off the desk." The quiet change avoided unnecessary backlash from well-meaning, concerned patrons. Librarians were still available "at *their* desk," developing programs, providing individual research consultations, and answering triaged reference questions. The presence of RDAs at the desk is no secret. The message communicated to students and faculty regarding desk staffing is that the highly trained students are glad to help on demand at the desk, and librarians are always available for individual meetings.

> When I began my first semester of graduate school in couples, marriage, and family counseling, I knew that I wanted to have a part-time position that enabled me to work on my communicative skills with diverse sets of people. I was fortunate enough to get a position as a Research Assistant at the Research Desk of the main campus library; not only have I learned about the research resources that are available to affiliates of the college, but I have also been able to work on my interpersonal and customer service skills with eclectic patrons throughout the area.
>
> *Tyler Key, Research Desk Assistant, College of William and Mary*

Hiring

A lesson we quickly learned in the first year of the program was the need to begin the search for RDAs early. The search now begins in late spring/early summer for new RDAs who will start in the fall. Starting the search early and acquiring a large pool allows selection of the students with the best communication skills and good fit for the department. We prefer that RDAs are incoming graduate students. After losing four of five RDAs due to graduation after the first year, we also prefer students who are enrolled in a two-year program. Hiring students upon their arrival at the college ensures they will be on the team as long as possible, providing the best return for their extensive training. Excellent reference service is not a skill learned overnight; students who continue in the RDA program in their second year have more confidence, effectively answer more difficult inquires, and are great partners in training of incoming RDAs.

We found that five RDAs is the optimal number of students to employ at one time for staffing the scheduled research desk hours while meeting students' scheduling needs. Five students provide everyone with enough hours while maintaining flexibility to cover for schedule conflicts. To recruit students, the following job description is posted on the Swem Library student employment opportunities website:

> The Swem Library Research Department has openings for Research Desk Assistants. The students in this position will work up to 20 hours per week. Training will be provided. While some flexibility in scheduling is available, applicants should be prepared to commit to regularly sched-uled shifts. Assistants will spend a majority of their time shift at the Research Desk. We will work around your other commitments.

Responsibilities

- Often serves as the first point of contact for thousands of patrons a year who come into the library.
- Frequently works at a high pace while multi-tasking; interprets myriad library poli-cies and procedures for patrons.
- Assists students in finding library resources using the library catalog and various databases.
- Answers questions in person, by phone, email, and instant message.

Additionally, to increase exposure and communication with the target recruitment audi-ence, academic departments with graduate programs are contacted directly. We request that graduate program directors and advisors distribute the job description to incoming students who will not receive departmental funding. Graduate students enrolled in any of the programs at the college who are not funded through any other assistantship of paid college employment are eligible to apply for a position.

Because the hiring process is begun before students are likely to be on campus or even in the state, we conduct many student interviews using Skype. Video interviews are the next best thing to in-person interviews for a public-facing position. The Skype inter-view is optimal for capturing a student's personality and potential for engagement with a patron. While face-to-face communication is a skill that many students have mastered, to effectively communicate via video chat is indicative of excellent communication skills.

One can teach a student to use research tools, but a friendly disposition must come natu-rally. Communication skills are critical for success as an RDA and are the number one criteria of evaluation. The interview questions center on a student's customer service experience; e.g., "What is the best thing about working to help someone in a difficult situation?" and research experience, e.g., "Tell me about your favorite research tool in your undergraduate library." Interviewees also are asked to confirm their schedules because we require all RDAs to work at least two night or weekend shifts per week.

TRAINING

The Research Desk Assistant program serves a dual role, supporting both the research needs of the diverse array of student, faculty, and community library users and the professional librarians at the Earl Gregg Swem Library. For this reason, we view student employees as crucial members of the library's research team. Without them, it would be increasingly difficult to staff the research desk on nights and weekends while expanding liaison librarian roles and fostering an environment of engagement across the campus. In order for the students to provide service at the exceptional level expected by our users, a large amount of time and effort is devoted to the RDA training program.

We continually evaluate our training sessions based on feedback from RDAs, assessment of RDAs, and the needs of the library. Lessons learned in the first two years of the program have been used to streamline and improve training efforts. Effective training of student assistants is critical for a quality program. A well-designed training framework and schedule provide the groundwork for successful training.

> Working as a research desk assistant has improved my ability to "dig deeper." Students often do not come to the research desk with a clear picture of what they are looking for, and it is only through the continued research interview that their needs are uncovered. As a counseling student, I have applied these skills to my clients, using similar techniques to discover their concerns, goals, and emotions.
>
> *Morgan Reid, Research Desk Assistant, College of William and Mary*

Development of the Training Program

In developing our training, we drew from the professional literature but also relied heavily on information sharing through professional LISTSERVs and personal experiences. The Peer Research Advisor program at Davidson College, highlighted in the article "We aren't just the kids that sit at the front,"[1] was an inspiration for the student program. Student employees, especially those serving as the face of the department, providing research assistance to other students, must be treated as learners as well as departmental colleagues, inspiring their best efforts. Inquisitive, empowered, and responsible research team members who value the mission of the research service point and strive to always answer a question to the best of their ability are the type of student workers we want. The training goal is to set the RDAs up for success in that endeavor.

We do not expect that RDAs advise a student in a semester-long research project or dissertation. We do expect that the RDAs be knowledgeable enough to accurately answer, find an answer, or direct to someone who can answer the myriad of questions streaming through the research desk on a daily basis. For long-term, large-scale, or difficult research inquiries, students are trained to refer the patron to a research librarian using LibCal, our consultation scheduler. Developing the RDAs' skill in triage is a goal in the training sessions. The students are partners in success and are not filling the role of a professional research librarian.

The training program takes place on and off the research desk. Before students begin their role as an RDA, they must attend an eight-hour training session. The original plan was to cover the entirety of materials in one day; however, move-in, graduate program orientations, and attendance to other required events made it difficult to schedule a full day of training in the short time between student's move-in and the beginning of the semester. To accommodate schedules, training was divided into two half-day sessions, using Doodle (http://doodle.com) to identify meeting times to fit everyone's busy schedule.

In our face-to-face training, students receive a notebook with physical copies of all materials used in the sessions. Training materials also are all available for reference for RDAs on their private LibGuide. The RDA training packet contains:

- The official training checklist
- Schedules
- A description of the position
- RDA code of conduct
- Liaison departmental list
- Building partners list
- Maps of the Library and Campus
- Research desk procedures
- Triage methods
- RUSA Guidelines for Behavioral Performance of Reference and Information Service Providers (RUSA 2013)
- Reference Interview from University of Illinois (Slater 2011)
- Helping Multiple Patrons from University of Illinois (Slater 2013)
- "Learn to Swem"—the main tools of library research
- Database searching tips and tricks (See Appendix A. Database Searching Tips and Tricks)
- Practice questions

Training: Day One

Known as the "introduction to everything" day, the goal of day one is to familiarize new RDAs with the library, their coworkers, and the nature of the position. It begins with an overview of the position and the code of conduct. Students then go on a tour of the library building—a very important tour because many questions asked in the early part of the semester will be directional and Swem Library has many building partners: Academic Advising, Writing Center, The Center for Geospatial Analysis, and The Omohundro Institute for Early American History & Culture. After the tour, we cover the RUSA guidelines and the reference interview process. While some training programs we referenced taught this information through a PowerPoint presentation format, we chose a more informal approach. Trainees, returning RDAs, and librarians gather to read the RUSA Guidelines[2] and input from librarians' personal experiences to engage students in. Sitting around the conference table from the start imparts the message to students that they are members of the team and that their input and integration is valued. Throughout the day of training, students meet the liaison librarian and department heads and, much like any first day on the job, they leave after four hours with more information than they can absorb. So, they are sent home with their materials and instructions to spend time reviewing and bring questions to day two.

Training: Day Two

The second day focuses on practical hands-on training. We begin with answering questions from day one's materials, of which there are always several, then move directly into library research training 101. It is not expected that the students master the library's large number of databases, course guides, and government information holdings in a single session, but we do expect that they will quickly develop a working knowledge of how to get started in research. The RDAs are graduate students and the majority enter the position with research experience from their undergraduate career. The training begins with an overview of frequently used resources, aptly named "Learn to Swem," a presentation featuring the library catalog, discovery layer (Summon), top databases, research guides, and RDA resources. Using "Tips and Tricks for Database Searches," the coordinator demonstrates sample search strategies. This segment of the training functions like a fast-paced information literacy class.

After the coordinator gives the RDA a whirlwind tour of the William and Mary Libraries online environment, the next two or three hours are spent as a group working through "Common and Not So Common Questions," a handout featuring thirty-five practice questions developed to touch on all ranges of questions fielded at the research desk. Questions range from detailed research questions, which would require the answer "let me help you book a research consultation with a librarian," to catalog searching, policies, directional questions, and everything in-between. Students take turns answering the sample questions until the group has formulated answers to all the questions. The exercise serves as both an introduction to staffing the research desk and a team-building conversation starter, encouraging communication among RDAs.

Continued Training

Following our whirlwind training days, students begin working their scheduled shifts at the research desk. For their first few shifts, students work alongside a seasoned reference librarian. During their first shifts at the desk, students continue their introductory training. They learn how to open and close the service point, transfer phone calls, locate resources, answer chat questions, and input statistics into LibAnalytics—all skills best learned through the hands-on environment, not group discussions. The first shifts of a semester are always wildcards, generally busy with many questions related to directions and policy interspersed with occasional in-depth research questions from faculty or continuing students. One RDA described fielding the vast array of questions as a continuous need to "press the panic button."

> Coordination of the Research Desk Assistant program has been a challenging yet wonderfully rewarding task. I have improved my leadership skills by guiding the research department through this change and expansion of research services in the library and I am greatly impressed with the results thus far. Working with a great group of students is an added bonus.
>
> *Lauren Manninen, former Science Librarian,*
> *College of William and Mary*

Because there is much to learn on the desk and students will work with any of the reference librarians, each RDA brings their training checklist, which is started during the training days and is completed through on-the-desk training. The checklist gives the student and librarian a reference point for what has been covered and what is still to learn. Once the basics are covered and the checklist is signed by the coordinator and student, the RDA spends time reviewing library resources in-between answering questions. During the training time frame, librarians often take the lead in answering research questions while the student observes.

After a week of working alongside a librarian, the students are generally ready to take flight. Feedback from the first-year RDAs indicated that having a librarian shadowing students consistently over an extended period of time impeded student confidence.

Prolonged shadowing may also impart an impression that the librarians did not trust the students or value RDAs' work. So, after a week, RDAs staff the desk solo. During the daytime hours, librarians keep a quiet yet consistent watch, ensuring someone is available to support students, answer difficult questions, and drop by the desk periodically to check on the student. During the evening hours, however, the students are left on their own, with backup from the circulation desk and the cell phone numbers of their training coordinator, head of research, and librarians who volunteer their knowledge after hours. The flow of the semester generally supports this method of student learning on the job, with librarians' help during the day and building their skill set to draw upon during evening shifts. By the time the semester reaches a point where research inquiries increase in number, the students have the experience to field many of the questions that come their way.

Training Communications

Group emails are frequently sent to keep RDAs and the department informed about what happens at the desk. Emails are sent to ask questions, share information about a particular course project likely to bring a number of students to the desk, odd requests, or to communicate training opportunities. During the first year, email was the exclusive form for group communication among RDAs. The coordinator sent weekly emails addressing students' questions, praises, and areas for improvement. We discovered that this method was not completely effective. Students seemed to lose information and were often confused about issues communicated through email, which required that each student be addressed individually in person. Email is currently used for information sharing and to communicate time-sensitive issues but not for ongoing training.

In the second year of the RDA program, face-to-face team meetings were held every other week. The group meeting significantly improved communication among students and serves as a team-building opportunity within the group, providing a time to communicate with each other beyond shift changes. Meeting time is used to answer questions, provide feedback, and to host guest speakers for ongoing training sessions. Students learn how to use more in-depth library resources that they will be called upon to use at the desk, improving the level of service we provide during night and weekend hours. At each meeting, guest librarians from across the libraries are invited to discuss and train on topics, including using the government information collection, finding and using microfilm/microfiche, subject-specific databases, genealogy resources, branch libraries, and customer service skills.

Projects

Students also continue to learn and build skills through on-the-desk projects. The desk does experience "down-time," and in that time, students are provided with projects to both enhance their research skills and assist librarians. In the first year, RDAs tackled the arduous task of reformatting the links boxes in more than 400 LibGuides to enable a more seamless transition of the research guides to LibGuides Version 2.0. The LibGuide project encouraged students to learn more about library resources and to develop relationships with individual liaison librarians. Students also search the library catalog for lists of purchase requests or publisher's catalogs to help with collection development and literature reviews.

Triage

The most difficult aspect of training RDAs is developing their knowledge and ability to triage effectively and appropriately. While we want the RDAs to be knowledgeable, it is not expected that they will know everything. It is stressed throughout training that students should call upon librarians to answer detailed reference questions when a librarian is available but that in the times when no librarians are available they should feel empowered to help a patron to the best of their ability. Determining when to tackle a question or to reach for help can be difficult, so we suggest that RDAs encourage patrons to follow up with an individual research consultation after assisting with detailed research questions. In fall 2015, LibCal scheduling software was implemented, allowing patrons to easily schedule individual research consultations at a desired available time. Since the adoption of this service, there has been a great increase in the number of follow-up meetings.

CODE OF CONDUCT

Our students are expected to present themselves and behave as professionals because they are the face of the department. RDAs sign both the library code of conduct and one created specifically for the department. The code of conduct was written to capture the purpose and mission of the research desk service and includes the following:

1. Always remember that you are the face of Swem Research Department. Please remain approachable, welcoming, and attentive at all times.
2. Please refrain from using your cell phone, eating, or having ongoing personal conversations at the desk.
3. If you need a break, put up "the sign" and set chat to "away." If you have backup, let them know. Remember to set chat to "available" upon return.
4. If you need to miss a shift, it is your responsibility to find coverage. Please ask your team members if they can cover your shift and inform your department contact ASAP. In an emergency, please notify the research department ASAP.
5. Attendance at biweekly training meetings is mandatory. Please plan on regular attendance.
6. While you are working on the research desk, you are likely to remain busy assisting patrons and working on librarian-assigned projects. Should you complete all required tasks and find yourself in a lull, homework is acceptable. However, it must

not interfere with your ability to attend to your responsibilities. The privilege to work on personal work may be revoked at any time.

7. If you don't know the answer, ASK!

8. Remember to refer difficult research questions to librarians, encourage research consultations, and end each transaction with an open door for the patron's return if needed.

9. Try not to say "No." Always try to provide an alternative.

10. Please check your email regularly; email is a primary method of contact in the department.

11. SMILE!

ASSESSMENT

Swem Library tracks all research desk questions through LibAnalytics, tallying all directional, technology help, policy, and research-related questions asked through any communication medium. RDAs are trained to accurately record research desk statistics, which not only demonstrates the need for staffing the service point but enables the coordinator to review RDA performance. The coordinator conducts periodic reviews of research questions answered by RDAs lasting ten or more minutes. Questions that were answered ineffectively or that missed a critical resource are chosen to discuss anonymously during team meetings. The RDA reviews are not conducted as a policing activity, realizing that everyone, including professionals, makes mistakes; they are used for learning opportunities. Excellent answers to research questions are also pulled to highlight the awesome work the RDAs perform on a daily basis.

Librarians also track statistics for individual consultations. Since beginning the RDA program, there has been a dramatic increase in the number of one-on-one research consultations scheduled with research librarians. The RDAs are one of the main reasons for the increase in research consultations. By staffing the desk and increasing the promotion of the one-on-one model, they are allowing the research department to expand services. Research questions answered at the desk have remained stable, which indicates that the research department is serving a greater number of patrons, one of the main goals of the RDA program.

Drawing on assessment methods of the student assistant program at the University of Portland (Senior, 2014), RDAs conduct self-assessments at the end of each shift. They use an internal form to respond to three questions: (1) What did you do well?; (2) What could you improve?; and (3) Do you have any questions, comments, or concerns? The coordinator reviews the entries prior to the biweekly team meetings and addresses comments and questions with the group. The individual reflections are helpful to address issues at the desk and determine future training sessions.

REFLECTIONS

Several years of the RDA program has provided the opportunity to learn lessons, adapt to needs, make changes, and improve the services. The number one lesson learned is that to implement a large-scale change in services, such as the Research Desk Assistant program, planning is key. Many hours must be devoted to discussions around the role of the students, how they fit into the department, when they will be hired, and how to train them.

Librarian understanding, involvement, and buy-in are critical. In the planning stages of the RDA program, there were some speed bumps with implementation due to concerns about a possible decline in the quality of services provided at the desk. There was also confusion as to what the exact role of the RDA was, but after two years of teamwork, we struck an optimal balance among service, skills, and librarian availability. After taking part in training sessions, librarians agree that students are well-trained and feel confident with their work at the desk. Positive feedback from stakeholders across our campus further solidified librarian acceptance of and—dare we say—embracing of the RDA program. The research team continues to interact with steadily increasing numbers of students and faculty, engaging in innovative methods for information literacy instruction and individual research consultations.

The long-term benefits of an RDA program are numerous. The research department increased its ability to communicate with the university community. Librarians continue to participate at the research desk service point, answering questions and working with RDAs during busy times. Librarians now have the freedom to integrate in new ways, such as engagement with the new curriculum at the college, sharing expert advice related to scholarly communications, and becoming involved in university committees. The RDAs have expanded support of research across the campus and community.

The Research department plans to continue to support and improve the RDA program into the foreseeable future. RDAs provide valuable services to the Research department and William & Mary campus community at large. It is our hope that through their experiences working in public services that they develop a robust research skill set which will transfer to their professional lives. Overall, the Research Desk Assistant program has been a major success for the Research department at the Earl Gregg Swem Library. Librarians are engaging with their liaison areas more than ever and are providing new services all the while supporting the availability of drop-in research assistance. Through the Research Desk Assistant program, Swem Research has accomplished large goals with a small team.

APPENDIX A

DATABASE SEARCHING TIPS AND TRICKS

Keywords are words or phrases which describe your information need/research topic.

Tips for determining keywords:
- Use a variety of resources including books, reputable websites, and popular news to get background information on your topic.
- How would a researcher describe your topic? Make sure you use formal terminology, including scientific names for organisms and full phrases in addition to abbreviations.
- Are there many ways to describe the same concept? Think of all synonyms for your keywords!

Search tools are used to link your keywords together for an effective database search. The top search tools you need to remember are:

1. Boolean operators: AND, OR, & NOT
   a. AND links together the main concepts in your search
   b. OR is used to locate synonyms
   c. NOT should be used with caution, as it excludes whatever word or phrase is marked with "NOT"
2. "Quotation marks": "quotes" are used around a specific phrase in order to tell a database, find these words together, not separate.
3. The asterisk (*): The asterisk is used at the end of the root of a group of words to find all forms of a word (ex: diet* yields, diets, diet, dieting, dietitian, dietary, etc.)

Sample search:

Topic: How might corals be analyzed or dated using archaeological techniques?

Search statements are combinations of keywords and search tools for use in database searches:

	Coral*
AND	analy* OR dat*
AND	Archaeolo*

Brainstorm! Try multiple strategies! Ask a Librarian for assistance when needed!

Practice makes perfect!

Your Topic:

Possible Keywords:

Search Statements to Try:

NOTES

1. Cara Evanson, "We Aren't Just the Kids That Sit at the Front," *CR&L News* 76, no.1 (2015): 30–33.
2. Reference and User Services Association division of the American Library Association (RUSA), "Guidelines for Behavioral Performance of Reference and Information Service Providers," last modi-fied 2013, http://www.ala.org/rusa/resources/guidelines/guidelinesbehavioral.

BIBLIOGRAPHY

Evanson, Cara. "We Aren't Just the Kids That Sit at the Front." *CR&L News* 76, no.1 (2015): 30–33.
Reference and User Services Association division of the American Library Association. "Guidelines for Behavioral Performance of Reference and Information Service Providers." Last modified 2013. http://www.ala.org/rusa/resources/guidelines/guidelinesbehavioral.
Senior, Heidi E. K. "Student Workers at the Reference Desk." *OLA Quarterly* 16, no. 2 (2014): 5–6.
Slater, Robert. "The Reference Interview." Last modified August 12, 2011. https://www.library.illinois.edu/staff/training/resources/graduate_assistants/trainingmanual/refinterview/.
———. "Helping Multiple Patrons." Last modified August 2, 2013. http://www.library.illinois.edu/training/resources/graduate_assistants/trainingmanual/multiplepatrons.html (site discontinued).

REFERENCE ASSOCIATE PROGRAM AT FLORIDA STATE UNIVERSITY:
Training Future Librarians

Emily Zoe Mann

Getting your foot in the door of academic librarianship can be a Sisyphean task. After finishing my MLIS, it took almost three years of cobbled-together part-time paraprofessional library work before I was able to get my first professional librarian job. Along the way, I collected a good amount of job-hunting and professional development tricks and tips as well as a passion to help other new librarians avoid my fate. The Reference Associate Program at FSU was born of this desire to mentor new librarians as well as the need to offer peer-to-peer reference that matched the rest of the peer-to-peer service model FSU Libraries had already implemented.

FLORIDA STATE UNIVERSITY LIBRARIES

Florida State University (FSU) is a large public university with an enrollment of more than 41,000 students, about 32,000 of which are undergraduate students. The FSU library system consists of seven libraries. The largest is the Robert Manning Strozier Library, which serves the needs of both undergraduate and graduate students. Strozier Library is an extremely popular study location for FSU students and is affectionately nicknamed "Club Stroz." The university also has a school of information that awards ALA-accredited MLIS degrees.

There are several distinct student areas in Strozier, including the Scholar's Commons for faculty and graduate students, the Learning Commons for undergraduates, Special Collections, and the stacks. The Reference Associate Program was created to assist patrons in the Learning Commons located on the first floor. While this area is geared toward undergraduate students, it is the first point of contact for all library patrons and is open to everyone.

Reference Associate History and Objectives

Strozier Library moved to a combined service desk model with peer-to-peer services in the mid-2000's after an extensive ethnographic study. The goal of the combined service desk was to staff the service point with undergraduate student workers who specialized in a specific area, such as technology, outreach, circulation, or reference but were cross-trained in all areas. Each student was hired for their specialization by a supervisor who also specialized in that area; they then received cross-training from specialists in other areas. While there was a triage and consultation system in place, many patrons were unaware of walk-up reference services, and the student workers at the desk were not being specifically trained to help with reference. The combined desk did not have designated areas for a particular assistance; instead, patrons stood in one line and went to the first open employee. After the combined service desk was instituted, there was a sharp decline in recorded reference transactions. This could have been due to a number of factors, including student workers not knowing when to mark a transaction as reference, the lack of a clear reference desk, or the new peer-to-peer model. This model had been in place for several years at FSU when I arrived as the reference librarian.

The Reference Associate Program was developed with two goals in mind. The first goal was to meet the need for peer-to-peer reference services, and the second goal was to give aspiring librarians an opportunity to improve their reference and library service skills.

Due to a vacancy in the reference librarian position, there were no undergraduate students specializing in reference at the combined desk when I began. However, rather than continue with providing reference at the main service point, I decided to create the Research Help Now (RHN) desk within eyesight of the combined desk. This desk still works with the peer-to-peer model but allows students a space to get more focused reference help. We chose to call it Research Help Now since students are not always familiar with the term "reference." The physical desk is simply a table with a computer that faces the combined desk and is set to only login for library staff. Originally, the only signage was a digital sign that said "Research Help Now." After the pilot proved itself, a permanent sign reading "Research Help" was put into place.

Rather than use cross-trained undergraduate students, I decided to staff the RHN desk with graduate students currently in or recently graduated from library school. Florida State University has MLIS students, and the Reference Associate Program was created with the idea of taking advantage of this while also providing its students with the opportunity to gain practical library experience. The FSU Reference Associate Program was influenced by the University of North Carolina at Greensboro's Reference Intern program, which I had previously helped supervise. FSU's human resources (HR) system allows hiring of both current students and recent graduates for this job. Because students often leave library school without any experience, it is important to make the program available to recent library school graduates as well. This also increases the job hiring pool since the majority of FSU MLIS students are online and not located in Tallahassee. The Reference Associate Program works because the students are motivated to get library experience. Since the inception of the program, former reference associates have gone on to work in museums, public libraries, and academic libraries. One hiring manager told me that a former reference associate has applied for an entry-level position, but once they came in and talked about the experience they had gained as a reference associate, the library planned to offer them for a more advanced position with higher pay, thus showing the value of the experience.

> The skillset I have attained in working as a research consultant is highly valuable. Not only have I gained knowledge regarding effective customer service, but I have also become a more proficient user and learner of the library in general.
>
> *Sila Lott, Research Consultant, Florida State University*

In order to hire recent graduates, the program is not set up as a traditional internship; however, the program acts as an internship in all but name. Students work at the reference desk, attend required training, and are required to create professional output. The program allows reference associates to stay with us for only four semesters as we do not want them to see it as a permanent job but rather an opportunity to prepare for a permanent job. This frequent turnover means a larger time commitment and more work on the part of the trainers, but the quality of work we receive as well as the ability to help new librarians start on their path to a professional position makes this a worthwhile endeavor

The program was piloted for a semester with four reference associates and then assessed. Assessment was done in three ways, first in the form of daily question tracking on a Google Form that allowed us to see how many questions we received as well as the kinds of questions being answered. Second, we monitored virtual reference and read transcripts to see the quality of the answers as well as sitting in at the desk to watch transactions. Finally, we conducted a summative assessment in the form of an anonymous survey that the reference associates filled out. This feedback helped us create a more comprehensive program with clearer goals and assessment that will be addressed later in this chapter.

Location and Hours

Because the combined service desk was overwhelmingly busy with circulation transactions and technology troubleshooting, we decided to create a separate RHN desk. The new RHN desk is close to the main combined desk, and this cluster of service points is making it easier for our students to find help. There are several positives to this model. For example, student workers at the combined desk are able to quickly point out the RHN desk, which helps us reduce the number of patrons that might leave rather than continue to seek help. Our current location also allows reference associates to see students approaching from the front of the library and the back of the library, allowing them to reach more patrons. Being visible is crucial for success, particularly when the service point was new.

We made several decisions about hours and staffing based on the needs of our institution and statistics gathered at both the combined service desk and the RHN desk. When planning for your own program, it is important to look at when librarians are available, when the desk is busiest, and how much time you can budget for each reference associate to work.

> This position has challenged me to continue growing, to continue learning, and to keep evolving in a day and age where library users become more interdependent with technology.
>
> *Sila Lott, Research Consultant, Florida State University*

A summary of our staffing model:

- Ideally, the RHN desk is staffed from 10 a.m. until midnight Sunday through Thursday, but when faced with a labor shortage or budget constraints, we opt to fill the later hours, which is when FSU students tend to seek library assistance.
- The reference associates cover in-person and virtual reference while at the desk but have virtual reference backup from staff so they can focus on face-to-face interactions.
- Reference associates cannot work more than twenty-nine hours a week because we are not budgeted to offer them benefits.

- Librarians are available weekdays from 8 a.m. to 6 p.m., so it's important to schedule reference associates during the later hours when no librarians are available to help.
- The RHN desk is not staffed on Fridays due to lack of traffic; however, we do staff on Saturdays since there are no librarians in the building.

It is essential that you do a quick assessment of your own needs, limitations, and services before you set up your own program.

ADMINISTRATION
Management and Staffing

This program is a part of FSU's Learning Commons. This program is run by one full-time librarian with assistance from one full-time evening staff member. This system works well as the librarian is available during the day, while the staff member is available until 10 p.m., which allows for consistent supervision for the reference associates. Although reference associates work independently at the RHN desk, supervisors are always available as back up. In addition, there are other Learning Commons staff members in the building at all times with the reference associates so they are never too far from help.

It is important to have more than one staff member working with the students for several reasons. First, it's an extensive time commitment to ensure the program is successful. Strategically planning training and having several staff members involved makes it more manageable. Second, having staff members who work different shifts can offer more consistent supervision for reference associates. The more people involved in hiring, training, and planning, the stronger the program will be. Having a diversity of viewpoints is also essential to building a successful program and even more essential to sustaining the program. I can only bring in my own experiences and ideas, but having the experiences and point of view of my staff has been tremendously beneficial to myself and the reference associates. Looking at any program through multiple lenses is one of the best ways to ensure its success. Collaboration strengthens any program.

Budgets and Funding

The budget for the Reference Associate Program comes from the Learning Commons student worker budget. We have a fixed budget and plan for the entire academic year at the start of the fiscal year. Priority is given to staffing the RHN desk during the fall and spring semesters when more students are on-campus, therefore the summer sessions (we have three) have a much more limited schedule.

When considering the budget, we looked at several models of pay rates and staffing hours. While we could have paid a higher rate but staffed fewer hours, we chose to staff more hours with lower pay. The reference associates are at a slightly higher pay range than the undergraduate student workers and work around twenty hours each. We hope that the professional benefits, such as professional references and experience for future library jobs, help compensate for the pay rate. This information is made clear in during the hiring process and we let potential reference associates know that while it won't be a high-paying job, it will give them a great deal of experience and marketability. This will depend on the institution you are working at as some institutions require higher pay for graduate students.

Promoting the Program

Marketing and promotion have proved to be one of the more difficult parts of this program, simply because of the size of FSU. The first step in developing promotion was to create signage. At the time of the pilot there was a general signage redesign planned so we were asked not to create permanent signs that might not match the anticipated sign design. We worked around this by having a digital sign created by the library's graphic designer. This sign is displayed on a second computer monitor at the RHN desk and faces patrons. This could also work on a digital picture frame. We also had a web banner created to cycle on the main library website. Clicking on this banner leads to a separate site that lists the hours. In addition, we have handouts with information about the program that we give out at the circulation desk, at information literacy classes, and at library outreach programs. Once the new signage redesign was done for the entire floor a permanent sign was created that reads Research Help.

HIRING

Recruitment

Recruiting quality applicants can be difficult. The majority of library school students at our institution are distance students, so the pool of potential applicants is limited. While we would like to hire distance students to help with virtual reference, this is not something our HR is currently set up to deal with. This is why we also hire newly graduated MLIS students and do not require that students be in the Florida State University MLIS program. In order to recruit, we send an email to the Information School listserv, advertise with the FSU ALA student chapter, and put an advertisement on floridalibraryjobs.com. The supervisors also attend the FSU ALA student chapter meetings so that students are aware of the program. In addition to these advertising methods, we ask our reference associates to talk to their classmates and encourage them to apply. As word has gotten out about the program, our pool has grown with each hiring cycle.

Applications and Interviews

In order to apply for the job, potential candidates are asked to submit a cover letter and résumé. This not only lets us see their job history but also gives us an idea about their experience and knowledge in creating job application materials, something we train them in later.

After the initial screening, we bring in potential candidates for an in-person interview in order for the supervisors to get to know the candidates. We seek candidates who have good customer service skills, positive attitudes, and are not afraid to ask for help. We strive to make it clear to our candidates that we do not expect them to know everything from the start, but we expect them to be willing to learn. We begin by telling them:

> I started working more hands-on with the reference associate program in the fall of 2015. I knew that the program was good; I just wished that I knew how effective it was. I now get to see first-hand how well the students are accepting it and much it is being used.
>
> *Supervisor, Florida State University*

The person in this position works to provide reference in the learning commons both in-person and virtually. Because we know we are hiring students/recent graduates, we will be providing weekly training sessions as well as giving an extensive training at the beginning of the semester. We will have some homework and expect the people hired to treat this as both a job and learning opportunity. We will have a semester-long project for each student and will expect some output by the end of the semester. You will not be expected to work extensively outside of your paid hours (other than some homework) but you will be expected to treat this as a true work position and not work on outside homework or socialize with friends during work hours. Our hope is to make you marketable as librarians once you graduate with a greater understanding of providing in-person and virtual reference.

In the interview, we ask general questions, such as why they are interested in the position as well as what strengths they bring to the position. We also ask them several specific questions about their professional and personal goals as well as their comfort in asking for help. These questions include:

- What type of library are you interested in working in? Why do you think this position will be helpful in achieving this goal?
- What are some of your personal goals this year?
- What areas of libraries are you particularly interested in? What kind of research areas interest you?
- What would you do if a patron asked you a question about a topic you are not familiar with?

We have found that these questions not only help us get to know the candidates but also let the candidates know our expectations upfront.

TRAINING
Instructional Design

One key to success with the Reference Associate Program has been solid instructional design. Reference associates are student workers and are employed for both the pay and the learning opportunity. In order to deal with this dichotomy, the program is designed as if it were a yearlong class. The instructional design for this program is based on Fink's integrated approach to designing college courses, which requires a backward design with both formative and summative assessment.[1] This instructional design method looks at the needs of the learners, creates learning objectives, and then assessment based on the objectives. After this process, the activities for instruction are created. The Reference Associate Program coordinators met for a full day of instructional design and created the following training program and learning objectives.

Learning Objectives

Fink's integrated approach involves identifying learning objectives for the course. These learning objectives are then used to create an easily used assessment matrix (see Appendix A. Criteria for Assessment) that is given to both the trainers and reference associates so there is full transparency in the assessment process. The following learning goals or objectives were created for the program:

1. Reference associates will be able to evaluate and assess whether or not a reference interaction is a teaching moment.
2. Reference associates will have the confidence to try to answer questions they are unfamiliar with but the respect to refer the question to the appropriate person when necessary.

3. Reference associates will show empathy and interest to patrons as well as to themselves.
4. Reference associates will be able to assess and use library resources effectively.
5. Reference associates will understand and use reference interview techniques for patron interactions.

These learning objectives are based on observations from our first semester with the Reference Associate Program as well as the feedback we received from the pilot program. Having these learning objectives made it simpler to create a training program and to assess how students were doing. Assessment will be discussed later in this chapter.

Communication

We use our Learning Management System (LMS) system to communicate with reference associates. Because students are accustomed to being on the LMS for class, this is currently the best place to house the manual, weekly journal, and schedule. In general, it is a good communication tool that allows the supervisors to talk with everyone at once and provides a good place for shift swaps.

> I have the great pleasure of working with the past and present reference associates. I got to see the creation of the program and the current state, and through it all the focus has been on helping our patrons. Both the students and the associates get to benefit from this program. To me, our program centers on the patrons while teaching our associates the tools that they can use in their future endeavors.
>
> *Supervisor, Florida State University*

Reference Bootcamp

After the reference associates are hired, they are required to meet for a week of training known as Reference Bootcamp. This training aims to give them the tools they need to successfully act as the first point of contact for reference questions. Having an extended training as a group also has the added benefit of allowing the students to bond, creating a stronger group dynamic. (In addition to the reference associates, we invite any library staff member who is interested in improving their reference skills or getting a "reference refresher" to attend whichever sessions they would like.) This Reference Bootcamp takes place for one week. We meet for several hours on Monday, Wednesday, and Friday, with homework and reading in-between. (See Appendix B. Training Agenda.)

The activities are based on successful information literacy active learning activities. Even the homework incorporates active learning; rather than give them the link to the articles, we provide them with citations and ask the students to use the skills they have just learned to find the articles. (See Appendix A.) We then discuss the methods they used in the next meeting.

While going over the databases, we not only talk about how to use particular databases but what a database is, what journals each one pulls from, how to use the thesaurus, and best practices for searching. The reference associates bring laptops into the classroom in order to follow along with database and resource demonstrations, so it's a more interactive experience.

It is essential to build in time for questions. There is a huge potential for information overload in this bootcamp and it's important that the reference associates leave feeling prepared to work on the desk but not overwhelmed with the amount of information and skills they were expected to learn over the last week. Honestly, there will be some feelings of doubt, so we also make it a point to remind the reference associates that we are always available for them when they have questions.

After Reference Bootcamp, reference associates work at the combined circulation desk for one week in order to be truly cross-trained. They then begin working at the RHN desk and we continue to meet as a group once a week.

> What I have attained in the program has been a stepping stone to my future career goals and aspirations. The program reaffirms my passion for libraries.
>
> *Sila Lott, Research Consultant, Florida State University*

Weekly Training

After the initial training, there is weekly training during which supervisors and reference associates meet for an hour. This training is divided into several parts. The first part is a review of virtual reference and journals. This is a time when the supervisors can discuss the work that reference associates are doing on virtual reference. Exemplary chats are shown and discussed. If there seem to be general issues that reference associates are having in virtual reference, this is a good time and place to address the problems and work on them together. We also discuss what was reported in the weekly journals and offer time to ask questions. After this, we host invited speakers, go on field trips, or one of the supervisors does a presentation on a particular topic.

Examples of weekly meeting topics:

- Microfilm tour of collections and how to use it
- Using and teaching citation management tools
- Tour of Special Collections at our library
- Tour of the public library
- Instructional design
- Scholarly communication
- Data management
- Collection development
- Working with patrons with Autism Spectrum Disorder

This list, however, is in no way complete. We try to get an idea about what the reference associates are interested in and then plan speakers, workshops, and tours that will be beneficial to them.

Professional development is an important part of training because this is often skipped in library school. One session that is very popular is the presentation on conferences. This presentation reviews how to find conferences, how to navigate them, how to present at them, and how to find scholarships. Another training that the reference associates look forward to is the cover letter and résumé/CV workshop. This training gives them information on how to create a viable résumé or CV, and we create a cover letter together on Google Docs using a real job advertisement. During an ALA annual conference, many of the reference associates visited the ALA JobList Placement & Career Development Center and were told that their CVs and résumés were very well-crafted and showed a great deal more professionalism than many other recent graduates. I also give them advice on the job hunt, such as resources to look for jobs, what to expect on an academic job interview, and general behavior guidelines, like who to address cover letters to as well as thank-you letter etiquette.

Because the reference associate training calendar is based on the school year, there can be repetition for reference associates who have been with the program for more than two semesters. Reference associates who have already seen a particular training are allowed to miss that training, but often it changes just enough from semester to semester that they still can get something out of it. That said, we still try to create a yearly schedule that avoids duplication.

When planning the training calendar, we contact our guest speakers to select mutual training session dates. Then we schedule the remaining open dates for training sessions by supervisors, such as cover letters, citation management, and conference guidance.

Semester-Long Project

Reference associates are given a semester-long project to work on at the start of the semester. In addition to the weekly training and the hours scheduled at the RHN desk, reference associates are allotted one hour a week to work on their semester-long project. During the first weekly meeting, they are given a prompt and asked to work as a group. Here is an example of a semester-long project prompt:

> At the end of this semester, the reference associates will create and present an online training tool together. What this tool will be is up to the group. Communication will take place at the weekly reference associate meetings and via email. You all have one hour of paid time to work on this per week. You can also work on your own parts during downtime at the desk.

Criteria

This can be any type of online training tool you want; however, it must meet the following criteria:

- Be ADA accessible
- Have at least one learning objective
- Create some form of assessment
- Be useful to the undergraduate population

First Steps

- Create a timeline.
- Think about what you want to accomplish. What is the problem you are trying to solve? (For example, Citation Fox was created by a library to help with difficult citations.)
- Create one or more learning objectives you want your tool to accomplish.
- Think about what platform you will use. I have no money to offer you, so it will need to be free or something the library already has (a very real-world experience for you!)
- Please feel free to use me or any other librarian/student/professor as a resource.

They are also given deadlines for the project description, a mid-semester presentation, and a final end-of-semester presentation. The reference associates are encouraged to talk with the different speakers from the weekly training to see if they can use some of their experience or knowledge to help them with the project. An invitation is sent to all the previous speakers as well as all library staff to watch the final presentation.

This particular project was highly successful and led to the reference associates getting experience in project management, presenting to large groups which included library administration, and being accepted to present their findings at the Florida Library Association annual conference. The project was embraced by the digital scholarship and technology department of the library, and the project continued into the next semester with the idea of implementing the tool. You can see an iteration of the tool at https://rhnfsu.wordpress.com. Even more impressive, during an ALA annual conference, one reference associate spoke to a vendor about the project and the vendor invited the reference associates to give a webinar about the project through the vendor's webinar series. Having the reference associates work on a project that has a practical application is a great opportunity to create tangible evidence of their work and to make a visible impact on the library and library world.

> I think that peer-to-peer reference is a good idea because it is a learning experience for both sides. It also may be less intimidating working with someone that you think that you can relate to.
>
> *Supervisor, Florida State University*

ASSESSMENT
Tracking Sessions

We keep statistics of every interaction at the RHN desk. Currently, we use Springshare's LibInsight for this record-keeping, though in the past we used LibAnalytics and a free Google Form. From each interaction, we gather the following information: how the patron was helped (in person, online), type of question answered, a brief description of the question, and the reference associate who helped the patron. LibInsight also does an automatic time stamp so we know what time and day the interactions take place.

Keeping track of this information is essential for proving the value of the program. It also lets us see when we are getting the most and fewest interactions, which is helpful when we have to cut or add hours to the desk. These numbers are also important in assessing the usefulness of the program, as we can see the number of interactions that take place. Because we have been keeping this kind of information for years, we were able to see a 13 percent increase in reference questions in the first two years the RHN desk was put into place.

Student Assessment

We ask for two types of assessment from our reference associates: self-assessment and assessment of the program. In order to allow for formative and self-assessment throughout the semester, reference associates are required to keep a weekly journal on our LMS site. This lets them check in and see if they are meeting the learning objectives of the program as well as ask questions about things that happened on the desk. The added bonus of having these journals on the LMS is that both the supervisors and the other reference associates can comment, making the journals collaborative. Feedback has shown that reference associates prefer a particular prompt each week rather than just writing about their time at the desk.

We have a summative assessment at the end of each semester in which reference associates fill out an anonymous survey evaluating the Reference Associate Program as a whole. The comments in the surveys are important in reshaping any part of the program that is not working. The reference associates also do a final journal entry and assess if they met all the learning objectives over the semester.

Evaluating Reference Associates

There is informal evaluation throughout the semester for each reference associate, with communication taking place one-on-one as needed. (See Appendix B.) There are also two formal evaluations. The first one takes place mid-semester and is a good time to reflect on how each reference associate is doing and if they need any changes. This also is a good time for the supervisors to make sure the training is in line with reference associates' needs. At the end of the semester, the supervisors collaborate to write a formal evaluation letter. This letter is presented to the reference associate and is saved by the supervisors to help with reference letters in the future.

REFLECTION

Working with reference associates has proved to be challenging but rewarding. The fact that reference associates all want to become professional librarians makes them enthusiastic and results in a great work ethic. This makes them a pleasure to work with and also helps reinvigorate the librarians working with them. The mentor relationship that the supervisors are able to form with the reference associates is a rewarding one that is mutually beneficial. Librarians and staff members are able to pass on knowledge while at the same time learn to see the process with new eyes. When we do the same thing over and over, it becomes too easy to see it as routine and boring. Watching reference associates get excited about answering questions that might strike me as run-of-the-mill helps to remind me why I got into the profession in the first place.

Challenges and Success

Creating the Reference Associate Program from scratch presented a number of challenges as well as successes. One particular challenge was setting up the comprehensive training program. The training described earlier is a direct result of lessons learned from the pilot program. Approaching the training program as a class and using instructional design made planning the program easier and also made the program more successful. Using an integrated approach as well as making the learning objectives clear from the start was also more beneficial to the reference associates.

> I am happy that I got to witness this program from the start and to watch it grow. I am very proud of the small part that I played, and I think that this program has done a great service to the library as a whole.
>
> *Supervisor, Florida State University*

Future Plans

Since writing this chapter I have left my position at Florida State Universities, but the reference associate program continues and evolves under new management. One of the best things about this program is that the reference associates help to direct its future. Changes are made based on the successes and failures of the semester. The program has continued to grow and show its worth. Thanks to the proven success of the program, budget significantly increased and the reference associates continue to be valued.

I am fortunate to have had the experience of collaborating with the reference associates because they are not just library school students; they are my future colleagues. The reference associate program will continue to grow and change just as the field of librarianship does. And as it does, I am excited to see the librarians it will help to produce.

APPENDIX A

CRITERIA FOR ASSESSMENT

Learning Objective	Poor	Acceptable	Exceptional
Reference associate will be able to evaluate and assess whether or not a reference interaction is a teaching moment.	Reference associate always tries to teach the full process of finding reference material without taking time to understand patrons' needs. *Or* Reference associate provides a resource with no explanation.	Reference associate answers question, explains how they got the answer, does not perform full reference interview.	Reference associate performs full reference interview to understand needs of patron and gauges their reactions to teaching. Student asks patron if they would like to learn how to do more of the same sort of research. Reference associate does not force teaching if it is not wanted by patron. Reference associate offers referral for further learning if appropriate.
Reference associate will have the confidence to try to answer questions they are unfamiliar with but the respect to refer the question onto the appropriate person.	Reference associate says "I don't know," and ends interaction there. *Or* Reference associate spends over 15 minutes on the question, does not find an answer or refer patron to correct person for help.	Reference associate makes an effort to find the answer if they can't they refer patron to supervisor. *Or* Reference associate spends less than 10 minutes on the question and refers it to appropriate person if they can't find answer.	Reference associate shows reflective listening skills and makes an effort to find the answer while keeping patron informed. If after 5–10 minutes of searching and interacting Reference associate cannot find answer, they will refer patron to the appropriate subject librarian, staff member, or librarian.
Reference associate will show empathy and interest to patrons as well as to themselves.	Reference associate has closed-off body language and doesn't look up from the computer. *Or* Reference associate dismisses patrons' perceived needs. *Or* Reference associate makes assumptions about patron without doing actual reference interview.	Reference associate makes eye contact and smiles. Student listens to the question but may not use reflective language or continue with the reference interview after a certain point.	Reference associate projects empathy with eye contact, smiling and open body language. Reference associate takes the time to listen to patron fully, uses reflective language, and checks back with them frequently to make sure they are on the right path for research.

Learning Objective	Poor	Acceptable	Exceptional
Reference associate will be able to assess and use library resources effectively.	Reference associate has one or two go-to resources and does not make an effort to learn and use new resources.	Reference associate uses the most popular databases, catalog, and the "I need to" section of the website.	Reference associate uses research guides, subject databases, and guides outside of the library website to find information.
Reference associate will understand and use reference interview techniques for patron interactions.	Reference associate answers the initial question without doing any reference interview. *Or* Reference associate leaves out two reference interview steps: greeting, asking open questions, finding resource, follow-up, and kind sendoff.	Reference associate leaves out one reference interview step. *Or* Reference associate answers question but doesn't do follow up.	Reference associate performs complete reference interview with all steps and answers question correctly. If they can't find the answer, presents a good referral. Reports questions/concerns to supervisor.

APPENDIX B

TRAINING AGENDA

The bolded words have active learning activities associated with them.

Monday: 1 p.m.–4 p.m.
1:00–1:15 **Introductions**
Have students interview each other, then introduce each other to the group.
1:15–1:45 Blackboard/general policies
1:45–2:30 Library tour
2:30–2:40 Break
2:40–3:00 Library website
      Catalog, journal finder, databases, research guides
3:00–3:45 **Reference Interview**
3:45–4:30 **Keywords**

Homework:
- Post reflection in Blackboard.
- Read: Harmeyer, D. "Hybrid Reference: Blending the Reference Interview and Information Literacy." *Reference Librarian*, 51(4) (2010): 358–362.
- Read the student manual and sign.

Wednesday: 9:30 a.m.–3:30 p.m.
9:30–9:50 Logging hours, desk in office, space to put things
9:50–10:20 Circulation
10:20–10:30 Break
10:30–11:00 Discuss reading and thoughts concerns so far
11:00–12:00 **Virtual Reference**
12:00–1:00 Lunch on your own
1:00–1:30 Learning objectives and assessment
1:30–3:00 Academic search complete/**database activity**
3:00–3:30 FAQ
      Book reviews, opinions, peer-reviewed articles, newspaper articles

Homework:
- Read: Schwartz, H. R., & Trott, B. b. "The Application of RUSA Standards to the Virtual Reference Interview." *Reference & User Services Quarterly* 54(1) (2014): 8–11.
- Find one article about emerging trends in libraries that interests you. Read and summarize. Be prepared to explain your research process to the group on Friday.

Friday 9:30 a.m.–2:30 p.m.
9:30–10:00 Discuss reading and article you found
10:30–11:00 Reference databases
Opposing viewpoints, Oxford Digital Reference Shelf, Biography in Context
11:00–11:30 Citations
11:30–11:45 Triage
11:45–1:00 Lunch together (my treat for reference associates)
1:00–2:00 **Threshold concepts**
  • 2:00–2:30 Wrap up, time for questions

Homework:
Post Reflection in Blackboard

Bootcamp Activities

Introductions

This is a simple activity that lets reference associates get to know each other, practice their interview skills, and practice their presentation skills. Reference associates are paired up (if there is an odd number, a supervisor pairs up) and given the following questions to ask their partner:

  • Name
  • Kind of library they want to work in
  • Where they are from
  • Interesting fact

After a few minutes of letting the reference associates interview each other, they take turns presenting their partner to the group.

Reference Interview

In order to learn about reference interviews, we first go over a PowerPoint presentation that explains the reference interview (http://bit.ly/1NBPFUH). For the activity, we split reference associates into groups of two. If there is an odd number, one of the supervisors acts as a partner. Each reference associate is given a sheet of paper with a scenario and a prompt. One reference associate plays the "patron" and the other is the "librarian." The patron reads the scenario to themselves and only asks the prompt. It is then the job of the librarian to figure out what the patron actually needs, using the reference interview. It is a good idea to have the reference interview steps available for reference associates to refer to during this activity. The students take turns playing the librarian and patron and then go in front of the group with different scenarios and prompts. We then discuss the activity and why it's so important to do a full reference interview.

Examples
1. Scenario: You are a freshman in a Biology 101 class that wants to find out when cats were domesticated.
   Prompt: I need some help finding information on cats.

2. Scenario: You are an underclassman taking a sociology class about modern slavery. Your professor has told you to write a paper about any topic on modern-day slavery but you must have three resources, one book, one article, and you get bonus points if you have a primary source.
   Prompt: Are there any books on slavery here?

3. Scenario: You have never cited anything before but your professor has told you that you need to cite three articles for your paper in APA style. You found the articles through one search but are not sure how to cite them.
   Prompt: Hi. I need some help with citation.

Keywords

This activity is intended to get reference associates thinking about keywords and understanding the different ways people might describe the same thing. The reference associates are divided into two groups and given whiteboard markers and whiteboards. Then a series of pictures are shown. These pictures tend to be full of activity, one example being a man dressed as Elmo being arrested in Times Square. Each picture is put up for a few minutes, during which each team must write as many keywords that they can come up with to describe the picture or aspects of the picture. After each picture, we look at the keywords and phrases each team comes up with and discuss the different ways things can be described. We generally show three or four pictures and then show several research questions and ask them to come up with keywords.

Virtual Reference

This activity gives reference associates the opportunity to practice with virtual reference. We first go over best practices for virtual reference and how to use our software. Then the reference associates take turns coming to the main screen and answering chat questions that the supervisor sends in. It is important if you are using your live chat service that you let other librarians on virtual reference know there is training going on. You can also create a separate training queue if your software allows for this. While the reference associate is in front of the group, the other reference associates are encouraged to help them and they all work together to answer chat questions.

Database Activity

This activity is done after they have been introduced to Academic Search Complete. It aims to teach reference associates how a database works so they can provide better reference.

Reference associates are divided into groups of two. Each group is given a database. You can allow the students to pick their own databases that they are interested in or you can assign ones you think will be helpful for everyone to know. The reference associates are then given a worksheet with the following questions to answer.

1. What subject does the database cover?
2. Can you find what resources the database is using? List some of the resource or journals and be ready to show the group.
3. What are some of the limiters?
4. What tools are available?
5. How can students save the articles or get back to the articles?
6. What is unique about this database?
7. Are there any other things you want to tell the group about this database?

The reference associates then present to the rest of the group and in the process learn about database structure as well as finding out about some specific databases the library has.

Threshold Concepts

This is a simple discussion. We hand out a copy of the ACRL *Framework* and give everyone a chance to read over them. There is then a led discussion about how we can incorporate these ideas into reference and virtual reference.

NOTES

1.   L. Dee Fink, "A Self-Directed Guide to Designing Courses for Significant Learning," Dee Fink & Associates, last modified August 2005, http://www.deefinkandassociates.com/GuidetoCourseDesignAug05.pdf.

BIBLIOGRAPHY

Fink, L. Dee. "A Self-Directed Guide to Designing Courses for Significant Learning." Dee Fink & Associates. Accessed July 20, 2016. http://www.deefinkandassociates.com/GuidetoCourseDesignAug05.pdf.

PEER RESEARCH MENTORS AT GETTYSBURG COLLEGE

Clinton Baugess, Mallory Jallas, Meggan Smith, and Janelle Wertzberger

OVERVIEW

Musselman Library at Gettysburg College developed a Peer Research Mentor (PRM) program to expand the library's formal research and instruction program. (See Appendix A. Job Description—Peer Research Mentors.) Designed and coordinated by a group of research and instruction librarians, the PRM program is built around a cohort of eight undergraduate students from a variety of class years and disciplines. Each PRM has a librarian supervisor. The PRMs participate in intensive training, provide reference service alongside professional librarians at the Research Help Desk, and develop outreach projects to better connect student patrons with library collections and services.

Training

Our intensive "boot camp" training workshop is scheduled over two days before the start of the fall semester. (See Appendix B. Peer Research Mentor Boot Camp Schedule.) The core curriculum addresses challenges that student researchers face: getting started, defining a topic, finding articles in library databases, and evaluating sources. Training modules were collaboratively developed, taught, and assessed by pairs of librarians. Librarians build upon boot camp training during biweekly cohort meetings throughout the semester. (See Appendix C. Topics Covered at Biweekly Meetings.) In the fall, librarians select topics, design lessons, and facilitate the meetings. In the spring, PRMs take the lead, with support from librarian supervisors.

> I am familiar with more databases than I ever knew existed! Tough research topics don't daunt me anymore because I know I have a variety of places to search and I know how to redefine my search terms if something isn't working.
>
> *Peer Research Mentor, Gettysburg College*

Reference Services

PRMs co-staff the Research Help Desk with librarians. Working together allows the PRMs to practice and build their knowledge and skills with support from experienced colleagues.

Outreach

In consultation with their supervisors, PRMs design outreach projects that bring together specific student populations with library services. PRMs have promoted and taught library tools, created workshops for classes, and developed instructional videos.

ADMINISTRATION (PROMOTING THE PROGRAM) OR TRAINING (INVOLVING OTHER STAFF)

As our Peer Research Mentor program has grown, we have cultivated relationships with other campus groups and organizations. Some of our strongest connections are with the Office of Academic Advising, which includes the Honor Commission, and the Intercultural Resource Center, which is part of the Office of Multicultural Engagement. Working with these offices has simultaneously enhanced PRM training and promoted our program to the larger campus community.

For example, librarians and PRMs collaborated with the Intercultural Resource Center to create drop-in workshops for international students. When our next hiring cycle began, their director promoted the program to international students and we received several PRM applications. We hired two international students and subsequently integrated PRMs into international student orientation. As a result, new international students receive much more than the traditional library tour at the start of the academic year.

Gettysburg's Dean of Academic Advising approached librarians about supporting efforts to promote academic integrity on campus and collaborating with the Honor Commission. We invited her to co-facilitate a biweekly meeting with a PRM. The lesson plan included a jigsaw reading from *Cheating Lessons: Learning from Academic Dishonesty* by James M. Lang and a discussion with the Dean and a student member of the Honor Commission. As a result of this training, one of the PRMs joined the Honor Commission and served as the library liaison to coordinate future events and programming.

> I might do some teaching in some form in the future, and I think the aspect of mentoring other students as a PRM has been useful for working with students on a one-on-one basis, answering their questions, and explaining how to look for sources. Even if I don't teach in the future, that experience will be helpful in any job where I will need to work with other people.
>
> *Peer Research Mentor, Gettysburg College*

Training (Boot Camp)

In order to prepare peer research mentors to participate in the program, librarians in the Research and Instruction Department developed an intensive, two-day "boot camp" training for new PRMs. Boot camp is designed around the research process and provides PRMs with a helpful framework to use when assisting students. The training focuses on areas in which undergraduate students often struggle—getting started with research, generating keywords, evaluating sources, and locating and accessing materials. PRMs participate in active learning exercises and formative assessments throughout the training (assessments help librarians identify areas where further training is needed). PRMs also spend time learning about relevant library services, collections, and staff; the reference interview; and best practices when working with peers.

Boot camp training materials are organized in a binder filled with daily schedules, outlines for each section, additional resources, employment forms, and contact information. The outlines include the main training topics, sample research questions that might apply to the topic, and reflection questions. Short periods of time for reflection and writing are provided throughout the boot camp. Reflections are initially discussed during boot camp; librarian supervisors continue debriefing these with PRMs during their first week of work.

> I am familiar with a host of database platforms and I understand when certain information might require a library subscription and how I might get around these obstacles. Open access resources may have some information when a paywall gets in the way of finding a given article. I can also use my knowledge of search engines to enhance searches I conduct for research material.
>
> *Peer Research Mentor, Gettysburg College*

Training (Ongoing)

The training process for peer research mentors continues throughout the semester via biweekly cohort meetings, weekly research questions and resource exploration, and one-on-one meetings with a librarian supervisor.

The biweekly meetings are facilitated by librarians or PRMs and can be used to build upon concepts covered during boot camp or to introduce new content. Topics have included citations, discipline-specific resources, using special collections, and library technology (microfilm readers, digital scanners, and assistive technology). Additionally, the meetings enable the cohort to work together on shared questions and issues experienced either at the Research Help Desk or with their outreach projects.

PRMs continue to develop their own research skills and explore new library resources by engaging in exercises delivered via our course management system. PRMs work on practice questions while working at the Research Help Desk and are encouraged to discuss them with the librarian on duty. The questions are selected from our database of Research Help Desk questions and anonymized as needed. In alternating weeks, PRMs are asked to explore specific library resources chosen to expose them to a wide range of research tools. Answering the weekly research question or exploring the resource of the week helps ensure that PRMs are continually building their knowledge.

Regular meetings with supervisors provide an additional opportunity for PRMs to work through and discuss the questions and exercises. These meetings are designed to function as regular check-in points on their outreach projects and as a means to provide additional one-on-one training when needed.

HIRING

Research and instruction librarians developed a job description detailing the three core components of the peer research mentor position: training, reference service, and outreach. The description made clear that we were seeking students who were interested both in enhancing their own research skills and sharing these skills with fellow students.

We advertised the position in the campus newspaper, via email, and on library social media. We also contacted faculty we felt could recommend strong student applicants (we targeted instructors of first-year seminars and our teaching partners in the Education, English, and History departments). During our second hiring cycle, we reached out to campus offices that might help us diversify our applicant pool. They shared contact information for various student groups on campus and encouraged individuals to apply to the program.

> Working with a multitude of people and personalities is another aspect I will use in my life. No two people are the same, and being able to treat them all with respect and according to their individual needs is something that will take me far.... Becoming more confident here by working with different patrons and understanding that people here care for me and are willing to help will allow me to be more of a team player.
>
> *Peer Research Mentor, Gettysburg College*

Applicants were required to submit a letter that expressed their interest in the position, described their education and/or career goals, and listed relevant course experiences and references. Research and instruction librarians reviewed applications and identified candidates to interview. In later hiring rounds, we invited interested current PRMs to join the interviews. Interview questions focused on the applicants' research skills, relevant coursework, public service, and mentoring experience. We also shared important information (such as the time commitment, including the required boot camp training dates and biweekly meeting times) and left time for applicants to ask questions. Following interviews, references were contacted and all candidates were discussed within the department before making final hiring decisions.

APPENDIX A

JOB DESCRIPTION—PEER RESEARCH MENTORS

The Research & Instruction Department of Musselman Library invites Gettysburg College rising sophomore and rising junior students to submit applications to become a peer research mentor for the 2020-21 academic year. A peer research mentor is a student who works alongside librarians to support students engaged in research, while also improving one's own research skills. This position is open to rising sophomore and rising junior students in any major. The peer research mentor team intentionally includes students representing a range of class levels, academic backgrounds, and student experiences. If you love information and helping people find exactly what they need, this could be the position for you!

Peer research mentors will engage in three main areas:

1. Training: Mentors will participate in a concentrated series of training sessions in August before classes begin, as well as ongoing training throughout the year (one hour bi-weekly). Training topics include basic customer service principles, navigating our online and print library collection, understanding today's information environment, search strategies, evaluating information, the inner workings of the library (from cataloging to interlibrary loan), current library issues, and other topics of interest to the mentors.
2. Reference service: Mentors will work at the library's main research help desk two to four hours per week, partnered with a professional librarian. In addition, qualified mentors may meet with students during scheduled research appointments.
3. Outreach: Mentors will design and implement an outreach program each semester. Each mentor will consult with a supervising librarian in order to customize a project that reflects the mentor's interest and skills. For example, a mentor might create a web research guide that supports a class assignment, meet with students completing a particular assignment, or promote reference services in other ways. This component is flexible and should support the mentor's academic interests.

Qualifications:
- Desire to learn, improve, and master research skills in more than one academic subject area
- Interest or background in education, mentoring, and/or tutoring
- Strong communication and organizational skills
- Ability to work effectively with diverse groups of students, faculty, staff, and community members

Preferred Qualifications:

- Interest or background in education, mentoring, and/or tutoring

Peer research mentors will be part of a learning community supported by each other as well as Fortenbaugh Interns, the Holley Intern, and librarians. Peer research mentors will mentor other students while becoming more successful researchers themselves.

Peer research mentors will work six to eight hours per week while classes are in session, in addition to about fifteen hours of paid training during the last week of summer break. The pay rate is $8.50 per hour.

To apply, submit a letter indicating your interest in the position, your education and/or career goals, any relevant courses, and the names and contact information for two or three references (references should be faculty members who can tell us about you and your work in the classroom, and/or your supervisor in a campus job or other relevant job). Please be specific about why you would like to be one of our peer research mentors. Application materials must be received by Friday, April 17, 2020 to be considered.

Have questions? We'd love to chat with you! Drop by the office (room 102, main floor, Musselman Library) or contact one of the current peer research mentors.

APPENDIX B

PEER RESEARCH MENTOR BOOT CAMP SCHEDULE

Move-In Day

- 9:00 a.m.–4:30 p.m.: Pick up key from Residence Life
- 5:00–6:30 p.m.: Kick-Off Dinner (Library Dean's home)

Day 1 of Boot Camp

- 8:00–9:00 a.m.: Breakfast, Introductions, and Warm-up Discussion
  Discuss: What is a library? What is our library? What has your library experience been like? How do you use libraries in general? Share your personal favorite library story.
- 9:00–10:15 a.m.: Give Us a Library Tour
  Each PRM explores a floor of the library and prepares to present important features to the other PRMs and librarians. Librarians fill in as needed.
- 10:15–10:30 a.m.: Break
- 10:30 a.m.–Noon: Introduction to Research
  Introduce the research process which outlines the Boot Camp training. Assign research topics for remainder of training, and start with reference sources (print and online).
- Noon–1:00 p.m.: Lunch
- 1:00–3:00 p.m.: Discovery & Access: Books!
  Local catalog vs. WorldCat, searching strategies (keyword vs subject; advanced search tips), LC Call Numbers, Course Reserves, Textbooks, ILL, etc.
- 3:00–3:30 p.m.: Break
- 3:30–5:00 p.m.: Practice
  Library Olympics: Book relay race, Where in the library is it?, and "Hot seat" (practice reference questions). Receive homework: Reflection—What confuses you? What do you hope to learn? What are you excited about?
- 5:30–7:00 p.m.: Dinner

Day 2 of Boot Camp

- 8:00–9:00 a.m.: Breakfast, Meet & Greet, and Warm-up Discussion
  Introduce key library staff (Systems Librarian, ILL staff, Circulation, Building Manager). Discuss reflection questions.
- 9:00–10:15 a.m.: Discovery & Access: Finding Articles
  Articles, Journals, Databases, and One Search—oh my! Includes what is a database, identifying the right resource; searching and advanced search tips, etc.

- 10:15–10:30 a.m.: Break
- 10:30 a.m.–Noon: Discovery & Access: Journal Locator & Evaluation
  How to use the Journal Locator to identify, locate and access individual journals and articles in library collection, retrieving full-text, or utilizing Interlibrary Loan. Cover distinguishing among types of sources (books vs. articles, primary vs. secondary, etc.) and critically evaluating information sources (popular vs. scholarly, peer-review process).
- Noon–1:00 p.m.: Lunch
- 1:00–3:30 p.m.: Research Help Desk Basics
  Reference interview with practice questions. Research Help Desk minutiae: LibAnswers, READ Scale, printing, and technology troubleshooting.
- 3:30–4:00 p.m.: Break
- 4:00–5:00 p.m.: Library Olympics & Closing Ceremonies
  "Find that citation" and "Can you help me?" (Research Help Desk scenarios). Medals and closing ceremonies.
- 5:30–7:00 p.m.: Dinner & Final Reflections
  Receive reflection homework for first one-on-one meeting with librarian mentor: "How can the library help students become better researchers?"

APPENDIX C

TOPICS COVERED AT BIWEEKLY MEETINGS

- Citation and bibliographic management tools
- Using Special Collections and Archives
- Open access and introduction to scholarly communications
- Designing outreach projects
- Historical resources for research on the American Civil War
- Dealing with end-of-semester reference questions
- Interlibrary Loan and off-site storage
- Ebooks
- Science resources (PRM-led)
- Academic integrity and the honor code (PRM-led)
- Funky technology in the library: microfilm readers, assistive technology, and more (PRM-led)
- Music resources (PRM-led)
- Image sources (PRM-led)

RESEARCH TUTORS AT GRINNELL COLLEGE:
Collaborating and Transforming

Phil Jones and Chris Jones

OVERVIEW

In the spring of 2010, librarians at Grinnell College decided to draw upon and to develop our student staff members' talent in teaching academic research. To do so, we carefully recruited and trained the first cohort of student assistants to work at our research desk. In the years since, these student staff positions have undergone title changes—first assistants, then fellows and, for four years now, research tutors—but what has remained constant is the creative and quality work students bring to the provision and promotion of research services at Grinnell. The core work of our research tutors is teaching their peers to discover and consider a range of promising material and to imagine, even at an early stage, how potential sources might advance a project or paper. But the impact of the tutors' work extends beyond the research desk. All of Grinnell's librarians—including our director— help train and provide continuing education for our tutors, and this consistent contact sparks insight, changing the way librarians work with other student staff and student researchers. In this chapter, we first profile our successful research tutor program, followed by an extended example of how supervising research tutors for just one semester transformed how our special collections librarian works with student staff members.

We consulted professional literature before beginning to recruit, train, and collaborate with students to provide reference services. What we found was decades-old material, such as a case study of the University of Michigan's Peer Information Counselor Program, which focused on helping minority students.[1] Although a number of helpful articles profiling programs similar to ours have been published since we began working with research tutors,[2] we initially found it necessary to consult a wide range of literature, such as techniques and strategies for training students working as book shelvers to help patrons with research inquiries at circulation desks and throughout academic libraries.[3]

> Much like a narrative, research projects are a creative activity for which the rules are up to a student's interpretation and seeing them play with the limits of a prompt is particularly interesting. I have never been able to shake off that feeling that, when students come to the desk, they are sharing with me some part of themselves that is personal: their projects. I find it humbling to be witness to the creation and production process and to be trusted enough to be allowed to help them.
>
> *Research Tutor, Grinnell College*

ADMINISTRATION

Research tutors are part of Grinnell's campus-wide peer education program and are supported by a grant from the Arthur Vining Davis Foundations.[4] Our campus program includes both student mentors and tutors, positions with distinct but complementary duties. Faculty members can request a peer mentor to work with his or her students in and outside of the classroom to review disciplinary content and assignments. Peer tutors provide schedulable or walk-up academic assistance at service points, such as the libraries' research desk, the campus foreign language labs, or Grinnell's data and social inquiry lab. Peer tutors are also available from Academic Advising for more traditional, one-on-one tutoring for a range of humanities and social science disciplines. And science and math tutors are available in Grinnell's Science Learning Center and Math Lab, respectively. Tutors work both afternoon and evening shifts, Sunday through Thursday, at the research desk in Burling Library, home to both Grinnell's librarians and collections serving humanities and social science academic departments. Grinnell students, faculty, and staff, as well as members of the greater Grinnell community, contact our tutors and librarians in person, by email, instant messaging, text, and phone.

Each of these peer educator positions has a job description, including both common and specialized elements, and peer tutors working across campus are paid the same hourly wage. When we began our research tutor program with three tutors, their salaries were covered by the libraries' student employment budget. Over the next few years, the program grew to six research tutors and a library donor came forth to help fund these student staff positions.

Faculty and staff supervising Grinnell's network of peer educators meet regularly to discuss, for instance, ideas for improving student training, job performance, and satisfaction. We also plan and schedule paid, collective continuing education opportunities for our peer educators. Some of these sessions have been conducted with large groups of more than 100 students; other sessions have brought small groups of peer educators together for discussions with, for example, a representative from our campus office of Careers, Life and Service to consider how work as a peer educator can be included and described on résumés, cover letters, and applications for employment, scholarships, and graduate school.

HIRING

Careful selection of research tutors is central to our program's success. We build a pool of student applicants by sharing a position description like the one below with a range of faculty members and requesting nominations of excellent students who are successful researchers and good communicators:

Job Description: Research Tutor

For the spring semester, Grinnell College Libraries (GCL) will hire and train one Research Tutor (RT) to work up to ten hours each week. Duties include afternoon, evening, and weekend shifts at Burling Library's research desk helping patrons with directional, basic, and more in-depth information questions plus working with librarians to develop and promote GCL's research services. RTs complete training on topics such as the use of reference sources, GCL catalog and web pages to support research, databases and indexes, web searching, and research desk and library procedures. Candidates must be second-year Grinnell students by the time they begin work as a Research Tutor, have successful customer service and academic research experience, and facility with the Microsoft Office Suite and interest in online social networking tools. Work experience in a library is welcomed but not required.

We also like to honor the initiative of promising students by considering anyone who has inquired or applied for a research tutor position or for a position in Grinnell's libraries. For each open position, we typically have three to five applicants, and we interview all students who apply. Each interview runs about thirty minutes and is conducted by two persons—some years, by two librarians; other years, by a librarian and a current research tutor. For interview questions, see Appendix A. Following interviews, we contact the finalists' references, typically professors or work supervisors on campus. And finally, with an eye to a diversity of academic majors, class years, and foreign language skills, we offer research tutor positions to the students we believe are most engaged and passionate about academic research and teaching.

TRAINING

Research services are provided at Grinnell through a progressive triage model. We begin this work by training all students and staff members working at the two busiest public service desks in Grinnell's libraries to answer basic information questions and to make appropriate referrals to the research desk or to a librarian. The topics covered in this training—access options for journals, magazines, and newspapers, location and use of our online guides for disciplinary research, for instance—came from conversations with supervisors and student staff members as to the types of questions asked at our public service desks. For a basic information services training checklist, see Appendix B.

For new research tutors, training begins the first full week of a semester with the same basic information service training all public service desk students and supervisors complete. This way, our tutors have an idea of the type of assistance any patron referred to the research desk will likely already have had. The subsequent, in-depth training our tutors complete consists of eight to ten hours of meetings with a range of librarians and draws on readings[5] and discussion of topics such as library and research desk services, reference interviewing, the libraries' catalog and website, intellectual freedom, and an overview of the 600-plus databases to which Grinnell provides access. For the research tutor training agenda, please see Appendix C. And training continues each week, both fall and spring semesters, as one or more librarians meet with all research tutors, for instance, to review questions received during recent shifts at the research desk, for continuing education in specialized areas such as research in the humanities, data and statistical sources, and Grinnell's special collections, and for discussion of relevant topics such as ebooks, academic journal pricing, and scholarly communication. Additionally, we ask each of our tutors to select one or two areas of specialization in which they would like to receive additional training: primary sources, images, and gender, women's, and sexuality studies are examples of training areas tutors have recently requested. For this focused training, tutors meet individually or in pairs with the librarian serving a particular academic department or concentration for conversation and an overview of disciplinary research tools and strategies.

We also rely on tutors to help improve and promote research services. Since our tutors are interested in and well-informed on libraries and academic research, we frequently discuss ideas we are considering for our library's website or Facebook page. Research tutors' services are promoted on the Students section of the libraries' website with a page describing services provided, a photo of each tutor, and a listing of their areas of research interest. An enjoyable and effective way of promoting the fact that peer educators work at the research desk has been to create eye-catching posters in large and small formats for strategic placement around campus, everywhere from a prominent spot near the campus cafeteria to bulletin boards in classrooms and dormitories to restroom stalls around campus (the latter is, of course, a research tutor suggestion). Recent examples of successful posters include homages to *The Brady Bunch*, the Beatles' iconic *Abbey Road* album cover, and Harry Potter, which was photographed in a campus building noted for Gothic design. As seen below, tutors also help us promote a range of services with posters, such as Library Labs, the research consultations students or faculty schedule with a librarian:

ASSESSMENT

Our tutors work alone at a walk-up service desk without direct supervision, so evaluating their work with other students or patrons has proved to be a challenge. Nonetheless, we have developed a range of assessment methods that provide our tutors with formative and summative feedback in both quantitative and qualitative form. Tutors keep a record of each research desk transaction, recording actual questions asked as well as question type and duration and the tutor assisting. We then explore in our weekly meetings a range of possible approaches for addressing these queries. Where might one turn for information on a Chicago city administrator at the time of the Great Fire in 1871? Suggestions from discussion: an email inquiry to the Chicago History Museum website. Or is there much scholarship on the decline of French New Wave Cinema? Suggestions from our discussion: try the major database for film studies, but search also the databases of allied disciplines, such as history, language, literature, and even sociology. And consider primary sources like movie reviews or interviews with directors and actors or their letters and diaries. Discussions such as these allow librarians to hear suggestions tutors share with their peers, but we also learn if the tutors are approaching inquiries received at the research desk creatively and if they are teaching their classmates to draw on a range of potential material from a number of academic disciplines. Of great importance here is that these discussions of research inquiries allow our tutors to teach and to support one another as they grow and refine their skills and strategies for academic research. We also ask our tutors to write a reflective essay during the spring semester in response to a prompt such as, "As a research tutor, what have you taught and what have you learned?" Librarians and tutors then dedicate an hour-long meeting to hear and discuss the ideas developed in these essays. Representative quotes from our tutors' written reflections appear throughout this chapter.

> It should go without saying, then, that my own ability to think critically has expanded greatly during my time at the desk. In some ways, this development has been obvious, such as my newfound ability to understand statistical sources and those sources which are found in the natural sciences. In other ways, however, my growth at the desk has been more intangible, but I can still sense that by helping patrons with their information needs, I have become more adept at serving my own.
>
> *Research Tutor, Grinnell College*

REFLECTION

What follows are the reflections of Chris Jones, Grinnell's special collections librarian and archivist of the college, who served as supervisor of the research tutors while Phil Jones was on sabbatical. Chris's reflections show that the benefits of a program like Grinnell's research tutors extend well beyond a reference desk; indeed, working with our research tutors helped him to imagine and create new ways to draw upon and honor talents of students working in our Special Collections.

> Every student has a different question, and every student has different styles of doing research, and a research tutor must learn to adapt to get their point across in a way that others can understand—preferably, without too much obvious scrabbling around in front of other students. A successful research project is, in the end, the result of the hard work of the student, and we are at the research desk to help others do their best.
>
> *Research Tutor, Grinnell College*

In Grinnell's Special Collections and Archives, we have always tried to emulate the training that the research tutors complete, and during the semester I supervised these students, I learned that we are definitely on the right track. However, I also learned that we could expand how we train and work with our own students and include them in more (and creative) ways.

In Special Collections, we have followed many of the examples set by the larger research tutor program, including conducting a job interview that more closely resembles a professional job interview than a *pro forma* meet-and-greet. Due to our small staff size (two FTE), we have chosen to adapt other aspects of the research tutor program to help alleviate the pressure on staff. For this reason, our student assistants act as peer educators in two ways. The first is by assisting patrons, whether students, staff, faculty, or off-campus non-student researchers, who visit Special Collections or get in touch with us in some way (e.g., email, telephone, etc.). Our students are now trained to conduct basic reference interviews, as are the students who staff the libraries' research desk, and to retrieve materials from our secure storage area. We have also adapted the peer educator model to our needs by relying on our student assistants to help one another as needed. It has been our experience that students often feel more comfortable asking for help from peers than from figures of authority. As there can be anywhere between three and five student assistants working in Special Collections at one time, our student assistants sometimes find it easier to consult one another rather than staff members, who naturally have a broader variety of responsibilities. We have found this peer mentoring to bolster the confidence of the student staff as well as to provide leadership experience that can be recorded on a résumé or CV.

In addition to aiding patrons with reference questions and mentoring one another, the student assistants in Special Collections also help in improving and promoting the primary resources available in the libraries. While working with the research tutors, I learned that they take great pride in sharing what they do with their friends and peers, so I decided to try to bring a similar experience to our student assistants. Students have taken an increasingly active role in curating exhibitions in Special Collections, including one large exhibition housed in the cases in the Burling Library Gallery and two smaller cases in the reading room of Special Collections. One of the smaller cases in the reading room houses "flash exhibits" that get changed out once a month, on average, during the school year. The second case houses a slightly longer-term exhibit. Each of the smaller cases is regularly curated by students with minimal staff involvement. And our student assistants generally take the lead in organizing the larger exhibitions in the Burling Library Gallery, which are rotated at the beginning of each semester.

> The past year has also been the most challenging in terms of the number of people who ask for help. There are shifts when someone is asking questions on IM and two people are at the desk or the phone rings. In this example, I have learned to keep calm and approach each student one at a time. Even if it means asking one of the students to wait, it is necessary for helping everyone and being a good tutor.
>
> *Research Tutor, Grinnell College Libraries*

In the spirit of peer mentoring, we also began another collaboration with our student assistants several years ago. One of our student staff members first conceived of—and curated—the event "Break Open the Vault" in consultation with Special Collections staff. Because there are many resources and artifacts housed in Grinnell's Special Collections, and patrons are not allowed into the secure storage area, a student assistant decided it could be fun and engaging to pull some of those materials out into the reading room to create small informational placards for each item and to invite the campus and Grinnell communities to walk through the space and enjoy these resources. The staff was consulted each step of the way, but the student did all of the curation work himself. By the end of the first Break Open the Vault event, which was only an hour long, we had more than sixty students and campus staff members visit our reading room, the majority of whom had not previously visited the space. We took this as a huge success, and this event has now been regularized to happen once a year, toward the end of the spring semester, and serves as an open house for Special Collections. For subsequent events, student assistants create posters and Facebook announcements; the event consistently attracts up to 100 people, many of whom come when the door opens and stay for the full hour (and sometimes longer). During the event, the student curators mingle with the public and respond to questions, ask questions designed to engage the visitors with the exhibit items, and converse generally about the materials chosen for display. These events frequently lead to return visits by Break Open the Vault guests, which is good for the libraries, and follow-up questions, which are good opportunities for the students who respond to them. Because this event was a successful example of student leadership inspired by the research tutor program in the libraries, the Special Collections staff has decided to further emulate that program by consulting with their student assistants more frequently. For example, we are currently exploring ideas for a fall semester event in Special Collections, which would rely and build on the leadership our students have already displayed. Our hope is that the student assistants in Special Collections will continue to be a driving force in shaping our reference and research activities to the same degree that the research tutors have participated in and shaped the reference and research program for the Grinnell College Libraries.

> I begin by giving the student room to explain their research process—the tools they typically use, the course they're writing for, what they've tried so far, etc. I like to keep the dialogue open and welcoming so the student feels they have a voice and are not being patronized. I also try to do this in my work as a writing mentor on-campus—so to some extent, these two jobs are a great combination. In a sense, I have the opportunity to help students at every stage of the process—research and all the various writing stages. I am excited to continue on in these two positions in the coming semesters.
>
> *Research Tutor, Grinnell College Libraries*

I have also led a continuing education session for the research tutors in Special Collections. As to the purpose of this annual visit, first and foremost, I want the student tutors to leave the session with a stronger idea of the materials contained in Special Collections, and I want them to be more familiar with how to access those materials. During their visit, we cover topics such as: what are the major collections; that we have printed physical guides to the collection (including a card catalog) in addition to the finding aids online; and when, and how, to direct researchers to Special Collections. We also cover the basics of citing the various kinds of materials found in Special Collections.

Because this part of the continuing education visit can tend to be very information-dense, I always end the session with a visit to our vault. While Special Collections enjoys a certain mystique, we frequently hear of students who graduate without ever making use of the materials we have to offer. Therefore, if we can provide an enjoyable experience to our research tutors, we can count on them to talk to their friends about the rich, amazing collections we offer and to be able to assure researchers that they are welcome to visit and to make use of these materials. The vault tour also serves to reinforce why we have such facilities to care for these special resources in the first place. During their continuing education session, I invite the tutors to touch and handle a range of items from our collections, including rare books, college records, and literary manuscripts. I intentionally pull resources that are not in the most pristine condition so that the tutors are forced to consider the physicality of the materials in conjunction with the climate-controlled space in order to gain a better understanding of why we have special rules governing the use of the collections.

By far, the most gratifying thing to me—and I believe the most beneficial aspect for the research tutors—is when the continuing education sessions become less about me teaching a class-like session and it turns into more of a discussion. This is usually the result of a certain comfort level being achieved, and a more relaxed atmosphere seems to invite more discussion, which, I feel, leads to more information being retained.

CONCLUSION

In coming semesters, we would like to expand the reach of our tutors beyond the research desk: might research tutors collaborate, for instance, with Grinnell's writing mentors and disciplinary tutors to help students discover and use a range of source material in academic work? Our research tutors consistently surprise and please us with the quality and thoughtfulness of their work as peer educators. We look forward to more unexpected and successful collaborations.

APPENDIX A

INTERVIEW QUESTIONS FOR RESEARCH TUTOR APPLICANTS

1. What interests you in this position?

2. Describe your customer service experience. What was enjoyable and challenging?

3. Describe how you like to do research. (We're not looking for a librarian answer here.)

4. Describe research processes that students tend to use. Can librarians and research tutors draw on any of these approaches as we help students at the research desk?

5. After a training period, research tutors will work much of the time alone at Burling's research desk. Describe a situation in which you've worked alone and with little direct supervision.

6. Explain how you'd help a student who:
   a.   Didn't have a clear research topic.
   b.   Wants more information and research options after you have shown them all the resources and search techniques you know.

7. What are some good ways of making research desk services more appealing, visible and useful for Grinnell's students? We communicate with students via Facebook, chat/instant messaging and texting, for instance. What other ways might you suggest to reach and help our patrons?

8. You'll complete two weeks of training before working at Burling's research desk. What would you most like to learn to help you succeed as a research tutor?

APPENDIX B
BASIC INFORMATION SERVICE TRAINING CHECKLIST

Training goals: All students working at the libraries' public service desks will A) be able to answer directional and basic information questions and B) know when and how to refer a student for more in-depth help.

A. Basic website and catalog searching

1. _____ 3Search: *what is this tool?, "keyword" vs. "subject" on sleep* AND *dreams, e.g.*

2. _____ Request materials: *when checked out, not available yet, etc.*

3. _____ My Account features: *checked out item, renewing items*

4. _____ Interlibrary Loan: *locating request link, signing into ILLiad*

5. _____ Connecting from off-campus: *access databases through GCL website*

B. Research pages [goal: point to the webpage and basic use.]

6. _____ Doing research: *a progression to guide your academic work*

7. _____ Subject guides: *pick guide useful for your academic major*

8. _____ Database A–Z list: *briefly review and search a database*

9. _____ ".PDF full-text" and "Search for full text:" *follow links in database search results*

10. _____ ILL: *if GCL doesn't have the article, chapter, or book*

11. _____ Journal finder: *do we have access to* Southern Review?

C. Referrals

12. _____ Why important? *We want to help students learn, so if you can't help, try to find someone else who may be able to.*

13. _____ When to refer? *How to refer? You may refer a patron for additional help when…*
    - You don't know the answer to their question
    - You're uncertain if you've fully answered their question
    - A student's question exceeds your level of training or comfort

14. _____ Getting help: librarians and research tutors available at research desk, on-call, IM, texting, email, phone, by appt. Note Chat with us! widget.

15. _____ Consulting librarians page: each librarian helps several academic departments. See Find Your Consulting Librarian under Doing Research or under Faculty on left-side of GCL homepage.

16. _____ Library Lab: research consultation with librarian

17. _____ Library hours and calendars: *find out when libraries open, services available*

Thank you for helping fellow students strengthen their academic research skills.

APPENDIX C

RESEARCH TUTOR TRAINING SCHEDULE

Session #	Topic	Date	Time	Location	Leader
1	Research Services, Burling Library tour	Tues 9/1	4:15–5:15 p.m.	Burling Research Desk	Phil Jones
2	Research Desk Procedures	New tutors schedule session between 9/2 and 9/10	TBD	Burling Research Desk	Meredith Drake, Sophie Donlon
3	GCL Website and 3Search/Catalog	Wed 9/2	4:15–5:15 p.m.	Burling Computing Lab	Sara Peterson
4	Research Services, Part 2	Thur 9/3	4:15–5:15 p.m.	Burling Research Desk	Phil Jones
5	Databases	Mon 9/7	4:15–5:15 p.m.	Kistle Science Library	Kevin Engel
6	Research Tutor weekly meeting	Tues 9/8	4:15–5:05 p.m.	Burling Computing Lab	Phil Jones, librarians
7	Beyond Grinnell	Thur 9/10	4:15–5:15 pm	Burling Computing Lab	Julia Bauder
8	Shadow a Research Tutor	Schedule this session after October 1st	1 hour	Burling Research Desk	Meredith Drake, Sophie Donlon

Suggested Training Session Topics
Sessions 1) and 4) Research Services, Library Tour

- Research Tutor/Basic Information Service (BIS) program overview: students helping, mentoring students at public service desks in Grinnell College Libraries
- BIS training checklist, Library of Congress (LC) handout
- Discuss reading on research service, interviewing (to be distributed at training)
- Reference collection as a place to start, a microcosm of the library

- Research collection/web resources: print collection, limiters in catalog, Research Universe, Reference Sources, Subject Guides, Google/web, Doing Research
- Research area, roaming versus sitting
- Library tour: tour handout provided for students; goal: big-picture understanding
- GC Libraries Student Staff Handbook: current version available via Employment link on library homepage

2) Research Desk Procedures

- Share with Research Tutor how you provide research service.
- Procedures: phone calls, query email, IM research service, Science-Direct/Pioneer-Web, ITS Help Desk/Portal, Research Tutor statistics spreadsheet

3) Grinnell College Libraries Website and 3Search/Catalog

- 3Search and classic catalog, basic and advanced searching, subject searching
- Fields, operators, limits, sorting: What's within reason?
- Examples of sources in GCL catalog, Google Preview, ebooks, etc.
- GCL web pages to support research: "Find It" drop-down menu items, "Doing Research" and GCL home page left-side links

5) Databases: multidisciplinary versus disciplinary, searching, accessing sources, RefWorks, whatever else you deem important

6) Beyond Grinnell: WorldCat.org, Center for Research Libraries, Google (basic, advanced search, Scholar, Book Search, e.g.), anything else you want to cover

7) Shadow a Research Tutor:

- Experienced tutors share their tips for effective research service
- Any advice, encouragement you'd like to provide

NOTES

1. Barbara MacAdam and Darlene P. Nichols, "Peer Information Counseling: An Academic Library Program for Minority Students," *Journal of Academic Librarianship* 15, no. 4 (1989): 204–09.
2. Megan S. Mitchell, Cynthia H. Comer, Jennifer M. Starkey, and Eboni A. Francis, "Paradigm Shift in Reference Services at the Oberlin College Library: A Case Study," *Journal of Library Administration* 51, no. 4 (2011): 359–74, *Library, Information Science & Technology Abstracts*, EBSCOhost, accessed December 18, 2015.
3. Luke Vilelle and Christopher C. Peters, "Don't Shelve the Questions Defining Good Customer Service for Shelvers," *Reference & User Services Quarterly* 48, no. 1 (2008): 60–67, *Library, Information Science & Technology Abstracts*, EBSCOhost, accessed December 18, 2015.
4. The Arthur Vining Davis Foundations, http://www.avdf.org.
5. Kay Ann Cassell and Uma Hiremath, *Reference and Information Services: An Introduction*, 3rd ed. (Chicago: Neal-Schuman, an imprint of the American Library Association, 2013); Catherine Sheldrick Ross, Kirsti Nilsen, and Marie L. Radford, *Conducting the Reference Interview: A How-to-do-it Manual for Librarians*, 2nd ed. (New York: Neal-Schuman Publishers Inc., 2009); American Library

Association, "Code of Ethics of the American Library Association," accessed December 29, 2020, http://www.ala.org/tools/ethics.

BIBLIOGRAPHY

American Library Association. "Code of Ethics of the American Library Association." Accessed December 29, 2020. http://www.ala.org/tools/ethics.

The Arthur Vining Davis Foundations. http://www.avdf.org http://www.avdf.org.

Cassell, Kay Ann, and Uma Hiremath. *Reference and Information Services: An Introduction.* 3rd ed. Chicago: Neal-Schuman, an imprint of the American Library Association, 2013.

MacAdam, Barbara, and Darlene P. Nichols. "Peer Information Counseling: An Academic Library Program for Minority Students." *Journal of Academic Librarianship* 15, no. 4 (1989): 204–09.

Mitchell, Megan S., Cynthia H. Comer, Jennifer M. Starkey, and Eboni A. Francis. "Paradigm Shift in Reference Services at the Oberlin College Library: A Case Study." *Journal of Library Administration* 51, no. 4 (2011): 359–74. *Library, Information Science & Technology Abstracts*, EBSCOhost. Accessed December 18, 2015.

Ross, Catherine Sheldrick, Kirsti Nilsen, and Marie L. Radford. *Conducting the Reference Interview: A How-to-do-it Manual for Librarians.* 2nd ed. New York: Neal-Schuman Publishers Inc., 2009.

Vilelle, Luke, and Christopher C. Peters. "Don't Shelve the Questions Defining Good Customer Service for Shelvers." *Reference & User Services Quarterly* 48, no. 1 (2008): 60–67. *Library, Information Science & Technology Abstracts*, EBSCOhost. Accessed December 18, 2015.

ASK YOUR PEERS AT JAMES MADISON UNIVERSITY:

Developing a Peer Reference Service

Stefanie E. Warlick, Kelly N. Miller-Martin, and Jonathan R. Paulo

OVERVIEW

Summary of the Program

The Ask Your PEERS service is a peer-to-peer reference service designed to meet the needs of student users during prime hours of building use when traditional librarian reference and research assistance is unavailable. Ask Your PEERS was staffed by four JMU Libraries student employees who completed an extensive training program focused on building skills in peer mentorship and research support. Before JMU Libraries fully integrated and adopted the service in spring 2015, the service successfully ran as a pilot project for a full year.

The primary areas of planning included the development of an intentional service model, operating budget, organizational buy-in, recruitment, and training methodology and approach. To inform the process, the planning team gathered and analyzed student staffing and pay model information as well as building use data. Additional sources of information included attending an institute on how to develop peer mentor programs, completing an on-campus exploration of existing peer services, and reviewing the relevant literature on peer reference and peer education.

JMU Landscape

James Madison University (JMU) is a comprehensive public institution in Harrisonburg, Virginia. The student population is primarily comprised of residential undergraduates, who account for 19,000 of the approximately 21,000 total students. At JMU, the Libraries includes campus educational technology, digital scholarship, and online learning services alongside foundational library collections, resources and spaces, scholarly communications and data/information literacy services, and collaborative teaching and research support. The two main buildings, Carrier Library and Rose Library are open to the campus community until 2:00 a.m., five nights a week, with shorter hours on the weekend.

> The most crucial and helpful parts of our training, in my opinion, were the observations of the Ask a Librarian desk. Here we could see how our librarians interact with patrons and handle research questions, and the one-on-one meetings with specific librarians helped us become better acquainted with various research techniques.
>
> *Peer Reference Specialist, James Madison University*

When the Ask Your PEERS service was originally implemented, library services across the two facilities include a suite of research and access support services. Rose Library operates under an integrated, tiered referral model through a single service point supported by student and part-time employees and supervised by full-time library specialists. Librarians in Rose Library are available for referrals on weekdays, generally during regular business hours. In contrast, Carrier Library operates with a distributed service model that includes a traditional reference desk (the Ask Desk) staffed primarily by librarians and is available as late as 8:00 p.m. during the week. Both libraries are supported by a cross-library chat and email reference service during regular business hours.

Outside of the times and days that the Ask Desk and the virtual services are staffed, high-quality reference and research support are not available as a frontline, on-demand service. To offset this reduction in on-hand expertise, evening and weekend library staff receive training to meet basic information-seeking needs and are expected to refer when appropriate. Building traffic data emphasized an existing imbalance between dedicated reference and research support and high-volume building use. In 2012, library service point managers began considering ways to address this imbalance. Based on observed successes from other units on campus and personnel constraints within the libraries, library service point managers explored the feasibility of creating a peer-to-peer reference and research service.

Peer Education Landscape

Peer-to-peer education is an established model within higher education. Many student services on academic campuses have widely adopted peer models, not simply because students often report feeling more comfortable talking with their peers, but also for more substantive reasons, such as to support affective and cognitive growth and development.[1] While highly successful models exist, academic libraries have been slow to adopt peer-based models as evidenced by a lack of research and discussion in the literature. The peer education model is more visibly prevalent in student services such as writing centers and academic tutoring. As peer-led learning continues to grow in higher education, and reference and research support models evolve in academic libraries, the timing seems right for a more wide-scale adoption of peer-led reference and research support.

Locally, peer education is evident throughout the JMU campus, and the JMU Libraries have hosted these activities in library spaces for several years through partnerships with the JMU Learning Centers' offerings such as science and math, writing, and anatomy tutoring. Direct benefits of these hosted services are expanded walk-in access during evening hours and increased visibility to the campus community. The partnership arrangement, in particular, the peer-to-peer approach and the expansion of operational hours, provides a mutual benefit for the libraries, the learning centers, and most importantly, the academic community.

With the notable success of these long-standing partnership programs in the libraries, it was appealing to both round out peer offerings on campus to include reference and research support and to expand the suite of library services. As the library location with no dedicated reference and research support after 5:00 p.m., Rose Library was the most acceptable site for the Ask Your PEERS pilot. Library service point managers began gathering information to create an implementation plan that would be shared with the library administration for ultimate approval.

ADMINISTRATION
Service Model—From Concept to Implementation

The planning team analyzed hourly space use data to confirm the perceived gap in reference and research services during high-traffic times. Collected by library student employees, this data is regularly used to inform a range of service and space planning activities and, in this case, reinforced the decision to offer quality reference and research support during busy evening hours. Taking note of the successful implementation of other JMU peer-based services and pairing the evidence of building traffic, we set the target hours of operations for this pilot service at 7:00 p.m. to 10:00 p.m. Sunday through Wednesday.

Operating Budget

Library administration expected they would receive no additional budgetary requests for this service. Therefore, we analyzed student staffing in the library, as well as pay-rate information from other peer-based services on campus, to set a realistic pay scale for the Ask Your PEERS staff that fit with the existing student employee budget. In order to offer these student employees (self-named PEERS) a higher pay rate than the baseline student employee positions in the library, without the benefit of additional funding, we slightly adjusted student staff levels at the Rose Library Information Desk. While it required a close look at existing service point staffing and a little creativity, the increased pay rate was a priority for the planning team because it reflected the additional level of training and responsibility that would be expected from the PEERS.

> I know that I personally used to struggle when I needed to do research for my classes. I thought that it would be a personal gain and a great way to help other people learn how to overcome researching obstacles.
>
> *Peer Reference Specialist, James Madison University*

Organizational Buy-In

The support of the larger organization was an essential part of moving toward successful implementation of the new service. In particular, buy-in from the reference librarians was fundamental to offering the kind of robust training program and skill growth necessary to support the intended level of peer-led reference and research service. Initially, the planning team shared a draft of the training program with reference librarians in order to receive feedback during the planning phase. Some of the additional strategies for developing buy-in and support included consistent, concise, and transparent information on the purpose, goals, and specifics of the service throughout the implementation process and the creation of opportunities for research experts to participate in the training program. By offering mentorship and guidance, librarians were able to contribute to the development of the students' skills and have more confidence in the level of service the students would be able to provide once their training was complete. We also shared the finalized training program within the organization via an informational poster presentation and email communication. These efforts to share information allowed everyone to see the level of thoughtfulness involved in skill building for these students and the expectations that were established for offering this new service. Although not all librarians or all departments were involved in the training, widely sharing the training program increased awareness and understanding of our preparation and goals. We believe these efforts were important because the service was public-facing and was a new approach to reference service at JMU.

Timeline

The planning team established a target implementation date after almost a year of information gathering and planning. We considered and established general approaches for recruitment and training, but additional work was necessary before rolling out the pilot service. Limiting the amount of uncertainty the PEERS would experience during the pilot was a priority. We also wanted to present a finalized training outline that explicitly addressed operational complexities and included a high level of detail regarding explicit roles and timeline expectations for library staff involved in the training program. After investing an additional semester in solidifying details, we hired and began training with the inaugural cohort of PEERS in January 2014.

Naming and Branding

The service's branding and visibility were essential components of success, especially since peer-led reference was a new offering from the JMU Libraries. To help the PEERS develop ownership of the service, they participated in both the naming and branding of the service. During an initial group meeting, the students created the formal Ask Your PEERS name. Allowing students to participate in the naming process and direction for the branding and promotion of the service resulted in stronger team cohesion and enthusiasm and a sense of ownership for the mission and vision of the service. Some of the initial promotional efforts included print and digital signage within the libraries, flyers around campus, tabletop advertisements within the libraries and in the dining halls, advertisements on the projection screen in the campus theater before movies, a social media campaign, a T-shirt design for the service "uniform," and Ask Your PEERS swag such as pens and notepads.

Example of promotional material: Postcard

HIRING

Recruitment

Hiring students to work as PEERS required the development of a new position description (see Appendix A. Peer Reference Specialist Job Posting) and the creation of a series of clear recruiting and operational guidelines (See Appendix B. Ask Your Peers Guidelines for Reference Service). It was critical to fully understand the implications of creating and filling a student position that required a higher level of training and responsibility. The planning team intentionally chose peer reference specialist as the position title in order to express the elevated level of student worker employment as well as to carefully define expectations. We purposely limited recruitment to existing library student employees who had completed base-level service point training and had been employed at Rose Library for at least one semester. By recruiting from a pool of students already equipped with foundational knowledge of library services, the training for the PEERS could focus on new job responsibilities unique to the peer reference specialist role. Applicants submitted an essay of 500 words or less describing their interest in the peer reference specialist position and the ways in which their experience would transfer and serve to benefit the service. The essay, in addition to the existing working relationships with the student applicants, allowed the hiring manager to identify and select students who showed a natural interest in research and an inclination for serving successfully as peer educators.

Relevant literature suggests the following peer mentor characteristics lead to a greater chance of success: trustworthiness, supportiveness, strong communication, interdependent attitudes, empathy, enthusiasm, and flexibility.[2] These characteristics offered insightful guidance for recruitment given the necessary level of responsibility, social interaction, and instructional skills.

A final aspect of the recruitment and staffing approach was to have the PEERS maintain some working hours at the Information Desk. The differing pay rates for peer reference specialist and student assistant positions meant that PEERS students would need to technically hold two library positions simultaneously and expectations for maintaining boundaries for these different roles had to be clear. Essentially, we had a limited budget for offering the higher pay rate. The Ask Your PEERS service only offered six hours per PEER per week, and we had four students who were accustomed to working up to eighteen hours per week. In order to provide our students with access to sufficient hours as a library employee, we chose to have them hold two positions with two separate time sheets and we communicated limitations on how many hours they could work in each position per week. The initial work of creating operational guidelines was offset by the mutual benefits of PEERS maintaining strong connections with the Information Desk. PEERS could remain informed about library services at the Information Desk, and in addition, PEERS would naturally bring new knowledge back to the front line service point, subsequently modeling their newly acquired skills and customer service techniques for fellow student employees.

TRAINING
Philosophy

Development of a thoughtful training plan was a critical step. A review of the literature helped inform this process. In 2014, Bodemer explored the question of whether or not undergraduates should provide peer-led reference and found that "historical attempts to employ undergraduates in reference reveals varied motivations, reservations, and technological shifts that inform a more considered answer."[3] One of the central themes of the Ask Your PEERS training program was an expectation that students were not asked to be librarians but rather to provide a level of research and assignment help consistent with their training level and to appropriately refer students to librarians or other experts. Bodemer strongly encouraged academic libraries to adopt peer-led education and concluded that "the role of the librarian is not to lead every instruction session or answer every question but, rather, to provide the training and tools so that peer providers can serve as optimal vehicles for student learning."[4]

Kolb's Learning Style Inventory provided a theoretical framework for the creation of a training program. Kolb's theory includes a four-stage learning cycle comprised of experience, reflecting on the experience, learning from the experience, and trying out what was learned.[5] Opportunities to reflect and observe, conceptualize abstract concepts, actively experiment, and have concrete experiences are examples of the incorporation of Kolb's learning theory into the PEERS training program. The range of training activities included observation, hands-on practice, group meetings, team building, reflection, discussion, video tutorials, role-playing examples, and quizzes. We provided a variety of learning methods in order to accommodate various learning styles and to provide a more thorough training program and depth of experience for the PEERS.

Methodology

The resulting training program was spread out over five weeks with six hours of training scheduled per week (See Appendix C. Peer Reference Training Schedule.) Activities incorporated into the Ask Your PEERS training program primarily fell into four training categories: observation, hands-on practice, individual assignments, and group meetings.

Sample Training Week	
2 Hours	View all video tutorials (required and complementary) for: • Research Essentials—Evaluating Information (10 minutes) • Research Essentials—Citing & Fair Use (21 minutes) • Complete the Madison Research Essentials practice exercises • Evaluating Information • Citing & Fair Use • Work on 33 Questions (See Appendix B. 33 Questions.) • Answer 10 questions
1 Hour	Observation/Hands-on Practice/Reflection session with Rose Librarian • Library Services/Spaces Overview
1 Hour	Observe Ask Your Peers in Rose Library When desk is not busy: Browse through at least 5 Subject Guides located on JMU Libraries homepage. Go through each tab, familiarizing yourself with how subject guides are organized in order to refer students to these guides for help with research
2 Hours	Team-building event for all Peer Reference Specialists Tentative Agenda: • Thoughts and advice from returning Peer Reference Specialists regarding training and providing peer reference service • Review Peer Reference interactions in-person and chat • Discuss ideas to market and promote the service

The majority of observation time was dedicated to shadowing reference librarians at the Ask Desk and, after the initial semester, shadowing the returning PEERS at the Ask Your PEERS service point. The observation time served as an opportunity to understand these service points and also to strengthen relationships with the reference librarians and fellow PEERS.

Students also observed other peer mentoring services on campus such as the writing tutors.

The hands-on practice portion of the training was mostly one-on-one work with reference librarians, which offered a variety of Kolb's Learning Style inventory activities such as observation, reflection, hands-on practice, and concrete experiences. For example, the PEERS and librarians reviewed chat reference transcripts together, talked through how to respond to sample questions, and practiced using general databases for working through common assignments and frequently asked questions.

> Research is a lifelong requirement, and the PEERS program is a great opportunity for students to sit down with us and learn how to research on their own so they can apply it in the future."
>
> —*Peer Reference Specialist, James Madison University*

Individual assignments included the completion of locally created online information literacy modules and accompanying quizzes, assigned readings, and practice questions. Information literacy modules assured that students mastered base levels of information literacy skills, while readings helped students understand the tenets of peer-led education. The practice questions included various types of questions that the PEERS were likely to receive at the service point. During the training period, the focus was less on finding the correct answer and more on how to respond, especially highlighting the need to ask open-ended questions.

Finally, group meetings were important for creating team cohesion and building a community between the planning team and the PEERS. This was especially true during the initial semester the service was offered. Talking and getting to know each other over pizza and a few quick icebreaker games helped create a more comfortable and informal team-based environment for learning and communicating, build excitement for the service model, and develop a consistent commitment to the Ask Your Peers service. Most importantly, these team-building meetings gave students a sense of ownership by allowing them to brainstorm marketing ideas and also provided them with an opportunity for continual feedback on any ongoing training needs or issues related to the service. During the inaugural training period, group meetings served as an opportunity to name and brand the service. In addition, a panel of students from other peer-led campus services joined the final group meeting and helped make connections to common and best practices of peer education and allowed seasoned peer mentors to share insights from their own experiences. One of the last group meetings during the initial semester included role-playing, with librarians acting as students. This activity offered a final opportunity to demonstrate some of the concepts introduced during training, bolster confidence for the newly trained PEERS, and highlight the growth in their skills to the librarians who had been involved in training.

ASSESSMENT
Training Assessment

Assessment methods for the training program included both formative and summative elements. The formative assessment helped indicate progress and identify areas for adjustment along the way, while summative assessment measured the overall effectiveness of the training program. Weekly journaling during the training period ensured that training activities were meeting the stated learning objectives. During training, PEERS were required to write one journal entry per week summarizing knowledge gained from each week of training. In addition, journaling provided students with a tool for reflection and accountability. Much of the training happened autonomously, either through individual work, observation, or working with other library staff. Journaling not only indicated student progress but also held students accountable for independent training activities.

Pre and post-tests served as summative assessment. During the first group meeting, prior to receiving any training, the PEERS completed a pre-test comprised of ten research-related questions that covered important concepts, skills, and commonly asked questions (See Appendix E. Peer Reference Specialist Pre-Test Assessment.) The post-test was presented at the final group meeting at the conclusion of the training period (See Appendix F. Peer Reference Post-Test Assessment.) Average pre-test scores across training cohorts were sixty-seven out of 100, and average post-test scores were 90 out of 100. Good performance on the pre-test, before any training began, was most likely a result of exposure to information literacy instruction in the JMU curriculum and library student employee orientation. The post-test results indicate significant improvement and mastery of some of the key concepts necessary for providing quality peer reference.

Communication

Multidirectional communication was key during the pilot training program and throughout the initial semester. Maintaining communication required a deliberate effort since the service hours were in the evenings when most librarians and managers were not available. The PEERS completed service log entries and communicated with each other, the planning team, and librarians using online discussion boards. By participating in discussions alongside the PEERS, as well as monitoring the log entries and chat transcripts, the planning team was able to proactively offer support and guidance as needed and address any issues that arose. These supportive teaching moments and check-in team meetings held throughout the semester were crucial components of ensuring the skill and confidence of the PEERS and maintaining the desired level of quality for the service. The service log also allowed the peer reference specialists to communicate with each other regarding common questions or assignments, helpful tips, or any other concerns. For example, the students sometimes wrote notes to each other offering each other support and encouragement.

Service Statistics

The PEERS log every service interaction. We require them to enter specific data about each question they receive, including the question asked, a general summary of how the question was addressed, the type of question, and the duration of the interaction. As a result, the planning team was able to monitor the usage of the service in terms of the type of questions and trends.

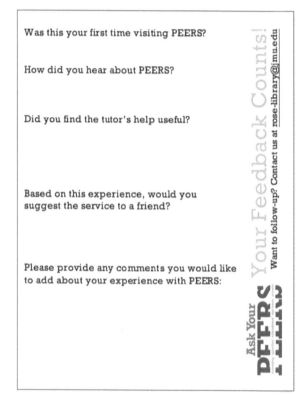

In addition, PEERS collect user comments on paper feedback slips to assess the success of the specific interactions and the overall service. An unanticipated hurdle in collecting this feedback directly from users was that the PEERS felt uncomfortable soliciting comments in-person immediately following an interaction. Soliciting direct feedback from users is an ongoing challenge.

Feedback slip

One of the earliest benefits of tracking and counting sessions was the realization that in-person visits were slow to catch on and that the peer reference specialists had the capacity to also staff the chat reference service, especially with two students staffing the physical service point at all times. PEERS answered chat questions only during Ask Your PEERS service hours. This change in service staffing extended the availability of chat reference by twelve hours each week. The PEERS welcomed the additional level of responsibility and potential for helping more students.

Across all four semesters, our PEERS logged a total of 375 interactions in-person (seventy-three) and via chat reference (302). While we couldn't fully predict what the business for this service would look like, if pressed, we would say we probably expected more in-person and were surprised by the overall higher number of chat questions. Approximately 80 percent of the total interactions were reference questions. Without the Ask Your PEERS service, a significant amount of questions would have either not been asked, required an asynchronous response on an email reference form, resulted in a referral, or been answered by an evening/weekend staff member who would not have been fully prepared to answer because of their level of training. Instead, the peer-led reference service provided a quality level of research and assignment help at the time of need, through the increasingly popular model of peer-led education.

> I've seen the effective use of peer learning in the classroom through team-based learning and group activities. From early conversations with these students, I find that these students are excited and motivated to both expand their skills through interactions with librarians and share this new knowledge with their peers.
>
> *Carolyn Schubert, Health Sciences and Nursing Librarian,*
> *James Madison University*

REFLECTION
Challenges

Organizational buy-in was important on many levels. Librarian concern for the level of quality that peer reference specialists would be able to offer was an anticipated challenge during the planning phase; however, in the case of Ask Your PEERS, hesitancy from librarians was not an issue. The lack of concern was possibly a result of an intentional effort to cultivate buy-in, communicate with the organization, and include librarians in the development and facilitation of the training program.

One pair of the major challenges was brand recognition for the service among the campus community and visibility of the service within the library space. Maintaining service visibility through promotional materials was an area in constant need of attention but important and worth the effort. We found that it was effective to start the service with an eye-catching logo that could be repeated in a variety of promotional materials and formats. With a clean and consistent logo, we were able to proactively pull together an initial marketing plan and more readily take advantage of promotional opportunities that arose through our campus network (See Appendix G. PEERS Marketing Outline and Appendix H. Promotional Copy Sent to Newspaper). As far as physical location, although there was space available at the central service point, separating the PEERS was an intentional way to draw more attention to the new service. Separating Ask Your PEERS also allowed the service to be collocated with other peer-led services taking place in the library during evening hours. This location decision affected subsequent planning considerations, such as a need for access to mobile technology and power sources. Eventually, and with a limited budget, we were able to secure dedicated laptops for the PEERS to use at their designated service location.

The maintenance of open and informational communication channels required thoughtful effort and consistency throughout the training and implementation of the program, and there was a need to maintain strong relations between the planning team and the peer reference specialists after the training period was complete. Streamlining communication involving multiple groups and channels was an initial challenge, and improvements based on direct feedback from the PEERS led to increased consistency. Identifying opportunities for continuing education for the PEERS was also helpful to retain close connections as a team as well as for ongoing development of skills and keeping students informed about new and important resources. Following through with ongoing training was initially a challenge, especially in terms of students' schedules and availability, the planning team's workload, balancing the amount of ongoing training with the initial training program, and avoiding duplicative content.

> Although the number of patrons we get each night varies, there are always meaningful questions and opportunities to teach someone new about the benefits of our program and the research help we can offer.
>
> *Peer Reference Specialist, James Madison University*

Successes

Ask Your PEERS is a distinguished service, explicitly set apart from other JMU Libraries service offerings. Thoughtful and focused service implementation required the creation of clear documentation and expectations while remaining flexible and responsive to inevitable unknowns and challenges. This work required time and attention but ultimately resulted in success.

Overall, the Ask Your PEERS program achieved successful outcomes related to the training program, service promotion, team development, use of service, and organizational buy-in. The following outcomes served as evidence of success:

- Pre-test and post-test assessment revealed an overall increase in skills and knowledge due to the completion of training.
- Marketing and promotion were intentional and reached diverse audiences in the campus community.
- Peer reference specialists effectively worked together as a team, developed ownership of the service, and delivered quality services.
- In-person visits and chat reference during the pilot phase justified formal adoption and continuation of the program.
- The broader organization vocally supported the program, with administration ultimately funding the service and officially adding Ask Your PEERS to the suite of library service offerings.

The root of these overall successes can be attributed to comprehensive and thoughtful development and implementation of the pilot program. Taking the time to organize a pilot project mitigated the inevitable challenges of the steep learning curve for a new service. A clear vision, thoughtful planning, and a flexible planning team that was able to make minor adjustments and improvements along the way helped drive progress within the program and ensure ultimate success.

> What better way to demonstrate that we are an engaged university than to enable our own student workers to provide a high level of service? The possibilities for outreach, engagement, involvement, community building, and advancing the profession are better than any other program I know of for undergraduates at our desks!
>
> *K.T. Vaughan, Director of Rose Library, James Madison University*

Future Plans

Prior to a phased reorganization that resulted in a move from a distributed service point model to a more consolidated and centrally managed model that included Ask Your PEERS elements, the planning team and library administration intended to expand the Ask Your PEERS service. At the time, our future plans included several questions and priorities. Offering the service in additional library locations raises questions about funding, recruitment, sustainable staffing models, and consistency in service provision, but has potential for reaching a broader audience and greatly extending the times, days, and hours when research and assignment help is offered by the JMU Libraries. Promotional efforts will continue in an effort to further establish and maintain brand recognition and ultimately increase usage of the service. More importantly, marketing and branding efforts will transition from solely highlighting Ask Your PEERS as a new library service to focus on promoting the full suite of library service offerings. In addition, we will give more attention to developing an anonymous online user survey to capture feedback on service transactions to more fully assess the service from the user perspective and to offer an additional layer of quality oversight for the service and provide additional evidence of success.

Continuing education is also a priority. Although general supporting resources are in place for the PEERS, providing ongoing support and training is essential in order to continually advance skills and remain connected to peer-led education and reference theory and practice. Examples of continuing education activities we have experimented with include sharing relevant readings, organizing panel-style sessions with subject experts, and offering informal conversations with a favorite librarian. We will continue to work with the PEERS to identify valuable opportunities to support their growth as service providers while balancing the demands of their academic commitments and our limited resources.

As the field of peer-led education continues to grow, staying informed of trends and new directions will be important. Libraries continually seek to develop student-centered services, and peer-led reference is a powerful opportunity to align with other peer-led services on campus. As seen with Ask Your PEERS, well-trained peer mentors and peer-led services can expand reference and research support on campus without lowering the overall quality of service offerings and can ultimately improve the academic support available to students.

APPENDIX A

Position documentation for peer reference specialists. In lieu of advertising on the broader campus job boards, the following is emailed to current JMU Libraries Student Assistants as a means of advertising and recruiting for the position.

PEER REFERENCE SPECIALIST JOB POSTING

General Info
Rose Library Peer Reference Specialist

Rose Library seeks current Student Assistants to apply to work as Peer Reference Specialists. Students in these positions will provide excellent customer service and reference assistance to a diverse population of library users by staffing the Peer Reference Service. Applicants must complete a 6-week training program before their regular Peer Reference shifts begin.

After completion of the training program, the schedule will be 8 hours per week and will include two, 3- hour Peer Reference shifts (the service operates Sunday through Wednesday from 7:00pm–10:00pm) and two, 2-hour Information Desk shifts. During exam weeks, the schedule may be subject to change. This is a part-time student position working 10 hours per week over the course of a calendar year with no benefits. Hourly rate for Peer Reference Specialists is $8.25; hours worked as a Student Assistant at the Information Desk are at an hourly rate of $7.25.

Duties and Responsibilities

Provide excellent customer service, demonstrate effective communication skills, and conduct effective reference interviews. Provide library outreach by connecting students with library resources and services through consultations involving assistance with research and assignments. Recognize when to use the appropriate referral methods in accordance with a tiered reference model. Initially staff a reference service point, but service could evolve to including roving reference and chat reference. Peer Reference Specialists are expected to adhere to and enforce library policies and procedures and abide by RUSA Guidelines for Behavioral Performance of Reference and Information Service Providers. Successful applicants will demonstrate a willingness to be flexible depending on the University's and library's needs and calendars.

Qualifications

Competitive candidates will demonstrate excellent customer service and reference skills, intermediate computer skills and an ability to address individual patron's reference needs. Candidates must be dependable, approachable, encouraging, pay strict attention to detail, and have basic reference skills or the strong desire to learn them. Preference will be given to students who are able to commit to one year of service as a Peer Reference Specialist.

To Apply for this Position

Please submit an essay of 500 words or less explaining your interest in the position and the ways in which your experiences will transfer and serve to benefit the Peer Reference Service.

APPENDIX B

Handout provided to Peer Reference Specialists during training as well as in the service operation binder as a ready reference document.

ASK YOUR PEERS GUIDELINES FOR REFERENCE SERVICE

Conducting a Reference Interview:

- Avoid looking too busy; remain visible and approachable.
- Make patrons feel welcome and comfortable.
- Implement your listening skills; allow patrons to fully state their information needs in their own words before you respond.
- Seek clarification if you are unsure or confused; confirm that you correctly understand the question.
- Use open-ended questions to seek additional information.
  - o "Please tell me more about your topic."
  - o "What information have you already found?"
  - o "How much information do you need?"
- Ask what class the assignment is for and when the assignment is due to gain perspective on what type or level of information is needed.
  - o Is it upper-level research or general information?
    - ▪ Do they need background information or more in-depth research?
    - ▪ You can recommend appropriate Subject Guides or Course Guides.
  - o How far into the research process is the patron?
    - ▪ Do they need sources to help with getting started or to finish an assignment?
  - o What type of information is needed, and how much is needed?
  - o Ask to see the assignment if the information need is unclear.

Research Assistance:

- Help patrons with topic development in order to develop search terms.
- Identify appropriate sources that are most likely to contain information relevant to the patron's information need.
- Work with the patron to narrow or broaden search words when searches bring back too little or too much information.
- Explain what you are doing each step of the way, and why you are recommending each step, in order to enable patrons to improve their research and assignments.

- You should not do the research for the patrons, but simply guide and help them to find the right path, allowing them to answer similar questions on their own.
- Encourage patrons to return after trying out your recommendations and suggestions.
- Be aware of time spent with one patron, especially if others are waiting, and be aware of how much time patrons have for your help.
- Ask patrons if you have fully answered their questions.

Referral:

- Don't attempt research help beyond your abilities. Be comfortable referring patrons to librarians.
- Give a business card, refer patrons to appropriate Subject Guides, or help patrons complete the email reference form for further help with recommended resources and further research assistance.
- See the *Referral Methods for Peer Reference Specialists* document for more detail and referral suggestions.

APPENDIX C

Training schedule provided to peer reference specialists and participating librarians during the fall semester 2014 training period.

PEER REFERENCE TRAINING SCHEDULE
Fall 2014

During training, Peer Reference Specialists will be required to write weekly journal entries in the Canvas course. These weekly entries should reflect on all of the training activities from that week, including a brief summary of what was learned, feedback about the effectiveness of each training activity, and any additional questions or comments. Peer Reference Specialists, will be asked to complete their training hours at the Rose Library, except for any times scheduled elsewhere (i.e., Carrier Library Ask a Librarian Desk).

August 28 (6:30–8:30)	
2 Hours	**Group Meeting:** Introductions and pizza, welcome two new students and two returning students Overview of Peer Reference Handbook • Job Responsibilities, Supporting documents and guidelines Overview of LibChat and RefAnalytics Pre-Test Icebreaker Overview of Pilot Project • Rationale, part of other library services • Timeline for pilot and decision to implement • Lessons learned from 1st semester of pilot project Student contributions to the development of the service Referral Methods Review of Training schedule
4 Hours	Pick up shifts at Rose Information Desk
September 1–September 7	
2 Hours	View all (required and complementary) video tutorials for: • Research Essentials—Discovering the Library (23 minutes) • Research Essentials—Information Formats (21 minutes) Complete the Madison Research Essentials practice exercises • Discovering the Library • Information Formats Begin 33 Questions (finish by September 21) • Answer 5 questions

September 1–September 7	
1 Hour	View all (required and complementary) video tutorials for: • Research Essentials—Finding Information (25 minutes) Complete the Madison Research Essentials practice exercises • Finding Information Work on 33 Questions • Answer 5 questions
2 Hours	Observe Ask Your Peers in Rose Library
1 Hour	Observation/Hands-on Practice/Reflection session with Rose Librarian: Library Services/Spaces Overview

Fall 2014

September 8–September 14	
2 Hours	View all (required and complementary) video tutorials for: • Research Essentials—Evaluating Information (10 minutes) • Research Essentials—Citing & Fair Use (21 minutes) Complete the Madison Research Essentials practice exercises • Evaluating Information • Citing & Fair Use Work on 33 Questions • Answer 10 questions
1 Hour	Observation/Hands-on Practice/Reflection session with Rose Librarian: Library Services/Spaces Overview
1 Hour	Observe Ask Your Peers in Rose Library • When desk is not busy: Browse through at least 5 Subject Guides (located on JMU Libraries homepage). Go through each tab to become familiar with how subject guides are organized in order to refer students to these guides for help with research.
2 Hours	Team-building event for all Peer Reference Specialists Tentative Agenda: • Thoughts and advice from returning Peer Reference Specialists (regarding training and providing peer reference service) • Review of Spring 2014 Peer Reference interactions in-person and chat • Discuss ideas to market and promote the service

September 15–September 21	
2 Hours total (1-hour with each librarian)	Observation/Hands-on Practice/Reflection session with 2 Rose Librarians: *Notes for facilitating librarians:* Observation: Use any of the following options, or something similar of your design, to guide your time together. • Use a Library Instruction session, Undisciplined Research class, or Research Consultation for observation. • Review chat transcripts or reference question statistics. • Illustrate how you would conduct searches on example topics. Hands-on Practice or Reflection: Use any of the following options, or something similar of your design, to include practice or reflection. • Discuss your design and strategies for the instruction session or research consultation. • Have the Peer Reference Specialist practice answering similar chat transcript or reference question examples. Have the Peer Reference Specialist conduct searches on example topics.
1 Hour	Work on 33 Questions • Answer all remaining questions. Browse through Background Information page (located on JMU Libraries homepage) and review Reference Universe, Issues & Controversies, Opposing Viewpoints, and Sage Knowledge in order to know how to search for information in these resources.
2 Hours	Go to Carrier Library and observe Carrier Library Ask a Librarian Desk.
1 Hour	Observe Ask Your Peers in Rose Library.

Fall 2014

September 22–September 28	
1 Hour	Observe a Writing Center peer tutoring session at a satellite location.
2 Hours total (1-hour with each librarian)	Observation/Hands-on Practice/Reflection session with 2 Rose Librarians: *Notes for facilitating librarians:* Observation: Use any of the following options, or something similar of your design, to guide your time together. • Use a Library Instruction session, Undisciplined Research class, or Research Consultation for observation. • Review chat transcripts or reference question statistics. • Illustrate how you would conduct searches on example topics.

September 22–September 28	
	Hands-on Practice or Reflection: Use any of the following options, or something similar of your design, to include practice or reflection. • Discuss your design and strategies for the instruction session or research consultation. • Have the Peer Reference Specialist practice answering similar chat transcript or reference question examples. Have the Peer Reference Specialist conduct searches on example topics.
1 Hour	Read article on peer-tutoring (will be provided for you). Review Peer Reference Handbook documents (Appendix I), especially focusing on Referral Methods for Library Resources (Appendix J) and Providing Chat Reference documents (see Appendix K) .
2 Hours	Go to Carrier Library and observe Carrier Library Ask a Librarian Desk.

Training Activities during 1st week of working at the Ask Your Peers desk:

September 28–October 2	
6 Hours	New PEERS begin staffing Ask Your Peers desk
	Observe a Science and Math Learning Center Tutor session. During one of your Ask Your Peers shifts this week, from 7pm–8pm go to the Science and Math Learning Center tutors to observe for 1 hour.
2 Hours	**Final Training Group Meeting:** • Debrief on observing Writing Center and Science and Math Tutors • Debrief on observing and working with Rose Librarians • Debrief on observing Carrier Ask a Librarian Desk • Review and discuss peer tutoring article read during training • Use of LibChat and RefAnalytics • Reflect on training, what is needed/not needed for training improvements, questions, plan for beginning Peer Reference service • Post-test

Ongoing Training
• Remember to use Peer Reference Handbook documents for guidance in answering questions and referring questions.   • During slow-periods on shift, browse through Subject Guides to become familiar with resources in different disciplines.   • Review chat transcripts or reference question statistics.   • Conduct one formal peer-observation, using peer-observation form, during the Fall semester.   • December group meeting with everyone to review progress

APPENDIX D

Handout provided to Peer Reference Specialists during training program.

33 QUESTIONS

The following questions will help train current and new desk staff in some of the fundamental types of questions that are asked at public service desks. We receive questions about directions, policies, services, spaces, known items, research, and many other types of questions. Responses may change depending on the venue, such as face-to-face, on chat, or on the phone. For the following 33 questions, respond as you would for questions asked in-person. Lastly, some questions might not require an answer; here are some guidelines for these types of questions:

A question about finding a particular source could actually be a research question where the patron actually needs something else entirely, namely, help from a librarian. What question(s) would you ask to realize that the patron actually needs help with research instead of help finding a source that may or may not be appropriate given the assignment?

You might not want to respond with an answer, but with questions you would ask to clarify what is needed, based on various factors, such as the course, assignment, academic level, or prior research conducted.

How did you recognize that the question needed a referral to a librarian? For example, how would you deconstruct the question to find out right away that you should refer the question rather than after trying to provide help?

1. Where can I find some sources for my GCOM speech?

2. How can I renew my books?

3. How do I cite this book in MLA format?

4. How many books and DVDs can I check out and how long can I have them?

5. I am confused about where to find articles from the American Historical Review journal. I have citations, but the dates are both old and current and I can't find these articles.

6. I was told that various tutors are in the library now. Who is here and when can I meet with them?

7. I am having trouble printing wirelessly. Can you help me?

8. I don't have any money on FLEX. What are my options for printing?

9. The location for this book says Carrier Library Stacks. Where are the stacks?

10. Where can I find information about the cost of providing healthcare to employees?

11. How do I know if any group study rooms and laptops are available?

12. There is a book in Special Collections I need to use. How do I find it?

13. I'm writing a paper about the use of uniforms to prevent bullying and I need some sources.

14. I lost my JAC card. Do you have it here?

15. I need to find sources about reinforcement theory.

16. Can you help me find 2 peer-reviewed articles?

17. These articles I need are in Microform. How can I get them?

18. I need to find 2 magazine articles for my paper. Where can I find magazines?

19. How long can I have this book that my professor put on reserve for our class?

20. How can I find these articles that are listed in my textbook?

21. Where can I edit my video presentation?

22. I've never been to the Music Library. Can I have materials sent here to ECL?

23. Can you help me find sources for my HIST395 assignment?

24. I can't find any of the older journals on the shelves at ECL.

25. How can I compare international trade of different countries?

26. Do you know what software is on the library or Hillside computers?

27. I found some government documents in the catalog but don't know what I should do to find them.

28. Do you have a copy of Romeo and Juliet?

29. I need to find 3 primary sources about medieval history.

30. When I searched in JSTOR for scholarly articles for my paper, I couldn't find anything useful, do you know what I should do?

31. How am I supposed to cite this website in my paper?

32. I have to find 4 books for my assignment, but I couldn't find any.

33. Can I use these resources after I graduate?

APPENDIX E

Pre-test assessment given to peer reference specialists before training program began.

PEER REFERENCE SPECIALIST PRE-TEST ASSESSMENT

1. How should you begin peer reference interactions with students?
   a. Ask open-ended questions to listen and learn more about their topic.
   b. Search in a database to show them what is available before going further.
   c. Have students try searching first.
   d. Always start with Quick Search.
2. What would be most helpful when the search words you, or the student, are using are not bringing back useful or relevant information?
   a. Limit results by date.
   b. Use Interlibrary Loan to get materials from a different library.
   c. Search only for peer-reviewed articles.
   d. Brainstorm search words and related terms.
3. What should you do if a student has a research question that is exceptionally challenging?
   a. Spend extra time searching, especially in upper-level databases.
   b. Refer the student to a librarian or librarian's subject guide.
   c. Refer the student to the Writing Center.
   d. Try searching for dissertations, either in print or online.
4. From the JMU Libraries' homepage, what are two of the most helpful places to go when a student is looking for a general overview of their topic?
   a. Background Information page and Books/JMU Library Catalog
   b. Quick Search and Research Databases page
   c. Articles page and Research Databases page
   d. Quick Search and Periodical Locator link
5. What should you do if you are unsure what a student needs and the student has trouble expressing what they need?
   a. Ask someone else to try helping the student.
   b. Determine what you think the student needs and try searching for information.
   c. Ask to see the assignment or ask questions about the assignment.
   d. Have the student email the professor to get more information.

6. What are two of the best databases to use for a student in a GWRIT or GCOM course?
   a.   EBSCO or ProQuest
   b.   JSTOR or Scopus
   c.   Biography in Context or Communication & Mass Media Complete
   d.   Opposing Viewpoints or Issues & Controversies

7. Which of the following is NOT a helpful way to find a peer-reviewed article?
   a.   Use Quick Search.
   b.   Select the "peer-reviewed" search limit.
   c.   Add "peer reviewed" to your search words.
   d.   Look at a specific journal title and determine if the journal is peer-reviewed.

8. A student is conducting research for an ISAT course. What would be the most helpful place to find multiple resources directly relevant to ISAT?
   a.   Subject Guides
   b.   Quick Search
   c.   Background Information page
   d.   Periodical Locator

9. A student has the citation to an article. How would you help the student find the article?
   a.   Use the Research Databases page to pick a database.
   b.   Use Periodical Locator to search for the journal title.
   c.   Use JSTOR.
   d.   Use an EBSCO database.

10. How would you help students check their citations if they already completed them?
   a.   Have them create a RefWorks account from the JMU Libraries homepage.
   b.   Check their citations for them using a style guide to verify each citation.
   c.   Direct them to the Cite Sources link from the JMU Libraries homepage.
   d.   Use Periodical Locator.

APPENDIX F

Post-test assessment given to peer reference specialists at the end of the training program.

PEER REFERENCE POST-TEST ASSESSMENT

1. How should you begin peer reference interactions with students?
    a. Ask open-ended questions to listen and learn more about their topic.
    b. Search in a database to show them what is available before going further.
    c. Have students try searching first.
    d. Always start with Quick Search.
2. What would be most helpful when the search words you, or the student, are using are not bringing back useful or relevant information?
    a. Limit results by date.
    b. Use Interlibrary Loan to get materials from a different library.
    c. Search only for peer-reviewed articles.
    d. Brainstorm search words and related terms.
3. What should you do if a student has a research question that is exceptionally challenging?
    a. Spend extra time searching, especially in upper-level databases.
    b. Refer the student to a librarian or librarian's subject guide.
    c. Refer the student to the Writing Center.
    d. Try searching for dissertations, either in print or online.
4. From the JMU Libraries' homepage, what are two of the most helpful places to go when a student is looking for a general overview of their topic?
    a. Background Information page and Books/JMU Library Catalog
    b. Quick Search and Research Databases page
    c. Articles page and Research Databases page
    d. Quick Search and Periodical Locator link
5. What should you do if you are unsure what a student needs and the student has trouble expressing what they need?
    a. Ask someone else to try helping the student.
    b. Determine what you think the student needs and try searching for information.
    c. Ask to see the assignment or ask questions about the assignment.
    d. Have the student email the professor to get more information.

6. What are two of the best databases to use for a student in a GWRIT or GCOM course?

    a.   EBSCO or ProQuest

    b.   JSTOR or Scopus

    c.   Biography in Context or Communication & Mass Media Complete

    d.   Opposing Viewpoints or Issues & Controversies

7. Which of the following is NOT a helpful way to find a peer-reviewed article?

    a.   Use Quick Search.

    b.   Select the "peer-reviewed" search limit.

    c.   Add "peer reviewed" to your search words.

    d.   Look at a specific journal title and determine if the journal is peer-reviewed.

8. A student is conducting research for an ISAT course. What would be the most helpful place to find multiple resources directly relevant to ISAT?

    a.   Subject Guides

    b.   Quick Search

    c.   Background Information page

    d.   Periodical Locator

9. A student has the citation to an article. How would you help the student find the article?

    a.   Use the Research Databases page to pick a database.

    b.   Use Periodical Locator to search for the journal title.

    c.   Use JSTOR.

    d.   Use an EBSCO database.

10. How would you help students check their citations if they already completed them?

    a.   Have them create a RefWorks account from the JMU Libraries homepage.

    b.   Check their citations for them using a style guide to verify each citation.

    c.   Direct them to the Cite Sources link from the JMU Libraries homepage.

    d.   Use Periodical Locator.

APPENDIX G

Marketing outline document created to organize and share information related to promotion of the Ask Your PEERS service.

PEERS MARKETING OUTLINE

Overarching Ideas:
1. Market, PEERS as part of broader library services
2. Create internal message, then develop tailored parallel external message
3. Capture marketing impact through usage statistics or follow-up surveys

General Flow of Business:
Start Date: Roughly the second week of classes
End Date: The week before final exams
Not operational during academic breaks

Peak times are

Methods:

Baseline Information Sharing:
JMU Libraries Website
- Homepage: Visual in the feature box, events calendar, news item Ask the Library page: blurb, describing service

Foam-core poster, displayed during service operation
Table signs affixed to tables used during service; reserves space, lists service hours

Promotional Items Used During Service:
Staff T-Shirts:
- 24 shirts: Anvil Raglan Baseball shirt with PEERS logo

Pens:
- 300 Pens: White pens with purple accents
- File name resized to fit by vendor: Dart Pen Artwork.pdf
- File name to make edits: pen_logo_psd.psd

Notepads:
- Printed through the JMU Copy Center
- 50 half-sheet (8.5"x5.5") notepads printed on white paper
- File name to print: PEERS_Notepads_PDF for Printing.pdf
- File name to make edits: PEERS_Notepads.docx

Follow-Up Card:

- (Idea of using promo postcard or business card with service information as well as place for PEER to write liaison info, etc. and a link to a follow up survey to allow users to offer feedback)

Targeted Marketing:

Social Media
- JMU Libraries accounts: Facebook, Instagram, Twitter

Digital Signage:
- Slide posted in Carrier Library
- File name: Peers_slide promo for digital signage display

Postcards
- Printed through the JMU Copy Center
- Offered at service desks, distributed at orientation events
- File name to print: PEERS Promo Postcard_FA14_PDF for Printing.pdf
- File name to make edits: PEERS Promo Postcard_FA14

Flyers
- Printed in-house or through JMU Copy Center
- Posted in: Library buildings, campus buildings, on-campus housing
- File name to print: Peer Reference Signage 8.5x11 Poster_PDF for Printing.pdf
- File name to make edits: Peer Reference Signage_Poster and Table Tents.pptx

Table Tents
- Printed in-house and displayed throughout library spaces
- File name: Peer Reference Signage_Poster and Table Tents.pptx

Dining Services table tents
- Content must be 50 words or less and is submitted by completing a form for Events Management. Table tents will be posted in the dining halls throughout campus for one week. They are set out Sunday evenings. Requests must be submitted the preceding Tuesday.
- File name for content: Dining Services Table Tent.docx

Grafton-Stovall movie preview ad
- Submit slide request to University Program Board; fee is $75.00/month, $25/week
- Slide requirements can be found here: http://info.jmu.edu/upb/advertising
- File name: Peers_slide promo_psd.psd

APPENDIX H

Copy submitted to the JMU newspaper, *The Breeze*, for consideration. In this case the *Breeze* staff decided to interview one of the peer reference specialists and write their own copy, but it serves as an example of our attempt at promotion of the service.

PROMOTIONAL COPY SENT TO NEWSPAPER

JMU Breeze Article

Ask Your PEERS in Rose Library—Library service embraces peer/support model to provide research and assignment help during the evenings.

Have you ever needed research and assignment help during the evenings? Do you feel more comfortable asking one of your peers for help? Ask Your PEERS is a service in Rose Library that attempts to meet these needs. Located on the first floor of Rose Library, Sunday to Wednesday, from 7:00 pm–10:00 pm, this service is designed to give you more options to get the help you need during hours that librarian help is unavailable in Rose Library.

The Rose Library Ask Your PEERS pilot project was envisioned as a complementary service designed to provide familiar and quality service that is in/line with support from existing library staff and service points. The Peer Reference service meets student users during prime hours of building use and provides an additional area of outreach to connect students with resources. Much like other peer to peer tutoring programs, the Peer Reference Specialists have the ability to provide personal and uninterrupted reference and research help to their peers. Ask Your PEERS is currently staffed by four JMU Libraries student employees who completed an extensive training program focused on building skills in reference and research support. The service offers an additional way to get help and can further help you along the path of life/long learning; the research and assignment help you receive will easily be transferred to other courses, research needs, and personal and professional careers.

So why is this peer service a good thing? According to K.T. Vaughan, Director of Rose Library, "*What better way to demonstrate that we are an engaged university than to enable our own student workers to provide a high level of service? The possibilities for outreach, engagement, involvement, community building, and advancing the profession are better than any other program I know of for undergraduates at our desks!*"

This program falls right in line with the growing trend of peer tutoring and mentoring in higher education and across the JMU campus. The academic journal *New Directions for Higher Education* released a special issue, Peer Leadership in Higher Education (Spring 2012, Issue 157), which focuses entirely on peer education. JMU already has a variety of examples of peer leadership, including Writing Center tutors, Science and Math Learning Center tutors, Communication Center tutors, JMUTeach, MYMOM, Orientation, and various other examples of students providing tutoring and mentoring for their peers—Ask Your PEERS is another example of a JMU initiative that is offering help during a time when more traditional options aren't available.

Carolyn Schubert, Health Sciences and Nursing Librarian, also sees the potential value of a peer/education model: *"I've seen the effective use of peer learning in the classroom through team based learning and group activities. From early conversations with these students, I find that these students are excited and motivated to both expand their skills through interactions with librarians and share this new knowledge with their peers."*

The JMU Libraries are continually trying to develop partnerships with other departments on campus, such as the Writing Center, Science and Math Learning Center, Career & Academic Planning, and University Health Center all providing hours within the libraries, and often provided and led by students. The Ask Your PEERS service intentionally acts as a complementary service closely aligned with these peer/based campus partnerships currently offered in JMU Libraries.

Currently, the pilot service runs through Fall 2014 with hopes of providing the service in subsequent semesters. If you study during the evenings and prefer help from your peers, this new service is an excellent way to receive research and assignment support that saves you valuable time. As one of the first visitors to the Ask/your/PEERS desk said, "[You were] very helpful! I learned a lot!"

APPENDIX I

Peer Reference Specialist Student Employee Handbook, including cover letter used during the pilot year of the program. This document is provided to Peer Reference Specialists as a forward to the standard issue Rose Library Student Assistant Handbook.

PEER REFERENCE SPECIALIST HANDBOOK

Welcome Aboard!

You have been selected to be a Peer Reference Specialist at Rose Library. The Peer Reference service point is a dedicated, peer-to-peer service during evening hours that will supplement our current range of research and reference services.

This handbook will highlight information that is either slightly different from, or in addition to, the guidelines, expectations, and policies listed in the *Rose Library Student Assistant Handbook*. As a student employee maintaining two positions at Rose Library, you are expected to familiarize yourself with and abide by the content of both handbooks. If you have questions about any of the content or how it applies to your roles in the library, you are expected to proactively communicate with your supervisor.

The Peer Reference Service is a Pilot Program:

Please be aware that you are participating in a pilot program. This means that we are testing the waters with this service and expecting to learn a great deal about what works and what might need adjusting as we progress through this next semester together.

You will be asked to remain flexible and to contribute feedback routinely about different aspects of the service. Library staff will be assessing the success of this pilot and ultimately making a recommendation whether or not to continue the service.

Operations:

The service will operate Sunday through Wednesday from 7:00pm-10:00pm and be staffed by two Peer Reference Specialists at a time. The Peer Reference desk will be a table and four chairs located on the 1st floor of Rose Library.

The Job:

Responsibilities:

- Complete all steps required for training.
- Demonstrate proficiency at the Tier 3 competency level in the JMU Libraries Public Service Desks Core Competencies.

- Answer a variety of question types, especially research and assignment questions. Help with directional, technical, and informational questions as well.
- Provide library outreach by connecting patrons with library resources and services.
- Abide by the JMU Honor Code and respect patrons' confidentiality in all interactions.
- Use LibAnalytics to document activity at the service point; questions asked and answers given.
- Regularly communicate and ask questions through the Peer Reference notebook.
- Set up and take down the service point at the beginning and end of each shift, storing and securing all materials and equipment properly.

Service Expectations:

- Remain at the service location unless a reference interaction or time spent offering roving reference assistance requires you to move around.
- Please treat this as the separate position it is; you should not linger at, or behind, the Information Desk while on duty as a Peer Reference Specialist.

Conducting a Reference Interview:

- Avoid looking too busy; remain visible and approachable.
- Make patrons feel welcome and comfortable.
- Implement your listening skills; allow patrons to fully state their information needs in their own words before you respond.
- Seek clarification if you are unsure or confused; confirm that you correctly understand the question.
- Use open-ended questions to seek additional information.
  - "Please tell me more about your topic."
  - "What information have you already found?"
  - "How much information do you need?"
- Ask what class the assignment is for, and when the assignment is due to gain perspective on what type or level of information is needed.
  - Is it upper-level research or general information?
    - Do they need background information or more in-depth research?
    - You can recommend appropriate Subject Guide or Course Guide.
  - How far into the research process is the patron?
    - Do they need sources to help with getting started or to finish assignment?
  - What type of information is needed, and how much is needed?
  - Ask to see the assignment if the information need is unclear.

Research Assistance:

- Help patrons with topic development in order to develop search terms.

- Identify appropriate sources that are most likely to contain information relevant to the patron's information need.
- Work with the patron to narrow or broaden search words when searches bring back too little or too much information.
- Explain what you are doing each step of the way, and why you are recommending each step, in order to enable patrons to improve their research and assignments.
- You should not do the research for the patrons, but simply guide and help them to find the right path, allowing them to answer similar questions on their own.
- Encourage patrons to return after trying out your recommendations and suggestions.
- Be aware of time spent with one patron, especially if others are waiting, and be aware of how much time patrons have for your help.
- Ask patrons if you have fully answered their questions.

Referral:
- Don't attempt research help beyond your abilities. Be comfortable referring patrons to librarians.
- Give a business card, refer patrons to appropriate Subject Guides, or help the patron complete the email reference form for further help with recommended resources and further research assistance.
- See the Referral Methods for Peer Reference Specialists document for more detail and referral suggestions.

Time Sheets and Pay Rate Guidelines:
All time sheet guidelines in the *Rose Library Student Assistant Handbook* also apply to the Peer Reference Specialist position. Time sheets should be accurate at all times.

As a Peer Reference Specialist you will be responsible for completing a second time sheet each pay period. This second sheet will be used strictly to document hours worked at the Peer Reference Service (as a Peer Reference Specialist). You will maintain a separate time sheet for hours worked at the Information Desk (as a Student Assistant).

Because you will be receiving different rates of pay for each position, it is necessary that you track your hours accurately and on the correct time sheet. Any discrepancies will be viewed as intentional.

Intentionally falsifying or padding hours will be considered a dismissible offense.
   1st instance of discrepancy: Verbal Warning
   2nd instance: Written Warning
   3rd instance: Dismissal

Excused Absences, Illnesses, & Substitutions at the Peer Reference Desk

All illness, emergencies, excused absences, and substitution guidelines in the *Rose Library Student Assistant Handbook* also apply to the Peer Reference Specialist position.

In the event of an illness or emergency, please call your supervisor during business hours, or the Information Desk during evening or weekend hours, to discuss the situation.

Excused absences are absences pre-approved by your supervisor. These include substitutions. If it becomes necessary to miss a shift, you will be excused if you find a replacement for your hours or if you speak to your supervisor in advance.

To seek a replacement, contact the other Peer Reference Specialists. Due to the specialized training and difference in pay for Peer Reference Specialists, **you may not ask a Student Assistant to cover your Peer Reference hours**. You should give as much notice as possible and may need to contact your coworkers by e-mail or phone to request coverage. A list of phone numbers and e-mail addresses for student assistants is kept at the front of the time sheet notebook. Once arrangements are made to cover your shift, you are relieved of responsibility for the shift. If you agree to cover a shift for someone else it becomes your responsibility and you must work the hours agreed to or find a replacement.

If no one is willing or available to cover your shift, you must speak to your supervisor a few days in advance to discuss the possibility of having the absence excused. Please keep in mind that there are a very limited number of Peer Reference Specialists and it will present a significant impact on the service if you are absent or tardy. A doctor's note may be requested for absences due to illness or appointments. Excused absences should not exceed two per semester.

Shifts and Substitutions at the Information Desk

As a Peer-Reference Specialist, you are also required to work 2 hours per week at the Information Desk to ensure that you remain familiar with and up to date on policies, procedures, and services and continue to work as a member of the Information Desk team. You are expected to secure coverage for any of these shifts just like you would your Peer Reference hours, but a difference is that you may ask any of the Student Assistants to cover these hours for you.

Substituting for other Student Assistants is a way to pick up extra hours or to make up some of the hours you may have missed. **All hours worked at the Information Desk will be paid at the current Student Assistant rate of $7.25 per hour.**

You are expected to accurately maintain two separate time sheets, one for each position. Your total hours worked, Peer Reference and Information Desk combined, may not exceed 20 hours.

Continue on to review the *Rose Library Student Assistant Handbook*

APPENDIX J

Handout provided to peer reference specialists during training as well as in the service operation binder as a ready reference document.

REFERRAL METHODS FOR LIBRARY RESOURCES FOR PEER REFERENCE SPECIALISTS

Referrals play a central role in providing research and assignment help. You don't have to be a subject expert or a librarian; you simply have to know where to direct students. Here are various library resources to refer students to:

Subject Guides

- Most students don't know about these! Subject Guides are designed to provide instruction and research/assignment help. Simply refer a student to the subject guide related to their class or topic area. You can direct students to various tabs and sections of the Subject Guide, like Books, Articles, Statistics, etc. where databases will be recommended, often with tips and suggestions.
- Check the "Course Guides" tab to see if there is a guide for the specific class.
- Highlight the contact info on every guide. Encourage students to send an email to the librarian listed on the subject guide.

Background Information Page

- If a student needs background information or is simply getting started on a topic, encourage them to use the various resources on the Background Information page, especially:
  o Reference Universe
    ▪ Try doing a simple search for major concept of topic
  o Issues & Controversies and/or Opposing Viewpoints
    ▪ Useful for current issues and GCOM/GWRIT assignments
  o You can try a search in each database to compare results

Library Catalog

- If a student is having trouble with articles, finding them too narrow, off-topic, or overly research-based, encourage them to only search the library catalog for books, which might be more useful and relevant.
  o Search the JMU Library Catalog directly
  o Limit Quick Search results to Books and JMU Library Catalog

Quick Search

- If a student is having trouble with books, finding books too broad and not about a specific topic, encourage them to use Quick Search and search for their specific topic, possibly using various options to narrow and limit the search.

Research Databases

- If a student needs a specific type of resource, like biographical information, country information, newspaper articles, etc., try using the Research Databases page. There are databases listed by subject, and also by type (on the right), which will recommend databases for specific information types.

APPENDIX K

Handout provided to peer reference specialists during training as well as in the service operation binder as a ready reference document.

PROVIDING CHAT REFERENCE DURING ASK YOUR PEERS SHIFTS

Staffing Chat Reference:

- People approaching the desk should always receive your full attention. With 2 PEERS at the desk, try to have 1 person responsible for chat questions (feel free to rotate during an evening) and 1 person responsible for face-to-face interactions at the desk.
- Remember to Go Offline when done or if you step away from the desk for an extended time. We don't want to have missed chats if chat is available and you are not.
- Record all chat questions in RefAnalytics and include any chat issues/feedback in the notebook.
- Some of the most common chat questions involve:
  - Help with citations (be familiar with our citation resources and links)
  - Help with the check-for-full-text screen (be familiar with determining access to a journal, using links from the page such as the Google Scholar link or ILL/Article Delivery link)
  - Help with Interlibrary Loan/Article Delivery (be familiar with requesting items through ILL/Article Delivery)
  - Policy/resource questions about the library (be familiar with library policies and resources)
  - Help with finding an article or book (be familiar with finding known items)
  - Research help (be familiar with subject guides, sending links for suggested resources, sending links to search examples, and referring users)
  - Off-campus connection issues (be familiar with the Connect from Off Campus page)
    - You may want to ask users if they are on or off campus early on in the chat to avoid a longer chat where you didn't realize the issue was caused because they were off campus.
    - You also don't need to troubleshoot off campus access. Refer users to the page, the instructions, the troubleshooting guide, and contact info.

Customer Service and Best Practices:

- The basic principles of a reference interview are the same, regardless of environment.
  - Refer to the reference interview guidelines in your binder.
  - Continue to use reference interview techniques in chat, asking open-ended questions to clarify what information the user needs.
- Greet chat users quickly with a hello or personalized greeting. Chat is usually a less formal setting, so you can be casual, which helps humanize the interaction.
- Provide professional-level assistance, using the same resources and strategies you would for someone in person.
  - Sometimes patrons use chat from inside the library and you don't have to restrict your answers to online resources or suggestions, however hyperlinks to online resources are often easier for chat interactions.
- Information should be sent in small pieces, not large paragraphs.
- Strive for a hybrid combination of instruction and giving answers.
  - For example, responses should (when appropriate) include an explanation of the search process or strategy for finding the information.
- Questions lasting more than 20 minutes should be considered for continuation in- person or through email. If a chat question cannot be successfully handled in the chat environment, encourage the user to continue the interaction via email, a phone call, or an in-person visit.
- Ask the patrons if you have answered their questions completely.
- If unable to successfully answer the user's question, refer to the best source or person, using the same referral recommendations (referrals to resources or people) as suggested in your binder.

Ongoing Training:

- Review previous chat transcripts to get a sense of different questions asked, how different people respond to chat questions, and what type of help was offered to help answer the question.

NOTES

1.   Matthew R. Wawrzynski, Carl L. LoConte, and Emily J. Straker, "Learning Outcomes for Peer Educators: The National Survey on Peer Education," *New Directions for Student Services* no. 133 (2011): 17.
2.   Jenepher Lennox Terrion and Dominique Leonard, "A Taxonomy of the Characteristics of Student Peer Mentors in Higher Education: Findings from a Literature Review," *Mentoring & Tutoring: Partnership in Learning* 15, no. 2 (2007): 156.
3.   Brett B. Bodemer, "They CAN and they SHOULD: Undergraduates Providing Peer Reference and Instruction," *College & Research Libraries* 75, no. 2 (2014): 165.
4.   Bodemer, "They CAN and they SHOULD," 176.
5.   Saul Mcleod, "Kolb's Learning Styles and Experiential Learning Cycle," *Simple Psychology*, http://www.simplypsychology.org/learning-kolb.html.

BIBLIOGRAPHY

Bodemer, Brett B. "They CAN and they SHOULD: Undergraduates Providing Peer Reference and Instruction." *College & Research Libraries* 75, no. 2 (2014): 162–78.

Mcleod, Saul. "Kolb's Learning Styles and Experiential Learning Cycle." *Simple Psychology*. https://www.simplypsychology.org/learning-kolb.html.

Terrion, Jenepher Lennox, and Dominique Leonard. "A Taxonomy of the Characteristics of Student Peer Mentors in Higher Education: Findings from a Literature Review." *Mentoring & Tutoring: Partnership in Learning* 15, no. 2 (2007): 149–64.

Wawrzynski, Matthew R., Carl L. LoConte, and Emily J. Straker. "Learning Outcomes for Peer Educators: The National Survey on Peer Education." *New Directions for Student Services* no. 133 (2011): 17–27.

Case Study 9

COLLABORATIVE LEARNING AT JOHN CARROLL UNIVERSITY LIBRARY

Amy Wainwright, Katherine Baker, and Michelle Millet

On a typical Wednesday night at about 8:00 p.m. in John Carroll University's Learning Commons, we enter the lower level of Grasselli Library and see a multitude of whiteboard tables in front of us with groups of students working together. Some of the tables have signs on them with different subject areas, other tables are covered in equations, diagrams, and lists, and students are talking, gesturing, and adding to their whiteboard creations. The nearby individual study carrels are full by this time of the evening with more people practicing speeches, finishing projects with classmates, or working on papers in the midst of the activity around them.

Moving into The Den, Starbucks employees are quickly filling orders while students prepare for an evening of studying. Peer Health Advocate volunteers set up for a Wellness in the Stacks event in order to give all of the students who are hard at work a study break. Around the corner at the Relaxation Room, someone has almost finished their time using the massage chair and another student has signed up to use the yoga mat and relaxation audio when the room is available. The space is a balance between academic resources and wellness services designed to encourage John Carroll University students to live and study well.

OVERVIEW

In 2012, the new library director at John Carroll University partnered with the associate academic vice president for student success to pull together previously siloed activities into a central space for student support. This became what is now known as the Learning Commons at John Carroll University. The library director secured funds through the University Planning Group to buy some new furniture and whiteboards and hire students to facilitate peer-learning by strategically aligning the creation of the Learning Commons with the goal to increase access to student support and success.

When the new director arrived, there was already a Writing Center annex in the library and some energy to create something more, but no one was sure what that would be. The first peer-learning partner, biology, joined what would later become the Learning Commons in 2013, with the goal of targeting students in the introductory course, a class with a large number of students not passing. The Student Health department also enthusiastically partnered with the library the first year and created a series of bi-monthly events to encourage students to take study breaks and relax, called Wellness in the Stacks. These events were well-attended, but the director wanted to capitalize on the enthusiasm growing on campus to create an established space for student support and think bigger. The librarians weeded outdated media materials in order to clear out and repurpose space on the main floor of the library. Then, a group of campus faculty and staff—the Learning Commons committee—took trips to see other Learning Commons spaces, including those at Allegheny College and the College of Wooster, to get an idea of what others found to be working and not working.

The John Carroll University Learning Commons

By 2014, the Learning Commons grew to be the busiest peer-learning location on campus, supporting ten to twelve subjects for study tables, wellness events, counseling workshops, and résumé review. From the beginning, the heart of the Learning Commons has been the students who run it and use it. All it took was the right amount of energy, some new furniture, and the belief that less-siloed services would benefit our students. Today, the Learning Commons is arguably the most vibrant space for students on campus. It brings life to the library and continues to be an inspiration for growth and innovation.

ADMINISTRATION

The John Carroll University Library's Learning Commons has a unique place within the library's structure. The Learning Commons physically is confined to only the eastern half of the library's lower level. However, since we have created spaces for group work, designated a part of the floor as event space, and built a Relaxation Room outside of the eastern half of the floor, we are encouraging students to think of the whole floor as the Learning Commons. Long-term plans for the future of the Learning Commons include an expansion of the space to more officially incorporate the entire lower level. Within the library, the Learning Commons is considered a separate entity; for instance, the Learning Commons has its own branding and a separately funded staff. Despite this distinction, the Learning Commons embodies the spirit of the library in general and is integral to overall student outreach efforts.

The Learning Commons itself is almost completely run by students. A graduate assistant (GA) oversees the day-to-day functions in the Learning Commons and reports to the head of research, learning, and outreach. Other than offering a supportive and supervisory role, this librarian does not have much hands-on involvement with the Learning Commons. Essentially, the GA coordinates and maintains the Learning Commons independently. The role of the Learning Commons GA is to hire, train, schedule, and supervise all of the peer-learning facilitators (PLFs) who run study tables. Each semester, we hire approximately twenty PLFs to offer study tables that represent different subject areas (e.g., accounting, biology, Chinese) or specific classes (e.g., German 101, Political Science 300). The GA also promotes the Learning Commons and coordinates with other outside departments that are involved with our Learning Commons, such as Student Health, the Counseling Center, the Writing Center, and Career Services.

The library does not pay for any of the Learning Commons services out of our library budget. When we established the Learning Commons, there was a specific budget line created through a student learning initiative designated to pay the GA's stipend and the PLFs' wages along with a one-time budget increase to pay for a remodel of the Learning Commons space. Currently, we have fifteen PLFs who are funded through this campus budget line and five additional PLFs who are funded by the departments that they represent. This latter group of PLFs is a reflection of our growth on campus. Originally, some departments preferred to house all peer-learning options within their departments. As the Learning Commons has grown, many of these departments have shifted their PLFs to the Learning Commons space and yet still maintain the funding for these PLFs. For example, this year, study tables in accounting, economics, and physics were added to the Learning Commons, but they are paid through their respective departmental budgets.

As mentioned earlier, the GA handles a large portion of the promotion of the Learning Commons to our campus and interested users. Here is a table of our promotional activities and who manages them.

Promotional Method:	Managed By:	Types of Promotion:
Learning Commons Twitter	Learning Commons GA	Learning Commons study table schedule, hosted events, helpful study tips
Library's Facebook	Head of research, learning, and outreach, Learning Commons GA, and additional social media contributors	Study tips, student success advice, healthy living posts, promotion of Learning Commons events
In person	Learning Commons GA	Meets with campus faculty and staff to promote Learning Commons Services
Library's Twitter and Instagram	Head of research, learning, and outreach, and student outreach assistants	Cross-promotion of Learning Commons events
Library's website	Head of research, learning, and outreach	Prominent tab on the library's homepage directing students to Learning Commons information
LibGuide	Learning Commons GA	Study table schedule, the Learning Commons mission and overview, and additional resources
Dry-erase board calendar	Learning Commons GA	Regularly updated Learning Commons study table schedule and hosted events

Communication about the Learning Commons is handled in a few ways. Internal library communication about Learning Commons events, activities, and updates are the responsibility of the head of research, learning, and outreach The GA and librarian share some of the communication with departments outside of the library, but the GA is the main point of contact. The GA communicates with departmental representatives (designated faculty, administrative assistants, and occasionally department heads) at the beginning of each school year to confirm current study table offerings as well as check to see if there are new subjects we should be adding. When a faculty member feels there should be a study table specifically for their class, the GA is the person who carries out this conversation.

The homepage of the Learning Commons LibGuides page

Additional resources to help students and faculty understand some of the Learning Commons procedures

HIRING

The hiring process for our Learning Commons is heavily dependent on communication with academic departments. All of the students hired as peer-learning facilitators (PLFs) are recommended by a faculty member in their subject area, have excelled in this subject and are often upper-level students. The exception to the last condition is when we are filling positions in the foreign languages; the students hired to offer study tables in foreign languages are often native speakers of that language and therefore do not have to be upper-level students. At the beginning of each school year, the GA connects with each department to confirm whether we will be offering study tables in that area. If we do not already have a returning PLF, the GA will also ask for recommendations for strong candidates to interview.

Originally, we did not advertise or post job descriptions for PLFs because the hiring recommendations were coming directly from the faculty. As more students began to contact the GA with an interest in working for the Learning Commons, the GA created an online application and recommendation form. A link to the application is available on the Learning Commons website so that interested parties may apply more easily and so that the GA can send the recommendation form to faculty members listed by the applicants. This process is more formal and streamlined, which will be helpful as the Learning Commons continues to expand.

The interview process for the students is set up entirely by the GA. The GA gives an overview of the job to the student and asks some questions to focus the conversation on peer-learning styles and skills. Some sample questions are:

- "Why are you interested in this position, and what strengths do you bring to this position?"
- "What does collaborative learning mean to you, and how would you keep your sessions collaborative?"
- "Tell me about a time when you had to overcome a difficulty at work, in school, or at home, and how you solved it."
- "It can be tricky to balance schoolwork, friends, activities, and jobs during the semester. How would you plan to prioritize and balance your various responsibilities in order to get everything done?"
- "How do you feel about collaborating with a diverse group of students who have different needs and backgrounds at a study table?"

The GA makes the decision about which students to hire, in consultation with the head of research, learning, and outreach when necessary, and, if hired, the student provides availability for the study table schedule. Our Learning Commons is busiest during the evening, so most study tables are scheduled after 5:00 p.m. However, certain subjects regularly are scheduled earlier in the day to take advantage of breaks between classes. Each

PLF works either two or four hours a week; if they are scheduled for four hours a week, it is broken into two two-hour shifts. Finding an ideal way to schedule study tables to meet students' needs is an ongoing process, and each semester we try to improve the schedule.

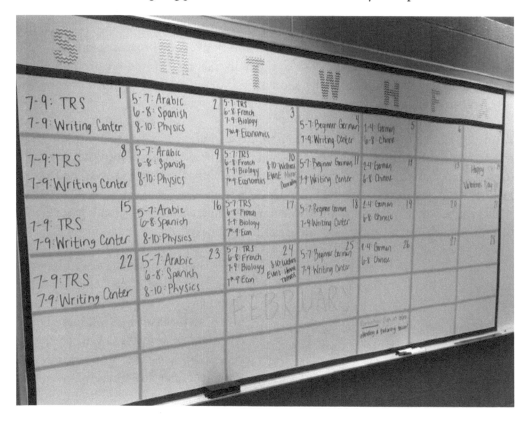

One of the many ways we promote the Learning Commons study table schedule. This is a dry erase calendar that the Graduate Assistant updates regularly.

Throughout the semester, there is the option to add study tables in new subject areas or specific classes when students, faculty members, or departments identify the need. In those circumstances, the GA follows the same procedure of requesting recommended students, interviewing them, and hiring. There is a point in the semester, often within a few weeks of midterms, when it is too late to add new study tables based on the timeline of the hiring process.

TRAINING

We begin each school year with a one-hour paid peer-learning facilitator (PLF) training session that is geared toward new hires. Study tables start during the third week of the semester, so we schedule the training session for the end of the second week or the beginning of the third week of the semester. Since the librarians would like to keep the Learning Commons applicable to student needs, the training offered to PLFs is still evolving. A few years ago, in order to begin more thoroughly assessing our training of PLFs, the Learning Commons graduate assistant (GA) created a brief, anonymous survey to gather information. PLFs answered questions such as "What do you wish you had learned during training that you instead had to learn on the job?" and "What suggestions do you have for future training sessions?" We continue to integrate suggestions from the PLFs as appropriate. The results from the anonymous survey and our planned changes are discussed in detail in the assessment section below.

Returning PLFs are invited to attend the training session each year so that they can share feedback and helpful hints with new hires, but their attendance is not required. The training session consists of presentations given by representatives from the Counseling Department, the Writing Center, and the Learning Commons. The GA meets individually or in small groups with all new PLFs who were unable to attend the initial training session. In this smaller session, the GA covers all topics in an abbreviated presentation.

The GA designed the training session to give PLFs the tools that they need to work collaboratively with students and identify when students need additional assistance. The training session begins with an introduction from the Learning Commons representative, typically the GA, who presents general procedures and encourages PLFs to direct any future questions or concerns to the GA. For instance, we tell PLFs how to check out subject signs from the library help desk so that students can easily identify where various study tables are in the Learning Commons. We also show PLFs how to sign students in for study tables; they are required to ask every student coming to the study tables to complete our online attendance tracking form. We use the information from the form to communicate study table usage and therefore justify continued funding for the program.

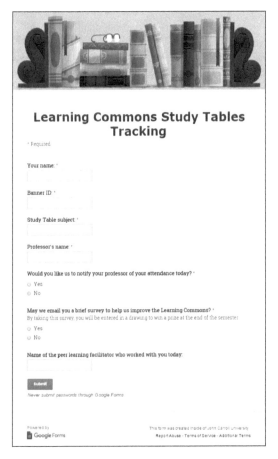

The form used by students who are attending study tables. This form captures basic information about the students and the sessions they are attending.

The GA reminds PLFs that they must remain present during scheduled study table hours and that they must give advance notice of absences. PLFs are permitted to do homework during their scheduled study table hours if no students have come for assistance, but they are instructed to use body language that makes them look approachable and ready to help when students do arrive. In the event that PLFs do need to miss a scheduled study table time, we permit the absence because we consider school to be the top priority for all employees. We have noticed that it is helpful to collect PLF cell phone numbers at the beginning of each semester because it is difficult to reach PLFs via email in time-sensitive situations, such as when they are running late to a study table and students have already arrived to participate.

The final piece of housekeeping that is covered by the GA is how to complete and submit timecards. This portion of the training session is most helpful for new hires, but returning employees may also benefit from hearing the procedures again. The library administrative services coordinator, who completes new hire paperwork and processes timecards, sets the payroll policies and maintains a private blog for student workers in the library. This blog serves as an employee handbook with information regarding how to get paid along with news updates and job expectations. This is a helpful resource for PLFs to access after training if they have any questions about how to complete their timecards and when to submit them.

After the GA discusses the basic Learning Commons operating procedures, the other presenters take over. The writing center director, Maria Soriano, uses a Prezi presentation to cover specific techniques and formatting suggestions for a student-centered approach.[1] Her presentation begins by discussing possible misconceptions that PLFs may have about peer-learning. PLFs learn that one strategy does not fit all students and that working as a PLF will be different from helping friends with homework. Then, the writing center director presents certain guiding thoughts to keep in mind while working as a PLF. These include a focus on collaboration, open conversation and demonstration rather than teaching, and an encouragement to rely on questions rather than statements in order to help students reach their own conclusions. Soriano recommends that PLFs use the first few minutes of a session to create an agenda together with the student, and she reminds PLFs to always be flexible in their approaches with students.[2] She presents dialogue examples to illustrate these recommendations, and PLFs read these aloud and discuss them as a group. Soriano finishes her presentation by reminding PLFs to place an emphasis on providing skills for students to become better learners instead of focusing on completing the assignment in front of them.

In addition, a counseling professor or a counseling graduate assistant from the Counseling Department gives a PowerPoint presentation titled, "Tutoring Through Motivation."[3] The presentation begins with a guided group discussion on what motivation is and what role it plays in a peer-learning relationship. The representative then defines motivational interviewing in a peer-learning relationship as a way to "elicit a student's internal motivation for academic improvement" and defines motivational interviewing techniques that PLFs can use.[4] These techniques are open-ended questions, affirmations, reflective listening, and summaries, and they can be remembered using the acronym OARS.

Dialogue Examples

Scenario 1--Creating an Agenda:

Tutor: "Hi, my name is Mark. You must be Sarah. How are you?"

Student: "I'm ok, thanks for asking."

Tutor: "What can I help you with for Biology today?"

Student: "We have a test coming up for Dr. Martin's class next week, and I'm so overwhelmed and lost. I don't understand ANYTHING."

Tutor: "You probably know more than you think! What in particular confuses you?"

Student: "Well, I followed the first few chapters, but when we got to Chapter 4, that's where I got totally lost."

Tutor: "That makes sense. Well, let's review those first few chapters, but focus on the principles in Chapter 4. Ok?"

Scenario 2--Flexibility:

Tutor: "Ok. So, with a thesis statement, you'll want to write a 1-2 sentence overview that specifically encapsulates the focus of your paper."

Student: "Yeah, that's the definition my teacher gave us, but I can't figure out how to do that."

Tutor: "Those can be tough. Why don't you tell me the argument of your essay?"

Student: "Well, I'm arguing that Apple made a bad decision for its business by making the iPhone 4C."

Tutor: "Interesting. Why do you have that opinion?"

Student: "Because it's not a well-made product."

Tutor: "Ok. Any other reasons?"

Student: "I also don't think it represents Apple's usual quality of technological devices."

Tutor: [after making notes] "That's great! If you look here, I've made notes on what you just told me. You have the material for your thesis here--now let's connect your statements."

These dialogue examples are used to stimulate a group discussion about flexibility and formatting. (Slide courtesy of the author from, "Learning Commons Tutor Training," by Maria Soriano. Prezi, September 30, 2013.)

MOTIVATIONAL INTERVIEWING TECHNIQUES

Techniques for using MI in tutoring sessions (Acronym **OARS**)

- 1. Open-Ended Questions
- 2. Affirmations
- 3. Reflective Listening
- 4. Summaries

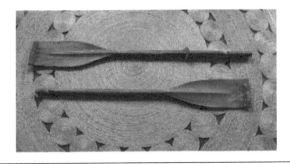

Visualization of the OARS motivational interviewing techniques. (Slide courtesy of the authors Nathan Gehlert and Christine Banks-VanAllen, from "Tutoring Through Motivation," PowerPoint.)

The representative presents examples of open-ended versus closed-ended questions and asks students to discuss why open-ended questions are more useful.[5] The main point that we would like students to understand is that open-ended questions avoid a simple yes or no response and allow PLFs to gather more information from the student. Next, the representative gives examples of affirmations, which are useful to convey a respectful and encouraging attitude. These affirmations should always be truthful and relevant to the subject, and they are best when focused on the hard work of the student.[6]

Certain motivational interviewing techniques are more useful in specific situations, as is evidenced through the discussion of reflective listening. In some situations, such as when a student is complaining about the difficulty of a course, an open-ended question such as "Why do you dislike this class?" only serves to encourage the student to continue wallowing in negativity and self-pity.[7] In such situations, it is instead useful to use reflective listening to mirror the student's statement by restating it and, if appropriate, adding emotional content to help students better understand the feelings they may not have voiced.[8] When a student says, "I really hate this class, the papers and exams are way too difficult," it is important for the PLF to make the student feel heard and understood. An appropriate response using the reflective listening technique would be, "It sounds like you are feeling over-whelmed with these assignments." Such a response acknowledges the student's state-ment and adds emotional content without encouraging the student to get bogged down in negativity.

Finally, the representative from the counseling department discusses how summaries are useful both throughout the peer-learning session as a way to ensure understand-ing before continuing on to new concepts and as a way to wrap up a session and provide future direction.[9] At this point in the presentation, PLFs break into small groups to talk through various role-play scenarios and discuss how the situations could be handled using the newly learned motivational interviewing techniques. Then they reconvene as a group and present their thoughts to other PLFs in a guided discussion.

On the anonymous training survey, in response to the question "What do you wish you had learned during training that you instead had to learn on the job?" one PLF responded, "How to motivate students and confront the ones that don't do their work." This suggests we may need to focus more on applying motivational inter-viewing techniques to real-world situations during training. We would like PLFs to use motivational interviewing techniques in order to avoid direct confrontation, which can cause defensiveness on the part of the student.[10] One way we may be able to improve PLF understanding is to add to the guided group discussion a specific role-play example addressing ways to motivate a student who does not complete assignments.

ROLE PLAY

Scenario 1. Samantha comes into the Learning Commons, seeking tutoring for biology. Samantha is solely interested in getting the right answers on her homework assignments, even though she does not seem to have a solid grounding in her overall biology knowledge.

Scenario 2. Bruce comes into the Learning Commons during the last week of the semester, saying, "I don't know anything. I'm confused on chapters 1-20, and my final exam is next week."

ROLE PLAY

Scenario 3: John comes into the Learning Commons, seeking help with statistics. In session, most of John's questions regard his new graphing calculator, which he does not know how to use.

Scenario 4: Wanda, a sophomore pre-med student, comes into the Learning Commons for tutoring in every class she has. Wanda frequently speaks quickly, and wants to ace every subject. Wanda indicates that she fears getting any B's on her transcript will hurt her chances of getting into Med School. Wanda has asked you to begin meeting her for twice the number of tutoring sessions usually offered to students.

These role-play scenarios are used to stimulate a group discussion on utilizing motivational interviewing techniques. (Slide courtesy of the authors Nathan Gehlert and Christine Banks–VanAllen, from "Tutoring Through Motivation," PowerPoint.)

The representative from the counseling department also starts a discussion with PLFs about how to set and maintain boundaries and how to recognize students who may need additional help beyond what a PLF is able to offer. PLFs are encouraged to talk to the GA if a student is pushing them to offer extra study table hours beyond the scope of their job requirements, if a student is being disrespectful or is exhibiting signs of depression or anxiety, or if they are afraid for a student's or their own safety, just as a few examples. PLFs are encouraged to brainstorm other possible scenarios in which they may need to consult with peers or a supervisor so that they are able to recognize such situations when they arise. We recently had a situation calling for the involvement of the GA when a student from a different college came to the accounting study table for assistance from the PLF. The PLF notified the GA, who was able to speak with the student directly and inform the student that John Carroll University is only able to provide free study tables to students who attend the university. This real-world example illustrates the importance of covering boundaries and asking for help in the PLF training session.

In the past, the GA has given PLFs handouts with helpful contact information, such as the phone numbers for the University Counseling Center, the Library Help Desk, the Center for Career Services, the Writing Center, and the Office of Academic Advising. In a future update to our handouts, we would like to better coordinate with the Counseling Department's training on maintaining boundaries and recognizing when students need more help. We would like to ensure that PLFs are able to distinguish between situations when it is appropriate to provide a student with the University Counseling Center phone number versus the Office of Academic Advising phone number. It may be helpful to add a group discussion of how to make distinctions between various student needs and the departments that are set up to serve them. As is evident, our PLF training procedures continue to evolve, but we hope our format will serve as a strong basis for the development of training procedures for new peer-learning programs.

ASSESSMENT

When the Learning Commons first began to take shape in 2012, there was not a system in place for assessment. The creation of the structure of the Learning Commons and marketing the services offered to the students and faculty were the largest areas of concern at the time. Therefore, the only usage statistics from the first school year the Learning Commons was open are estimates based on self-reporting from the PLFs. The data from this school year is not reliable.

In the 2014–2015 school year, a new sign-in procedure was implemented and continues to be used for students who want to join study tables. We created the sign-in form in Google Forms and is bookmarked on a dedicated laptop centrally located in the Learning Commons. The form gathers basic information from students: automatic time and date stamp, name, student identification (ID) number, study table subject, the relevant course professor's name, and the name of the PLF for the study table they are working at. Students strongly resisted signing in the first semester and were only a little more comfortable with it during the second semester. They were reluctant to give us any information that felt too personal. Often when students would sign in they would only leave their first name and possibly their ID number or their full name with no ID at all. The students also felt that having to go to the centralized computer to sign in was just enough of a hassle that they would put it off.

We began a small campaign to educate the PLFs about why we needed to collect this information in hopes that they could communicate it to the students attending their study tables. We also added signage near the designated sign-in computer. Both of these techniques are most likely what led to a slight increase in sign-ins by the end of the second semester. The last modification we made to the form was to include a checkbox requesting that the attending student's professor receive an email notification that the student sought additional assistance on their schoolwork. The GA manages those requests and sends a form letter to the faculty member.

The dedicated sign-in laptop in the Learning Commons

When the 2015–2016 school year started, we hired a new GA and there was some turnover with the PLFs from the previous school year. The new GA made it clear that it was the responsibility of the PLFs to ensure that the students were signing in to the study tables. She also created rewards for the two PLFs who had the most sign-ins throughout the semester. We created a bit.ly shortened link to the sign-in form so that if PLFs want to they can have students sign in on their laptops or phones. This increased our sign-ins by 500 percent (thirty-four sign-ins fall 2014 versus 179 sign-ins fall 2015). Some of this increase can be attributed to the popularity of the Learning Commons; however, we think it was also due to the changes we made in the PLF training process.

As an additional tracking tool, we created a shift report through Google Forms for PLFs to complete after each study table. For every shift report, PLFs must record the number of students who attended the study table and must confirm that all the students who attended did sign in online. If all the attendees did not sign in online, PLFs must provide an explanation. This has been useful information to gather from a supervisory perspective because it has allowed the GA to address technological issues and misconceptions along with habitual neglect of sign-in procedure with the respective PLFs. The information from the shift reports has also boosted the attendance numbers because we are catching more students who have attended study tables but have not signed in. In addition, PLFs record a brief description of what they covered with the students who participated in their study tables. This is helpful in tracking any themes that may arise in subject material or

Section from the training survey used to measure the effectiveness of current training sessions

assignments that students are struggling with. Although the GA cannot be present during all the times that the study tables are scheduled, the shift reports allow the GA to hear from PLFs each day and to provide specific feedback when PLFs do something positive or when an area for improvement arises.

As introduced above in the training section, we implemented an anonymous survey to find out how well PLF training is preparing PLFs for their jobs. The GA gathered information directly from the PLFs to find out how effective the training actually is and to collect suggestions for improvement.

Section from the training survey used to measure the effectiveness of current training sessions

We have gained several insights from the anonymous PLF responses. For instance, we originally called the session a tutor training session, but as one PLF helpfully pointed out in response to the survey, "I feel that the word 'tutoring' has a negative connotation among students, although the tutors know that this is not true. Maybe we could consider changing the wording to something like 'peer-learning' to avoid this stigma." We were already making efforts to use the terminology study tables rather than tutoring, but we had difficulty in determining an appropriate title for the students who worked at the study tables. The GA researched other options and we decided that the title peer-learning facilitator, used by University of California, Los Angeles, best fit the job description and did not carry the negative connotation that the title tutor does.

In the anonymous training survey, we also asked whether PLFs would consider a follow-up training session in which we discussed questions that came up in the first few weeks of work to be helpful to new hires. Most of the respondents indicated that such a follow-up training session would not be helpful, and when asked for suggestions to improve the training session, approximately half of the respondents indicated that they would not make any changes to the format. Based on this information, we did not add a follow-up training session to answer questions the following year, but we did discuss ways to make other improvements based on PLF suggestions.

For example, one PLF wrote in response to the anonymous training survey, "I wish we physically walked through exactly what to do when you get to the library to tutor for the first time (go to the front desk, get the sign, sit at an empty table, etc.)." Because of this response, we now request that all new hires stay after the training session for a brief walking tour in order to better acclimate new PLFs to the position. In addition, one survey respondent suggested learning more discipline-specific training approaches. We have been brainstorming the ways that we can encourage more collaboration between PLFs and faculty members, and one way that we are doing this is by implementing departmental liaisons who can serve as the point of contact for PLFs. We have also discussed the possibility of PLFs shadowing study tables run by PLFs in similar subject areas as a way to learn new techniques and share ideas. Although there are many potential changes for us to discuss, based on the PLF survey feedback we recently received, we are happy to know that PLFs consider our current material to be helpful and effective.

In the future, we plan to implement a new piece of assessment: we will compare the grades of students before and after participating in the Learning Commons study tables. We hope to find that when students use the Learning Commons they are able to maintain better grades in their classes. The student ID numbers that we collect on our sign-in form will be crucial to being able to gather this data.

REFLECTION

The Learning Commons has become an incredibly popular space for our students to work. As most of the Learning Commons is based on peer-to-peer interactions, this is a place students can go to receive support for their needs as a whole student. We include programming in the Learning Commons that can support students academically and co-curricularly. There are many ways for students to build leadership skills as well as learn to work better as a team.

Using PLFs to create an environment of academic support has been a learning process for those of us that maintain the Learning Commons. PLFs need to be given the right tools to effectively offer assistance to those students who are joining their study tables. Even PLFs who otherwise excel in their subject areas may need additional coaching to learn how to interact with students who have different learning styles.

In our Learning Commons, the best way to train the PLFs has been to include input from other departments on campus who have more specialized knowledge. The Writing Center has been training their consultants for a much longer time, and they can add their experience to our training. The Counseling Department brings new skills to the training that can improve the study table experience and communication for both the PLF as well as the students who come to study.

As we work to continuously expand our Learning Commons support, we look to add additional study tables from new subject areas. This might include some subjects that currently only offer peer-learning within their department instead of in the library. There are specific classes that may need dedicated study tables as well, and we may consider adding test-prep study tables specific to the GRE, LSAT, MCAT, and GMAT. In addition, we plan to look into the possibility of adding review sessions for midterms and finals that are more aggressively promoted by professors and that would hopefully be better attended. A few years ago, we began offering one-on-one study time in response to feedback; the PLFs can now schedule sessions directly with students in need of additional assistance for up to four hours a week in addition to their usual study tables. As a way to ensure that all PLFs are capable of collaborating with a diverse group of students who have different needs and backgrounds, we work with the Center for Student Diversity and Inclusion on campus to run separate sensitivity training sessions for PLFs in the Learning Commons.

Updating our study table offerings is part of the future of the Learning Commons programming, but we are also hopeful that we will expand the space of the Learning Commons. As mentioned earlier, the Learning Commons is situated in the lower level of our library but currently occupies only half the floor. The library director is in talks to expand the Learning Commons to fully utilize the space of the entire floor. If we are able to undertake this expansion, we could house a few additional student services in the space; for example, Services for Students with Disabilities, Career Services, and possibly Academic Advising. Plans for this change would prioritize student needs and multi-purpose space in order to ensure that the Learning Commons does not fill up with offices and take away collaborative learning spaces. Regardless of whether or not this expansion takes place in the future, we are pleased to have established a Learning Commons in the library, and its popularity with students on campus is evidence enough that there is a demand for such programming on many campuses.

NOTES

1. Maria Soriano, "Learning Commons Tutor Training," Prezi, last modified September 30, 2013, https://prezi.com/6zz3sqlhclyq/learning-commons-tutor-training/.
2. Soriano, "Learning Commons Tutor Training."
3. Nathan Gehlert and Christine Banks-VanAllen, "Tutoring Through Motivation," (presented at John Carroll University, 2015).
4. Gehlert and Banks-VanAllen, "Tutoring Through Motivation."
5. Ibid.
6. Ibid.
7. Ibid.
8. Ibid.
9. Ibid.
10. Ibid.

BIBLIOGRAPHY

Gehlert, Nathan, and Christine Banks-VanAllen. "Tutoring Through Motivation." Presentation, John Carroll University, 2015.

Soriano, Maria. "Learning Commons Tutor Training." Prezi. Last modified September 30, 2013. https://prezi.com/6zz3sqlhclyq/learning-commons-tutor-training/.

Case Study 10

PARALLEL PILOTS AT LEWIS & CLARK COLLEGE:

Augmenting Training vs. Developing an Accredited Practicum

Dan Kelley

OVERVIEW

The Aubrey R. Watzek Library is located at the heart of the undergraduate campus of Lewis & Clark College, a private liberal arts college in Portland, Oregon. Watzek Library serves both the College of Arts and Sciences (2,000 students, est.) and the Graduate School of Education and Counseling (750 students, est.). The building is open and staffed twenty-four hours a day, Sunday to Thursday. The reference desk is staffed by professional librarians 11:00 a.m. to 5:00 p.m., Monday to Friday. The research services department has reduced reference desk hours in recent years due to a decrease in the numbers of questions and an increase in the number of students making appointments with librarians for research consultations. Still, there are many hours when the library is open but the reference desk is closed. When the reference desk is closed, circulation student workers and staff answer and/or refer all questions; therefore, additional training has been needed at our library in order to provide patrons with quality service, even when librarians are not available. Over the years, we have addressed this in different ways.

In 2010–11, the research services department hired two students to work at the reference desk weekday mornings. Recruiting for these positions was difficult because we could only interview applicants who were: 1) recipients of federal work-study funding; 2) interested in a job in the library; and 3) available during morning hours. In the end, we did not feel that this initiative was very successful. We found that the students' skills and knowledge did not meet our expectations and after a single academic year we abandoned the effort.

> I can say with confidence that this practicum gave me valuable research skills. We did a few exercises that challenged us to find specific items in the catalog and from that alone, I learned how to use library resources that I didn't know existed. Helping others with their research forced me to improve on my own skills, and I used those skills throughout the semester while I wrote my thesis.... This practicum has also opened my eyes to other fields that a history education can lead to, such as archives and library sciences.
>
> *Sara Mills, Research Assistant, Lewis & Clark College*

In spring 2013, research services implemented a program to train circulation student workers to better handle questions. Each student would receive thirty minutes of training while shadowing a librarian at the reference desk. This program had potential, but we succeeded in training fewer than half of the twenty-four circulation student workers. Librarians and student workers alike were overwhelmed that semester because the library was migrating to a new Integrated Library System (Alma). So, we chalked it up to bad timing and resolved to try it again in the future.

In 2015, we renewed efforts to create training opportunities for circulation student workers (to be called "circulation consultants") to mitigate the problem caused by our empty reference desk and we planned to implement it in the fall semester. An additional idea was envisioned, inspired by a credit-bearing practicum between our special collections department and the English and history departments, where students worked behind the scenes in the library's archives: Why not create a similar practicum for our research services department in which students work at the reference desk as capable, competent research assistants?

History majors at Lewis & Clark College seemed best qualified for advanced library work because they are required to take a methods course, Historical Materials (HIST 300), in which they study the craft of historical and bibliographic research. In addition, the librarian liaison to the department had developed a very strong relationship with the faculty and consistently provided multiple library instruction sessions for the department. The librarian proposed the concept to the history faculty and they agreed that a practicum would be a valuable addition to the curriculum. Thus began the development of the circulation consultants and research assistant pilots.

The two pilots were administered simultaneously. The instruction services librarian worked with the supervisor of circulation student employees to manage the circulation consultant training. The history liaison collaborated with the history department to design and implement the research assistant pilot and acted as the "field supervisor." The following provides an overview and assessment of the respective pilots and their evolution over the next three years.

Circulation Consultant Pilot
Hiring
Research services does not participate in the hiring of circulation consultants. The supervisor in the access services department hires all students. Requirements for the positions include reliability, punctuality, and attention to detail. Students with experience providing customer service are desired, although some have no prior job experience. All student employees in the library receive federal work-study funding, and jobs in the library, particularly at the circulation desk, are some of the most popular on campus.

Training
The twenty-plus circulation consultants are library employees and have an existing spectrum of knowledge and responsibilities associated with their work at the circulation desk. We did not want to overburden them but to design attainable training and expectations; the primary goal was to teach them how and when to refer questions.

Circulation consultants already are required to attend two group training sessions to learn the essential duties for working at the circulation desk. The sessions are jammed with content, and we felt that adding more on reference work would be too much. We considered scheduling a third group session, but we couldn't find a common time to schedule one more session for a big group of busy students. We decided instead that the circulation consultants would do individual shadow shifts with librarians in order to ramp up their reference skillset.

We created the shadow training program as a collaborative project among all the research services librarians. Together we wrote learning outcomes, decided on the timing of the training, and eventually designed a wholly new, conversational style of student orientation. Each circulation consultant was invited to shadow a research librarian for thirty minutes during a regularly scheduled shift. Those not scheduled to work during reference desk hours and/or unable to complete a shadow shift during regularly scheduled hours were invited to make an appointment with a librarian for a thirty-minute consultation, which would be paid time.

Shadow shifts and consultations were scheduled to begin in the fourth week of classes. This gave new hires time to absorb their initial training and get comfortable with their circulation desk duties. We decided to do shadow shifts only when two students were present and the circulation desk was quiet enough to have one student leave for a bit. Only one librarian staffs the reference desk at a time, so shadow shifts occurred when the desk was quiet.

Curriculum and Learning Outcomes

The content of the shadow training for circulation consultants centered on five learning outcomes:

1. Librarians and circulation consultants will get to know one another in order to streamline the referral process.
2. Circulation consultants will learn to conduct reference interviews in order to best help patrons at the circulation desk.
3. Circulation consultants will learn to recognize when questions need to be referred to librarians in order to make sure library patrons are receiving the highest possible service.
4. Circulation consultants will become familiar with the liaison program in order to provide recommendations and also to highlight the research consultation service.
5. Circulation consultants will become familiar with the main library search tool in order to help patrons locate items.

Talking points evolved out of these outcomes and are on our training outline.* We wanted conversations that took place during the shadow shifts to flow, and the only essential outcome was the first one—getting to know one another. Librarians attempted to get a sense of how much experience the student had with the library and to tailor the rest of the conversation accordingly. We anticipated that students would use what they learned to provide better service at the circulation desk. But the conversations we had with students made us more aware that students needed to have confidence in their own library research abilities in order to help other students. For some students, this shadow training was the first time they had formal instruction about how to use the library. One librarian met with an international transfer student who was incredibly bright but altogether new to academic libraries in the United States. The student commented at the end of her shadow training that it had provided "clarity on what we do at the reference desk" and that she felt better prepared to use the library for her own research as a result. Our hope is that she was also able to demonstrate this new knowledge with students she worked with at the circulation desk.

---

* A copy of the training outline is available at http://bit.ly/1P5UFA5.

For the pilot, twenty-three students were hired to work the circulation desk. We created two spreadsheets[†] to help us schedule students for training. One sheet contained the names of all the circulation students and mapped their work schedules to the reference desk schedule. Four students were scheduled only when the reference desk was closed. They were invited to schedule consultations, and all four did. We felt that these students were especially important to train since they provide help at the circulation desk only when librarians are not readily available. The second sheet allowed librarians to track when they had completed a shadow shift. We were able to track the number of shadow shifts completed by various librarians and the dates when the shadow shifts took place.

Assessment

The purpose of assessing this pilot was to determine if the shadow training was a worthwhile and feasible use of time from the perspective of the consultants. We also wanted to know if or how they had applied what they learned in their work helping other students at the circulation desk. Additionally we wanted to know, from the librarians' perspective, whether the training seemed effective and manageable.

Methods for assessing the circulation consultant pilot were as follows:

1. Circulation consultants were invited to complete an anonymous survey about their experience with the training.
2. Librarians were invited to complete an anonymous survey about their experience with the training.
3. The coordinator discussed the training with the supervisor of the student workers.
4. The coordinator discussed the training with participating librarians.
5. The coordinator tracked training-related statistics.

Reflection

Of the twenty-three circulation consultants, twenty-two participated in reference training, either by shadowing at the desk or by scheduling a consultation. One student was unavailable for training despite being offered many options. Our success in reaching all but one student indicates that the training was attainable for busy circulation consultants, with varying schedules and competing job responsibilities. Their supervisor agreed that the training was both manageable and helpful.

In the survey, circulation consultants were asked to rate the value of the training across the five learning outcomes. The outcomes most frequently identified as valuable were getting to know a librarian and learning how to direct students to resources for particular academic programs (i.e., the liaison program). For students who did not already know about the liaison program and the corresponding research guides for majors and academic

---

† Copies of the spreadsheets are available at http://bit.ly/1ZaRls7.

programs, this part of the training provided an "aha!" moment. As one student put it, "I was able to learn to help others, but also I was able to learn about resources for my own major." In addition, the students' desire to learn belied our concern that the training would overload them. In fact, the most frequent suggestion for improving the training was to make it more in-depth.

> One of my favorite aspects of this class was analyzing the physical space of libraries. Our tours to Reed and University of Portland caused me to think a lot about how the space impacts how you use it. I had already thought about the difference between resources being online or offsite, but even compact shelving versus stacks in a dimly fluorescent–lit attic space versus in an aesthetically pleasing room changes how you interact with the materials.
>
> *Lindsay Mulcahy, Research Assistant, Lewis & Clark College*

Another survey question asked students to describe a time they used the shadow training to help someone at the circulation desk. Responses were thin; some students never perceived an opportunity to use the knowledge they learned in the training. The most affirming response had to do with the research guides: "When someone wanted to know where they could find academic search engines for their majors I [could show] them."

Circulation consultants do not currently track questions they answer, so we have no data on how many questions were answered involving the knowledge acquired in the training. Nor do we know for sure how effectively they applied what they learned. One student described, "I attempted one time with a patron that was looking to find more information on horse-shoeing; however, I had to give up because soon I realized that we both didn't know what we were doing." This, of course, would have been the perfect time to refer the question to a librarian, but it is unclear from the consultant's description if the question was referred or not.

Seven out of eight research librarians provided shadow training, either at the reference desk or by appointment; most librarians performed between two and four shadow training sessions. Librarians did not seem to be overburdened. Survey responses indicated that between two and four shadow training sessions seemed reasonable; those that did more still described the workload as acceptable. Librarians also felt that it was possible to do effective training in thirty minutes, though some notably skipped outcomes in order to stay within the timeline.

Librarians were asked in the survey to rank the five learning outcomes as either essential, supplemental, or more than necessary.

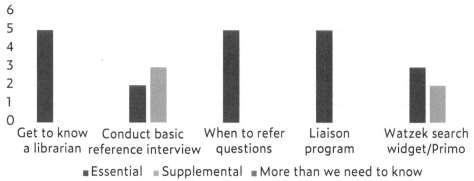

The shadow trainings centered on 5 learning outcomes, paraphrased below. Please indicate how you value each one.

■ Essential ■ Supplemental ■ More than we need to know

Librarians ranked circulation consultant training outcomes

The outcomes related to getting to know the librarian, referring questions, and the liaison program were ranked as essential. Like the students, librarians recognized the limited benefits of the training, like one who said, "I think it's a good idea, but it feels a little like a one-shot instruction session. To really connect with the circ students requires more. It's a start, and a good one, though."

Although limited in scope, the reference shadow training of circulation consultants helped enhance the knowledge base of our front-line student workforce, particularly in relation to the fourth outcome (becoming familiar with the liaison program). It also helped librarians and students develop face/name recognition and rapport. We could have done a better job evaluating the effectiveness of the program. Student response to the survey, for example, was insufficient. It would have been better not to conduct the survey during final exams. Enthusiasm for the circulation consultant program merited its continuation, with some important revisions.

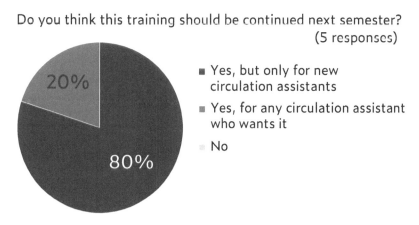

Do you think this training should be continued next semester?
(5 responses)

■ Yes, but only for new circulation assistants

■ Yes, for any circulation assistant who wants it

■ No

Librarians recommend continuing the circulation consultant training

The following spring, there were only six new student hires at the circulation desk. We assumed we would provide training to new students but also considered offering a second training to interested students to build upon the first training. Unfortunately, none of them took us up on the offer for additional training which may have indicated a lack of interest and engagement. A librarian suggested the addition of assignments to be done by the circulation consultants before or after the training sessions to help them practice. This would have an additional benefit of providing assessment data. It also could increase their contact with librarians if they were encouraged to ask for help if they needed assistance with the assignment.

Another suggestion from the librarian survey was to implement secret shopping, in which we track responses to a few pre-arranged reference inquiries at the circulation desk after students have received shadow reference training. This was implemented in 2017, and allowed us to gauge how circulation consultants put their training into practice and enriched our assessment data.

Librarian and student input both demonstrated that the outcome related to conducting reference interviews was too complex for such a short training. The intent of this outcome was to remind students to ask simple questions like "What class is this for?" or "What is your major?" in order to help them steer users to relevant library resources, such as subject guides. Teaching how to conduct high-quality reference interviews proved untenable and was removed from the learning objectives of the training.

In passing, a senior who had the shadow training commented, "Every E&D class should get this sort of info and how to use search engines, even Google Scholar." E&D refers to a required core course for first-year students in which many—but not all—of the sections receive formal library instruction to prepare them to write a research paper. This comment points to a couple of things: first, that not all students receive library instruction/orientations in the first year; and second, that the shadow training can help fill the gap for students who work at the circulation desk and have not received library training through other venues.

Circulation student workers serve a pivotal role in the library, interfacing with students and faculty. Our goal in training them as consultants was to enable them to provide a higher level of service to library users, especially when librarians are not available. Showing them how and when to refer questions and find subject guides and liaison librarians remains our highest priority. Other skills—like expertly searching the discovery interface, knowing the databases, and conducting reference interviews—are good for them to learn but required significantly more time than we had allotted.

Research Assistants Pilot

Hiring

Unlike the circulation student workers, the research assistants are not employees of the library; they are enrolled in the practicum course, HIST 244. The history librarian reviewed transcripts and faculty recommendations and then interviewed the students, identifying those who demonstrated intellectual breadth, interpersonal communication skills, and a strong service orientation. Curiosity about academic libraries and a desire to help other students were also highly valued. In 2016, 2017, and 2018 the practicum consistently had more applicants than spaces, and students had to be turned away.

Training

We had much more leeway in planning the training for our two research assistants, which occurred during a semester-long practicum, HIST 244. The practicum was designed to challenge them intellectually, and we also wanted them to be competent answering advanced questions that required deeper understanding of the research process. Like the circulation consultants, the research assistants needed to be able to recognize when to refer questions to others, but we hoped they would be able to answer questions beyond the scope of what we would expect our circulation consultants to do. Conducting successful reference interviews and knowing when to refer questions is a surprisingly nuanced process. We were initially mindful of this and wary of creating confusion for anyone in the library about the degree of help users could expect from the various people working behind our two (then separate) service desks.

Comparing our two consultant pilots:

	Circulation Consultants	Research Consultants
Student library employees	X	
History majors in a practicum, HIST 244 Library Reference		X
Reference shadow training	X	X
Semester–long curriculum around reference practice and librarianship		X
Trained to provide basic reference help at the circulation desk	X	
Trained to provide advanced reference help at the reference desk		X

The prerequisite for the practicum is HIST 300, which provides foundational training. This methodology course is required of all history majors and offered every semester by tenured history faculty. The learning outcomes state that by the end of the course, students should be able to demonstrate

1. knowledge about the goals and methods of the discipline of history;
2. research skills in a variety of historical materials, including electronic databases,
3. bibliographies, government documents, maps, newspapers, manuscripts, oral interviews, photographs, art and architecture, and documentary film;

4. the ability to edit and annotate a primary document and to place it in historical context;

5. skill in written communication; and

6. skill in making oral presentations.

To achieve these outcomes, HIST 300 has two components vital to our training program. The first is a project in which students annotate a checklist of sources on Zotero, such as bibliographies, indexes, gazetteers, archival guides, research databases, and subject encyclopedias and dictionaries.* Annotations are required to evaluate and suggest possible uses for the source and indicate its strengths and weaknesses, including its scope and any particularities. In short, students are required to describe and think critically about many of the tools that academic librarians use.

The second component of the class is an editing project. Each student selects a primary historical source and prepares a rigorously annotated edition of it. After selecting a source, students are required to

1. write an introduction placing the selection in its historical context;

2. write a statement of editorial methodology, explaining what decisions they made about spelling, grammar, missing words, headings or subheadings, or other insertions of their work into the document;

3. provide appropriate maps and illustrations and enumerate these in a list of figures;

4. prepare informational annotations in the form of side notes identifying obscure persons, events, and places, citing their sources for such information;

5. write an *analysis* of the source, interpreting its content and historical value and significance, taking into account relevant published historical scholarship on this topic; and

6. compile a bibliography of the sources used in editing the primary document.

It is important to recognize that these tasks (especially the third, fourth, fifth, and sixth) require the students to use the knowledge and skills they gained from working with the checklist during the annotation project. The editing project often lays the groundwork for the required senior thesis.

There are four mandatory texts for HIST 300. Two focus on methodology and one is a style guide, but the last contributes to the students' abilities as research assistants and improves their broader understanding of libraries. Jenny L. Presnell's excellent book, *The Information-Literate Historian: A Guide to Research for History Students*, introduces a variety of reference sources as well as library catalogs, subject indexes, maps, archives, images, and statistics. This book also provides some very useful case studies, which demonstrate how those tools can be used in scholarly research.

---

* The 2015 and 2020 HIST 300 syllabi are available at http://bit.ly/29ZKTjR and https://bit.ly/3ikBQNk. The HIST 300 checklist is available at https://www.zotero.org/groups/hist_300_lc/items. The spring 2018 syllabus for HIST 244 is available at https://goo.gl/yosgKa.

Research assistants in the stacks—Emma Hoch-Schneider and Hannah Swernoff

The first three weeks of the research assistant program were devoted to training. During New Student Orientation, the research assistants led library tours in order to learn the intricacies of the building. They shadowed two librarians at the reference desk to become familiar with the major tools of disciplines and the research librarians. The practicum supervisor met with them to review best practices for conducting reference interviews, developing exercises using chapters three and four from *Conducting the Reference Interview: A How-to-do-it Manual for Librarians*. The research assistants also practiced known-item searching with the discovery system and learned how to decipher cryptic holdings information. Research assistants needed to have a deep understanding of the library's subject guides and the discovery tool in order to be able to answer the most common reference questions, and the practicum supervisor relied on *The Oxford Guide to Library Research* to help explain complex search techniques. In the third week of the semester, the research assistants began staffing the reference desk in the evenings.

Curriculum and Learning Outcomes

We worked alongside our students and history faculty to write the learning outcomes for the research assistant practicum:

1. Practicum students will learn to interview patrons in order to apply research methods and sources based on need, circumstance, and type of inquiry.
2. Practicum students will participate in a variety of events and readings in order to evaluate how academic libraries contribute to scholarly conversation.

3. Practicum students will continue to improve and explore their own research abilities.

After the initial training, research assistants were required to attend an event, participate in a webinar or site visit, or read an article or book each week. The practicum supervisor sought out controversial topics, conducive to stimulating discussions, and convened with the consultants on Friday mornings to discuss over coffee. During the six semesters that HIST 244 was offered the readings evolved (the syllabus from the spring of 2018 can be viewed at https://goo.gl/yosgKa). However, curricular content over the course of the semester consistently included:

1. attendance at a library-sponsored lecture on campus;
2. participation in an ACRL webinar;
3. observation of a library instruction session;
4. reading of articles about contemporary contentious issues impacting libraries;
5. two field trips to local academic libraries; and
6. reading of texts concerning publishing, information, and/or libraries.

The research assistants attended a campus lecture, "Google Searching for Black Girls: Old Media Stereotypes in New Media Practices," by Dr. Safiya Noble, in which she discussed how search systems in the digital age reproduce racist and gendered stereotypes. This talk exposed students to the important role librarians can play in educating information seekers about the bias and commercialization of search. They also participated in a webinar entitled "Designing Collections for Collisions: Preserving Library Serendipity in a Digital World," which discussed serendipity in library stacks and how spontaneous research discoveries happen with physical collections.

The research assistants then attended a library instruction session for first-year students. The in-class activity required students to use the discovery tool and/or the two service desks to locate and obtain diverse items in the collection. The students then described what they found and how they found it to the class. The librarian chimed in with pointers and anecdotes about the collections, the discovery tool, the services, and the building. After the class, the librarian explained why he had structured the session the way he did and how he had collaborated with the professor. By observing a first-year class, the consultants learned how librarians teach and clearly saw the challenges first-year students face when using academic libraries.

The research assistants then took two field trips to academic libraries accompanied by the practicum supervisor. The first was the Clark Library at the University of Portland which was completely renovated in 2013. According to the wiki "Celsus: A Library Architecture Resource," the major renovation transformed a building previously focused on books and quiet study into a building dedicated to the "technology-driven collaborative learning style." The research assistants toured the building, noticing how students used the space.

Then they met with a librarian for a discussion about the renovation, the staffing of the service desks, and collection development.

The second field trip taken was to the Hauser Library at Reed College, a very different animal than the Clark Library. Brimming with books, the library at Reed made reading and contemplation a priority. We met with the director of the library and the deputy chief information officer and discussed IT-library collaboration, liaison roles, and the library building, comparing and contrasting Lewis & Clark College's approach with Reed College's. After the conversation, a Reed student library worker gave the research assistants a tour.

> Overall, this practicum has been eye-opening. Having spent so much of my time at Lewis & Clark in Watzek Library, I was excited to engage directly with the "behind the scenes" aspects.... Working the reference desk allowed me to utilize the skills I learned in Historical Materials directly while refining and improving my own research abilities. I have been able to apply these skills directly to my current history and biology courses and will continue to do so as I begin to tackle my senior history thesis and future biological research. Learning how libraries can be used, what information is available, and how to convey these resources to my fellow students, has made this practicum both academically and personally fulfilling.
>
> *Emma Hoch-Schneider, Research Assistant, Lewis & Clark College*

The research assistants read *Words Onscreen: The Fate of Reading in a Digital World* by Naomi Baron. Baron, a professor of linguistics, contrasts reading on a screen to reading on paper and introduced some academic literature on reading comprehension. The author considers the spectrum of "types" of reading and the role that reading plays in building critical-thinking skills. This reading yielded a Friday morning conversation about learning styles, liberal arts education, and collection development practices.

Assessment

The purpose of assessing the HIST 244 pilot was to ensure that the students were intellectually engaged and were well-prepared to provide advanced research assistance to others. Formative assessment happened during the semester, and summative assessment was conducted by both the librarian and the chair of the history department. The methods for assessing the research assistant pilot were as follows:

1. The practicum supervisor met with the research assistants every Friday morning and solicited feedback on all aspects of the program.
2. The research assistants wrote a two-page reflection about the practicum to the chair of the History Department and the librarian supervisor.
3. The practicum supervisor created a survey in which the research assistants ranked the initial training and the weekly experiences on how much they contributed to the learning outcomes for the practicum and how intellectually engaging they were.
4. The practicum supervisor obtained verbal feedback from research librarians and from the circulation supervisor about the job performance of the research assistants.
5. The practicum supervisor interviewed the research assistants about their experience with the practicum during the final meeting of the semester.

REFLECTION

As the proverb goes, "Self-praise is no recommendation." However, feedback from the research assistants and library staff suggests that this pilot surpassed expectations. Research assistants' statements were very positive; they described the experience as "wonderful," "fulfilling," and "eye-opening." We confirmed that HIST 300 provided a solid foundation for the assistants, but librarians felt that our training for known-item searching (specifically for articles) was inadequate. The research assistants also requested additional practice conducting reference interviews. The research assistants found the readings and field trips to be intellectually stimulating and helpful in meeting the learning outcomes. The Friday morning conversations were a venue for the exchange of bigger ideas and yielded informed, innovative ideas from the research assistants about library spaces, collections, policies, and instruction. The assistants reported that the desk was not busy (they only answered about sixty questions over the course of the semester) and that other students did not understand their role.

After the initial pilot, the research assistants, who were all strong readers, engaged with challenging texts including:

- Gleick, James. *The Information: A History, a Theory, a Flood*. 1st ed. New York: Pantheon Books, 2011.
- Joranson, Kate M, Steve I. VanTuyl, and Nina Clements. "E-Browsing: Serendipity and Questions of Access and Discovery" (2013). Proceedings of the Charleston Library Conference.
- Lewis, David. "Library as Place" in *Academic Librarianship Today*. Edited by Gilman, T. Lanham: Rowman & Littlefield, 2017.
- Petroski, Henry. *The Book on the Bookshelf*. New York: Alfred A. Knopf, 1999.
- Pyne, Lydia. *Bookshelf*. London: Bloomsbury Academic, 2016.
- Striphas, Theodore G. *The Late Age of Print: Everyday Book Culture from Consumerism to Control*. New York: Columbia University Press, 2009.

Research assistants—Lindsay Mulcahy, Sara Mills, Cade Brewer, and Melissa Dean-Treseler

These readings increased the intellectual rigor of the practicum and were well received by the students. Later changes to the practicum included increased involvement with library exhibits, collection development, and digital humanities. These changes provided the students with broader perspectives on the dynamic evolution of academic libraries. Over time, readings and projects will need to continue to evolve. The Friday conversations could be expanded to include interested faculty and staff, perhaps even from other local institutions.

One of the research assistants suggested having a long-term project during the course of the semester, perhaps in collection development, instruction, special collections, or the library website. The concept is appealing but could potentially overload the two-credit practicum. There is a four-credit history practicum we could employ if we decide to expand the scope of the program. Another option would be to create a second two-credit practicum that entailed a bigger project that would suit the requirements of both the student and the library.

Another opportunity would be to increase the coordination of our program with academic support units on campus. The Writing Center is one obvious option, but there may be other entities that would benefit from closer collaboration and would not dilute the strengths of the practicum. Connecting the research assistants more closely to the required first-year core class (which has a significant research component), the methods course (HIST 300), and the History Thesis (HIST 450) are also worthy of consideration.

Assessment of the program should be improved. Although we gathered feedback from the research assistants, we did not examine patron satisfaction or the accuracy of the assistance they received. Weekly systematic review and group discussion of authentic and challenging research questions proved to be very worthwhile in 2017 and 2018.

Expanding the size of the practicum was an obvious option and allowed us to provide more coverage on the service desk. In the spring of 2015, we accepted four students for HIST 244 and increased the hours students were available on the desk. Adding the students did not create much of an additional training burden and had no impact on the library budget. By spring 2018, the practicum had grown to include six students.

We also wanted to extend the opportunity to participate in the practicum to students from other departments, especially those who had completed a rigorous methods courses that included a strong bibliographic element. We realized that including other departments would necessitate creating customized training programs to suit those students. In the spring of 2018, non-history majors joined the practicum for the first time. Because those students had not taken the history methodology class the librarian did have to spend additional time training them, but the discussions were greatly enriched by the participation and perspectives of the students who majored in sociology, biology, and psychology.

We need to be more proactive about promoting the work that our research assistants are doing. Library patrons should be aware of the increased hours of service at the desk and the option of asking experienced peers for assistance. There are clearly students who prefer asking other students for help rather than librarians. In future iterations, we hope to coordinate both of the programs more than we have in the past. One idea is to have the research assistants receive the circulation consultant training so that they have a sense of our expectations for what the circulation student workers should be able to do and then can understand their own role more clearly. This is nuanced work, and we are still defining the parameters for both our circulation consultants and our research assistants. Clarifying the overlap and differences between these two programs is an iterative process, and we do not expect to completely eliminate the gray areas. Although the merging of the circulation and reference desks into a single service point in 2017 ostensibly created more opportunities for cross-training, it also made it more difficult for patrons to differentiate between the skills of the people who are offering assistance.

CONCLUSION

In the circulation consultant pilot, we prepared front-line circulation consultants to direct library users to information sources and services when librarians were not available. With the research assistant pilot, we developed a two-credit practicum, HIST 244, to help advanced undergraduates develop higher-level skills, providing research assistance to their peers while earning college credit and learning how academic libraries are evolving. Both programs helped us in our goal to provide better research help to students when librarians are not available. Both programs provided opportunities for students to serve as mentors for other students as they learn to do library work. Based on our assessments, the practicum provided better training to staff the service desks, aligned more closely with the culture of the institution, and produced a more engaging and intellectually rigorous experience for the student participants. The concept of a "practicum" also appeals to students who value opportunities that might stand out on a resume or job application. Five of the students who enrolled in the practicum have continued on with graduate work in information science.

> Obviously, this practicum aided research for various academic works I had this semester, and it also helped me to understand and appreciate various kinds of sources and their usefulness at different stages of research. However, in a more reflective manner, evaluating Watzek in comparison with other nearby academic libraries provided me with a new perspective through which I could reflect on how Watzek is used by students, and evaluating it within the context of more abstract library theory allowed me to consider how it could be or should be used. As a history minor (and a nerd in general), I am a huge proponent of physical books and libraries, and I believe they do and should hold a pivotal role in scholarship. That said, I do agree with some of the arguments for moving in a more digital avenue: allowing for increased space to permit continued collection growth, the ability to search an entire document for a keyword, and the altruistic hope of democratizing information. In short, it's complicated.
>
> *Melissa Dean-Treseler, Research Assistant, Lewis & Clark College*

We hope to foster in both our circulation consultants and our research assistants an appreciation for the subtleties involved in helping other students navigate the research process in academic libraries. Understanding the complex nature of the work will make both groups more effective ambassadors of the library and ultimately help our patrons.

Acknowledgements

The author would like to acknowledge the contributions that his former colleague Kate Rubick made to this chapter. He would also like to extend his appreciation to his library colleagues at Reed College and the University of Portland for supporting the practicum. Lastly, he offers heartfelt thanks to the faculty and students in the history department at Lewis & Clark College. It was a pleasure working with you and learning together.

BIBLIOGRAPHY

Bell, Steven J. "Designing Collections for Collisions." Association for Library Collections and Technical Services. Accessed August 10, 2020. http://www.ala.org/alcts/confevents/upcoming/webinar/091615.

Gleick, James. *The Information: A History, a Theory, a Flood*. 1st ed. New York: Pantheon Books, 2011.

Joranson, Kate M, Steve I. VanTuyl, and Nina Clements. "E-Browsing: Serendipity and Questions of Access and Discovery" (2013). Proceedings of the Charleston Library Conference. Accessed August 10, 2020. http://d-scholarship.pitt.edu/20367/.

Lewis, David. "Library as Place." In *Academic Librarianship Today*. Edited by Gilman, T. Lanham, MD: Rowman & Littlefield, 2017.

Mann, Thomas. *The Oxford Guide to Library Research*. 4th ed. New York: Oxford University Press, 2015.

Noble, Safiya Umoja. *Algorithms of Oppression: Race, Gender and Power in the Digital Age*. New York: New York University Press, 2018.

Petroski, Henry. *The Book on the Bookshelf*. New York: Alfred A. Knopf, 1999.

Pyne, Lydia. *Bookshelf*. London: Bloomsbury Academic, 2016.

Presnell, Jenny L. *The Information-Literate Historian: A Guide to Research for History Students*. 2nd edition. New York: Oxford University Press, 2013.

Ross, Catherine Sheldrick, Kirsti Nilsen, and Patricia Dewdney. *Conducting the Reference Interview: A How-to-do-it Manual for Librarians*. New York: Neal-Schuman Publishers, 2002.

Striphas, Theodore G. *The Late Age of Print: Everyday Book Culture from Consumerism to Control*. New York: Columbia University Press, 2009.

University of Wisconsin—Milwaukee, School of Information Studies. "University of Portland-Clark Library, Portland, Oregon (renovation)." https://libraryarchitecture.wikispaces.com/University+of+Portland-Clark+Library,+Portland,+Oregon+%28renovation%29 (site discontinued).

WRITING CONSULTANTS AT THE UNIVERSITY OF DAYTON:

A Collaborative Cross-Training Approach

Heidi Gauder

OVERVIEW

The creation of a new learning commons at the University of Dayton Roesch Library not only highlighted the research and writing support available to students, but it also led to an entirely new library-led cross-training program for writing center student employees. Prior to the new learning commons, the writing center occupied spaces on the upper floors of the library, and the staff of the two units enjoyed a friendly, albeit distant, relationship for many years. The new learning commons, named the Knowledge Hub, brought the library research team directly together with the writing center, both in terms of proximity and workflows. Library and writing center student employees work together at a shared service desk, while research librarians and student writing consultants share the same consulting workspace. With a mandate to provide integrated services, the library and the writing center developed a shared mission and have been working to articulate a common culture as well as developing a multi-faceted training approach. This chapter describes the development of Knowledge Hub training, with a focus on staffing, service philosophy, cross-training approaches with the writing center, and assessment efforts to date.

History

The impetus to create a learning commons came from multiple factors. LibQUAL+ surveys revealed a growing demand for study space, while the library and writing center both desired increased visibility for the research and writing services. The reference desk was already located on the first floor in what was to become the Knowledge Hub. The writing center, on the other hand, was located on a different library floor; to access the writing center, users had to walk past rows of bound journals which obscured visibility and made it difficult for students to find. The writing center itself occupied an open library space and shared an understanding with the library that the space and furniture were available for anyone to use when the writing center was not open, as study tables are at a premium throughout the library. However, library floor counts indicated that very few people occupied that fairly sizable space other than during the writing center hours. Thus, the library saw benefits in sharing a more visible space with the writing center, which would free up additional study space once the writing center relocated.

It also helped that the library and writing center already had an existing relationship. In addition to being neighbors, librarians had participated in writing center training sessions and both of the unit coordinators sat on the English Department composition committee. The librarians and student writing consultants share responsibility for teaching academic integrity across campus, and there is a general appreciation of each other's role in providing academic support. Because the research and writing processes are often interconnected, these two units seemed like a natural fit. The Knowledge Hub opened in September 2014.

The Knowledge Hub space includes workstations, printers, tables and chairs for group or individual study, and more. Staffing for the Knowledge Hub is located at the main service desk and there is a nearby space for research and writing consultations. The consultations take place in an open area, which is available for anyone to use; there are no doors or walls enclosing the consultation area. The writing center works from a peer-support model, with both the writing consultants and service desk employees either undergraduate or graduate students. The library utilizes paraprofessional staff and student employees at the service desk, while librarians primarily conduct the research consultations.

Philosophy

As the Knowledge Hub became a reality, the stakeholders wrote a mission statement for the new space and services to help guide how we would work together. The library and writing center both came to this process with a strong focus on customer service and academic support, and our existing relationship made the creation of the mission statement a relatively easy process. This mission statement has become the basis for our training efforts, our communications, and our work focus:

> The Knowledge Hub staff seek to provide writing and research support for members of UD's community in a comfortable, collaborative environment where learning can flourish. Staffed by Roesch Library research librarians and Write Place student writing consultants, the Knowledge Hub will help to empower individuals by offering easy access to the resources they need to succeed.

This mission statement and our library-writing center collaboration philosophy were informed by the work of others. James Elmborg, University of Iowa, argues for greater connections between the research and writing domains,[1] as does Janelle Zauha, Montana State University, who notes, "When research and writing services are located near each other but are kept entirely separate, however, the signal is also given that both librarians and tutors feel these processes can and should be carried on in separate spaces, that it is as normal for students to move smoothly from the task of research and on to writing as if stepping between two rooms of the house, closing doors as they go."[2] Elise Ferer's literature review of library and writing center collaborations also helped us understand how other libraries approached these efforts and what we might consider for our local situation.[3] Elmborg and Hook's edited volume included a theoretical basis for such collaborations as well as case studies about libraries and writing centers working together.[4]

This work helped shape and supported our conception of what an integrated space might be. Practically speaking, we realized early on in the planning that our users would expect service desk assistance from Knowledge Hub employees, regardless of the reporting structure. The mission statement, with an emphasis on customer service, and the work of others writing about library-writing center collaborations helped us develop the cross-training program for writing center student employees.

Hours/Location

The Knowledge Hub takes up considerable space on the first floor of the library. A large service desk welcomes users to the area, which includes twenty computer workstations, two printers, a smaller reference collection, and three wall-mounted monitors for group work. The remaining space has study tables, large and small, for individual and group work. Some of the tables are reserved for writing and research consultations when the services open.

The writing and research consulting services are available Sunday through Friday in the Knowledge Hub. These hours are coordinated so that research and writing opportunities—and cross-referrals—are available mostly at the same time. The Knowledge Hub service desk opens at 8:00 a.m. Monday through Thursday and closes at 10:00 p.m. on those days. It is staffed Friday through Sunday as well. The service desk hours are longer since we also provide technical support for the Knowledge Hub computer workstations and printers. During the summer, only the writing center has a presence in the Knowledge Hub; drop-in research questions are fielded at the Knowledge Hub service desk and redirected to librarian offices.

ADMINISTRATION

The Knowledge Hub comprises two units: the University Libraries research team and the Ryan C. Harris Learning Teaching Center (LTC) Write Place. The research team is led by the director of education and information delivery and includes librarians, paraprofessional staff members, and student employees. The research team reporting lines are listed below:

- Director of education and information delivery
  - reference and instruction librarians (2)
  - life and health sciences librarian
  - communications and outreach librarian
  - coordinator of research and instruction
    - reference assistant (part-time)
    - reference assistant
      - student employees (10)

The paraprofessionals and student employees staff the Knowledge Hub service desk and the librarians staff drop-in research consultation shifts in the Knowledge Hub space. The University Libraries are managed by the dean of libraries.

The Write Place (writing center) is managed by a full-time coordinator, who supervises a student staff of approximately forty. This group includes six Knowledge Hub service desk student employees and about thirty-four writing consultants. The service desk employees manage the intake process for writing consultations, who work primarily with drop-in clients. The Write Place reports through an associate provost.

There is no Knowledge Hub manager but rather a Knowledge Hub administrative team, which includes two librarians and two staffers from the LTC. This team meets regularly to address issues of shared concern, including training, hours of operation, communication, and outreach. These meetings are vital since the operation is managed by units that have different reporting lines, budgets, and work cultures.

TRAINING

Because the Knowledge Hub area includes a shared service desk and a consultation area, training is multi-faceted. Some training components focus on camaraderie and job understanding among the different employee categories, while others address customer service and task acquisition, and yet another looks closely at the integration between writing and research. Most of this cross-training is organized by the coordinator of research and instruction and the Write Place coordinator.

The training process focuses primarily on library and writing center student employees, although there is some cross-training for the library staff. Student employee training is differentiated by job function, yet we also conduct training so that both the library and writing center staffs have an understanding of the job functions that support the Knowledge Hub services. Much of the training occurs at the start of the school year, with supplemental sessions and meeting opportunities throughout the year.

The training process outline:

- All-staff Knowledge Hub orientation: overview of Knowledge Hub services and mission; opportunity to meet new and returning staff
- Training for Knowledge Hub service desk: library paraprofessionals, library student employees, and writing center service desk student employees
  - Group meeting to review basics
  - One-on-one training
- Writing consultant training
  - Group meeting for writing consultants and librarians to discuss the role of librarians and research in the writing process
  - Follow-up meeting to continue discussion
- Social opportunities as they arise

The training program is vital in meeting the Knowledge Hub's mission of a collaborative work environment for academic support. The training prepares the student employee staff of both the library and writing center to provide effective service, despite the differences in our work tasks and despite the fact that one service is provided primarily by full-time employees and the other service is facilitated mostly by undergraduate students who attend school full-time.

Team Building: All-Staff Training

Given the large number of library and writing center staff who provide Knowledge Hub services, both units place importance on getting to know each other as well as understanding and valuing the various roles within the Knowledge Hub space. The Knowledge Hub administrators have created opportunities throughout the year to foster socialization.

Orientation

One of the most important training events occurs at the start of the school year when the library and the writing center hold a joint mandatory orientation. It is one of the few times that all staff can come together, and includes full-time reference librarians, full-time writing center administrators, library reference student employees, and writing center student employees. In fact, the library makes attendance at this meeting a condition for library student employment. During the orientation, we deliberately seat different employee types together so that the two staffs have an opportunity to meet. Orientation includes snacks and simple ice-breaker questions and then moves quickly to a focus on the shared service aspect of Knowledge Hub. We ask small groups to respond to prompts about the Knowledge Hub mission, addressing the following questions in particular: "What actions can you take individually and collectively to contribute to the mission? What new opportunities do you envision for the space and our work?" We then come back together to discuss and share as a group. The goal for this question is to encourage students to situate their own work within a larger Knowledge Hub context and to begin making connections among the services offered in this common space.

We host another all-staff meeting in January, right after the start of classes. This orientation continues the goal of developing an understanding of the Knowledge Hub as a shared service point and how each employee can contribute. This session asks everyone to consider Knowledge Hub goals for the coming year, again using small groups with mixed staff to develop the goals and then coming together to finalize the results.

Staff Directory

In addition to the all-staff orientation, the library and the writing center produce a staff picture directory to help learn and remember names beyond the one-time event. We request everyone to submit a staff photo and fill out a brief form that asks staff to share interesting facts about themselves. The photo directory is a fun, easy way to engage staff. The staff directory is a print resource but will move to a secure online space for even easier staff access.

Other Social Opportunities

The Knowledge Hub administrative team uses holidays to recognize our student employees and promote staff interactions. We celebrate Halloween with candy packets for all student employees and recognize Christmas with a "Deck the Hub" party for the student employees and adult staff. For the Christmas party, we set up craft stations and use construction paper and discarded books to make simple ornaments and decorations for the space. An invitation to wear an ugly Christmas sweater, along with cookies and hot chocolate, sets the stage for staff and student employees to meet one final time before the end of the semester. We also celebrate Valentine's Day with candy for all the Knowledge Hub student employees and wish them well on their spring semester final exams with encouraging words and snacks.

Customer Service and Desk Skills: Service Desk Employee Training

Successful service desk training forms the basis for a successful Knowledge Hub experience. This section describes the need for service desk training, a training timeline, shared documents, summer term training, and cross-training for writing center tasks.

The Knowledge Hub is anchored by a large service desk, which is staffed by student employees from the library and the writing center as well as the research team's paraprofessional staff. It is here, in particular, where the library and writing center staffs must be able to perform certain tasks regardless of reporting lines, as our shared service philosophy focuses on providing effective and efficient customer service. Thus, library student employees must be knowledgeable about the writing center intake process, and the writing center student service desk employees must be familiar with basic library technology issues and library services.

For these student employees, we conduct a fairly structured training program at the start of each semester. Both the library and the writing center hire new student employees after each semester, as students graduate or move on to other opportunities. The beginning of each new semester provides a small window of time when we can do group training for new student employees and remind returning students about work details they might have forgotten as well as any recent changes in procedures and technology. Student employees are given an outline of customer service expectations that set the tone for providing Knowledge Hub help, rather than simply the rules or best practices for only the writing center or the library.

Appendix A contains the introduction and one part of our customer service standards document. Although the library created the document, it has the support of the writing center administration. In addition to describing the Knowledge Hub service philosophy and standards for behavior, we also share an outline of tasks students should be able to accomplish, absent a library staffer. We then work with student employees and review these basic tasks, including answering the phone and proper greeting, troubleshooting basic technology issues, using service desk software accurately, and how to check in research consultations.

During the fall and spring semesters, we do not provide reference-related training for the writing center student employees, as we have librarians and paraprofessionals readily available to provide that support. The writing consultations occur in the same open area where the research consultations take place, so a referral can be easily facilitated as the need arises. Since the Knowledge Hub service desk is double-staffed with library and writing center staff, the library research team members can easily handle ready reference questions or check in students for research consultations.

The Knowledge Hub service desk includes two workstations, one for a library employee and one for a writing center employee. During the academic year, the desk is double-staffed, so remedial training occurs on the job in collaboration with the writing center coordinator. We also maintain a shared Knowledge Hub binder that includes many training materials and basic instructions. These efforts are further enhanced by an email distribution list and a shared Google Docs folder for writing center-related items.

Shared Knowledge Hub binder contents:

- customer service standards
- list of cross-training tasks
- basic instructions for technology issues
- library and writing center phone numbers
- library and writing center staffing schedules
- data entry procedures for consultations
- writing center protocols

During the summer term, writing center student employee training is more extensive, as they staff the service desk alone for part of the day. These student employees are expected to answer ready reference queries in addition to directional and technical questions. Reference training focuses on enabling the writing center student employees to answer questions that begin, "Do you have this book/library resource…?" We also work to identify when questions should be referred to librarians, namely those that indicate a need to research a particular topic.

In the summertime, we monitor the reference work of the writing center student employees more closely to ensure that responses are accurate. We review queries recorded in the reference tracking software (we use LibInsight Lite), and the student employees also report "New to me" questions in a Google Form to which both library staff and the student employees have access. Between these two venues, librarians provide feedback, whether by email or in the form itself. Throughout the summer, we supplement an initial training session with a series of scenario-based questions using the university's learning management software. Please see Appendix B for sample questions. One question, for example, asks student employees to respond to a textbook inquiry. To answer this question successfully, student employees must understand library textbook policies, textbook editions, and access to our statewide library consortium catalog in addition to patron-initiated borrowing.

Training at the Knowledge Hub service desk is primarily focused on customer service, facilitating client check-ins for consulting services, fixing technical issues associated with our computer lab, and successfully directing users to various library services. Because we have both research and writing consultations, the writing center also cross-trains librarians and library student employees on their Knowledge Hub service desk processes.

Although similar to a research consultation check-in, their work is slightly more compli-cated due to multiple writing consultants and consultation volume.

Cross-training for writing center work is focused around the Knowledge Hub service desk tasks. Like research consultations, an initial client interview is conducted to determine the type of help needed and familiarity with a writing consultation, so that expectations can be set for meeting outcomes. During the cross-training, the library employees learn about the software used to record consultations, communication protocols between the Knowledge Hub service desk and the writing consultants, and the paperwork associated with appointments and waiting lists. The writing center operates primarily on a drop-in basis, so coordination between the Knowledge Hub service desk and writing consultants is essential when multiple clients are waiting for help.

As we work more closely together, we are looking at points where training is duplicated and we can share the efforts. The writing center, which reports through another unit, uses the university's learning management system to deliver training modules about general safety and Title IX issues. The library supervisor for the Knowledge Hub student employ-ees likewise uses the learning management system to develop online training modules for her employees.

Referral Skills: Writing Consultant Training

The writing consultant training is more nuanced. We have found that these student employees have often attended library instruction sessions and may have asked simple questions at a library service desk, but few have actually met with a librarian one-on-one to discuss research. The writing consultant training, then, works from the perspective of teaching writing consultants about the role of librarians in the context of the writing process, with the end goal of effective referral services.

Survey

When the Knowledge Hub first opened, we surveyed writing consultants to see what they knew about librarians and librarian training. The simple survey comprised three multiple-choice questions and asked the following: list the circumstances in which they had worked with a librarian; identify tasks associated with a librarian position; and select education requirements for librarians. The full survey is included with Appen-dix C. The survey allowed us to begin a conversation about the structure of libraries, namely that not everyone in a library is a librarian and that to be a librarian requires additional training and education beyond the undergraduate degree. Because many writing consultants have continued their employment for several years, we have not repeated the survey. Upon further reflection, this survey was discontinued, as we found that it had a chilling effect on meaningful conversation between librarians and writing center consultants.

Because the survey results indicated that few student writing consultants had direct experience working with librarians on research consultations, the training sessions for writing consultants now include librarian participants. We have also asked the writing consultants to discuss their own research needs with a research librarian so that they have first-hand knowledge of a research consultation. In the workplace, all student employees wear name badges and the librarians have individual nameplates when they staff the research consulting area. These activities, along with a new Knowledge Hub all-staff photo directory, help both sets of staff to recognize each other and to develop a deeper understanding of each other's work.

Second, training has also focused on helping student writing consultants recognize when a client could use additional research support. The writing consultants are taught to use a hierarchy of writing needs, including content, organization, mechanics, revision, and documentation, during a writing consultation. As the Knowledge Hub construction was coming to completion, the Knowledge Hub administration team identified the potential for referrals when student writers use outside sources to support their claims. Cross-training for the student writing consultants centers around helping this group recognize when support or evidence is weak or missing.

Authentic (or Nearly Authentic) Learning

The writing consultant training is facilitated with a writing sample that is evaluated for evidence of particular information literacy skill levels. We try to use authentic writing samples but cannot always do so. In situations when we are not able to use an authentic sample, we share a text written by a librarian with sources and evidence that are less than ideal. Appendix D is an example of a librarian-written text that we use for this exercise. The samples are short, five or six paragraphs, but long enough to construct an argument and brief enough to read quickly. Evaluation is conducted with an information literacy-specific rubric. We adapted one developed by librarians at the University of Houston[5] for this exercise, and we continue to use this rubric. For the training session, we pared down the rubric content because of time limitations.

The writing consultants and librarians work in pairs or small groups to read and evaluate the writing sample. Each group must work together to score the sample using the supplied rubric. The scores are reported out, which are recorded and shared on a classroom whiteboard. Sharing the results is important, as it allows the groups to provide a rationale for their scores, and it is the rationale that prompts real discussion about the sample quality. Following this discussion, the large group brainstorms ways the writing consultants can draw out more information about the client's research efforts.

This exercise involves writing consultants and librarians working together. In previous iterations, the librarians rated the sample independently of the writing consultants and scores were compared during the training session. Although this approach was useful in seeing how the two different groups scored the samples, it did not help build the rapport and understanding that is useful for the two groups. In working together, the librarians and the writing consultants also benefit from hearing the same message together. Any future training sessions with the writing consultants will likely involve librarians for these reasons.

This training exercise sought to provide some direction to the writing consultants as to when they might refer their clients to a research librarian. In particular, we wanted them to look closely at the external evidence their clients were using, to identify weak synthesis effort, and to realize that poorly constructed citations might be a hallmark for other research issues. We also wanted to call to their attention when sources were insufficient for assignment requirements.

We realized early on in the partnership that a second session would be beneficial for the writing consultants. They were managing multiple writing needs during their consultations and could benefit from a more direct approach, rather than a framework, about evaluating source quality in their clients' work. We timed a second presentation for the middle of the semester when we traditionally saw an uptick in research and writing visits. We again used writing samples for this training session, but instead of a rubric to guide evaluations, we asked the writing consultants to discuss the merits of the sources with a partner. We instructed them to pay attention to source quality and synthesis with respect to the research paper directions. As part of this discussion, we included a list of writing instances that might be an opening for a discussion about sources. These examples include keyword topic help at the pre-writing stage, a works-cited list with popular or undetermined sources instead of scholarly ones, irrelevant quotes that do not support a thesis, and poor documentation style. See Appendix E for conversation prompt examples.

Because the writing center's goal is to help students become better writers with the help and support from peers, the consultations are in-depth conversations filled with guiding questions. In that vein, this training session looked to provide them with some guided prompts that they could use with their clients.

Cross-training for writing consultants focuses not only on understanding our respective roles in this combined service area, but it also sought to provide writing consultants with tools that would help them look at a writer's source content more closely. Our hope is that once the writing consultants understand the one-on-one help we can provide, then they would be better able to recommend such help when they identify such needs for their clients.

ASSESSMENT

At this point, there is no formal assessment of student employee library-related work. Because the librarians and research paraprofessionals are actively working with the writing center's student employees, we can easily address issues, especially at the Knowledge

Hub service desk, on a case-by-case basis. The writing center student employees who staff the Knowledge Hub service desk in the summer are evaluated when they begin working by themselves at the service desk, as mentioned previously. We have started to develop a year-round training and evaluation program for the library student employees; as soon as that training is in place, we likely will work with the writing center coordinator to determine if program components would be useful for the writing center student employees.

Our collaboration with the writing consultants remains a work in progress, and developing an appropriate assessment process will likely take a while. When we opened the Knowledge Hub, we anticipated that we could measure, in part, the success of integration by a growing number of referrals. If we taught the writing consultants how to look for weak or poorly researched sources, the thinking went, then they could, in turn, bring a librarian into the conversation or refer their clients to us. However, there are multiple aspects we are contending with in this combined service area, not the least of which is that we are still hard at work creating a Knowledge Hub culture where everyone recognizes their respective work unit's contributions to providing academic support as well as the contributions of the other unit.

There are other reasons why this measure is a difficult gauge for assessing Knowledge Hub success. Many students view writing as a linear rather than recursive process, and so for them, research needs happen at a different stage than when they seek out writing assistance. We also recognize that the staff members providing writing and research support are very different: the librarians are full-time employees with advanced degrees while the writing consultants are primarily undergraduates who work part-time and attend school full-time. The librarians are seen as research experts and writing consultants are very skilled peer mentors, another difference that this training seeks to bridge. As a result, we have shifted focus for the time being away from a quantitative approach for assessment to focusing on efforts that contribute to a shared Knowledge Hub culture from which collaboration arises.

As the cross-training grows and matures, we will also find ways to effectively evaluate student employee performance and learning, whether is it with the library Knowledge Hub student employees or with the writing center consultants. The library student employees are assessed via tutorials in the learning management system already. We also have some assessment in place for writing center students who handle ready reference queries at the Knowledge Hub service desk, but there is opportunity to do even more. As the shared Knowledge Hub culture grows, the ways in which we collaborate with the writing center assess other aspects of the cross-training program will likewise become evident.

REFLECTION

We created the Knowledge Hub with the understanding that the library and writing center would be more than good neighbors occupying the same space. We would be working together, sharing certain work tasks and needing to understand each other's work so that we could effectively work with our users. We believe that successful operation of the Knowledge Hub requires a keen understanding of our respective units, excellent customer service, and a mastery of tasks, both library- and writing center-related, associated with the service desk. Our cross-training efforts to date have focused on all of these aspects in close collaboration with the writing center coordinator.

We recognize that this cross-training program also has limits. Assessing for success with a strictly numbers-based approach proved to be difficult. At this point, we have shifted focus to making sure that the writing consultants know who we are, what we do, and what help we can provide. We acknowledge that the consultations are hosted by two very different groups—research librarians and peer writing mentors—and each group brings a particular dynamic to consultations. We have no plans to cross-train librarians on writing consultations or writing consultants on research sessions, although we acknowledge a shared responsibility in helping students with citation questions.

There is great potential for building upon the cross-training program that we have started. We recognize now that we need to provide such opportunities throughout the year, whether for training or social interactions, not just at the beginning of the academic year. We see opportunity for greater student employee involvement in leading cross-training efforts as well as the need to examine overlap in our individual training programs so that we can achieve more efficiency in scale. We will continue to examine the roles of the librarians and writing consultants in the writing process and experiment with ways that we can work together for the shared goal of providing academic support. One possibility could include greater discernment at the Knowledge Hub service desk and would involve training on how to recognize when a student writer could benefit from a joint research and writing session. And we will maintain a training focus on realizing a shared Knowledge Hub culture and mission while considering how to measure student employee performance and overall Knowledge Hub success.

APPENDIX A

INTRODUCTION AND ENTRY FROM THE KNOWLEDGE HUB SERVICE DESK MANUAL

Knowledge Hub Service Desk and Customer Service Expectations

The Knowledge Hub service desk assists many users who are looking for all kinds of help. The staffers at this desk interact with students, staff, faculty, community users, and other visitors. We work with people of all ages, both in person or on the telephone.

As a Knowledge Hub service desk staffer, you represent both Roesch Library and the Write Place. Our users do not distinguish or even know who we report to when they are asking a question—they want someone who can provide an answer or else lead them to someone who can answer their question.

It is vital that you come ready to work as a Knowledge Hub staffer, as someone who can manage both Library and Write Place tasks. On any given shift, you will likely be trouble-shooting printer issues, answering the phone and directing questions, asking our users about their needs and facilitating them to the right person, using the appropriate workplace software, and more.

Because we deal with a variety of users, the standards for behavior and appearance differ at the Knowledge Hub service desk than what you experience as a writing consultant. The standards below were created so that we could ensure a professional, welcoming experience for anyone who visits the Knowledge Hub. We do not want our users to think that they are interrupting a staffers' homework, movie/music, conversation with friends, or lunch. We do want them to think, however, that we take our jobs seriously by the manner in which we dress and maintain the service desk area. It is OK to do homework during down times, but the primary emphasis during your shift should be on making sure that our users feel welcome and that we are there to lend assistance.

At the Knowledge Hub Desk

The Knowledge Hub service desk is staffed by both students and full-time staff. We sometimes have students with needs that are more easily addressed if they join us on the staff side of the desk, so it can be confusing to users to figure out who is and who is not a staffer. Nametags are worn to help our users identify who is available to help them.

The service desk area is a shared public space, so it is important to remove any potential obstacles off the floor and out of the public, like backpacks. We also strive to maintain a professional atmosphere, so extra bags and coats need to be stored in the reference workroom where we have a coat rack and other storage options.

- ALWAYS wear your nametag at a visible level.
- Backpacks and coats must be stored in the reference workroom.
- Shoes must stay on your feet.
- Make sure that you are using appropriate language, and keep conversations appropriate to the workplace.

APPENDIX B

TRAINING QUESTIONS DELIVERED THROUGH THE LEARNING MANAGEMENT SYSTEM

Question 1: Someone comes up to the Knowledge Hub desk and says, "I'm a UD alum and I'm here early for Reunion Weekend. I sent myself old UD pictures before I came here. Can you give me a wifi password for my laptop and show me how to hook up to these printers?"

1. List a question you might ask to get clarification on what this person is trying to do.
2. Write out a response as to how you might answer this request.

Question 2: A student needs the most recent edition of the textbook *Engineering Economics Analysis* by D. G. Newnan, as she says the title is not available at the bookstore.

1. Describe how you will search for this title. What statements would you make or clarifying questions might you ask?
2. Include a URL for a relevant catalog record, if you find one.

APPENDIX C
WRITING CONSULTANT SURVEY

Have you ever worked with a University of Dayton librarian? Check all that apply.

- ☐ You asked a question at the Information desk.
- ☐ A librarian met with your class to discuss research.
- ☐ You met with a librarian at the Research Desk to discuss research.
- ☐ You met with a librarian in his or her office to discuss research.
- ☐ You were on a committee with a librarian.
- ☐ I've talked with a librarian but not about research.
- ☐ I have never worked with a librarian.

What do you think are the main responsibilities of UD reference librarians?

- ☐ Refill staplers
- ☐ Help people find articles and books to write papers
- ☐ Show people how to cite sources correctly
- ☐ Fix printer problems
- ☐ Buy books for the library
- ☐ Answer directional questions like, "Where is the bathroom? Host tours and scavenger hunts activities for students
- ☐ Teach classes about how to do research
- ☐ Plan events and exhibits
- ☐ Build webpages
- ☐ Make online tutorials and videos
- ☐ Read books
- ☐ Write articles and give conference presentations
- ☐ Check out books

What kind of education and training do you think is needed for a librarian job?

- ☐ Bachelor's degree
- ☐ Bachelor's degree plus computer certification
- ☐ Master's degree
- ☐ Two Master's degrees
- ☐ A Ph.D.

APPENDIX D

WRITING SAMPLE USED FOR TRAINING WITH WRITING CONSULTANTS

Hypothetical first-year writing course assignment: Identify a problem on the University of Dayton campus. Write a researched paper to explain the problem and provide a solution. Include at least 3 quality articles (minimum 1 scholarly) to support the argument.

Let's Eat Local!

Looking around the University of Dayton's dining halls, I see many food choices. You could eat pizza every day if you wanted to or you could eat lots of varieties of food. You could drink Pepsi for breakfast, lunch, and dinner if you wanted to as well. Although I see a variety of food, I also see many GFS (Gordon Food Service) trucks in the dining hall delivery zones. Thus, it is clear that much of our food is pre-packaged and pre-made before it arrives at the University of Dayton. I believe this reliance on GFS for food supply is a problem and that we need to do more to support locally grown agriculture. I propose that the University of Dayton become involved in Community Supported Agriculture (CSA) efforts because it is more nutritious and because it supports the local economy.

We need to add more locally grown fruits and vegetables to the menu options in the dining halls because it is more nutritious. Studies have shown that freshman students gain, on average, fifteen pounds during their first year of college. Many are on their own for the first time in their lives and do not have to live by mom and dad's rules. Many are excited to make their own decisions about food choices and thus pick their favorite foods but they might not be the most nutritious. Students may also be depressed or homesick and overeat in order to deal with their feelings (Jio). With pizza, burgers, and potato chips ever-present on the dining hall menus, it is no wonder that students gain weight. Although ordering food from GFS in bulk is cheaper, it leads to poor eating habits for students. Thus, if the University of Dayton ordered more locally grown fruits and vegetables, this food could replace some of the less nutritious items that are constantly on the dining hall menus.

Another reason why we should buy from CSAs is because it would support the local economy. The University of Dayton is a leader in the city of Dayton's economy and by buying locally grown fruits and vegetables, our school could set an example for other companies to buy locally. Even more important, our school would be helping the local economy and it would create a trickle-down effect. According to Samuel Staley, Dayton's economy is stagnant. "Few people would recognize Dayton, Ohio, of 2008 as the industrial powerhouse it was less than one hundred years ago. Once a beacon of manufacturing success, Dayton claimed more patents per capita than any other U.S. city in 1900." We still need to find ways to give it a boost. Just imagine how much money could be put into the local economy instead of into the pockets of a "food corporation" that makes millions of dollars a year if we were to use some of that money on Community Supported Agriculture! Dayton has a number of CSAs that could easily be supported by the University of Dayton (Green People). Clearly, then, for reasons of health and economy, the University of Dayton needs to stop shopping so much at GFS and spend more on Dayton's own CSAs.

Bibliography

Green People. "Buying Club / Community Supported Agriculture listings by state and country." http://www.greenpeople.org/Community-Supported-Agriculture.cfm.

Jio, Sarah. "Did You Gain Weight in College? Natalie Portman on Gaining the Freshman 15." *Glamour Magazine*. December 16, 2010. http://www.glamour.com/health-fitness/blogs/vitamin-g/2010/12/did-you-gain-weight-in-college.htm (article discontinued).

Staley, Samuel R. "Dayton, Ohio: The Rise, Fall and Stagnation of a Former Industrial Juggernaut." *New Geography*. August 4, 2008. http://www.newgeography.com/content/00153-dayton-ohio-the-rise-fall-and-stagnation-a-former-industrial-juggernaut.

APPENDIX E

CONVERSATION PROMPTS FOR WRITING CONSULTANTS

The intended use is during writing consulting sessions to help writing consultants discern research quality.

"The evidence that you are using here"…

What kind of source provided this information?

Tell me more about how this information supports your thesis.

"The quote that you are including here"…

Who is the author of this quote? What are his/her credentials?

What is the purpose of this quote? Will it provide emotional, moral, or expert support to your thesis?

"Your bibliography here…"

If you need to use scholarly sources, which ones are scholarly?

How did you go about finding your sources?

NOTES

1.   James Elmborg, "Locating the Center: Libraries, Writing Centers, and Information Literacy," *Writing Lab Newsletter* 30 (2006): 7–11.
2.   Janelle Zauha, "Peering into the Writing Center: Information Literacy as a Collaborative Conversation," *Communications in Information Literacy* 8 no. 1 (2014): 1–6.
3.   Elise Ferer, "Working Together: Library and Writing Center Collaboration," *Reference Services Review* 40 no. 4 (2012): 543–57.
4.   James Elmborg and Sheril Hook, eds., *Centers for Learning: Writing Centers and Libraries in Collaboration* (Chicago: Association of College and Research Libraries, 2005).
5.   Christina Gola et al., "Developing an Information Literacy Assessment Rubric: A Case Study of Collaboration, Process, and Outcomes," *Communications in Information Literacy* 8 no. 1 (2014):131–44.

BIBLIOGRAPHY

Elmborg, James. "Locating the Center: Libraries, Writing Centers, and Information Literacy. *Writing Lab Newsletter* 30 (2006): 7–11. https://wlnjournal.org/archives/v30/30.6.pdf.

Elmborg, James, and Sheril Hook, eds. *Centers for Learning: Writing Centers and Libraries in Collaboration.* Chicago: Association of College and Research Libraries, 2005.

Ferer, Elise. "Working Together: Library and Writing Center Collaboration." *Reference Services Review* 40 no. 4 (2012): 543–57. https://doi.org/10.1108/00907321211277350.

Gola, Christina, Irene Ke, Kerry Creelman, and Shawn Vaillancourt. "Developing an Information Literacy Assessment Rubric: A Case Study of Collaboration, Process, and Outcomes." *Communications in Information Literacy* 8 no. 1 (2014):131–44. https://pdxscholar.library.pdx.edu/comminfolit/vol8/iss1/5/.

Zauha, Janelle. "Peering into the Writing Center: Information Literacy as a Collaborative Conversation." *Communications in Information Literacy* 8 no. 1 (2014): 1–6. https://pdxscholar.library.pdx.edu/comminfolit/vol8/iss1/8/.

Case Study 12

PEER RESEARCH CONSULTANTS AT THE UNIVERSITY OF MINNESOTA–TWIN CITIES:

Student-Driven Success

Kate Peterson, Jody Gray, and Andrew Palahniuk

OVERVIEW

Background

Since the mid-eighties, libraries have demonstrated success with Peer Information Counselor (PIC) programs. It has been common practice for PIC programs to focus on diversity outreach as a primary goal. This is most often accomplished by hiring students from traditionally underrepresented groups to work in public service sites and provide reference assistance. According to Welburn, "Institutional responses that deliver on a promise of promoting stronger hetero-ethnic and cross-cultural engagement among students from diverse backgrounds are more likely to improve the overall campus climate and increase student persistence and success over those that try to wash out differences."[1]

At the University of Minnesota-Twin Cities, a large, urban university with about 30,000 undergraduate students,[2] an initiative began in the mid-2000s to bring together services to support students academically in centralized locations. This program was called the SMART Learning Commons and was housed in three libraries on campus. As part of the development, a Peer Information Counselor (PIC) program was proposed as a service within the Learning Commons that would support undergraduates' research and increase outreach to students of color and American Indian[3] students attending the University of Minnesota.

In addition, the Office of Equity and Diversity (OED) identified several priority areas for the University of Minnesota campus. Two of the areas were to

1. improve campus climate for diverse student, faculty, staff, and visitors and
2. engage internal and external communities in re-imagining strategies for achieving the university's retention and success goals for diverse students.[4]

It is because of these priorities that we strategically partnered with the Multicultural Center for Academic Excellence (MCAE). MCAE primarily serves undergraduate students of color and American Indian students and focuses on the first-year experience through scholarship programs and Living Learning Communities.

The University of Minnesota Libraries collaborated with these campus units to develop a Peer Research Consultant (PRC) program. We launched the program in 2009 with three students who identified with underrepresented groups. The program goals were to

1. provide information literacy skills through individual peer consultations to support campus-level undergraduate student learning outcomes[5] and
2. promote and provide diversity and cultural competency and training among the student workers to support the Office of Equity and Diversity's vision.

Table tents used in promotion

Audience

The initial audiences for this program were first-year writing students, students of color, and American Indian students, with a particular focus on those associated with MCAE and its academic support programs and scholarships. The First-Year Writing programs and first-year students are continually the largest numbers of students using the PRC program each year. However, there is an increasing number of courses and upper-level undergraduates using the services. Over time, we found that international students were big users of our program and they have become one of our targeted audiences.

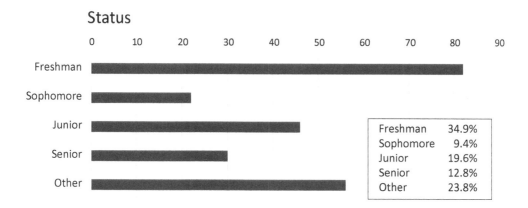

Freshman	34.9%
Sophomore	9.4%
Junior	19.6%
Senior	12.8%
Other	23.8%

Status of students using PRC Program. "Other" includes non-degree-seeking students, which is the status for some English-language programs on our campus.

What the PRCs Do

As it says on our website (https://www.lib.umn.edu/smart/prc) and promotional materials, "the Peer Research Consultants provide one-on-one assistance to develop the research strategies needed to write an excellent research paper." One of our first PRCs came up with the tagline, "Research your way to an A!" PRCs are available through drop-in hours or by appointments. We advertise our service by saying that the PRCs will help students

- find scholarly or academic articles;
- narrow down your paper topics;
- create thesis statements or research questions;
- navigate the libraries' website and locate good databases for a topic;
- choose good keywords for searching; and
- evaluate articles and websites.

We offer both drop-in consultations and appointments. These both typically last thirty minutes. PRCs also have staffed special paper-writing clinics and the end-of-the-semester Exam Jam, which is coordinated with MCAE and the SMART Learning Commons.

> I think the Peer Research Consultant program is (and has proven to be) an excellent way for students to get personalized research help. The program is set up to offer walk-ins and appointments to meet nearly any student's schedule—this really makes it wonderfully accessible.
>
> *Andrew Palahniuk, Lead, Peer Research Consultant Program and Libraries Instructional Design, University of Minnesota–Twin Cities*

Hours and Space

Each semester, we evaluate and consider the hours and locations. Hours are determined by PRC availability; as a result, we do not have the same set hours from semester to semester. In any given semester, we have between two and four PRCs working. Our basic guidelines for hours are a few hours each day, Monday through Friday, anywhere from 9:00 a.m. to 5:00 p.m. Sometimes we have overlapping shifts at different locations. We typically offer between twenty-five and thirty-five service hours per week. We are busier in fall than in spring and have the majority of consultations between weeks four and eleven of the semester. We have tried evening hours but didn't have enough consultations to sustain it.

The PRC program location is very malleable. We offer the majority of our hours in our Walter Library SMART Learning Commons. Walter Library is the Science and Engineering Library. It is also the busiest SMART location in terms of total tutor hours. The core service in the SMART Learning Commons is another successful peer-tutoring program. This large program, administered by our Office of Undergraduate Education, offers tutoring in more than 150 subjects, including math, chemistry, economics, foreign languages, writing, and more. Walter Library is centrally located on campus and busy with undergraduates from all colleges and majors. We also offer PRC hours in the MCAE Instructional Center in an adjacent building housing other campus support units. We have also offered PRCs hours in two other libraries, an Office of Information Technology Collaborative space, and the International Student and Scholar Services office. We are always on the lookout for new spaces that might be a good match for the PRC program.

Appointments

We added appointments, in 2011, to our existing drop-in consultation service. Appointments are available during our drop-in hours and over time has been managed using email, Google Calendar, Google Forms, and recently LibCal appointment software from Springshare. We ask students why they are making an appointment (Goals/Potential Topic field in the form), which helps the PRC prepare in advance. If the topic seems more specialized, we might connect the student with the subject librarian or ask the subject librarian to advise our PRCs. The appointment forms are a great way to help ensure we are well-matched with why students are seeking the service and that our PRCs are trained to support (see Appendix A: Sample of Appointment Requests).

Our PRCs sit at a designated table in busy Walter Library. The large sign helps students find the PRCs.

ADMINISTRATION

Management

Initially, the development of the PRC program was assigned to the diversity outreach librarian, a position that was created as a collaboration between the libraries and MCAE. In 2008, an information literacy librarian position was created, hired, and quickly became the co-coordinator of the PRC program. These two positions complemented one another in developing this PRC program. Both positions were created to support evolving library needs as well as the university's strategic plan, which included several new initiatives:

- A newly created First-Year Writing program to serve all incoming first-year students
- Adoption of undergraduate student learning outcomes[6] focused on the academic experience and student development outcomes focused on experiences outside the classroom
- Restructuring and hiring the first vice president and vice provost for equity and diversity (OED) (MCAE is part of OED at the University of Minnesota)

During subsequent department re-organizations and position changes we added an additional staff member to coordinate much of the day-to-day aspects of the program. Here sample of major duties:

1. Recruitment, hiring, and maintaining the relationships with the partner units.
2. Training, promotion, communications, and integration within the First-Year Writing curriculum.
3. Day-to-day supervision of the PRCs, signing time cards, keeping up the website and the appointment process, assisting in the scheduling, and general troubleshooting.

> I am surprised at how popular this program is with international (non-native speaking) students. I feel this is because peer–tutoring is very accessible to a wide spectrum of students, plus instructors realize the value of using such a program and encourage their students to seek it out.
>
> *Andrew Palahniuk, Lead, Peer Research Consultant Program and Libraries Instructional Design, University of Minnesota-Twin Cities*

HIRING

We are very intentional about our hiring process. One of our goals is to hire students of color, American Indian students, first-generation students, or low-income students. Our philosophy is we are giving more than a job; we are giving them an experience that is an asset to their education and professional development at the University of Minnesota. We try to limit barriers to both recruiting and retaining our student staff. One way to accomplish this is to pay attention to the policies that may be putting up unintentional barriers (see Appendix B: Sample PRC Job Description). For example, we do not require work-study. Often, a student's contributions from parents are one thing on paper but another in real life. Some cultures have very specific belief systems about loans which may prohibit some from accepting parts of the financial aid package. By not requiring work-study, we have widened our pool of applicants. International students are another group of students we can hire when work-study isn't required.

We recruit in close consultation with the MCAE staff. We are able to utilize their expertise and experience with students of color and American Indian students. We only hire students in their second year and above. During a student's first year, the MCAE staff work closely with them and learn more about their personalities and level of responsibility. They are able to suggest that a particular student apply and give recommendations to the PRC coordinators in their hiring process.

In order to be accessible to all students from any marginalized identity (e.g., international, GLBT, first-generation), however, we do not limit the search to only MCAE students. We do an open call for anyone to apply. We ask students to provide a reference from a former employer, staff, or faculty member. It is these references that make all the difference in the final hiring decision.

Required Qualifications	Preferred Qualifications
• Successfully completed Writing 1301/1401 or equivalent with a B or higher • Acceptance and current enrollment at the University of Minnesota as an undergraduate student with a status of sophomore or higher	• Prior tutoring experience • Effective communication and interpersonal skills • Work–study eligible
Must provide a letter of recommendation from faculty or advisor addressing the following: • Academic performance • Interpersonal and communication skills • Leadership skills	

Experiences in the areas of information literacy are not part of the hiring process. We train the students in everything they need to know to do the job. That makes the other factors, such as recommendations, important. We want PRCs who demonstrate good communication and interpersonal skills. Because they are often working independently, they need to be self-motivated and very responsible. We also look for students who are comfortable in leadership roles. We have hired many orientation leaders and presidents of student organizations.

This, in turn, can be a challenge when developing our schedule; active student leaders tend to have very full schedules and have more restrictions on their time. We try to make this mutually beneficial. We are flexible as much as we can be, and, in return, we know these students will talk about the PRC program and thus provide great word-of-mouth publicity within their groups. We want to encourage our PRCs to continue being active in their college careers.

We are also clear that if a student takes the role of a PRC, they will have that position until they graduate or decide to leave. We have carved out room to accommodate extra learning experiences, such as study abroad. Several of our PRCs have taken advantage of this option. In their absence, we provide fewer hours.

Lead PRC

A few years ago, we began to offer one "lead PRC" position each semester with additional responsibilities. Primarily, they staff the libraries table at more than thirty-five new student and transfer orientations during the summer. The lead PRC also works on a variety of special projects, from working on the libraries' web content to an inventory of study spaces and more. The lead PRC pulls together class schedules and creates the PRC semester schedule. He or she also pulls together data and statistics and draft reports about the PRC program. The lead PRC often sits in on planning meetings with coordinators to give the student perspective and they become another contact for our partners. This is yet another opportunity for mutual benefit: we provide additional professional development skills for these students and they promote the program at orientation.

Promotion and Marketing of PRCs

Like many other aspects of the program, we have tried many promotional strategies. We know the most effective way of getting students to use the service is a referral from a course instructor, so we work with the First-Year Writing instructors at many points during the semester, including orientation sessions for new instructors. We hand out hundreds of PRC bookmarks during the in-class session, Intro to Library Research, taught during the First-Year Writing courses. We also make bookmarks available at our services desks and at orientation.

We use an email campaign to reach various units across campus. We continually add to this list, but a few examples of our targeted email audience includes

- First-Year Writing instructors and Center for Writing staff;
- MCAE staff;
- First-Year Seminar and First-Year Experience instructors;
- International Student and Scholar Services (ISSS); and
- academic advisors.

We offer class visits and will send promotional materials such as our bookmarks or posters to these various units around campus. We also share with our own large library staff and ask subject librarians to promote the service during classes when appropriate.

We continue to experiment with ways to reach our target audiences. Experiments have included

- table tents in the dining halls;
- posters around campus;
- various social media channels;
- "ads" on the campus portal;
- digital signs; and
- blurbs in the undergraduate newsletter.

We have found that promotional work is never done and it can be challenging to keep up momentum each semester. (See Appendix C: Peer Research Consultants bookmark and Appendix D: Peer Research Consultants poster, both created by Andrew Palahniuk.)

> I feel that being a PRC is one of the most dynamic jobs a student could do. It is because we are constantly growing and developing ourselves when different students with varied research ideas meet us. The training offered is absolutely essential to get through the technical aspects of being a PRC and it prepared us to manage our time with the students very well. However, being a PRC also entails that you have to go beyond the technical training and improvise based on needs of different students. Thus, all and all, the PRC program teaches us important professional and life skills and I feel it should be offered at all libraries.
>
> *Peer Research Consultant, University of Minnesota—Twin Cities*

Additional Student Support and Other Projects

Throughout the program, we have added duties to the PRC position description. As mentioned above, we have an in-class session called Intro to Library Research integrated into the First-Year Writing program. We also have an online tutorial. One element of the tutorial is an online worksheet in which students complete authentic research tasks, such as telling us about their topics, selecting keywords, and identifying three sources that might be helpful for their topic. Students also have the option to request "follow up by a librarian." During slow times, our PRCs will follow up with those students via email with additional database and search strategy examples in addition to information about the PRC program. About 10 percent of students ask for follow-up and between 200 and 350 students complete the worksheet each semester.

TRAINING

Our training program is grounded in two principles:

1. Train PRCs with the students we are consulting with in mind.
2. Value student's existing research experience.

Over the eleven years of our program, we have modified our training based on these principles. Initially, we began with a "What do we want PRCs to know?" frame but have since shifted to a "What do our PRCs need to know to be able to help students during a consultation?" frame. Though subtle, this difference has led us to eliminate "nice-to-know" elements, like the history of the libraries, and focus more on thinking about the research process.

Our training program involves the following elements:

1. College Reading & Learning Association (CRLA) training on how to be a tutor
2. information literacy and library research training
3. intercultural communications training
4. service desk training

College Reading and Learning Association (CRLA)[7] Tutor Training

As established earlier, the PRC program collaborates with other peer-tutoring programs in the SMART Learning Commons and around campus. These units provide joint training for all students each fall during a one-day intensive training session before the start of the semester. Training materials and outcomes are based on the CRLA certification process. CRLA Tutor training topics included the following:

- tutor responsibilities
- do's and don'ts
- ethics
- setting goals in tutoring sessions
- communication skills
- referral skills
- learning styles and study skills
- critical thinking
- assertiveness/handling difficult students
- understanding cultural differences

About sixty to one hundred students attend this session and the various units take the lead in presenting the identified topics. The biggest benefit of this setup is the connections made between peer-tutoring groups across campus. This training is infused with active-learning techniques including case studies, role-playing, small-group work, and community building exercises. Throughout the day, the tutors are talking and learning with each other. We have seen long-term benefits from this as the students become comfortable making referrals among these various peer services.

> We have had some amazing Peer Research Consultants. They are self-motivated, smart, and engaged with the job. I truly believe it is the relationship with the Multicultural Center that has driven our ability to recruit students that we know are invested in their academics and their college experience. The staff at the Multicultural Center are able to call on their knowledge of students they have been building a relationship with for an entire year or more before they recommend them to be a PRC.
>
> *Jody Gray, Director of the Office of Diversity and Inclusion for the College of Food, Agricultural and Natural Resources Sciences, University of Minnesota–Twin Cities*

Diversity Training

Part of the CRLA training covers intercultural communication. We have also asked the International Student and Scholar Services (ISSS) office to provide training. This was prompted when we realized that a large number of international students were using our service. Many of the students who come from MCAE have had lots of exposure to diversity, but we still want to encourage them to continue learning. When we can, we bring in speakers for them. Other times, we pay them to attend workshops that are already happening on campus.

Information Literacy and Library Research Training

When we initially began the PRC program, a small working group developed the Information Literacy and Library Research training, using a backward design process, to determine our learning outcomes and training activities. This training is given during in-person sessions during the first four or five weeks of the semester.

Our training uses active learning with a combination of short videos, worksheets, practice exercises, and homework. Students also complete some of our regular workshops offered at the beginning of each semester that focus on our citation managers tools such as Zotero and Mendeley. The final activity is a case study that puts the PRC in their role of helping example students through their research questions. It is "graded" using a rubric and returned with feedback. Based on a student's performance, we determine if additional training is needed and we will tailor it to the student's needs. The training is reviewed each year and modified based on new search tools, such as the addition of our discovery layer, new databases, etc.

PRC Information Literacy Learning Outcomes

A PRC will be able to help a student

- narrow/expand topic to fit the requirements of the assignment;
- identify the key concept for their topic and provide assistance in identifying keywords and synonyms;
- organize the keywords into a search strategy using AND, OR, quotes, title searching, etc.;
- select different databases to find information based on topic/needs;
- navigate "Find It" screens to locate full text, use interlibrary loan services, email, save or print articles they find;
- determine whether a chosen article is scholarly or popular and determine whether a source is appropriate/useful for their topic; and
- evaluate sources on criteria such as authority/credibility, useful/relevant, timely/current, and appropriate/audience and to identify "red flags" of bias in a source.

Below is a general outline of our training sessions.

Orientation Session

We go over logistics, including introductions, name tags, time cards, getting paid, introduction to training, registering for libraries wide workshops, and an overview of PRC handbook. The PRC handbook is a Google site which includes all the forms, policies and other materials we frequently refer to and use. We make this guide for PRCs to use on their own and encourage them to add useful information they may discover.

Session 1

- We review CRLA tutor training and discuss PRCs' research experience. (Examples: Draw your typical research paper process. How do you usually go about doing research? Which tools do you use most often?)
- We teach a modified "Intro to Library Research" session. We give background on the First-Year Writing course.

Homework: Complete the Intro to Library Research worksheet with a topic of their choice and watch videos such as *Picking your Topic is Research*[8] from North Carolina State University Libraries. We also ask the PRCs to use our "Chat with a librarian" service with a real research question to become familiar with the service and answer a few reflection questions on how it went.

Session 2

- We review homework and introduce the concepts of the reference interview and asking open-ended questions. We show "bad reference" videos and discuss them. The PRCs write five to ten questions they imagine they may need to ask students they are working with. (Examples: Ask to see the students' assignment. What class is it for? When is it due? Do you need specific types of sources?) This is added to a PRC handbook.
- We talk about how to select a database, demonstrate our subject guides and course guides, the role of our subject librarians in creating these guides and their role as collection experts, and how to model the use of these during a consultation.
- PRCs do a "dissecting a database" exercise modified from University of California-Los Angeles Library. Each PRC selects five databases from a list of the common databases for first-year writing topics (e.g., Ethnic NewsWatch, Sociology Abstracts, JSTOR, Opposing Viewpoints, CQ Researcher, ProQuest Newsstand) or unusual databases either due to search interface or content (e.g., Ovid interface for PubMed, First World War primary source database, Opinion Archive, etc.).
- We talk about techniques to help students narrow research paper topics. For this exercise, we give PRCs a broad topic similar to the topics selected by first-year students (e.g., steroids, school violence, etc.), then ask them to brainstorm how they could narrow the topic (e.g., subtopics, time, place, industry, company, specific event, etc.).

Homework: Complete the "Dissect a Database"[9] and a worksheet with incomplete citations (e.g., from articles, books, book chapter, dissertation, conference proceeding, etc.) and ask PRCs to see if we have the full text.

Session 3

- We review the homework and discuss database pros and cons, and when each database might be useful. We try to frame these around example research topics or research assignments.
- We talk about reading citations and finding the full text if we have it. We introduce our interlibrary loan service and talk about how to request an item.
- We talk about sources and terms such as primary, secondary, empirical, peer-reviewed, refereed, academic, scholarly, review article, qualitative, quantitative, etc. We show the video called *Scholarly vs. Popular*[10] from Coastal Carolina University

Library. We talk about the peer-review process. We review how to limit your results to specific types of sources and review Ulrich's Periodical Directory. We discuss evaluating sources based on timeliness, credibility, relevance, authorship, etc.

- We talk about making referrals within the libraries.

Session 4

- We review advanced search techniques, including using subject headings, using a bibliography, and cited reference searching including Web of Science and Google Scholar.
- We review common types of assignments like annotated bibliographies, literature reviews, etc.
- We discuss Google search tools, including the pros and cons of Google Scholar and Google Books.
- We talk about the purpose of an elevator speech and ask PRCs to prepare one about the PRC program. We expect the PRCs to be able to do a five-minute class visit.

Homework: PRCs complete a web searching worksheet, which includes evaluating web pages, and prepare an elevator speech on PRC service.

Session 5

- We practice delivering PRC elevator speeches for class visits.
- We talk about making referrals outside of the libraries, such as for writing help, etc., and to the counseling center and other non-academic student services on campus.
- We spend time brainstorming what makes a good consultation and talk about what a tutor is and isn't.
- We troubleshoot a variety of scenarios, including poor research topics, crying students, students who don't have enough time (and tips on how to ask for an extension), how to deal with researching an offensive topic, abusive students, and other unlikely scenarios.
- We review plagiarism and how to support citing, including showing students our citation tools and free citation tools and guides.

Homework: Our final homework is a series of case studies asking PRCs to help hypothetical students on their research topics. The PRCs should be demonstrating what they have learned during our training. We have a grading rubric and will follow up with any additional training as needed.

Ongoing Training

We include training as part of our bi-weekly staff meetings. This has included assignment-specific training for a bio-medical engineering course, a visit to our Archives and

Special Collections, and we take example PRC questions and work on them as a group. We also continually ask PRCs what training they feel they need based on the questions they are getting in their work with students or even through own course work.

Service Desk Training

At a few points during our program, we have experimented with PRCs working on our reference desk and, since 2014, on our combined service desk. For example, PRCs have staffed one of our service desks during the first three weeks of the spring semester when there is little demand for research consultations. We were able to offset the schedules of our course reserves staff during their busiest time. The PRCs received an additional four hours of training focused on circulation, helping patrons identify books, finding books on the shelves, using our reference tracking software, and other common service desk questions.

ASSESSMENT

Intake

Tracking the consultation sessions is a vital part of the program. It gives us an opportunity to determine if the program is reaching the intended audience. Using Google Forms, PRCs fill out two forms for every consultation; the first is an intake form, which gathers demographics, such as name, email, status, subject and/or course number, location of consultation, and if the student is part of an MCAE program.

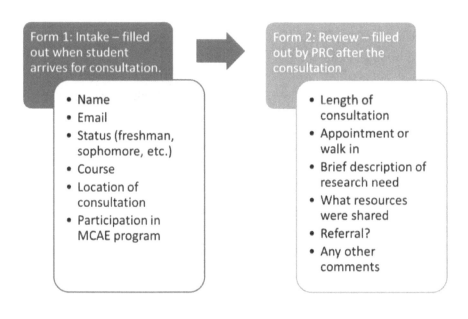

Form 1: Intake – filled out when student arrives for consultation.

- Name
- Email
- Status (freshman, sophomore, etc.)
- Course
- Location of consultation
- Participation in MCAE program

Form 2: Review – filled out by PRC after the consultation

- Length of consultation
- Appointment or walk in
- Brief description of research need
- What resources were shared
- Referral?
- Any other comments

The second is completed after the consultation and collects information about how long the consultation lasted, if it was an appointment or walk-in, a brief description of the assignment or research need, what sort of help student needed, what resources were shared, if a referral to other service was made, and any other comments. We periodically review this data for trends and to identify areas for future training.

Student Feedback on Consultations

About a week after the consultation, we send an email to students asking them to evaluate the service by rating his or her agreement with the following:

- "The PRC was professional and courteous."
- "The information provided was useful for completing my assignment."
- "Overall, I am satisfied with my experience with the PRCs."

We have space for comments if he or she would refer the service to a friend and how he or she heard about the PRCs. We use this data as an overall evaluation of the service. Here is a sample of responses:

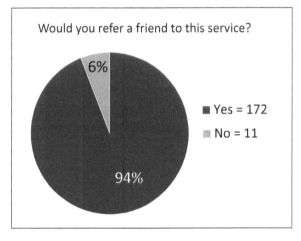

- "She was so nice and friendly! She gave me all these tips to help me find scholarly articles in the future! I'll definitely be back for any other research projects!"
- "I found it very helpful. She helped me find credible resources and make my topic more specific."
- "The tutors helped me a lot in finding sources and forming the thesis statement. They were very welcomed and I felt comfortable asking them!"
- "The Peer Review Consultant I met with was very patient and good at teaching me how I could use resources like the U of M library website in future projects as well as the paper I was doing."

Student Success Measures

The PRC program is part of a larger Library Data and Student Success project begun in 2011, which gathers data on student use of the libraries. This project partners with the Office of Institutional Research to bring in additional demographic data and student success data, such as GPA and retention. This project didn't single out the PRC program specifically but did find evidence of correlations between first-year student use of the libraries, in which the PRCs were one example, and higher GPA and retention for the second semester.[11] We also studied the relationship between socioeconomic indicators and first-year student use of academic libraries, including the PRCs.[12]

> The students who work for the Peer Research Consultant program are incredibly dynamic individuals—nearly everyone has proven to be a leader both within the program and at the university. This program has become much better based largely on the ideas and strategies thought up and implemented by the students themselves. I feel very fortunate to be able to work with these students; they teach me a great deal about innovation and taking ownership of one's work.
>
> *Andrew Palahniuk, Lead, Peer Research Consultant Program and Libraries Instructional Design, University of Minnesota–Twin Cities*

REFLECTIONS AND FUTURE DIRECTIONS

The PRC program is one of the foundations of our undergraduate services. With the changing duties of our subject librarians and the changing service models at our desks, this program fills a gap for students who need and want one-on-one support. This peer-tutoring model is a good fit in our service portfolio. Our twin foci of teaching information literacy skills and promoting diversity and cultural competency align perfectly to support the academic success of our students, contribute to the student learning and development outcomes,[13] and the vision created by the Office for Equity and Diversity.[14]

The PRC program has grown and changed along with our libraries and campus strategic plans. For example, our campus has a new program of Grand Challenge courses and we are working on ways the PRCs can support this initiative. We reviewed and revised our existing program using the threshold concepts, frames, and dispositions of the ACRL *Framework for Information Literacy Framework for Higher Education*.[15] In 2017, due to some changes on campus a new group was formed, the Learning Support Network. This group brings together units which support peer tutoring. One outcome of this was a new website (https://success.umn.edu/), which bring together these services in a more student-friendly hub.

In 2017, we were also able to demonstrate the need for and hire a fifth Peer Research Consultant paid for by an internal grant. The allowed us to offer more consistent hours and expand our role in supporting in-class instruction to multi-lingual First Year Writing sections and a student success course called LASK 1001: Mastering Skills for College. In fall 2020, the grant funding had ended but we were able to continue the funding for a fifth PRCs by splitting the cost between the Libraries and the First Year Writing program.

In Fall 2019, we add a new service—support for students who wanted to get started with Undergraduate Research, sometimes called faculty-sponsored research. We knew there was population of early undergraduates who were interested in getting started but were unsure of how to navigate our large campus and begin. We worked with the Office of Undergraduate Research (OUR) to develop training for our Peer Research Consultants on these topics. This included an overview of the OUR programs, using our Experts@Minnesota (https://experts.umn.edu/) profile system to identify possible faculty mentors, and helping students look up past research posters in our University Digital Conservancy (http://hdl.handle.net/11299/45100). We also offer a workshop called "Think Like a Researcher" in partnership with OUR for same audience. Our PRCs now support the teaching of this workshop. This proved to be a valuable addition to the program. For example, in Fall 2019, 32% of our consultations were on getting started with faculty-sponsored research.

The Peer Research Consultant program has thrived in spite of changes in the organizational structure and support. We attribute this to our extensive training, distributed administrative structure, and focus on students. As for replicating this program at other institutions, the key is flexibility. The changing landscape of higher education, technology, and diversity demand diligence, reflection, and an entrepreneurial spirit.

SPRING 2020 PIVOT

The Covid-19 global pandemic caused the University of Minnesota-Twin Cities to abruptly start distance learning in March 2020. The Library buildings were closed. With the end to face-to-face consultations we quickly pivoted to offering 30-minute online appointments with Google Meet and Zoom. Although there was an overall decrease in usage like many of our online services, the online PRC appointments proved to be popular. We were also able to reach new audiences virtually than in person. For example, we have a program called College in the Schools where students take UMN courses such as First Year Writing in their high schools. Traditionally students would have had to travel to our space, but now they are able to get help from our PRCs. We will also be offering our training to our new PRCs synchronously for fall 2020. All of higher education will be changed as a result of the pandemic, but for our program, this new delivery method both for training and consultations is here to stay.

APPENDIX A

SAMPLE OF APPOINTMENT REQUESTS

- I have a research paper due this week and my topic is about abuse in nursing homes. I need help finding good sources that pertain to my topic.
- Analyzing the rivalry of Magic Johnson and Larry Bird and the impact of race on that rivalry.
- Main topic: cultural/collective/societal memory Indonesian Genocide of 1965 using art to portray tragedy.
- I'm doing a research paper on dogs. I'd like to go over the thesis and a few articles so I can pick which information I should put in the paper.
- I would like to get sources about how cold weather affects people's mentality of looking for socializing.
- Research paper, 3 sources required.
- I need help finding scholarly articles for my research paper. I've done a little searching but so far all the articles I've found have little to do with my topic.

APPENDIX B

PRC JOB DESCRIPTION

University of Minnesota Libraries
Peer Research Consultant Job Description

University Libraries Peer Research Consultants connect students with the information resources they need to succeed in their courses. Working in the SMART Learning Commons (http://smart.umn.edu/), Peer Research Consultants work one-on-one with a diverse group of students in first-year writing and other research enriched courses. Consultants assist these students in locating and evaluating relevant and credible scholarly and popular sources on a research topic, in using a standard format for citing these sources, and in using bibliography creation tools.

Peer Research Consultants complete an extensive training program designed to build a strong foundation of research and tutoring skills. This training includes apprenticing with librarians at library reference desks and in the classroom as well as taking part in the SMART Learning Commons Consultant's training series. The knowledge and skills developed in this position will contribute to Peer Research Consultant's own research and study skills.

The SMART Learning Commons offers drop-in tutoring in specific gateway courses at various locations on the East Bank, West Bank, and St. Paul campus as well as special events such as academic success workshops and pre-exam review sessions. Peer Research Consultants work with students on a drop-in basis at the center to which they are assigned and may also participate in the delivery of special events. The libraries are seeking energetic, personable individuals particularly apt at working with a diverse group of students.

In alignment with the University of Minnesota Student Development Outcomes, the successful Peer Research Consultant staff member engages in activities which develop and demonstrate achievement in the following areas.

Specific Skills and Development Outcomes/ Success Outcomes for PRC:
Responsibility/Accountability

- Makes appropriate decisions regarding his/her own behavior by serving as an Ambassador for the University of Minnesota Libraries
- Meets agreed-upon expectations by being punctual and maintains a stable attendance record and attending and actively participating in scheduled training sessions and staff meetings

- Takes responsibility for his or her own learning by meeting deadlines for assignments given during training sessions

Independence/Interdependence
- Appropriately determines when to act alone and when to work or consult with others by asking appropriate questions about subject matter and assignments
- Demonstrates the ability to initiate action and effectively engage others to enhance outcomes by exploring (in person or virtually) the University of Minnesota Libraries locations and partner locations for SMART and MCAE
- Works with minimum supervision, whether it is alone or within a group by getting to know the other PRCs by name as well as the librarians who work the reference desks and the staff at the Multicultural Center for Academic Excellence

Goal Orientation
- Manages energy and behavior to accomplish specific outcomes by following through on emails and important messages from coordinators, finishing consultation paperwork during shift
- Demonstrates effective planning and purposeful behavior by recognizing different learning styles and adapting his/her consultation style to match the student's
- Does not allow distractions to prevent timely completion of tasks by finishing assigned projects during the time when no students are in need of assistance and not having visitors during office hours

Self-Awareness
- Maintains and projects an optimistic perspective by being courteous and willing to help
- Expects the best from self and others by never doing the student's homework, being respectful and considerate of cultural differences and by assisting students through the peer consultation process by establishing a rapport conducive to positive personal and professional interactions
- Accurately assesses and articulates (when appropriate) personal strengths and weaknesses by attending library workshops outside the required training and referring students to libraries' reference services
- Demonstrates the ability to help others adapt to new situations by asking questions to ensure that you understand the issue or problem and by having an awareness of intercultural communication. Speak more slowly and simply if it will help the student or rephrase comments or questions.

Resilience
- Able to recover from disappointment or bad experience and continue to work successfully by seeking assistance following a weak performance on an assignment

Appreciate of Differences

- Seeks out others with different backgrounds and/or perspectives to improve decision-making by being open to new ideas and courteous when you disagree
- Appreciates the importance of diversity and conveys this value to others by respecting differences in background, opinion, ability, motivation, and desires and/or being inclusive to all
- Understands and respects the values and beliefs of others by attending the required cultural competency training to identify body language, personal space, and the different communication styles

Tolerance of Ambiguity

- Can work under conditions of uncertainty by understanding that not all issues or questions have a black or white answer

APPENDIX C

PEER RESEARCH CONSULTANTS BOOKMARK

Created by Andrew Palahniuk

APPENDIX D

PEER RESEARCH CONSULTANTS POSTER

Created by Andrew Palahniuk

NOTES

1. William Welburn, "Creating Inclusive Communities: Diversity and the Responses of Academic Libraries," *portal: Libraries and the Academy* 10 (2010): 355–63.
2. "Fall 2015 Enrollment Data," University of Minnesota, accessed December 18, 2015, http://www.oir. umn.edu/student/enrollment/term/1159/current/13223 (page discontinued).
3. Throughout this article we refer to students of color and American Indian students as two separate categories due to the unique relationship of American Indian communities with the United States Government.
4. "Reimagining Equity and Diversity: A Framework for Transforming the University of Minnesota," University of Minnesota, accessed December 10, 2015, http://www.mcohs.umn.edu/wp-content/ uploads/2014/07/ReimaginingED_Dec2009.pdf.
5. "Student Learning Outcomes," University of Minnesota, accessed December 18, 2015, http:// academic.umn.edu/provost/teaching/cesl_loutcomes.html.
6. "Student Learning Outcomes," University of Minnesota.
7. College Reading & Learning Association," https://www.crla.net/.
8. "Picking Your Topic *is* Research," North Carolina State University Libraries, accessed November 18, 2015, http://www.lib.ncsu.edu/tutorials/picking_topic/.
9. "Dissecting a Database: Teaching Yourself How to Search," Louise M. Darling Biomedical Library at the University of California, Los Angeles, accessed November 18, 2015, https://www.bluecc.edu/ home/showdocument?id=358.
10. "Scholarly Sources vs. Popular Sources," Kimbel Library at Coastal Carolina University, accessed November 18, 2015, https://vimeo.com/13186317.
11. Shane Nackerud, Jan Fransen, Kate Peterson, and Kristen Mastel, "Analyzing Demographics: Assessing Library Use Across the Institution, *portal: Libraries and the Academy* 13, no. 2 (2013): 131–45.
12. Krista M. Soria, Shane Nackerud, and Kate Peterson, "Socioeconomic Indicators Associated with First-Year College Students' Use of Academic Libraries," *The Journal of Academic Librarianship* 41, no. 5 (2015): 636–43.
13. "Student Learning Outcomes," University of Minnesota.
14. "Reimagining Equity and Diversity," University of Minnesota.
15. *Framework for Information Literacy for Higher Education*, Association of College and Research Libraries, accessed December 20, 2015, http://www.ala.org/acrl/standards/ilframework.

BIBLIOGRAPHY

Association of College and Research Libraries. *Framework for Information Literacy for Higher Education*. Accessed December 20, 2015. http://www.ala.org/acrl/standards/ilframework.

Louise M. Darling Biomedical Library at the University of California, Los Angeles. "Dissecting a Database: Teaching Yourself How to Search." Accessed November 18, 2015. https://www.bluecc.edu/home/ showdocument?id=358.

Nackerud, Shane, Jan Fransen, Kate Peterson, and Kristen Mastel. "Analyzing Demographics: Assessing Library Use Across the Institution." *portal: Libraries and the Academy* 13, no. 2 (2013): 131–45.

Soria, Krista M., Shane Nackerud, and Kate Peterson. "Socioeconomic Indicators Associated with First-Year College Students' Use of Academic Libraries." *The Journal of Academic Librarianship* 41, no. 5 (2015): 636–43.

University of Minnesota. "Fall 2015 Enrollment Data." Accessed December 18, 2015. http://www.oir.umn. edu/student/enrollment/term/1159/current/13223 (page discontinued).

———. "Student Learning Outcomes." Accessed December 18, 2015. http://academic.umn.edu/provost/ teaching/cesl_loutcomes.html.

University of Minnesota, Office for Equity and Diversity. "Reimagining Equity and Diversity: A Framework for Transforming the University of Minnesota." Accessed December 10, 2015. http://www.mcohs. umn.edu/wp-content/uploads/2014/07/ReimaginingED_Dec2009.pdf.

Welburn, William C. "Creating Inclusive Communities: Diversity and the Responses of Academic Libraries." *portal: Libraries and the Academy* 10, no. 3 (2010): 355–63.

Case Study 13

RESEARCH MENTOR PROGRAM AT UNH MANCHESTER:
Peer Learning Partnerships

Carolyn White Gamtso, Annie Donahue, and Kimberly Donovan

OVERVIEW
Summary of the Program

At the University of New Hampshire at Manchester (UNH Manchester), the librarians, the Center for Academic Enrichment (CAE) professional staff, and the First-Year Writing Program faculty established a rich collaboration for supporting undergraduate students throughout the research process. The UNH Manchester Research Mentor Program trains peer writing tutors in information literacy skills so they can better assist students with research-based papers. After the completion of their training, the peer writing tutors earn the designation "research mentor." This effort was realized by adapting a highly effective peer-tutoring program, integrating basic information literacy instruction skills into the tutor training curriculum and incorporating the research mentors within library instruction classes and activities.

The Research Mentor Program started with a pilot project in fall semester 2003 in which three experienced peer writing tutors underwent ten hours of one-on-one training with an instruction librarian to develop and hone basic library research skills, thus becoming research mentors. These newly trained research mentors were each assigned to a first-year composition class and worked with the classroom instructor and an instruction librarian to assist students as they navigated the research cycle, from brainstorming ideas to researching specific topics to writing and editing drafts. White and Pobywajlo provided a detailed examination of that pilot project and the valuable lessons learned.[1]

> Learning about how to choose appropriate sources, and how to direct tutees to appropriate sources, was helpful. As a writing tutor, I might be working with students in disciplines different from my own. It is important to be able to evaluate sources for their relevance to the topic being explored, and this applies to sources which are allowed under a tutee's assignment but would not be permissible in my area of discipline.
>
> *Research Mentor, University of New Hampshire at Manchester*

One of the strengths of the Research Mentor Program has been the deliberate effort to adapt and evolve the program in response to assessment findings over the years of operation. Following a successful pilot, the program was implemented and all peer writing tutors were trained as research mentors. Working with the instruction librarian, research mentors participated in the classroom instruction depending on their individual confidence level leading an activity. Outside the classroom, research mentors provided one-on-one tutoring sessions that integrated research and writing holistically.

Originally, research mentor training was crafted to focus on resources and techniques suitable for supporting students in the First-Year Writing course, but gradually the scope broadened to include discipline-specific needs from gateway to capstone courses. For the first ten years of the program, the UNH Manchester Information Literacy Instruction program aligned with the Association of College and Research Libraries (ACRL) *Information Literacy Competency Standards for Higher Education.*[2] Information literacy instruction for first-year students focused on three of the ACRL standards: (1) students determine the nature and extent of information needed, (2) students access needed information efficiently and effectively, and (3) students evaluate information and sources critically. Instruction was delivered through three in-class workshops deliberately scaffolded to meet students' developmental abilities.

As the Research Mentor Program matured, information literacy instruction evolved from a tool-based to a skill-based pedagogy, and teaching styles progressed from demonstration of resources to active engagement with resources. The information literacy components of the curriculum were integrated into the Tutor Development course, and the instruction librarian served as co-instructor responsible for developing and delivering that content.

A decision to redesign the Tutor Development course curriculum in summer 2014 was predicated on several factors, including a recent leadership change in the CAE, the findings of a June 2014 research study that updated the 2005 review of the program's pilot semester, and ACRL's introduction of the *Framework for Information Literacy for Higher Education*.[3] This course redesign did not critically impact administration or tutor hiring processes but did have a significant impact on the training aspect of the program. This chapter focuses on the current iteration of the Research Mentor Program, describing these recent changes, and examining valuable lessons learned throughout the program's evolution.

ADMINISTRATION

The management of the CAE falls under Academic Support Services at UNH Manchester. The research mentor training program, while co-taught with one of the UNH Manchester Library's instruction librarians, is part of the CAE's peer-tutor program; therefore, CAE professional staff assume overall responsibility for training, supervising, paying, and evaluating the research mentors. The unit's organizational chart (see Appendix A, Unit Organizational Chart) demonstrates the reporting structure: the CAE Director reports to the associate dean and the two other professional staff, who are also involved in research mentor training, report to the director.

The professional staffing of the CAE includes a full-time, year-round director who is also the writing support coordinator, an 80 percent-time science support coordinator, and a 100 percent-time math support coordinator, all supported by a full-time administrative assistant. The CAE is closely allied with the multilingual learner support coordinator, whose expertise informs training practices.

The CAE is funded in the college's general budget as a discrete organization. The budget accommodates salaries and fringe benefits of the unit's four staff members. Salary expenses for the research mentors, math tutors, and science tutors make-up approximately 10 percent of the unit's total budget. A generous allocation for supplies and services includes travel and conference support, allowing both the professional staff and peer tutors to attend several regional conferences annually.

The CAE and the library share the responsibility of training research mentors through the Tutor Development course (UMST 521). CAE professional staff create, implement, and assess the general tutoring curriculum. The participating instruction librarian develops and teaches the information literacy components specific to the research mentor training aspects of the course. Research mentors, who are dual-trained as peer writing tutors, are enrolled in the same section of UMST 521 as the math and science tutors. All students participate in the weekly general tutoring sessions but only peer writing tutors attend the sessions focused on information literacy, which are led by the CAE director and the instruction librarian and include specific research mentor training activities.

The CAE strives to ensure that current and prospective students are aware of the services and programs available to them. The Research Mentor Program is promoted through a variety of embedded strategies, such as

- open house events;
- admissions and orientation tours;
- presentations in first-year seminars;
- presentations in individual writing and writing-intensive courses;
- print materials;
- visual messaging on monitors placed throughout campus; and
- the university blog.

The CAE communicates to faculty and the college community primarily through email and via the college's website[4] and Facebook page.[5] Students are able to book tutoring appointments directly through the CAE Facebook page or website. The website provides further information about the CAE mission, services, and policies.

Hiring

The CAE hires peer writing tutors/research mentors before both the fall and spring semesters, starting recruiting approximately six weeks prior to the end of each semester. Faculty are asked for potential tutor recommendations; also, because UNH Manchester is mainly a commuter campus with a large share of non-traditional students, recruitment likewise takes place face-to-face at tables staged at the entrance of the campus building and staffed with current peer tutors/research mentors. This method has proved to be the most successful at garnering tutor/mentor applications (see Appendix B, Center for Academic Enrichment Tutor Application).

Prospective tutors/research mentors are given a list of the job criteria, which includes a cumulative GPA of 3.0 or higher and a B+ or above in all courses the prospective tutor/mentor plans to tutor. Tutors are required to enroll in Tutor Development (UMST 521) for two or four credits as well as attend and embed as a tutor/ research mentor with a writing course. They also commit to at least five hours a week of tutoring. Research mentors also need to have completed First-Year Writing (ENGL 401), and transfer students must be in their second semester of college. In addition, applicants must submit a writing sample. A faculty recommendation is also required to complete the application packet (see Appendix C, Faculty Recommendation for Prospective Peer Tutor).

Subsequently, the prospective research mentor is interviewed by two CAE staff members. The interview questions are predetermined to ensure consistency, and the staff members take turns asking questions (see Appendix D, Peer Tutor Interview). At the end of the interview, one of the staff members role-plays a student with a paper, and the potential research mentor attempts to tutor the staff member. After this mock tutorial, the interview is complete and the staff subsequently makes the decision to hire.

> I really enjoyed learning about the different frameworks. They gave me a whole new perspective on conducting research as a college student. They made me realize that college students' voices matter just as much as scholars' and other authority figures'. When tutoring students on research methods in the future, I will ensure that I emphasize that their research matters beyond the scope of receiving a passing grade. I also appreciate how the frameworks provide tips for evaluating sources and determining what information is pertinent to a topic.
>
> *Research Mentor, University of New Hampshire at Manchester*

TRAINING
The Tutor Development Course (UMST 521)

All trainee peer tutors at UNH Manchester are required to take a credit Tutor Development course (UMST 521) as preparation for working with students in the CAE. This interdisciplinary course is team-taught by the director of the CAE and either the math or science support professional of the CAE along with the participating instruction librarian for the information literacy portion of the research mentor sessions. The trainees study theories of learning and adult development as well as approaches to tutoring in the writing, math, or science discipline. The trainees also practice their tutoring and communication skills. The trainee research mentors accomplish these course goals through participating in experiential learning activities, reading pertinent articles, assessing themselves with questionnaires, reflecting on their understanding in writing, and collaborating in and out of class. They may take the course for either two or four credits.

An instruction librarian co-teaches the writing portion of the class with the CAE director; the two collaborate to ensure that the librarian-led information literacy units mesh with the theories and pedagogy of the entire course. The librarian's primary goal is to demonstrate to the mentors that high-quality research is an essential component of high-quality academic writing. Indeed, both the librarian and the CAE director stress that appropriate source choice is a "higher-order concern"[6] in a piece of student writing, so mentors must help students assess their sources as part of any tutorial involving a research assignment. Through the information literacy portion of the Tutor Development course, mentors are provided with the skills necessary to help tutees position themselves in the public or scholarly conversation around an issue, brainstorm topic ideas, develop researchable questions, use background sources (such as print and online encyclopedias) to explore and refine topics, and critically evaluate sources before incorporating them into a paper or project. The mentors are not trained to search the library's catalog or periodical databases with the tutees (although they have already learned the basics of these skills in their own first-year writing courses). Rather, the mentors are instructed to ascertain when a reference librarian's intervention is necessary to move a student's research forward and to walk with the student to the librarian at the Library and Information Technology Help Desk (co-located with the CAE in the college's Learning Commons).

The librarian uses the Association of College and Research Libraries' *Framework for Information Literacy for Higher Education*[7] as a touchstone document throughout the course. The ACRL Framework document, adopted in 2016, identifies six threshold concepts for information literacy that library instructors are encouraged to explore as foundational ideas that can inform their pedagogy. According to Townsend, Brunetti, and Hofer,[8] "threshold concepts are the core ideas and processes that define the ways of thinking and practicing for a discipline, but are so ingrained that they often go unspoken or unrecognized by practitioners." Jacobson and O'Keeffe[9] note the pedagogical sea change necessary to shift from teaching through the use of standards, such as the ACRL's *Information Literacy Competency Standards for Higher Education*,[10] to teaching students to engage with theoretical concepts; the shift is one that serves students well by preparing them for the realities of the current informational environment. Teaching threshold concepts requires library instructors to "occup[y] the role of coach, animator, or advisor leading the discussion, while encouraging students to become active agents in their own learning."[11] The librarian discovered that the reimagined Tutor Development library sessions did involve a transformation of her teaching style as she and the research mentors learned together and from each other, exploring the threshold concepts as lifelong learners on the same path.

Each of the five ninety-minute in-person information literacy units focuses on one of the six frames, with five of the frames covered during the course. (Because the mentors are advised not to instruct their tutees in the use of the online catalog and periodical databases, the instruction librarians have elected not to formally introduce the mentors to the frame Searching as Strategic Exploration. The mentors are instead encouraged to bring their tutees to an instruction librarian for in-depth research queries.) Research mentors come to class having read the session's frame for homework, and each class begins with a discussion of the research mentors' thoughts regarding the frame and its implications for them as students, as researchers, and as research mentors.

Using a course-specific LibGuide as a platform,[12] the librarian leads the research mentors through a series of exercises that apply the frame's concepts to real-world information-gathering scenarios. The class is interactive and dynamic, encompassing hands-on activities, short films, and ample group discussion time. At the end of the class period, the librarian and the research mentors examine how the frame might inform their work with students in a writing tutorial, including the practical applications of the threshold concept for developing researchers. The following section describes each of the library sessions in detail, demonstrating the scaffolded approach used by the librarian to introduce research mentors to the information literacy dispositions as detailed in the *Framework for Information Literacy for Higher Education*.

Session I: Scholarship as Conversation

The first librarian-led session in the Tutor Development course introduces the research mentors to the frame Scholarship as Conversation. The research mentors come to class having read the frame, and the class begins with the research mentors completing an advanced planner with reflection questions designed to stimulate discussion around the concepts presented in the frame (see Appendix E, Research Mentor Training: Discussion Questions). The librarian leads mentors in a conversation about how they, as students, have developed the knowledge practices and dispositions enumerated in the frame and how they, as research mentors, can help novice researchers develop those practices and dispositions. After the group discussion, the librarian shows the mentors a short video developed by the Oklahoma State University Library that ties the concepts of the frame to actual research practice.[13] The video describes the scholarly discourse of an academic discipline as a conversation with multiple threads and situates students in that discourse. The metaphor resonates with the research mentors, and the librarian focuses the discussion on the idea of students as creators as well as consumers of knowledge.

After discussing the video, the librarian asks students to brainstorm the ways in which information is disseminated, from newspapers to television to social media, and discusses these various media as part of a larger conversation about a particular topic or issue. The librarian uses an assignment suggested in an early draft of the Framework[14] to follow a national event with personal impact for the research mentors. The class traces coverage of the event from the earliest firsthand accounts in social media, through initial (often inaccurate) coverage in media outlets, to the researched conversation of scholars in the peer-reviewed literature of a variety of disciplines. The class ends with a discussion of the best sources for familiarizing oneself with a topic and where the research mentors should direct students for background and context (print and online reference sources).

Session II: Research as Inquiry

The focus of the second librarian-led session in the Tutor Development course is the frame Research as Inquiry. The librarian uses the frame to reinforce concepts introduced in the first session, including the need for a contextual understanding of a topic and the use of appropriate background resources to provide this understanding. The session expands on those concepts by encouraging the research mentors to practice brainstorming techniques to help students refine topics. The session introduces research mentors to specific background sources to use with tutees.

After a group discussion during which the librarian encourages the research mentors to share their thoughts regarding the frame, the class considers what information gathering needs to occur before making an important professional or personal decision (such as adopting a puppy). The class collectively considers all aspects of the decision and ascertains what information is necessary to ensure a well-informed and satisfactory outcome. By taking the processes of brainstorming and defining an information need outside the realm of academics, the librarian demonstrates that information skills learned "in school" are transferable to other areas of an individual's life; she also demonstrates that the research mentors—and by extension the tutees—have already developed some of those skills but may need to be guided to draw the correlation between one's approach to a "real-life" information need and the requirements of an assigned research project.

The research mentors then reflect upon how they can use the frame Research as Inquiry to help a developing writer understand the conversation around a broad topic of interest, formulate a researchable question, brainstorm prior knowledge of the topic, and conduct basic background research. The librarian plays the part of a tutee with an overly broad research topic, and the research mentors use guiding questions to encourage her to sharpen the topic's focus. The chosen topic links back to the previous session's touchstone event. After a group brainstorm session that encourages the "student" to explore her current understanding of the topic, the librarian introduces the class to two online reference sources that provide further information—*CQ Researcher* and *Opposing Viewpoints*—and asks the research mentors to explore the sources for information that would help clarify the issue. The class ends with the research mentors reflecting on how they can help students critically read the source entries (by looking at subject headings, for example) and use them to help tutees refine topics and begin thesis formulation.

Session III: Information Creation as a Process

The third session introduces the research mentors to a variety of bibliographic formats, with class discussions centered on an analysis of how and why the formats are created, vetted, and produced. After watching a video developed by the Oklahoma State University Library entitled *Inform your Thinking: Episode 5—How Is Your Information Created?*,[15] the research mentors are presented with print copies of periodicals in various formats, from popular magazines to trade publications to peer-reviewed journals. The research mentors are asked the following questions about the periodicals:

- What is the purpose of this publication? Is it political? Educational?
- What is the intended audience? Are they experts in a certain field of study? Do they share political views or social identities?
- What are some of the distinct attributes or distinguishing characteristics of the publication? Are the articles long or short? Do they contain photographs? Charts and graphs? Bibliographies?
- What was the process of creation for the articles in the publication? Are they based on original research or observation?
- Who are the authors? Are they academics? Doctors? Journalists?
- What other markers give the reader a hint at the purpose, audience, and authorship of the source? Are there advertisements? If so, what are they marketing? Are there cartoons? If so, what or whom are they satirizing?

After the research mentors have handled multiple periodicals, the class analyzes the nature of each format, including its purpose, authorship, and audience. More specifically, the librarian and the research mentors discuss how the print format of the periodical provides markers—such as political advertisements and cartoons—that help the reader situate the publication in the wider scholarly or political discourse. The class discusses the difficulty of assessing articles from these publications when they are accessed online through the electronic databases, where such markers are not present or are more difficult to locate. For example, after handling a print issue of the *National Review*, research mentors can easily identify it as a conservative magazine by reading the headlines and analyzing the cartoons. However, when presented with a PDF of a single article from the *National Review* out of the context of the entire issue, the process of assessment becomes more complex. Now the research mentors—and their students—must do due diligence by looking up the author (in an encyclopedia or on the internet) and the magazine (in *Ulrichsweb*) to find out more information about the publication's perspective.

Having completed the hands-on exercise with the print periodicals, the class takes part in an activity gleaned from an early draft of the ACRL's *Framework for Information Literacy for Higher Education*.[16] Together, the class reviews two articles on the same topic by the same author, one in a popular magazine and one in a peer-reviewed journal. The librarian asks the class why a scholar would choose to publish an article in a popular source, which leads to a discussion of authority and intended audience (foreshadowing a future frame). The class discusses how scholars may choose to extend their conversations to a lay audience so as to gain more widespread acceptance of their ideas. The exercise reinforces the processes by which information is created and disseminated, and for what purposes. The class concludes with a discussion of how research mentors can introduce the concepts of the frame Information Creation as a Process to their tutees when helping the tutees assess the sources selected for their papers and projects.

Session IV: Authority Is Constructed and Contextual and Information Has Value

The fourth library session begins with an in-depth exploration of the frame Authority Is Constructed and Contextual. The librarian asks the research mentors for their reactions to the frame, reactions which are always rich and animated as the research mentors respond to the ways in which the frame presents "authority" as a nuanced concept. The research mentors are drawn to the idea that expertise and authority can be possessed by those who may not have degrees after their names but whose personal experiences or research have resulted in new discoveries or new understanding. The class then discusses how authority can be erroneously granted (by media outlets or by the general public) to proclaimed "experts" without real competence in a discipline. A TED Talk by epidemiologist Ben Goldacre, "Battling Bad Science," presents this phenomenon in a humorous, compelling, and provocative manner.[17]

The librarian and research mentors trace a specific scholarly conversation in the popular media; the goal of the exercise is to analyze the nature of authority and to assess how that authority is granted and by whom. The research mentors explore articles by Harvard historian and law professor Annette Gordon-Reed and by journalist and independent scholar Henry Wiencek regarding Thomas Jefferson and slavery. The class discusses the difficulty of deciding which if either of the scholars has the greater authority. The research mentors also assess the forums in which these authors choose to take the conversation, including popular online sources such as *Slate* magazine and Smithsonian.com.

Although the research mentors come to appreciate the complexity of the issues around the concept of "authority," the class acknowledges that first-year writing students (who as novice researchers are only beginning to grasp the concept) need more direction when assessing the credibility and appropriateness of sources. The class discusses strategies for helping students evaluate sources using Mike Caulfield's "SIFT (The Four Moves)" method.[18]

The last part of class introduces the frame Information Has Value. After considering the various entities that serve to gain monetarily by controlling access to information, the librarian brings the theoretical discussion back to the practical task of assisting students with their research projects. The research mentors discuss the frame as it relates to intellectual property rights and the need to provide attribution and how the research mentors can help students with issues around correct citation of sources.

Session V: Mock Tutorials

The final library session presents the research mentors with an opportunity to bring together the skills they have practiced throughout the semester in small-group and class exercises through mock one-on-one tutorials. The librarian provides the research mentors with a handout that lists the preliminary questions they should ask tutees at the beginning of a session involving writing about research (see Appendix F, Mock Tutorials: Preliminary

Questions & Research Mentor Roles). The handout also reminds the research mentors of their roles, including assisting students with finding background information, evaluating sources, and seeking additional help from a reference librarian.

A second librarian visits the class to play the part of the tutee during the mock tutorials. The research mentors take turns conducting a tutorial with the librarian/tutee, which may involve reviewing a paper draft with inappropriate sources for the assignment, helping the librarian/tutee focus a broad topic, or guiding the librarian/tutee to appropriate background sources. At the end of each tutorial, the entire class discusses the challenges of each session, points out the strengths of the tutor's approach, and suggests how the session might have been even stronger.

ASSESSMENT
Measuring Student Learning

Earlier in the program implementation, a range of assessment efforts were employed to determine the effectiveness of the Research Mentor Program and its impact on student learning. Initial student learning measurement approaches included formative techniques similar to the "one-minute paper" or the "muddiest point" tools described by Angelo and Cross in their handbook of classroom assessment.[19] This assessment approach served as a checkpoint to determine what students were learning from library instruction sessions at a given point in the research cycle. In the First-Year Writing course, three instruction sessions were conducted across the semester. At the end of each instruction session, students completed the formative assessment tool and an online survey, identifying one learned concept and noting any uncertainties remaining. The results of these assessments were useful to confirm the effectiveness of the instruction session but were only an indirect measure of student learning.

Anecdotally, the program appeared to be successful but there was little firm data to confirm this assertion. Therefore, in January 2011, the instruction team developed an eighteen-month research study to gather evidence of the program's impact on student learning. A pre-test/post-test instrument was crafted using both fixed and open-ended questions designed to measure students' proficiencies on the first three ACRL Information Literacy Competency Standards. The open-ended questions were scored using a rubric. The study's findings demonstrated improved competency on each of the three information literacy standards measured: (1) ability to correctly use library resources, (2) ability to create an effective search strategy, and (3) ability to appropriately evaluate sources found. The positive results were encouraging and useful to informing curricular adaptation of the Tutor Development course.[20]

Within the Tutor Development course, research mentors were assessed through a variety of methods. Research mentors completed a pre-course reflection essay in which they identified their individual expectations for the course and the role of the research mentor, and in a post-course reflection essay, they described the impact of the course on their own learning and development growth. Throughout the course, research mentors demonstrated knowledge through role-playing the reference interview and participating in mock-tutorial sessions. In these authentic assessment activities, students displayed their abilities as the course instructors observed competencies met and areas requiring further training. If the research mentor was assigned to work with a specific First-Year Writing course, the students and course instructor completed an end-of-semester evaluation on the research mentor's effectiveness in supporting the research and writing process.

> Talking through how to spot bias or commercial interest in source material was also beneficial to me as a student, and as a tutor. Watching for bias is almost automatic for me at this point, which means that it's also challenging to help someone else understand my process. College students who are not as practiced at critical reading may need a tutor, a librarian, or a professor to assist with this important skill. The lessons in tutor development allowed me to brainstorm with other tutors about how to pass on the critical reading skills we use in our own research.
>
> *Research Mentor, University of New Hampshire at Manchester*

Further evidence of student learning among research mentors was explored in a six-month research study conducted in 2014.[21] This qualitative study utilized semi-structured interviews and a survey tool to gather data from a representative sample of eight research mentors who agreed to participate in the study. The research question sought to explore the impact of participation in the research mentor program on student learning from the perspective of the research mentors themselves. The study's findings validated that participants recognized an increased growth in their own information literacy, research, and writing abilities as a consequence of participating in the program. Furthermore, these participants credited the program with creating a reciprocal learning environment that enabled increased learning and development. An additional finding revealed that participants shared uncertainty and doubts about their abilities to initially succeed in the role of a research mentor. Participants recommended including additional practice opportunities with mock tutorials to assist new research mentors gain confidence in the role. Upon review of the study's findings, the Tutor Development course curriculum was adapted to incorporate additional activities and assignments that strengthen collaborative learning skills.

In the current iteration of the Research Mentor Program, reflective writing exercises connect applied concepts to weekly reading assignments. Practice reference interviews and mock tutorials provide a safe environment for gaining confidence in guiding the research process. At the close of each tutoring session, tutees are able to provide anonymous feedback on the support received from the research mentor, which is reviewed by the CAE Director with the mentor at appropriate points throughout the semester. Two applied projects, one at mid-term and the second at the end-of-term, allow research mentors to synthesize concepts presented and demonstrate the knowledge and skills developed through the course. Working in teams, research mentors complete a mock-tutorial assignment at mid-term in which they film two versions of a potential tutoring scenario—one that reflects good practice and one that does not. These films are viewed and discussed in class, the research mentor submits a self-reflection evaluating the work, and the project is assessed and graded by the course instructor. The final project requires each research mentor to write a collaborative learning case study integrating a variety of perspectives to make connections between theory and practice, thereby demonstrating learning acquired across the semester. A mix of graded and ungraded, formative and summative assessments measure student learning holistically and inform program effectiveness efficiently.

REFLECTION

The Research Mentor Program at UNH Manchester has evolved significantly since its inception in 2003, responding to tutor feedback as well as to broader philosophical shifts in information literacy pedagogy. The librarians and CAE professional staff members who oversee the project are all firm in their belief that an educational endeavor must be a constant work in progress; together, they engage in reflective practice and continue to ask what works in the program as well as what can be improved. When the results of the 2014 research study indicated that the research mentors at times felt overwhelmed by a perceived expectation that they were "research experts," the librarians responded by asking the mentors to help with background research and source evaluation but not with database searching. Such responsiveness is essential to maintain a strong program that best meets the needs of the research mentors and the students alike. The research study also indicated that, despite early feelings of trepidation, the research mentors did find that their own research and writing skills increased as a result of their participation in the Research Mentor Program.

The librarian and the CAE director are pleased with the current training model: the research mentors respond favorably to the use of the frames in the Tutor Development course as well as to the interactive, hands-on approach in the library sessions. While the librarian does not foresee immediate changes in the course's sessions, she hopes in the future to explore additional roles for the research mentors, such as including them in classroom library instruction sessions. Librarians and CAE professional staff anticipate the program to continue to evolve as new insights regarding threshold concepts, the Framework, and information literacy practice enter the profession's scholarly discourse.

APPENDIX A

UNIT ORGANIZATION CHART

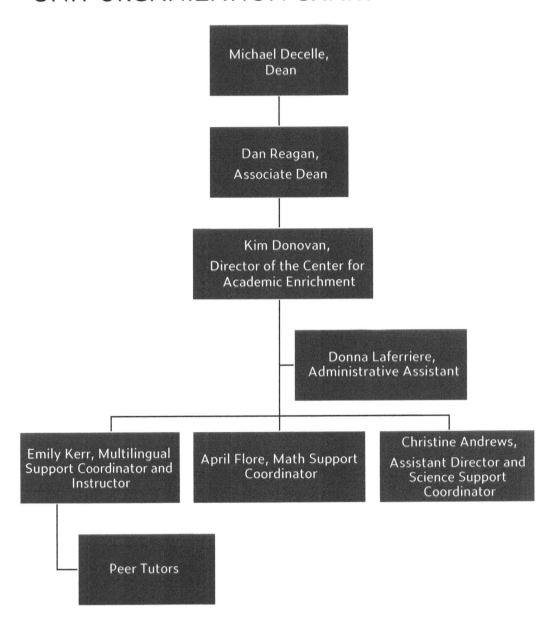

APPENDIX B

CENTER FOR ACADEMIC ENRICHMENT TUTOR APPLICATION

Complete & return this form to Center for Academic Enrichment
University of New Hampshire at Manchester • 88 Commercial Street, Manchester, NH 03101

Name:_____ Student ID: _____

Date:_____Address:_____

Phone—Cell :_____ Home:_____

Email:_____ Major:_____ Class Year:_____

Name of UNH Manchester Faculty Providing Recommendation:_____

Subject/courses to tutor (please be specific):

Do you have any concerns about enrolling in our Tutor Development class?

Do you plan to enroll for 2 or 4 credits? _____

1. Why do you want to be a tutor?
2. Please describe and comment on any previous tutoring, teaching, mentoring, or other related experience you have had.
3. What do you think would be your three best qualities as a tutor and why?
4. What are your strengths and weaknesses in the subject area you are interested in tutoring?
5. Describe one experience in which learning information, a skill, or a process was difficult for you. Describe how you learned it and when you realized learning had taken place.
6. What limitations are there on your tutoring time?

Please return this completed form to the Center for Academic Enrichment or email to kimberly.donovan@unh.edu

APPENDIX C

University of New Hampshire
at Manchester

Faculty Recommendation for Prospective Peer Tutor

> **Complete & return this form to Center for Academic Enrichment**
> Learning Commons, 88 Commercial Street • Manchester, NH 03101 • 603-641-4113

Student name:_____   Faculty name:_____

Student email/phone:_____   Faculty email/phone:_____

For what subject or skill do you recommend this student? _____

Briefly describe how you know this student: _____

_____

_____

Please rate the student on the qualities below:

	1 Poor	2 Below Average	3 Average	4 Above Average	5 Exceptional	Not applicable/ Don't know
Math skills						
Writing skills						
Reading skills						
Content area						
Interpersonal skills						
Reliability						
Trustworthiness						
Maturity						
Work Ethic						
Curiosity/Creativity						

Additional comments: _____

_____

Faculty signature: _____   Date_____

Recommendations will be kept confidential. Please return the completed
form to Kim Donovan via email (kimberly.donovan@unh.edu) or campus mail.

APPENDIX D

PEER TUTOR INTERVIEW

Student:

Staff Member:

Date:

- Why do you want to be a tutor?

- If you had previous experience as a mentor/tutor, describe that experience.

- Whom do you think uses the CAE?

- What do you expect to do as a tutor? ("Push" them on phrases like "help students." How? In what way? To what degree?)

- What concerns/fears do you have about being a tutor?

- Have you ever worked with a tutor as a student? If so, describe the experience.

- In what subjects are you confident you can tutor students? Would a faculty member confirm your ability to tutor in that subject?

- Becoming a peer tutor requires you to enroll and participate in a tutor development course. Are you able to do this?

- What hours would you be available to tutor? (courses enrolled in, other responsibilities)

- What questions do you have about becoming a tutor?

Mock interview notes:

APPENDIX E
RESEARCH MENTOR TRAINING— DISCUSSION QUESTIONS

1. Discuss the points that most struck you about academic discourse as described in the information literacy frame Scholarship as Conversation.

2. How have you, as a student, begun to develop the knowledge practices and dispositions listed under this frame?

3. How can you help the students you tutor to develop the knowledge practices and dispositions?

APPENDIX F

MOCK TUTORIALS—PRELIMINARY QUESTIONS & RESEARCH MENTOR ROLES

UNH Manchester

Tutor Development Class

- **Preliminary questions research mentors should ask students about a research-based paper at the beginning of a session:**
  1. What is the class?
  2. Who is the instructor?
  3. What is the assignment?
  4. Do you have a copy of the assignment with you? (Check myCourses if necessary.)
  5. What is your topic?
  6. What is your research question/thesis/controversy/position/policy? (For some instructors, students need to know the controversy around the issue and/or a policy.)
  7. What types of sources do you need to use? (Should be on the assignment.)
  8. Have you already begun your research? What have you found so far? (Assess whether the student has conducted background research or has understood the research thus far.)

- **The role of the research mentor regarding the research process:**
  1. Assess whether the student understands the controversy, knows a policy, or has a position.
  2. Assess whether the student has conducted background research or has understood the research thus far.
  3. Brainstorm and refine a topic if necessary.
  4. Identify key players, opinions, laws, etc. (who, what, where, why, when).
  5. Review any sources the student has found (in bibliography, draft, or in hand). Assess the student's understanding of the sources.
  6. Help the student find background information to help understand the controversy and/or find a policy (who, what, where, why, when).
  7. Identify if the sources the student used are not appropriate for the assignment.
  8. Walk the student to the Learning Commons Help Desk when necessary.

NOTES

1. Carolyn B. White and Margaret Pobywajlo, "A Library, Learning Center, and Classroom Collaboration: A Case Study," in *Centers for Learning: Writing Centers and Libraries in Collaboration*, eds. James K. Elmborg and Sheril Hook (Chicago: Association of College & Research Libraries, 2005), 175–203.
2. "Information Literacy Competency Standards for Higher Education," Association of College & Research Libraries, accessed December 18, 2015, http://www.ala.org/acrl/standards/informationliteracycompetency.
3. *Framework for Information Literacy for Higher Education*, Association of College & Research Libraries (ACRL), last modified February 2, 2015, http://www.ala.org/acrl/standards/ilframework.
4. "Center for Academic Enrichment," UNH Manchester, https://manchester.unh.edu/academics/academic-services/center-academic-enrichment-cae.
5. CAE Facebook page, https://www.facebook.com/UNHManchesterCAE/?fref=ts (site discontinued).
6. Thomas J. Reigstad and Donald A. McAndrew, "Training Tutors for Writing Conferences (Urbana, IL: ERIC Clearinghouse on Reading and Communication Skills, 1984).
7. *Framework for Information Literacy*, ACRL.
8. Lori Townsend, Korey Brunetti, and Amy R. Hofer, "Threshold Concepts and Information Literacy," *portal: Libraries and the Academy* 11, no. 3 (2011): 854.
9. Trudi E. Jacobson and Emer O'Keeffe, "SEEKING—AND FINDING—Authentic Inquiry Models for Our Evolving Information Landscape," *Knowledge Quest*, 43, no. 2 (2014): 26–33.
10. "Information Literacy Competency Standards for Higher Education," ACRL.
11. Colleen Burgess, "Teaching Students, Not Standards: The New ACRL Information Literacy Framework and Threshold Crossings for Instructors," *Partnership: The Canadian Journal of Library and Information Practice and Research* 10, no. 1 (2015): 2, https://journal.lib.uoguelph.ca/index.php/perj#.VnmdQk8eqy4.
12. UNH Manchester Tutor Development LibGuide, UNH Manchester, http://libraryguides.unh.edu/tutordevelopment2.
13. OkStateLibrary, "*Inform your Thinking: Episode 1– Research Is a Conversation*," online film, 3:22, May 18, 2016, https://www.youtube.com/watch?v=DmbO3JX5xvU.
14. "Welcome, Once More," Association of College & Research Libraries, last modified June 17, 2014, http://acrl.ala.org/ilstandards/wpcontent/uploads/2014/02/Framework-for-IL-for-HE-Draft-2.pdf.
15. OkStateLibrary, "*Inform Your Thinking: Episode 5—How Is Your Information Created?*," online film, 3:47, July 14, 2016, https://www.youtube.com/watch?v=ThQAmo4c66k.
16. "Welcome, Once More," ACRL.
17. Ben Goldacre, "Battling Bad Science," online lecture, 14:19, July 2011, https://www.ted.com/talks/ben_goldacre_battling_bad_science?language=en.
18. Mike Caulfield, "SIFT (The Four Moves)," *Hapgood*, https://hapgood.us/2019/06/19/sift-the-four-moves/.
19. Thomas A. Angelo and K. Patricia Cross, *Classroom Assessment Techniques: A Handbook for College Teachers* (San Francisco: Jossey-Bass, 1993).
20. Ann Elizabeth Donahue, "Charting Success: Using Practical Measures to Assess Information Literacy Skills in the First-Year Writing Course," *Evidence Based Library and Information Practice* 10 (2015): 45–62, https://scholars.unh.edu/unhmlibrary_pub/6/.
21. Ann Elizabeth Donahue, "But What's in it for Them? Understanding the Effects of Participation in the Research Mentor Program from the Mentors' Perspective" (paper presented at the 11th Northumbria International Conference on Performance Measurement in Libraries and Information Services, Edinburgh, Scotland, July 20–23, 2015).

BIBLIOGRAPHY

Angelo, Thomas A., and K. Patricia Cross. *Classroom Assessment Techniques: A Handbook for College Teachers* (San Francisco: Jossey-Bass, 1993).

Association of College & Research Libraries. *Framework for Information Literacy for Higher Education*." Last modified February 2, 2015. http://www.ala.org/acrl/standards/ilframework.

———. "Information Literacy Competency Standards for Higher Education." Accessed December 18, 2015. http://www.ala.org/acrl/standards/informationliteracycompetency.

———. "Welcome, Once More." Last modified June 17, 2014. http://acrl.ala.org/ilstandards/wpcontent/uploads/2014/02/Framework-for-IL-for-HE-Draft-2.pdf.

Burgess, Colleen. "Teaching Students, Not Standards: The New ACRL Information Literacy Framework and Threshold Crossings for Instructors." *Partnership: The Canadian Journal of Library and Information Practice and Research* 10, no. 1 (2015): 2. https://journal.lib.uoguelph.ca/index.php/perj#.VnmdQk8eqy4.

Caulfield, Mike. "SIFT (The Four Moves)." *Hapgood.* https://hapgood.us/2019/06/19/sift-the-four-moves/.

Donahue, Ann Elizabeth. "But What's in it for Them? Understanding the Effects of Participation in the Research Mentor Program from the Mentors' Perspective." Paper presented at the 11th Northumbria International Conference on Performance Measurement in Libraries and Information Services, Edinburgh, Scotland, July 20–23, 2015.

———. "Charting Success: Using Practical Measures to Assess Information Literacy Skills in the First-Year Writing Course." *Evidence Based Library and Information Practice* 10 (2015): 45–62. https://scholars.unh.edu/unhmlibrary_pub/6/.

Goldacre, Ben. "Battling Bad Science." Online lecture, 14:19. July 2011. https://www.ted.com/talks/ben_goldacre_battling_bad_science?language=en.

Jacobson, Trudi E., and Emer O'Keeffe. "SEEKING—AND FINDING—Authentic Inquiry Models for Our Evolving Information Landscape." *Knowledge Quest*, 43, no. 2 (2014): 26–33.

OkStateLibrary. "Inform Your Thinking: Episode 1—Research Is a Conversation." Online film, 3:22. May 18, 2016.

OkState Library. "Inform Your Thinking: Episode 5—How Is Your Information Created?" Online film, 3:47, July 14, 2016.

Reigstad, Thomas J., and Donald A. McAndrew. *Training Tutors for Writing Conferences.* Urbana, IL: ERIC Clearinghouse on Reading and Communication Skills, 1984.

Townsend, Lori, Korey Brunetti, and Amy R. Hofer. "Threshold Concepts and Information Literacy." *portal: Libraries and the Academy* 11, no. 3 (2011): 854.

UNH Manchester CAE Facebook page. https://www.facebook.com/UNHManchesterCAE/?fref=ts (site discontinued).

UNH Manchester. "Center for Academic Enrichment." https://manchester.unh.edu/academics/academic-services/center-academic-enrichment-cae.

———. Tutor Development LibGuide. http://libraryguides.unh.edu/tutordevelopment2.

White, Carolyn B., and Margaret Pobywajlo. "A Library, Learning Center, and Classroom Collaboration: A Case Study." In *Centers for Learning: Writing Centers and Libraries in Collaboration*, edited by James K. Elmborg and Sheril Hook, 175–203. Chicago: Association of College & Research Libraries, 2005.

ON NOT REINVENTING THE WHEEL:

Borrowing from the Writing Center Peer Consultant Model

Kate Hinnant and Jill Markgraf

OVERVIEW

When we developed the Peer Research Consultant program at the University of Wisconsin-Eau Claire's McIntyre Library, our goal was to give undergraduate students, in any discipline, the opportunity to help establish and staff the Research Center, a re-envisioned reference service. The program grew out of intentional and successive efforts to elevate the student "reference desk" work experience and contribute in a meaningful way to campus liberal education goals by providing high-impact practices. The exigency of a significant cut to the university's budget expedited our implementation of this program. Through a collaboration with the campus Writing Center, the Library's Research and Instruction department hires from a pool of undergraduate students who have successfully taken a three-credit tutor training course. In most cases, the students work in both the library and the Writing Center. Peer research consultants (PRCs), therefore, have already been vetted at one level and have developed a consultative disposition. Students staff the Research Center independently in the evenings and with librarian backup during weekday hours.

Background

Like most academic libraries, McIntyre Library relies heavily on student employees. Many of them work with us for several years, making their work experience—and relationships with library colleagues—among the most constant and lasting of their college careers. The impact of their work experience and work relationships extends beyond graduation. In a 2015 survey of McIntyre Library student employees from the past decade, 74 percent of students who had graduated indicated that they remained in contact with library staff. Sixty-three percent indicated that their work in the library impacted future career decisions. This comes as no surprise to those who work with library students. As librarians, who often straddle the divide between the curricular and co-curricular, we are uniquely positioned to see and maximize the connection between student academic and work experiences. At UW-Eau Claire, we engage in the curricular conversations on our campuses as well as the administrative and student supervision ones. When our campus adopted a new liberal education framework emphasizing integrative learning and high-impact practices, librarians considered how they might best contribute to the values and vision of the institution. Whereas the library does not have "majors" or its own students in the way that academic departments do, we recognized that our library employees were in fact "our" students, who would become "our" graduates. We began to embrace our roles as not only employers but mentors and teachers. This acknowledgment changed the way we regard, invest in, and nurture our student employees.

Student Employment as a High-Impact Practice

UW-Eau Claire has a goal that every student participate in a high-impact practice (HIP). Typically comprising experiences such as learning communities, first-year experiences, service learning, study abroad, collaborative research, internships, or a senior culminating project, HIPs share common characteristics. HIPs give students opportunities to

- engage in purposeful tasks;
- interact frequently with faculty and mentors and receive regular feedback;
- come into contact with people different from themselves; and
- reflect on, apply, and integrate knowledge into real-world settings.[1]

As librarians, we are tangentially responsible for supporting HIPs, but we were not really providing them. However, we realized that with intentionality we could infuse student library jobs with characteristics of a high-impact practice.

High-impact practices provide students with experiences, deep learning, and skills that are likely to be valued in their future career opportunities, but students are not always prepared to articulate what they have gained through their student work experience. Employer surveys reflect skills that employers say they want and they coincide with the skills students obtain working in the library. The National Association of Colleges and

Employers (NACE), for example, conducts an annual survey, and while it fluctuates from year to year, similar soft skills rise to the top: the ability to work in a team structure, the ability to make decisions and solve problems, the ability to communicate verbally with people inside and outside an organization, the ability to plan, organize, and prioritize work, and the ability to obtain and process information are among the top five.[2]

Similarly, a survey of employers conducted on behalf of the American Association of Colleges and Universities identified learning outcomes on which colleges should place the most emphasis: critical thinking and analytical reasoning skills, the ability to analyze and solve complex problems, the ability to effectively communicate orally and in writing, the ability to apply knowledge and skills to real-world settings, and the ability to locate, organize, and evaluate information from multiple sources.[3]

It is our goal not only to provide these experiences for students but to help them reflect on them and draw meaningful connections. We are taking steps to do this in the administration, hiring, training, and assessment of the peer research consultants.

Our initial efforts to maximize the library student work experience drew upon the literature as well as the experience, best practices, and interests of other student supervisors on campus. Librarians partnered with other campus leaders in developing and leading discussion groups, communities of practice, and student supervisor workshops all aimed at infusing on-campus student jobs with the elements that compose high-impact practices. The UW-Eau Claire Center for Writing Excellence emerged as a model for the kind of service the library was envisioning. The center recruits promising students from the first-year composition classes, inviting them to enroll in in-depth training through a semester-long course, Writing Center Theory and Practice. Students who successfully complete the course are then eligible to apply for paid writing assistant positions in the center.

Impressed with the quality and level of undergraduate student work in the Writing Center, research and instruction librarians consulted with Writing Center faculty and staff, visited the Writing Center Theory and Practice class to get a sense of the training that students received, and hatched a plan to hire from the pool of students who take the class.

Transition to Research Center

Our library, like most academic libraries, is experiencing a decline in traditional reference questions. At the same time, we spend more time and effort on in-depth research consultations. We decided we needed to rebrand our service to better reflect what we do and how we can support students. Hiring and training students to be in a position to handle more complex interactions was one part of the rebranding, but we also needed to take a look at our service point. The Writing Center provided further inspiration. Its service model and physical space are conducive to the sustained collaborative interactions that are supplanting quick factual "ready reference" questions at the traditional library reference desk. The library was ready to revamp its reference desk to better reflect and encourage these collaborations. Our traditional reference desk supported a service in which the librarian was largely in control of the interaction. The desk itself suggested a power differential where the librarian controlled the computer while the student looked on. Conversely, the Writing Center has tables where students and consultants sit side by side. Consultants are trained in strategies that encourage the student to take the lead. The library decided to adapt this model, replacing the standard desk with a small stand-up kiosk that serves as a home base for the librarian or PRC. This kiosk is flanked by tables with computers and space for student laptops, where the librarian or PRC can sit along-side the student, who will do searching and typing. This set-up enables the student to continue working independently after the consultation, something that was problematic with the traditional reference desk. The new arrangement is called the Research Center, better reflecting what students can expect to do there. The long-term plan for the Research Center includes removing a wall that sequesters librarian offices away in a suite so that the offices open up directly into the Research Center and are more accessible to students.

ADMINISTRATION

The peer research consultant model was conceived as a way to create a higher level, para-professional work experience for students. Its primary purpose was to provide student workers with a more valuable and educational experience. But it had the added benefit of providing a solution to a staffing challenge. While we were taking incremental steps to elevate the student work experience and laying the groundwork for a transition to a peer research consultant model, a state budget situation suddenly reduced our existing permanent staffing. We had to act quickly to devise a plan. Fortunately, we had one in the works; we just didn't expect to enact it quite so quickly.

Staffing

We lost funding for a full-time evening and weekend library assistant position. The new PRCs, with appropriate and ample training, assumed these hours. Rather than working alongside a librarian at the reference desk, as had been our previous student assistant practice, PRCs staff the new Research Center independently. PRCs are scheduled Sundays from 5:00 p.m. until 9:00 p.m., Monday through Thursdays from noon until 9:00 p.m., and Fridays from noon until 4:30 p.m. Librarians and a library assistant staff the service in the morning and provide backup during the afternoon hours.

Compensation

We wanted to recognize and reward the increased responsibility we were expecting from our students as best we could, given budget limitations. We made a case to library administration to hire PRCs at two dollars an hour more than the rate we had been paying. Even in a tough budget situation, this was workable, as we had given up a full-time permanent staff position. In looking at the results of our aforementioned library student survey, we found other ways we could "reward" or make the position more attractive beyond monetary incentives. In our survey, student feedback suggested that students valued opportunities for increased interaction with librarians. Historically, most of the training and day-to-day supervision of students were handled by the library assistant, with input from the department head (a librarian). In the new PRC model, an effort was made to have all departmental librarians involved in the initial and ongoing training and mentoring of the students. (We explain in the training section of this chapter how we built that component into the training.) We wanted to ensure that student-librarian interaction went beyond training, however. PRCs are integral members of the department and we wanted them to develop collegial bonds with librarians as well. In scheduling students, we aim to ensure that each PRC has some weekday hours so that they have an opportunity to interact with librarians. Librarians make efforts to chat with students during their work shifts, librarians are all included in PRC meetings, and PRCs are asked to join discussions regarding procedures, services, and future directions of the department and library. For example, PRCs suggested that we have lanyards made identifying those who work in the Research Center. Because the goal was to have library staff out from behind a desk and working among students, lanyards would make them more easily identifiable. Similarly, PRCs and librarians brainstormed what an ideal service point would look like, pooled ideas, and built a custom desk that is very much influenced by the ideas of the PRCs.

Promotion

Fall semester came quickly. The PRCs were hired and training was planned. The transition to the Research Center was still underway, though some elements—particularly those having to do with renovating our physical space—were put on hold for budgetary reasons. We ordered a standing vinyl banner, featuring a picture of students working together, to identify the Research Center. We included articles about the Research Center and the new Peer Research Consultant program in our biannual print newsletter and in e-newsletters that librarians send to their liaison departments. Initial promotional efforts focused on faculty and staff. Future efforts will be aimed at students and will be led by the PRCs.

HIRING

For the initial launch of the peer consultant model, we needed to hire three to five students, depending on how many hours they were each interested in working. We indicated a range of hours from four to ten, assuming that some students would be supplementing other jobs, such as Writing Center jobs, and may be interested in fewer hours. Two returning students who had staffed our reference desk for several years were informed about the planned changes in service and expectations. Both were eager to become peer research consultants.

The timing of events, including the implications of the budget cuts and our decisions to transition to a Research Center and the peer consultant model, meant that we needed to hire over the summer. This posed challenges as most students were away from campus, not necessarily checking email or job announcements. Fortunately, our colleagues in the Writing Center offered assistance in reaching and promoting our new positions. They emailed position descriptions to students who had taken or were enrolled in the Writing Center Theory and Practice course for the upcoming year and posted an announcement of the positions in a Facebook group for Writing Center assistants.

Beginning with recruitment, we wanted the PRC experience to project a consistent philosophy and communicate the educational value of the position. The position description was written to emphasize liberal education goals, such as critical thinking, communication, and ability to demonstrate respect, sensitivity, and discretion in dealing with diverse populations. The position description also included language clearly articulating the value of the work. It listed benefits of the job:

- Development of high-level research skills to assist in academic and lifelong learning
- Mentoring from library faculty and staff
- Opportunity for independent work and high level of responsibility
- Development of valuable professional skills, including problem-solving, communication, customer service, and critical thinking
- Increased awareness of the many different aspects of campus life and activities

We intentionally designed the application and interview processes to emulate a professional experience. Deviating from a standard student employment form, which asked for little more than availability and GPA, we asked for a cover letter, résumé, and references. Recognizing that this might well be the first time students have ever been asked for a cover letter, we included language gently describing what it should include: "A brief letter describing any work experience, coursework, or other background that you think would make you a good fit for this position." From the pool of applicants, we selected students for interviews. Though ideally we wanted to provide a comparable experience for all candidates, it was more important to us to accommodate students, including those who were not in town over the summer, and be respectful of their varying levels of access to technology. As a result, we offered students the option of Skype, phone, or in-person interviews. Students opted for either phone or in-person interviews.

Thirty-minute interviews were scheduled. Three librarians and the library assistant formed the search committee that interviewed each student. As with the position description, interview questions were crafted not only to prompt responses but also to communicate the philosophy of the department. For example, one question was, "As a peer research consultant, you will have some skills and knowledge that your peers don't. Instead of simply telling your peers what to do, how do you think you will make your consultations truly collaborative?"

Once students were hired, they read and signed an expectations document that further communicated the philosophy of the department. In addition to covering practical and professional matters like absences and dress policies, it included the library and departmental mission and vision statements, with expectations for PRCs in upholding and contributing to those ideals. It also asked students to read and uphold the ALA Bill of Rights and campus computer use policies.

TRAINING

When we designed our initial peer research consultant training, we divided our training tasks into two different focuses. The functional orientation, covering routines, locations of supplies and tools, and the physical and digital practicalities of staffing the desk was best done in the Research Center itself. But we also wanted to work with our students on the dispositions and practices required to do actual peer-to-peer consulting. These, in addition to topics related to unpacking patron's questions and working with the library's search tools, were tackled in a six-hour weekend retreat after the second week of classes. After this beginning of the semester training was completed, we followed up with weekly online discussions of topics and questions related to peer consulting as well as with in-services at peer research consulting meetings.

We were working with both returning student workers and new recruits from the pool of students who had been trained as Writing Center Assistants. The returning student workers had the advantage of being familiar with the functional aspects of our department, but their previous experience at the desk had been under our old, more traditional reference desk model. They were used to showing and telling during interactions that typically took three to ten minutes. Our new recruits knew nothing about working in a Research Center but had ample experience with the back and forth of peer-to-peer consulting and the practice of letting the patron steer the consulting experience. As a result of this disparity, it was a challenge to design an initial training plan that could bring them into congruence.

Initial Training

We decided to do the functional training as the students came to their various shifts during the two weeks of the semester. We divided a list of topics and tasks to be covered among the department staff, including using chat, emergency procedures, mapping shared calendars, and timesheets. Each student had a checklist, and the idea was that the assigned staff would get to the students as they could. In reality, the scheduling of the students, some of whom mainly worked evening hours, made it difficult for the staff to connect with them. The department was also down two staff members that week, shifting the burden of training onto the shoulders of the remaining staff. As a result, training on the practical elements of the job was more haphazard than planned, with the Research and Instruction department supervisor doing much of the evening training and some students not being fully up to speed on the research desk, procedures, or locations until the second or even third week. Based on student feedback, one of the casualties of our unusually sporadic training was that our newer peer research consultants did not feel that they got much of an orientation to the physical space of the library.

Training Retreat

At the end of the second full week of class, after everyone had had at least a shift or two in the library, we held our one-day weekend training retreat. Four staff members from the Research and Instruction department participated, along with all five of our student trainees. After a brief ice-breaker, our morning agenda covered ways of being approachable, how to engage or be attentive, how to actively listen, and how to determine what student patrons need by asking follow-up questions. In order to convey the importance of this material and the dispositions we hoped our peer research consultants would develop, we devoted significant time to these topics. We gave short presentations followed by group discussions expanding on the presentation using their previous experience. For each topic, we also had the students perform related exercises, such as brainstorming, reflecting, and improv-based scenario exploration, so that they could apply or explore what we had discussed. A PowerPoint kept us on task, but only contained one or two slides per topic so as to keep the group focused on what was being said, instead of on the screen.

An important shift that we wanted our returning peer research consultants to make was a conceptual one: instead of thinking of themselves as mere dispensers of information about how to obtain library resources, showing and telling students where to go, we wanted them to adopt a more collaborative approach. One of the essays that all students in the Writing Center Theory and Practice course read is Jeff Brooks' "Minimalist Tutoring: Making Students Do All the Work."[4] This essay lays out, in concrete steps, the way a writing tutor can shift from the role of active editor to becoming an educator, one who grants the student the time and encouragement to focus on the task of writing. Like in a "minimalist tutoring" context, we wanted students seeking help from the Research Center to be "primary agents," responsible for making the key decisions in their own research. And as a writing tutor might convey the message "Your paper has value as a piece of writing," we also wanted our PRCs to broadcast that they were willing to listen and hear what their fellow students were inquiring about. Some of the advice Brooks gives is straightforward, such as positional advice: "Sit beside the student, not across a desk—that is where job interviewers and other authorities sit." Other advice required more unpacking and practice: "Get the student to talk." This material was old hat for the three PRCs who had been through the tutor training, but we felt it was important to devote some time to it on our training day. And we wanted to make legible some of the possible connections between their tutoring experience and their work in the library. For the non-Writing Center students, this approach was distinctly different than their previous experience of dispensing directions.

After a lunch break, which provided more opportunity for the peer research consultants and staff to get to know one another, we shifted into library-specific resources. Because the morning session had concluded with how explicit questions, such as "Can you tell me where the books about the Middle East are?" often indicate more complicated research needs, the students were interested in learning more about the resources that they might use to anticipate the range of needs they might face at the desk. Before the Saturday training session, the students had completed the library's Guide-on-the-Side introduction to using Primo, our resource discovery layer, so they were familiar with searching, narrowing and widening their search, requesting resources, and emailing results. We had worked up a list of research prompts and had the students work on individual questions and share their findings with the group. We had intended to then move to individual subject-specific databases but were only able to briefly introduce a few and discuss the contexts in which they could be more useful than the discovery layer. We knew we would continue database instruction in our meetings with the peer research consultants, so we weren't overly concerned when this section got short shrift.

As part of our assessment of our new training program, we had students complete a brief survey and we conducted a group interview. We expected, based on our own observations, that there would be some divergence in the students' responses depended on which group they fell into—those with Writing Center experience and those with prior experience in the library. We predicted that the repetition of some material learned in the Writing Center course would be seen as less valuable. Without self-identifiers, it is difficult to confirm this, but we did gain some constructive observations. For some, the section on "approachability" went on too long: "Personally, I did not need much training in being approachable or how to 'kindly' interact with my peers.… " But the "active listening" and "understanding the question behind the question" sections were brought up positively in both the survey and the discussion interview: "For me, the time we spent going over active listening and negotiating questions was the most valuable (followed closely by the time we spent going over library resources). The activity used to demonstrate active listening was a great way to identify individual strengths and weaknesses. One of the returning student workers even expressed the wish that she had practiced this earlier in her college career."

The format for the morning session, with its short presentations and practice activities, turned out to be effective for many of the PRCs. As one student wrote on the survey, "I really liked the improv games because it helped me show what I knew and relate the situation to real life." Applying the concepts and dispositions discussed in the lesson almost immediately provided a low-stakes way for students to try them out, but it also had the added value of letting the students demonstrate what they themselves were bringing to the Research Center.

One thing that several of the students wanted more of was practice with real-life or probable research questions that they might face at the desk. Though these were included in the weekly discussions questions, it was clear that the students wanted their semester to be frontloaded with more experience responding to practice questions. In subsequent training day sessions, we cut back on some of the dispositional training and included more opportunities to work through Research Center scenarios.

Asynchronous Training

After the weekend session was complete, students were asked to engage in asynchronous discussions of questions the research librarians supplied each week. Discussion questions were posed at the beginning of the week in the Learning Management System (LMS) discussion area set up for the PRCs. Some were research "problems," scenarios that students were asked to consider how they would approach. Other questions were more reflective, asking students to think about an experience they had as a peer consultant. The first question of the semester asked students to consider an unsatisfactory reference interview, where a student asked for books about drawing and was dissatisfied to receive the call number of a volume titled *How to Draw: Drawing and Sketching Objects and Environments from Your Imagination.* Students were asked to think of follow-up questions or other strategies to determine what the student was really looking for. Another more reflective question asked the PRCs to think about a successful encounter at the desk and what made it stand out to them as a success. Some questions also invited students to comment about and make recommendations related to our new, evolving service model. For example, one post asked them to consider what furniture set-up would be most conducive to collaborative sessions. While not every discussion question led to exchanges between the PRCs, they read each other's responses avidly, and it was a good way for the PRCs to stay connected despite the disparate schedules. Librarians joined in on the discussion, commenting on strategies and sharing experiences. The weekly questions also provided a reason for students to check the shared LMS site, where important or amusing news was regularly posted.

In the online survey, the PRCs described the online sessions as a great way to stay connected during the semester, but they had other benefits, too. One student remarked that they were especially beneficial the first few weeks of the semester: "They gave me direction as I explored the library website and databases." Another student appreciated the opportunity to stand back and reflect on experiences at the Research Center: "The D2L discussion questions are great ways to keep thinking critically about the questions that come our way. It is great to see how other people respond so I can learn different approaches to a problem that I could use in the future when I have tricky questions at the desk."

Peer Research Consultant Meetings

For synchronous training during the semester, we turned to scheduled meetings. These meetings offered the tutors feedback on their work experiences and provided a venue for further training on the discipline-specific databases. Because of the difficulty of finding a common time to meet, the meetings have not been frequent. But they do present the opportunity for tutors to brainstorm about solutions to shared problems as well as to provide ideas about our evolving service model. Students could talk about the challenges of engaging their peers in collaborative sessions when they were expecting mere dispensing of information. At some points in the semester, the number of students seeking assistance was lower and the peer research consultants expressed their frustration at not being able to ply their skills. We also discussed ways of marketing our services and making the Research Center more appealing to the PRCs' fellow students.

ASSESSMENT

Assessment of the Peer Research Consultant program includes individual student assessment as well as programmatic assessment.

Student Assessment

As with the recruiting, hiring, training, and mentoring stages of working with student employees, we wanted the assessment stage to include elements of a high-impact practice. We turned to the University of Iowa's IOWA GROW program for inspiration. Iowa's program, based on the work of George Kuh, encourages students to make connections between their work experience and classroom learning by having them reflect on and discuss four questions:

- How is this job fitting in with your academics?
- What are you learning here that's helping you in school?
- What are you learning in class that you can apply here at work?
- Can you give a couple of examples of things you've learned here that you think you'll use in your chosen profession?[5]

We are now including variations of these questions in the formal annual review process, making performance evaluations more formative than summative. By beginning early on to get students to reflect on and articulate the value of their work experience, it is our hope that these ideas will be well-established and internalized by the time they graduate and move on to their professional lives.

PRC Program Assessment

In addition to assessing our students individually, it was also important for us to know how our efforts to implement the PRC program as a high-impact employment experience were faring. Through both the survey we administered online via Qualtrics and our group interview, we were able to gain some insights into the ways the PRCs were connecting their work experience in the Research Center with their campus experience, coursework, and future goals. Students described how their experiences assisting other students helped them think through their own research problems. The students who also worked in the

Writing Center found that being involved in the researched writing process from start to finish gave them new insights that helped them in both locales. Several students also recognized how important learning to check one's own assumptions would be to their future careers. One student, who wished to go on to be a counselor, stated that learning to listen to students taught her the importance of not quickly lumping issues into broad, known categories but rather hearing the specifics before responding. We plan to gather additional longitudinal data on the effectiveness of the Peer Research Consultant program through our biennial Library Satisfaction Survey and the Library Student Employee Survey. The former will provide feedback from library patrons on the service provided, and the latter will reflect student attitudes regarding the value of their work experience that we can compare to pre- and non-PRC student employee attitudes.

REFLECTION

In reflecting on our nascent Peer Research Consultant program, we can identify early successes as well as challenges.

We view the decision to recruit PRCs through the Writing Center as an unmitigated success. The students hired through the Writing Center are extremely engaged and successful in the PRC role. They bring with them a strong disposition for collaborative tutoring. We have observed that their passion for and commitment to service is infectious, raising the bar for the PRCs who were grandfathered in from previous reference desk student assistant positions. We have seen increased levels of engagement and effort in these returning students as a result.

Hiring high-performing students does pose a managerial challenge. Their high level of interest leads to greater expectations and demand for interesting, meaningful, and higher-level work. When traffic is slow in the Research Center, they are less likely to be content with unrelated or menial tasks. This is a good challenge to have, and we are developing new strategies for addressing it. PRCs have assumed responsibility for projects, including developing an FAQ for the library, creating videos and promotional media, and authoring LibGuides. We are incorporating the opportunity for PRCs to engage in faculty-student collaborative research on a topic related to their work in the library. We are also exploring the idea of credentialing additional self-guided training whereby students can earn certificates for completing additional training modules. A student may elect, for example, to complete a business information or legal information training module and receive a certificate.

We have long struggled with increasing diversity in our student staff. This challenge is exacerbated when we limit the pool of applicants to a pre-filtered population of students. The Writing Center staff actively recruits diverse students to take the Writing Center Theory and Practice course, but in our initial recruitment effort, none applied for the PRC positions. In subsequent semesters we worked with the Office of Multicultural Affairs to identify and encourage students to apply and have had more success.

Actively including all departmental librarians in the PRC training and mentoring roles has been another positive move, not only for the students but for the librarians. Several librarians have expressed an increase in job satisfaction emanating from their greater involvement with the students. This greater involvement has led to a wider range of more interesting projects for the students, addressing the challenge mentioned earlier. It also provides more continuity in supervising and communicating with students, as everyone shares a more cohesive idea of student expectations.

Toward the end of her first semester as a PRC, one student recently sent an unsolicited letter to Research and Instruction library staff in which she wrote:

> You all have taught me so much. Whether it is through answering my endless amount of questions or through our day-do-day discussions, I have a significant opportunity to learn. You provide guidance as I navigate through the complexities of the library (and life), which allows me to improve each day. The library has been a wonderful place in which I am able to grow and expand my mind at this university.

As far as reaching our goal of creating high-impact experiences for our students, we have more work and more assessment to do. But early indications suggest we are on the right track.

NOTES

1. George D. Kuh, *High-Impact Educational Practices: What They Are, Who Has Access to Them, and Why They Matter* (Washington, DC: Association of American Colleges and Universities, 2009), 9–17.
2. Susan Adams, "The 10 Skills Employers Most Want in 2015 Graduates," *Forbes*, November 12, 2014, accessed November 30, 2015, http://www.forbes.com/sites/susanadams/2014/11/12/the-10-skills-employers-most-want-in-2015-graduates.
3. Hart Research Associates, "It Takes More Than a Major: Employer Priorities for College Learning and Student Success" (Washington, DC: Hart Research, April 10, 2013), accessed November 30, 2015, https://www.aacu.org/sites/default/files/files/LEAP/2013_EmployerSurvey.pdf.
4. Jeff Brooks, "Minimalist Tutoring: Making the Student Do All the Work," in *The St. Martin's Sourcebook for Writing Tutors*, ed. Christina Murphy and Steve Sherwood (New York: St. Martin's Press, 1995), 88–95.
5. "Iowa GROW," University of Iowa, Division of Student Life, accessed December 9, 2015, https://vp.studentlife.uiowa.edu/initiatives/grow/.

BIBLIOGRAPHY

Adams, Susan. "The 10 Skills Employers Most Want in 2015 Graduates." *Forbes.com*. November 12, 2014. Accessed November 30, 2015. http://www.forbes.com/sites/susanadams/2014/11/12/the-10-skills-employers-most-want-in-2015-graduates/.

Brooks, Jeff. "Minimalist Tutoring: Making the Student Do All the Work." In *The St. Martin's Sourcebook for Writing Tutors*, edited by Christina Murphy and Steve Sherwood, 88–95. New York: St. Martin' Press, 1995.

Hart Research Associates. *It Takes More Than A Major: Employer Priorities for College Learning and Student Success: An Online Survey Among Employers Conducted on Behalf of the Association of American*

   Colleges and Universities. Washington, DC: Hart Research, April 10, 2013. Accessed November 30, 2015. https://www.aacu.org/sites/default/files/files/LEAP/2013_EmployerSurvey.pdf.

Kuh, George D. *High-Impact Educational Practices: What They Are, Who Has Access To Them, and Why They Matter.* Washington, DC: Association of American Colleges and Universities, 2009.

University of Iowa. Division of Student Life. "Iowa GROW." 2015. Accessed December 9, 2015. https://vp.studentlife.uiowa.edu/initiatives/grow/.

Part III

PERSPECTIVES FROM CAMPUS COLLABORATORS

Collaborators 1

NOTHING IS PERMANENT EXCEPT CHANGE:
The Adaptive Writing Center Training Model

Patrick Johnson and Melanie Rabine

OVERVIEW

In 2012, our writing center, the Fred Meijer Center for Writing and Michigan Authors (FMCFWAMA) at Grand Valley State University, joined two new programs, the Library Research Center and the Speech Lab, to create the Knowledge Market. To better serve multiple student populations and embody the student-centered design of the Mary Idema Pew Library, the Knowledge Market was designed to offer collaborative services in a central campus location. In creating the research consultant program, library administrators crafted their hiring and training model on our writing center, which had thirty-five years of steady growth and success.

We support a staff of sixty-plus undergraduate and graduate consultants, five campus locations, and an average of 12,000 consultations per academic year. The FMCFWAMA also provides in-class consultant support for every section of first-year writing (roughly sixty-two sections of twenty-eight students) as well as the two-semester version with a basic writing foundation (fourteen sections). We also offer multiple in-class workshops for any university course that incorporates writing. With GVSU hosting more than 25,0000 students, the FMCFWAMA plays an active role in writing across all disciplines. Much of our success can be traced back to our model for how we hire, train, and support our staff, which was developed by former director Ellen Schendel. Discussed in depth here, we offer this model to illustrate how our approach is grounded in established writing center theory and can be adapted to any peer-mentoring program.

ADMINISTRATION

The administration of the writing center is comprised of a full-time director (AP), a full-time office coordinator (AP), and a half-time training coordinator (AP). These three positions also work alongside a tenured faculty member who teaches the consultant training class and oversees Writing Across the Curriculum (WAC). The consultant staff is comprised of sixty to sixty-five undergraduate peer writing consultants, two or three graduate assistants, and three or four operational desk staff. We promote peer mentorship in both our mission and practice and we designate four to eight members of our staff to be lead consultants, who carry additional responsibilities to mentor and train new consultants.

HIRING

Goals

- Hire for the upcoming academic year by interviewing at the end of the previous one
- Extensive application process with scenarios, sample paper feedback, teacher recommendations, and writing samples
- Involve current staff in reviewing applications and interviewing applicants

The first and most important part of creating a strong staff of dedicated student workers is to ensure that you hire effectively from the onset. To achieve this, we do all our hiring for the fall semester at the end of the previous academic year. It's Michigan, so we call it a Winter Semester, whereas it is known as the Spring Semester in other parts of the country. There is not one kind of student we try to hire, but there are some qualities we look for in applicants, such as patience, intellectual curiosity, strong professional work habits, self-aware writing processes, good relationships with faculty, emotional unflappability, and solid oral/written communication skills. While administrators may implicitly and explicitly know what qualities are well-suited to being a writing consultant, we don't believe in hiring only one type of student. A thriving community of student workers benefits from diversity in all forms, whether it be cultural, academic, or personal.

Applications

All our application materials are available in Appendix A, and our goal with the application is to create a picture of a potential consultant by drawing on various aspects of their background, including the following:

- Demographic information:
  - Name
  - Phone and email address
  - Class standing
  - Major
  - GPA
  - Availability during the upcoming fall/winter semesters
- Qualifications and experience:
  - Other employment responsibilities
  - Types of writing-intensive courses taken
  - Habits in soliciting feedback on writing tasks
  - Previous consulting/tutoring experience
- Situational responses to a sample student paper
- Two hypothetical consultant scenarios:
  - Group meeting with disruptive students
  - Responding to negative student feedback
- Two academic writing samples
- Professor recommendation

Put together, these materials address how students participate in a variety of roles: as students, writers, and employees.

Our deadline for applications is the end of the second week in March, the week after students return from spring break. Leading up to the application deadline, we advertise in campus publications, on digital displays, and on billboards; however, our most important contacts are faculty themselves. Ideally, our staff reflects the students we want to serve and we strive to represent multiple majors in our center. Recruiting faculty in the process helps diversify our applicant pool and creates greater faculty awareness and appreciation of our program. Several times throughout the year, we email faculty who teach first-year writing and upper-division writing classes and ask them to recommend students who they believe would be effective writing consultants. Additionally, we solicit faculty recommendations when responding to faculty requests for additional services or questions about our staff/training in regard to assisting students from specific majors. When we begin actively soliciting applications (in early February) our office coordinator emails faculty recommended students and encourages them to apply.

Reviewing Materials

Normally, we receive between eighty and 120 applications for twenty to thirty openings. While it is time-intensive, we tend to interview roughly 90 percent of applicants because we recognize that the interview is the most essential part of hiring and we prefer to give all potential hires the chance. Those who are not granted an interview tend to demonstrate multiple areas of concern, such as lack of maturity, a fundamental misconception of the job/service, faculty concerns, and/or academic difficulties.

One of the best resources to draw on in the application process is the current staff. In our case, we utilize our lead consultants in the reviewing, assessing, and ranking of applications. Our approach is to use a two-reader system where two lead consultants review each application, though they are never allowed to evaluate or interview students they knew previously. We use a scoring sheet (Appendix B) to collect reader comments and ask each reader to score the application for both their application and their writing samples. Once all the applications have been reviewed, the administrative staff determines which applicants will be scheduled for an interview.

Interviews

All our interviews are group interviews involving four applicants and four members of the writing center staff (two administers and two lead consultants). Each interview lasts fifty minutes and is divided into two parts: group and individual. We begin with introductions both of the interviewers and the process, followed by asking prospective consultants to give their names and what made them want to work in the writing center.

After introductions, students have their applications returned to them. In it, they were all asked to provide sample feedback to a piece of student writing. We ask them to familiarize themselves with what they wrote and then have a group discussion with each other about providing feedback to the writer. Since a primary aspect of their work will be to function as an embedded consultant in a first-year writing course, it is essential we observe how candidates conduct themselves when working in a group setting. While the candidates discuss providing feedback with each other, each interviewer has a sheet to review one member of the interview group. Our scoring sheet (Appendix C) focuses on areas such as priority of concerns, tone (toward the student writer and each other), clarity of oral communication, and other aspects of their consulting instincts (e.g., use of praise, participation in the group, attitude, etc).

After ten minutes of discussion, we switch to an individual interview model where the four candidates move to the corners of the room and the four interviewers spend four to seven minutes speaking with each candidate. Each interviewer has a different set of questions that they ask of each candidate (Appendix D), including their professional work experience, their relationship with writing, their future goals, and two scenarios of challenging experiences they may have working in the writing center: negative feedback from a fellow consultant and a disruptive student group.

We end each interview with the opportunity for candidates to ask questions. Before they leave, we take a photo of each interview group so we can visually recall each applicant later in the process and give them a sheet with information about the rest of the process (interview timeline, notification date, training requirements, etc.). Following the interview process, administration informs between twenty to thirty applicants that they have been selected to become writing consultants. The number we hire is dependent on the number of graduating consultants from the previous year and the programmatic needs for the upcoming semester. During the summer, we contact them about their schedules (to make sure they can all fit our one credit consultant training course) and to give them details about orientation.

TRAINING

Goals

- Two-day orientation before the semester begins
- One credit class taken concurrently with first semester consultant hours
- Ongoing support and mentorship from lead consultants and administration

Our program believes that ongoing training is essential for a thriving center. Our orientation introduces new consultants to the features, responsibilities, and philosophies of our center, and those ideas are carried over into a one-credit consulting with writers course (WRT 306) as well as revisited in bi-weekly group meetings and professional development workshops. Each year, administrators and lead consultants revisit the previous year's orientation and adjust according to feedback and reflection. The outline of our approach utilizes an "I do, we do, you do" model, which transitions from observation into group discussions and activities, before asking consultants to engage in a consultation on their own. Once consultants begin working their regular hours, we provide multiple venues for discussion and reflection.

Orientation

The first part of our three-part training process is a two-day orientation, which covers all the essential aspects of the service, including our locations, services, and the various roles they will have as a writing consultant. The complete agenda for our orientation is available in Appendix E. Incoming consultants get to meet each other, the writing program administration, and the lead consultants who will play an essential role in their ongoing training. In addition, new consultants meet several instructors of first-year writing, whom they will be working alongside in classrooms. Finally, the orientation is the lynchpin of our training process as it is the first impression of the philosophies that guide our program. Up until this point, it is still possible for prospective consultants to assume they are going to be primarily editing student papers or correcting mistakes. Our orientation introduces them to the idea of having a dialogue with writers, forming a rapport, and adapting to the needs of each student and situation. Prior to attending, we ask all incoming consultants to read "Talking in the Middle: Why Writers Need Writing Tutors" by Muriel Harris[1] as it is a foundational text in defining the role of a consultant in the writing process. The first activity in our orientation involves discussing impressions of the article and how its ideas inform our service and approach to assisting students.

With the guiding philosophy in mind, consultants are asked to provide feedback on a sample student essay. Rather than put anyone on the spot, we run the discussion of the essay as a large group discussion, which allows everyone to hear and respond to various possible approaches. Had we not already introduced them to the work we do (in interviews and applications) and the philosophies that guide us (pre-reading Muriel Harris), the exercise could be a public outpouring of editorial and evaluative suggestions. However, these are usually rare, and any comments that position the consultant as the sole provider of knowledge or the one responsible for catching every mistake can be addressed for everyone in a discussion.

Next, new consultants will observe a consultation between two consultants. While we have experimented with designing a mock consultation that highlights important features and strategies, we have had the best success when asking our lead consultants to perform an actual consultation based on a piece of writing that is currently in process. Meanwhile, new consultants can compare the observed consultation to a sample drop-in script (Appendix F), which details the most common questions and categories of discussion for a consultation. Since the observed consultation is real and takes place between two consultants who already know each other (although we ask them to act like they don't), the comparison often leads to insightful questions about the numerous choices and adaptations consultants will face when working with students.

Day two puts the introductions from day one into practice. We begin with a guided exercise, covering their impressions of the role consulting plays in the writing process or asking new consultants to draw their own writing process, complete with roadblocks and frustrations. We recognize that the volume of information presented on day one can be overwhelming and we want to begin day two with an open conversation about how they see themselves as a writer and/or consultant. Next, we break into small groups and run through various scenarios of tricky and/or common occurrences in writing center work, including awkward conversations, dealing with silence, demanding students, etc.

The culmination of the training is a practice consultation, where new consultants are given an opportunity to try out the concepts and strategies they just learned with the returning members of our staff. All our returning consultants are given a paper to present as their own, and the new consultant is given thirty minutes to work with the writer on improving the draft. Following the practice consultation, we lead a discussion where each returning consultant offers a recap and praise for the new consultants' efforts. We want all our new staff to believe that this is work they can do, even if they still feel unprepared. Threaded throughout the day are opportunities for new consultants to get to know each other as people, through icebreakers, small group discussions, and a pizza lunch.

The end of day two includes having all new consultants complete brief administrative tasks, such as filling out their schedule of availability and signing a contract (Appendix G) that details the expectations of their position. With the orientation complete, the entire staff is gathered for an all-staff meeting, which recaps the previous year and looks ahead. At our university, every program must do an assessment project each year, and the staff meeting is when we share the data and impact of what was learned. Sometimes the assessment takes the form of updates or news, but oftentimes the assessment informs a change in policy or a new resource/training. The staff meeting is also when we discuss dates for upcoming conferences, training workshops, and special project opportunities. This orientation is the first part of our training model, and the ideas introduced there continue throughout the new hire's first semester in WRT 306 and mentor groups.

Training Course

WRT 306 is our training course, offered through the university catalog and required of all our newly hired consultants regardless of graduation class, previous professional experience, major, financial status, etc. The class is a one-credit course, and an instructor approved by the university teaches the material, which covers philosophical foundations of writing center work, best practices in working with student writers, and theories for peer-to-peer consulting. Consultants will read and discuss articles from Kenneth Bruffee, Steven North, Andrea Lunsford, and more. The standard textbook for the course is the *The Oxford Guide for Writing Tutors*,[2] which our center provides.

In addition to the primary textbook, the instructor provides supplementary articles culled from other sources. Because the instructor for WRT 306 is also the director of Writing Across the Curriculum, there is a larger perspective in both readings and assignments on the role consultants play in developing student writers at our university. For example, one assignment has consultants interview current teachers of upper-division writing courses to gain insights into common concerns as well as instructor priorities for their classes. Another assignment requires consultants to visit the writing center as a student. We do this to encourage empathy in consultants, many of whom have never visited the writing center. Because we hire high-achieving students, who exempt out of common courses or are in honors programs, we feel it is essential that we confront assumptions about the writing center acting as a remedial service.

All consultants are required to observe a first-year writing portfolio assessment group, where three instructors collaboratively determine grades through discussion of representative student papers. Many consultants reference the portfolio observation as a formative experience and it is often featured in their final writing assignment, a personal tutoring philosophy. These assignments and experiences are designed to develop a deeper understanding of university writing expectations, which directly affects their approach to assisting students. Finally, consultants may choose to do a research project on a particular area of writing center scholarship, which may lead to a conference presentation and/or a professional development workshop for our staff.

ONGOING SUPPORT
Goals

- Bi-weekly mentor groups with new and lead consultants
- Paid professional development workshops each semester
- Regular emails celebrating staff successes and upcoming opportunities
- Administrative availability and open-door policies

The support we provide to our staff is designed to be adaptive and ongoing. There are two mandatory supportive features provided by the writing center that are specifically unique to a consultant's first semester: WRT 306 and mentor groups. These two supportive features are specific to the first semester of a consultant's career, and they exist while consultants are working with students at our various locations. Since consultants are asked to begin tutoring already at the start of the semester, the WRT 306 training course and mentor groups exist as a hybrid of ongoing training and support.

Mentor Groups

Along with attending their assigned section of WRT 306, the new consultants attend mentor groups, where they receive professional and logistical announcements, consulting support, a safe closed-door space, and an opportunity to bond with other coworkers. One or two lead consultants facilitate a conversation intended to provide a venue for sharing their positive and negative experiences as well as problem solve as a group. The mentor groups, therefore, are peer-to-peer support groups, which extend our philosophy out into our continued-support program.

We see this mentoring experience as a necessary component to their continued learning as employees in the writing center. We recognize the importance of safety when working with student writers and we value consultants' needs to talk about their working experiences with each other without fear of administrative presence in the room; therefore, we see the lead consultant's role in the mentor group as a way to alleviate the pressure of evaluation from the space. In this safe space, we expect consultants to not only receive information about best practices from their fellow coworkers, but we also expect that consultants depressurize regarding the stress that can occur when starting a new job and/or working with student writers. Our mentor groups, therefore, are comprised of peers, and this helps create a learning-focused environment wherein consultants feel more comfortable voicing genuine concerns with their fellow class-mates and coworkers. Since we value the peer-to-peer model in consulting, we feel it is important to extend that model throughout our systems of on-going support within our mentor groups.

Additionally, the mentor group model helps us spread information in an efficient way. Our writing center is gifted with a large staff, and it is difficult to hear everyone's unique concerns, share specific and pertinent information face-to-face, and maintain a standard method of communication for all employees. Though we recognize the importance of all staff members receiving and sharing the same information, we feel especially concerned for new consultants who might not feel comfortable yet with our administrative open-door policy. The mentor groups, therefore, help us share timely logistical information with our newest members of staff on a regular basis, which in turn helps ease new consultants into their consulting identity and help develop their relationship with the administration.

Professional Development

Once writing consultants are hired, they are expected to continue their training by attend-ing a required two hours of professional development. These two hours of additional training come in the form of workshops, lectures, round table discussions, or special interest groups. The sessions are based on core writing center topics (e.g., ESL consulting, non-directive strategies, working with grammar, etc.), on topics that feel relevant but have not been covered in training (i.e., working with multimodal texts, collaborating with other services on campus, gender in the writing center, etc.), or on areas of interest that consul-tants have asked for specifically. These workshops may be facilitated by writing center administrators, lead consultants (who feel more confident researching and presenting in front of their peers), or consultants with a specific area of interest they wish to share with their coworkers. In other words, anyone can facilitate a professional development workshop; however, most often, consultants feel better prepared after having worked in the writing center for at least a semester.

Each year, we offer two all-staff meetings, one per semester. The first takes place immedi-ately following orientation and the second is offered at the beginning of the winter semes-ter. The second all-staff meeting is devoted to an area of training we consider essential for everyone. We have covered topics such as active-shooter training, maximizing their consultant experience in the professional job search, and introductions, overlaps, and intersections with other student support services on campus (such as the women's center, LGBT center, counseling center, disabilities center, and the office of multicultural affairs). Despite the fact that we feel writing consultants are ready to work with student writers immediately upon completing their two-day writing center orientation/training, we want to continually expose them to new ideas and provide opportunities throughout the year that address unanticipated problems for our service.

By extending the learning process beyond the original training event, our writing center sees training as an adaptive curriculum, requiring constant evaluation, adjustment, and integration of current research. Therefore, our professional development workshops are opportunities to challenge preexisting thought, theory, and practice within the field of writing center work. They are also considered learning opportunities that are fashionable, in that they relate to the current culture and climate of the writing center each semester. Most often, the writing center coordinator will poll the entire staff at the beginning of the year, collect topics of interest, and assemble workshops that address the staff's interests. Also, the writing center coordinator will help facilitate the consultants' interests in presenting their own personal projects based on what the current staff is working on at the time; therefore, the professional development program continues supporting the staff intellectually, academically, and practically based on the ever-changing community of the writing center. Because the staff proposes the topics, we ensure not only participation but relevance as well.

Furthermore, these professional development workshops often lead to greater projects, conference presentations, and/or résumé features for our staff; this aspect feels integral in another way our writing center provides on-going support. We value both the work of our staff and their academic and professional futures beyond the writing center. Our professional development workshop program, therefore, is typically an entry-level way of addressing ways in which consultants can develop their writing center work into a marketable, profitable, and enriching work experience.

Lastly, we encourage every member of our staff to consider attending the Michigan Writing Center Association conference. We value not only the experience of attending a professional conference devoted to peer mentoring, but the experience introduces them to conversations within the discipline, alternate approaches to services used by other centers, and possible research ideas that can be explored in the future. While the main tenants of our training (orientation, class, meetings) are required, we have several that are optional (conferences, research projects). A key philosophy that guides us is making sure we fully utilize the experience and knowledge of current consultants.

ASSESSMENT

- Creating university assessments that involve consultant projects
- Embracing a transparent process with regular opportunities to share data

Grand Valley State University requires all programs to perform internal assessments at various intervals: annual, three-year, five-year, and seven-year. The multi-year assessments include larger data trends, program outreach efforts, student satisfaction reports, total numbers, as well as reassessments of programmatic vision and its alignment with the goals of the college and university. The annual assessment addresses any unique or specific aspect of our service. Past assessments have studied the effectiveness of online consulting, collaborative consulting training/support, location and audience analysis, and the value of our program for unique audiences, such as multi-language writers, graduate students, and low-traffic majors.

As stated earlier, yearly assessment data is shared at the beginning of every year with everyone on staff. Not only does this increase program transparency, but it can often spark ideas for research projects that may later become assessment projects in the future. For example, a common route to training involves a discussion within a mentor group, that becomes a research project in WRT 306, that is converted into a professional development training or the creation of a resource, and, finally, the opportunity to present on the topic at a local or regional conference, which might further inspire other consultants to pursue research on similar or related ideas. This training loop utilizes consultant knowledge but also professionally empowers them to train each other and participate in academic and programmatic discussions in the field. A common axiom used in our center to describe this process is "to teach is to learn twice," meaning that asking consultants to teach and train each other creates a deeper understanding and creates a community of ongoing development and learning.

REFLECTION

After the first semester, we consider all consultants to be fully trained. The need for bi-weekly support meetings is replaced by monthly returner groups, which have a similar format, but with more specific topics of discussion. For example, the first returner group involves consultants reflecting on feedback from students they assisted the previous semester. All identifying data is removed, but consultants are given a copy of session notes, student evaluations, and comments. Upon reading feedback, there is often a need to talk through responding to constructive comments and recognizing trends in students they have assisted. While somewhat informal in practice, addressing feedback reinforces our program's goal to encourage ongoing reflection and training.

As an example of our reflective approach, we had a transgender student visit our center, who inspired a needed cultural and programmatic change. Our scheduling database connects to student records, and our consultants had been trained to refer to this data when learning the names of their upcoming clients in order to call for them in our space. On this day, the database identified the student as "Christopher" ; however, the student goes by Chris or Christine. Without intention, we had outed a student's transgender identity. The student was embarrassed, as were we. In response, we offered trainings about gendered pronouns (e.g., the use of they as opposed to he/she binaries), created new language for filling out session notes (e.g., asking each student for their preferred pronoun), and we changed how we address students. Before, we would call out a student's first name when their consultant was ready from the database, but following this experience, we now only use last names. We saw this reactive change to be a responsible adjustment given our mistake, but educating the staff required a flexible model of information sharing. This example also demonstrates how a learning opportunity in the writing center led to a change in service as well as a programmatic conversation, which we continued at local, regional, and national writing center conferences.

Academic conferences provide a context for consultants to develop their consulting identity by connecting their work and interests. We encourage all consultants to consider converting their WRT 306 project, a professional development workshop, or a personal academic project into a conference presentation. Though mentor groups, professional development workshops, and returner groups are required training and paid, we also consider attending and presenting at academic conferences to be an invaluable personal and professional experience. We do not require consultants to attend; however, we take great effort in advertising upcoming conferences, supporting consultants with every stage of the presenting process and guiding them through funding opportunities. Engaging in conversations that extend beyond our university fuels reflection and assessment within our center.

APPENDIX A

APPLICATION TO BECOME A WRITING CONSULTANT

GRAND VALLEY STATE UNIVERSITY
FRED MEIJER CENTER FOR WRITING AND MICHIGAN AUTHORS

- Turn in this application and two academic writing samples to the Fred Meijer Center for Writing (LOH 120). Late applications will not be considered.

- Please ensure that both writing samples are free of grades or professors' responses, and that at least one sample includes outside research and a works-cited/references list.

- Have a professor email a brief recommendation to the Writing Center—**virtualwc@ mail.gvsu.edu.** The recommendation should indicate in what capacity and for how long the professor has known you, and why he or she thinks you'd make a good writing center consultant.

- Applications are not complete unless your writing samples and recommendation are received in addition to this application form. Incomplete files will not be considered.

- For more information about the writing consultant position, please see our website: www.gvsu.edu/wc

Name _____   G Number _____

Current phone_____   Current email address: _____

Summer address _____
Be sure to include city, state & zip

Summer home _____   Summer email address _____ __

Your current class standing:
☐ Freshman ☐ Sophomore ☐ Junior ☐ Senior ☐ Graduate Student

Your Major(s): _____   Your Minor(s) _____

Current GPA   (At least a 3.0 cumulative GPA is preferred).

Please indicate your agreement with the following statements by signing below:

- I understand that if hired to be a Writing Consultant, I am obligated to attend two full days of training/orientation on August 27 & 28, occasional professional development seminars, and regular staff meetings.

- I understand that if hired, I will be required to enroll in the 1-credit course WRT 306: Seminar for New Writing Consultants. This course will be offered at three different times and at both the Allendale & Pew/GR campuses to accommodate different students' course schedules. Consultants are paid for attending orientation and meetings; they receive course credit for WRT 306. Please note that block tuition covers 12-15 credit hours.
- I understand that if hired, I will be required to work for the writing center at least 8 hours per week.
- I give the writing center permission to verify my GPA & class standing as listed on this application.

Signature _____ Date _____

Qualifications & Experience

Name: _____

Your current class standing:
☐ Freshman ☐ Sophomore ☐ Junior ☐ Senior ☐ Graduate Student

Your Major(s): _____ Your Minor(s) _____

Will you be a GVSU student   ☐ Fall 2020   ☐ Winter 2021
(check all that apply):

Will you be student assisting/teaching   ☐ Fall 2020   ☐ Winter 2021
(check all that apply):

Will you be studying abroad   ☐ Fall 2020   ☐ Winter 2021
(check all that apply):

> **Please note:** *Almost all consultant training activities happen in the fall semester, and we need a lot of daytime availability, since that is when the writing center is open and most WRT 098/150 classes are in session. Therefore, we can only hire students who will hold full-time status for the entire academic year, who will not study abroad in the fall, and who will not be student assisting/student teaching during the 2020-2021 academic year. See "Becoming a Writing Consultant" at www.gvsu.edu/wc for more information.*

Do you plan to work at another job while working as a writing consultant? ☐ Y ☐ N

If yes, about how many hours per week will you work at your other job? _____

Considering other commitments such as internships, jobs, leadership in organizations, church, sports, etc, what range of hours per week would you be able to work for the Center next year? (You are required to work at least 8 hours per week)_____

What Writing Department, SWS, or other writing-intensive courses have you taken?

How often and from whom do you seek feedback for your writing?

Please describe any previous teaching, tutoring, or other instructional experience:

Please describe any previous customer service experience you have, or other experiences working with people in a workplace, volunteer, or classroom setting:

Please describe any other experience relevant to the writing consultant position:

Situational Responses

1. **Please type answers to the following questions and attach those responses to the rest of your application.**

    Below is a student essay; the assignment was to respond to class readings on the topic of literacy. Imagine that you are a writing consultant giving the student some feedback. Please read the paper carefully and attach your typed responses to the following prompts. (You aren't required to write directly on the student's paper, but feel free to make notes in the margins if that is helpful to you.)

    A. Please list what you see as the main problems in this paper in the order that you would address them with the student-writer.

    B. Imagine you are talking with the student-writer. Address in a paragraph how you'd attend to the first issue on your list. Write as if you were talking to the student.

    C. After looking back at the essay again, select a few grammar or mechanical problems that you would want to discuss with the student. How would you address those issues? Of the essay's grammar/punctuation errors, why are these the most important to address?

Learning Through Interaction

Literacy is not just things that are learned in classrooms and textbooks, but rather by everyone sharing their knowledge through interaction. This argument is similarily posed in Heath's essay, "The Fourth Vision" and of Freire's essay, "The Banking Concept of Education."

Freire voices his opinion that the problem-posing method is better for education. This problem-posing method makes no authoritarian out of anyone. Rather it is a process in which everyone shares their knowledge, learns, and therefore grows. Learning from everyone in a classroom is beneficial not only to the student, but it is also beneficial to the teacher. For example, students usually fill out evaluations of the class at the end of the year, and their feedback helps the teacher to possibly figure out a different way to teach things so that students are able to understand. This is how the teacher-student relationships are developed.

Similarily, Heath states that people learn by talking and considering together. From this vision, three conclusions seem to point to past achievements that we must use to challenge both the future organization of institutions and simplistic definitions of literacy. "These include all of us-children and adults, students and teachers, shop workers and supervisors, clerical workers and managers-learn most successfully with and from each other when we have full access to looking, listening, talking and taking part in authentic tasks we understand. Secondly, we can complement each other in particular areas of expertise if we learn to communicate our experiences; sharing what we know helps bring the group higher performance than private reflections of individuals do. Finally, humans must move beyond information skills to meaning and interpretation for learning to take place and to extend itself" (Heath, 157). Both of these authors argue that we all can learn from each other to benefit everyone, whether it be at school, work, or home.

However, because the argument by both of these writers helps support the fact that the teacher is not the only "knowledge giver" does not mean that textbooks should be taken out of classrooms nor should lectures. Textbooks are a very important part of learning, but there is more to learning than just reading the text. I agree with this. To me, a good teacher is one who will respect the students equally and listen to them. I learn more if a teacher teaches the text, by relating it to our lives, rather then a teacher who gets up in the front of the classroom and rambles on about the text. For example, my English teacher during my senior year, would sit in a students desk and be part of the discussion when we would talk about Shakespeare. At times, some of Shakespeare's plays seemed to be too confusing , but with her interaction, I was able to understand on my level. This type of learning does not occur just in the classrooms, but also in the workplace. It makes the inferior person (student or employee) have a chance to be heard and from their knowledge, their overseer can learn more.

Some may disagree with this argument that everyone can and should learn from each other through interaction and cooperation. They may feel that Heath and Freire do not believe in teaching the text and instead they believe in just sitting around and talking. However, this is not true. I think, they still believe in the text, but they just feel everyone should have an equal chance to say what they feel instead of the teacher lecture the whole class. Maybe this is what Heath meant when she said, "Learning can be dangerous." Others may add, that this would give children a bigger role than what they should have. If we have the teacher-student relationships at school, the children may start to voice their opinion too much and take advantage of this when they are at home also. But I do not think this is so because the students would be in better learning environments if they were to ask questions to understand the material. Others may also add that people learn better by themselves through practicing. Of course, this is true, but is not the interaction of the teachers that first helps the students to understand what they are doing. Such as in Math class, if the teacher throws up a couple of problems on the board, chances are the students will be clueless. But, if the teacher explains how to do them and then walks around the room and checks to see if everyone is doing them right, they will understand better and then will be able to go home and be able to practice them on their own.

Just like Heath stated in her three conclusions, everyone learns best from each other—young or old. Teachers can really make a difference in the way they teach so can any authoritative figure for that matter. For example, I would much rather be in a classroom setting where you would sit around and discuss what you read, just like in English class, instead of sitting in my Chemistry class where my professor lectures for an hour that, to me, sounds like he is speaking some foreign language because I do not understand. I would be more inclined to not show up for the class that lectures because it would not keep my interest. In order to get more out of learning, one's interest level has to be high. Keeping one's level of interest is usually easier for the teacher when they interact with the students as they teach Literacy is gained by everyone sharing their knowledge.

—*Essay taken from: Straub, Richard and Ronald F. Lunsford.* Twelve Readers Reading. *Cresskill, NJ: Hampton, 1995.*

2. **Please respond to the following scenario (typed responses preferred):**

It is your fifth meeting with a WRT 098 group. (In WRT 098 groups, you facilitate a discussion about group members' drafts, trying to involve all students in the discussion). A student who seldom comes prepared arrives without having her assignment and without having followed any of your previous suggestions. Her next paper is due in two days, and she is constantly interrupting the group to demand special attention. It is obvious that she has not even read the assignment. How would you deal with this situation? (Be sure to consider both the student and the group.)

3. **Please respond to the following scenario (typed responses preferred):**

One of the students you work with in a WRT 098 class complains to you that your feedback isn't helpful. The student explains that his professor often gives advice that contradicts yours, and then the student suggests sarcastically that perhaps you need a good writing tutor. Even worse, all of this happens in a WRT 098 group session, with the other members of the group seeing and hearing everything—and waiting for you to respond. How would you answer the student's concerns?

4. **In a brief response (2-3 paragraphs is fine),** please explain the unique qualities, experiences, and abilities you possess that will make you an effective Writing Consultant.

Reminders:
- *Completed applications are due to LOH 120 by 5 p.m. on Friday, March 13.*
- *Incomplete or late applications will not be considered.*
- *Save room in your schedule for WRT 306! You can't enroll in the course until the summer, but if you're hired, enrolling in this one-credit course is mandatory. Your block tuition will cover this course if you stay within the 12-15 credit range (inclusive of WRT 306).*
- *See our website for more information about the position: www.gvsu.edu/wc*

We look forward to reviewing your application!

Final Checklist for Application:
- _ A complete application, which includes: Cover Sheet, Qualifications & Experiences, and Situational Responses
- _ Two academic writing samples (at least one of which must incorporate outside research and include a works cited/references page)
- _ Recommendation by a professor (emailed directly from the professor to the Writing Center (virtualwc@mail.gvsu.edu)

APPENDIX B

APPLICATION REVIEW FORM

Applicant's Name: _____

Reviewer's Name: _____ Date of Review: _____

Based on the front page, is this applicant able to be a consultant?   ☐ YES ☐ NO
(Possible issues include: enrolling in only one term, student-teaching in either term, no writing-intensive courses and no experience, can't work at least 8 hours per week, etc.)

Does this applicant respond appropriately to the student essay?   ☐ YES ☐ NO
(Possible issues include: missed the gross problems entirely, rude, fixated on grammar.)

     A.

     B.

     C.

Based on the situational responses, will this applicant work well with students? ☐ YES ☐ NO
(Possible issues: too rude, not direct enough, unethical.)

Based on the final application question, does this applicant have consulting-related qualities?   ☐ YES ☐ NO
(Possible issues: not a good employee, doesn't work well with others, is rude, etc).

Overall, can you imagine this applicant as a writing consultant? ☐ YES ☐ NO
(Possible issues: they were not articulate or well-written; they were incomplete; the answers were problematic.)

Application Rating: 1   2   3   4

Based on the writing samples, is this applicant qualified to talk about writing? ☐ YES ☐ NO

(Please consider the papers' organization, content, source documentation, and mechanics.)

Writing Samples Rating: 1   2   3   4

NOTES:

APPENDIX C

INDIVIDUAL INTERVIEW SHEETS
Round One: General Job Interview

Candidate's Name: _____ Date: _____

Interviewer's Name: PATRICK   Time of Interview: _____

Before you begin the interview, take a few moments to read carefully the bottom part of this page, which you'll complete after interviewing the candidate. Any notes you write under questions at the top of the page are to help you rank the candidate at the bottom of the form.

1. **Imagine that your last boss (or someone who supervised you in a volunteer setting, or perhaps a professor in one of your courses) were to speak frankly with me about your work. How would he or she evaluate you? What would this person say about your work ethic, your strengths and weaknesses as an employee?**

2. **How would this professor or employer evaluate your time management skills?**

3. **Tell me about a difficult situation you encountered on the job and how you resolved it.**

If time:

4. What do you see as the similarities and differences between being a teacher and being a consultant?

5. With what aspects of consulting will you feel most comfortable and able to do well? With what aspects of consulting will you feel the most uncomfortable and struggle?

***

A. Does the candidate ask any questions of you, the interviewer? [Note number of times and some examples]

B. Write a few sentences describing your impression of the candidate. When possible, offer examples. (You might address the candidate's comfort level, ability to think quickly, friendliness, expressiveness, professionalism, flexibility, intuitiveness, etc.)

Recommendation: 1   2   3   4

Round Two: Getting to Know the Candidate as a Writer

Candidate's Name: _____ Date: _____

Interviewer's Name: _____ Time of Interview: _____

Before you begin the interview, take a few moments to read carefully the bottom part of this page, which you'll complete after interviewing the candidate. Any notes you write under questions at the top of the page are to help you rank the candidate at the bottom of the form.

1. **What are your strengths as a writer? Your weaknesses?**

2. **What are the characteristics or qualities that make for an effective responder to writing?**

3. Tell me a bit about yourself as a writer—such as the kind of writing you regularly engage in, how frequently you write, what you like about writing.

 If time:

4. What is your writing process? What do you do from start to finish?

5. Tell me about your worst writing experience. What made it so bad? OR Tell me about your best writing experience. What made it so good?

***

A. *Does the candidate ask any questions of you, the interviewer? [Note number of times and some examples]*
B. *Write a few sentences describing your impression of the candidate. When possible, offer examples. (You might address the candidate's comfort level, ability to think quickly, friendliness, expressiveness, professionalism, flexibility, intuitiveness, etc.)*

Recommendation: 1   2   3   4

Round Three: Getting to Know the Candidate's Goals

Candidate's Name: _____ Date: _____

Interviewer's Name: _____ Time of Interview: _____

Before you begin the interview, take a few moments to read carefully the bottom part of this page, which you'll complete after interviewing the candidate. Any notes you write under questions at the top of the page are to help you rank the candidate at the bottom of the form.

1. Tell me about your scholarly and professional goals—what you want to do with the rest of your time at GVSU and once you graduate.

2. What do you want to get out of this job for yourself—your professional or scholarly development—that you think will contribute to those goals?

3. What particular skills do you think you bring to the job that are unique to yourself, given your previous employment/volunteer/scholarly experiences?

If time:

***

A. *Does the candidate ask any questions of you, the interviewer? [Note number of times and some examples]*
B. *Write a few sentences describing your impression of the candidate. When possible, offer examples. (You might address the candidate's comfort level, ability to think quickly, friendliness, expressiveness, professionalism, flexibility, intuitiveness, etc).*

Recommendation: 1   2   3   4

Round Four: Scenario

Candidate's Name:_____ Date:_____

Interviewer's Name:_____ Time:_____

Explain to the candidate that you are going to read a scenario to which you'd like him or her to respond. Give a copy of the scenario to the candidate. Read aloud the scenario exactly as it appears on this page. When you've finished reading, provide ample wait time for the candidate to respond. After you have read aloud the scenario, do not speak until after the candidate has responded. Feel free to take notes to help you fill out the questions appearing on the bottom half of this form.

Scenario 1:

You're working a shift of drop-in hours and have just spent 30 minutes working with a student on her paper for Writing 150. By the time the consultation was over, the student seemed to have a plan for revision. After the student leaves the Center, the other writing consultant on duty approaches you. She proceeds to tell you that she has some concerns about how you handled the consultation—that it didn't seem like you were doing a good enough job in addressing the student's concerns about the paper.

- How do you respond?
- Tell me about a time when you had to listen to criticism from a co-worker, class-mate, professor, or supervisor. How did that affect your working relationship?

***

A. *Note the candidate's response. Is it credible and useful?*

Scenario 2:

A student visits you during drop-ins with a paper that you find very offensive (racist, sexist, etc). How do you approach the session?

- In a small-group setting in Writing 150 classes, your role as a consultant is to facili-tate a discussion about the group members' drafts. How would you handle a similar situation in which one group member's draft clearly offends the rest of the group?

A. *Note the candidate's response. Is it credible and useful?*
B. *Write a few sentences describing your impression of the candidate. When possible, offer examples. (You might address the candidate's comfort level, ability to think quickly, friendliness, expressiveness, professionalism, flexibility, intuitiveness, etc.)*

Recommendation: 1   2   3   4

APPENDIX D

GROUP INTERVIEW OBSERVATION

Observation of Group Discussion of Sample Essay

Candidate's Name:_____ Date:_____

Interviewer's Name:_____ _____ Time:_____

Please read this sheet over before we begin. As you watch the discussion, please focus your attention especially on the candidate whose name is listed on this form. You will rank only that candidate's performance on this form.

Does the candidate offer any positive feedback? [note number of times, example(s)]

Does the candidate offer suggestions about what could be revised? [number of times, example(s)]

Does the candidate explain the "why" behind positive and constructive feedback, instead of making simply directive statements?

Does the candidate remain professional during the discussion, avoiding an abrasive or patronizing tone?

Describe the candidate's body language during the group discussion.

Does the candidate act as a facilitator at any point during the discussion?

Write a few sentences describing your impression of the candidate. When possible, offer examples. (You might address the candidate's comfort level, ability to think quickly, friendliness, expressiveness, professionalism, flexibility, intuitiveness, etc.)

Recommendation: 1 2 3 4

Poor **Strong**

APPENDIX E

CONTRACT FOR WRITING CONSULTANTS

Fred Meijer Center for Writing & Michigan Authors

I accept a consulting position in the Fred Meijer Center for Writing & Michigan Authors. I understand I have an obligation to continue my training while employed by the center and that my retention depends on satisfactory performance of my duties as evaluated by the director. I also understand that the number of hours depends on student demand but that the center requires a minimum of eight (8) hours of tutoring per week for incoming consultants. My hours will be determined by the schedule I provide at orientation.

Writing Consultants are responsible for:

- Keeping all scheduled commitments, and if unable to keep a commitment, contacting the office coordinator or administrator in time for a substitute to be arranged. If I arrange for a substitute myself, I will let the director know
- Filling out, correctly and on time, pay period paperwork, and post-session reports
- Participating in self-evaluation as assigned by the writing center's administration, such as observing a consultation or being observed by another consultant
- Attending and contributing to orientation, mentor group meetings, ongoing education seminars, staff meetings, and class (if applicable)
- Maintaining positive communication with faculty about the consulting that happens in their classrooms
- Behaving professionally and ethically when representing the center
- Writing handouts and completing special projects as indicated by the office coordinator and writing center administrators during drop-in hours, when not working with students

Consultants may be asked to carry out other duties, including serving on special committees, attending conferences, representing the center at campus functions, etc.

I understand that the initial training/orientation session is mandatory, as are mentor group meetings, ongoing education seminars, and satisfactory completion of WRT 306 (if applicable).

Signature _____ Date _____

Name (please print): _____

G# _____ Date of Birth _____

Local Address: _____

Phone Number: _____Email: _____

We will publish all staff email addresses on a contact list that is circulated **only to the center's staff and the WRT 098/WRT 150 faculty.** *May we include your phone number on this list?*

YES:_____ NO:_____

APPENDIX F

ORIENTATION AND STAFF MEETING AGENDA

GRAND VALLEY
STATE UNIVERSITY,
FRED MEIJER CENTER
FOR WRITING AND
MICHIGAN AUTHORS

Orientation Day 1

Thursday, August 27:

9:00–9:15	Getting to Know You: Introductions and an Overview of Today (PAT)

- Who we are: Patrick, Lisa, Lindsay, Melanie & the Leads
- **WRT 306 Registration!!!!!**

9:15–9:45	Discuss "In the Middle" by Muriel Harris (MELANIE+SYDNEY+MEGAN)
9:45–10:30	Discussion of a Student Essay (MELANIE+MICHELLE+TERESA)

- Discuss thoughts with consultants next to you (small group)
- (Large group) Discussion of what you notice about the essay—what should we do about this? Collect notes on board.
- Imagine student is in the room!
- Prioritize from gross to close
- Role of questions
- Role of telling
- Panel of Leads to share what they'd do w/ this paper

10:30–10:45	**BREAK & ICEBREAKER (CHRISTINA) Reconvene in LOH 120**
10:45–11:00	Introduction to Drop-In Script (MEGHAN)
11:15–11:30	Brief tour—how students move into the center (MEGAN & LEADS)
11:30–12:00	Observe a Consultation (look at drop-in script)—(SYDNEY & WHITNEY)

- Start to finish (checking in and out with ScheduleIT)
- Discussion of consultation (PAIGE)

12–12:30	**LUNCH—JIMMY JOHNS**
12:30–12:45	Getting a Resource Overview (WHITNEY & PAIGE)

- Dictionaries
- Genre guides
- Books
- Handouts
- Interwebs
- Quizzes (APA/MLA/Chicago & Grammar)

| 12:45–1:00 | Introduction to WC locations and services (MELANIE) |
| 1:00–1:15 | WRT 098 & WRT 150: What's Your Role? (PAT & LEADS) |

- Working in WRT 098 and 150 classrooms
  - Workshops
  - Group facilitation
- DSP and pf grading (LINDSAY and/or PAT)

| 1:15–1:30 | **BREAK (reconvene in LOH 164)** |
| 1:30–2:45 | Practicing Group Facilitation (CHRISTINA) |

Observe leads in a 15-minute group session and a 30-minute discussion

- Emphasize Wait Time
- Show how to direct students to writing activities
- Prompt participation from all
- Opening—establishing rapport
- Closing—wrap-up and looking ahead to using the info generated in groups

  Wrapping up activity: 1) What did you see? 2) What could you do? Share what happened in small groups, and look at handout—what can be added?

2:45–3:45	WRT 098 & WRT 150 Classrooms: Meet the Faculty (RICK, MARY, AIMAN, HEATHER)
3:45	What Not To Wear & What Not To Do (slide show) (MICHELLE)
4:00–4:30	Questions & Answers

Orientation Day 2

Friday, August 28:

9:00–9:30	Sacred Writing: What is the role of a writing consultant? (MELANIE)
9:30–10:30	What Would You Do? Scenarios (MEGHAN & TERESA)
10:30–10:45	**BREAK (reconvene in LOH 164)**
10:45–11:00	Professional Development: Office of Fellowships—Elizabeth Lambert
11:00–11:30	Practice Your Consulting Skills! (29 new/33 returners) (PATRICK)
11:30–12:00	How'd It Go? A Brag Session & Time for Reflection (PATRICK)
12:00–1:00	**LUNCH—PIZZA**
1:00–4:30	Staff meeting (see separate sheet)

Staff Meeting
Friday, August 28

| 1:00–2:00: | **What's New?** |

- Welcome back all!
- Revisit numbers and feedback from last year

- New downtown hours (EC, KM, CHS)
- New bus line (direct to CHS, no more shuttle)
- New pens (sorta)
- New tablets (great for finding new research/resources during downtime)
- New resources (Comics, team writing, PRE, resource wall)
- Professional development workshops start the first week of classes!
  - o Every consultant required to attend 2 per semester
  - o Check with Melanie for attendance and upcoming events
- Google Doc Training offered to all returners in week 1
- Mentor Groups (new folks) and Returning Consultant Meetings (with Melanie) will be scheduled along with hours
- Returning folks will be observing each other this fall; Leads will observe new folks; Pat & Melanie will observe the Leads (September)
- Conferences: MWCA (October 17) at Southwestern Michigan College (Dowagiac Campus): Blurred Lines: Focusing the Academic Kaleidoscope through Collaboration and Creative Thinking
- Moment of silence for Diana Hacker

2:00–2:15	**BREAK**
2:15–2:45	**Reminders:**

- We need your picture & bio! (email to Pat)
- Schedules available next Thursday
- Drop-ins and labs start Week 2
- 098 groups start Week 3
- Mentor groups start Week 3
- SNAPS!
- APA/MLA/Chicago Style Skill quiz
- Sub policy for September

2:45–3:15	**What I Wish I Knew/What I Need to Know**
3:15–4:15	**Policies & Contracts & Schedules:**

- Writing center policies
- Safety in the center
- Contracts
- Schedules

4:15–4:30	**Wrap up and Q&A**

Please have a Lead, Pat, or Melanie look over your schedule before you turn it in.

APPENDIX G

WALK-IN SCRIPT

Script for One-To-One Sessions (Drop-Ins, ESL & DSS Appointments)

Steps 3–8 work well when you're giving one-to-one help to a student in a WRT 098 or WRT 150 lab setting, too!

1. Greet the student.
   a. Ask if the student has visited the writing center before.
   b. Begin building peer-to-peer rapport.
2. Help student log into ScheduleIt.
3. Find out about the assignment the student is working on—look at the assignment sheet to ensure you (and the student) understand what is expected of the assignment. It is also important to ask when the paper is due.
4. Ask the student what he or she wants help with, specifically.
5. Based on information collected, determine the best approach to assist the student: Have the student read their paper aloud, read the paper silently, or just talk without focusing on what has been written.
6. Respond to the student's concerns first.
7. Raise additional issues *after* you have addressed the student's main concerns. Do not feel shy about pointing out specific areas for improvement.
8. End the session by recapping the main points the student will work on next. Be sure the student leaves with a plan to revise his or her work!
9. Offer the student the option of checking out a laptop to work further on the paper in the Center, and then encourage them to seek out more feedback from you or another consultant.
10. Ask the student if his or her instructor should be notified of the visit. If so, with the student, fill out the section in ScheduleIt that will email the professor a notification of the student's visit.
11. Help the student log out of ScheduleIt.
    a. If at a Knowledge Market location, use **#ref** if appropriate.
12. Thank the student for stopping by and invite him or her to come back.

Tips and Reminders

- Make sure the student has the power! Give the student your pen and, when appropriate, prompt him or her to write down ideas/reminders in the margins.

- Sessions stay focused and are more effective if you and the student work on only a few areas of the paper.
- Sessions of 30 minutes are about right; longer than that, and the student (and you) can lose focus; shorter than that, and you may not address the student's needs in a comprehensive manner.
- Offer the student handouts or show him or her websites (see www.gvsu.edu/wc) as necessary.
- Do not evaluate the student, their writing, or their instructor. Never discuss grades.
- Feel free to be yourself! Being a peer is an advantage.
- STUDENTS MUST LOG INTO ScheduleIt!

NOTES

1. Muriel Harris, "Talking in the Middle: Why Writers Need Writing Tutors," *College English* 57, no. 1 (1995): 27–42.
2. Melissa Ianetta and Lauren Fitzgerald, *The Oxford Guide for Writing Tutors* (New York: Oxford University Press, 2016)

BIBLIOGRAPHY

Ianetta, Melissa and Lauren Fitzgerald. *The Oxford Guide for Writing Tutors*. New York: Oxford University Press, 2016.
Harris, Muriel. "Talking in the Middle: Why Writers Need Writing Tutors." *College English* 57, no. 1 (1995): 27–42.

SPEECH CONSULTANTS AT GRAND VALLEY STATE UNIVERSITY:
Empowering Student Voices

Danielle R. Leek and Carl J. Brown

Kathleen J. Turner and Theodore F. Sheckels describe the foundation and evolution of college and university communication centers in the 1980s as a natural outgrowth of increasing attention to the value of oral communication skills and a concurrent need to improve student communication competency across the curriculum.[1] In 2011, Grand Valley State University in Allendale, Michigan, joined a growing community of communication center scholars and professionals by establishing the "Speech Lab."[2] The purpose of the Grand Valley Speech Lab is multifaceted. Primarily, the Lab exists to empower student-speakers via project-specific collaboration with highly trained consultants. Additionally, the lab promotes public speaking on campus and in the community. This chapter summarizes the purpose, structure, and administration of the lab in order to offer a more detailed description of how these elements shape the training of undergraduate peer consultants who provide instructional support (tutoring) for oral communication needs on campus.

OVERVIEW OF THE PROGRAM MISSION AND GOALS

The mission statement of a communication center serves a vital purpose. It defines the scope of the organization's efforts and guides the approach used in training peer consultants and serving students. The mission of the Speech Lab at Grand Valley is to empower speakers to shape their lives, professions, and society through confident and effective public presentations. This mission is grounded in the following values:

- *Listening* as an essential condition for empathy and learning
- *Audience* as the central feature of public messages
- *Speech* as a unique mode of inquiry
- *Voice* as the path to empowerment

The Speech Lab is designed as a community and campus leader for the development of knowledge and skills through speech activities and oral communication.

Program Practices

The Speech Lab is involved with numerous activities on and off campus. In the local community, for example, the Speech Lab helps sponsor high school speech and debate events. On campus, the lab offers curricular support for all instructors who encourage speaking in the classroom. For instance, the lab collaborates with university faculty to design oral communication assignments and to provide specialized assessment techniques for evaluating student presentations. These assignments include a range of speaking formats, including in-class discussions, debates, idea pitches, and panels. The Speech Lab also offers speaking workshops for student organizations, sponsors on-campus speakers, and partners with other relevant university programming.

This range of program activities is anchored by the Speech Lab's primary enterprise, which is providing peer tutoring for oral communication. The Lab's tutors are known as "speech consultants." To encourage multi-literacy, the Speech Lab collaborates with other peer services, including the University Libraries Peer Research consultants and the university Writing Center consultants, in what is known as the "Knowledge Market."

What Consultants Do

Speech Lab peer consultants are trained to work with students on all elements of the speechmaking process, including topic selection, organization, selecting supporting materials, and, most important, practicing delivery. During walk-in or scheduled appointments, consultants help with in-class assignments, such as informative speeches or group presentations, and with public presentations, such as sales pitches or special occasion speeches. Students who visit the lab can record their presentations in specially designed studio rooms and review their videos with a consultant. Consultants are available in multiple locations on campus and during morning, afternoon, evening, and weekend hours in order to best support the variety of student needs on campus.

ADMINISTRATION

With funding from the university's provost office, the Speech Lab is housed in the College of Liberal Arts & Sciences at Grand Valley. Both the organizational structure and the program's promotional strategy affect the hiring and training of peer consultants. These aspects of the Speech Lab are described in the following sections.

Organizational Structure

The Speech Lab is affiliated with Grand Valley's School of Communications. Two faculty professors from the school are given primary responsibility for the lab. The faculty executive director oversees budgeting, expenses, and lab policy. The executive director receives no compensation for this work and completes their role as part of the service expected from tenure-track faculty on campus. The faculty director oversees daily operations in the lab and has the primary responsibility for all employment decisions as well as training peer consultants. During the academic year, the faculty director receives course release time for their work. (The equivalent of 60 percent of teaching time is reassigned for Speech Lab duties.) Over the summer term, the faculty director receives a stipend for their on-campus work with the Speech Lab.

In addition to faculty positions, the Speech Lab is staffed by both graduate and undergraduate students from across the university. Students are hired to serve as peer consultants, office assistants, and interns. Interns work with the faculty director to manage communications and promotions for the lab.

Promoting the Program

A communication center has little value if students do not use its services. Yet, most center directors have expertise in pedagogy, not advertising or promotions. To manage this challenge, the Speech Lab follows Kyle Anne Barnett Love's step-by-step plan for marketing the communication center on campus.[3] Love argues that center directors must start with a clear plan for their marketing campaign. Using data about the center's current visitors, a strong campaign will set specific goals and engage in detailed audience analysis to craft a message that will reach the target audience. For many communication centers, including Grand Valley's Speech Lab, marketing needs to be done specifically for faculty because high levels of student communication anxiety on campus mean that students are reluctant to participate in consultations without direct incentives from their instructors.[4] Once a marketing message is designed, it should be shared using appropriate channels. These may include a website, email messages, social media, print ads, class visits, workshops, and special events. The Speech Lab has also produced promotional items that are handed out at campus events. These include pens, water bottles, stopwatches, and buttons. Often, students from Grand Valley's advertising and public relations program work with the Speech Lab to help design the center's most creative materials and campaign strategies. Appendix A includes an example of a recent Speech Lab promotional plugger that was distributed to faculty and students and published in the campus newspaper.

> The value of the Lab's services is centered on the idea that we treat each member of the campus community as the important and unique individuals that they are.
>
> *Carl J. Brown, Faculty Director, Grand Valley State University*

HIRING

Peer consultants are paid hourly and are expected to work approximately eight hours per week. On average, the Speech Lab employs fifteen undergraduates during the academic year. Consultants are hired in the winter term and begin their employment in the next fall semester.

Recruiting

The Speech Lab recruits peer consultants from programs across the university. Advertisements for the consultant position are published in the student newspaper, *The Lanthorn*, and posted on bulletin boards in all campus buildings. Social media is used to spread notices about hiring through various student organizations and academic departments. Consultants are also recruited directly from sections of the university's public speaking course. This course is required for students from a variety of majors, including advertising and public relations, communication studies, sports leadership, and computer science. Recruiting through multiple sources contributes to the diversity of the applicant pool and the Speech Lab consultant staff.

Applications

The application for employment as a peer consultant asks students to provide basic information, such as GPA and work history, as well as details about their experiences with speaking in public. Applicants are also tasked with writing brief responses to questions about the value of public speaking and the role of peer tutors. Applicants must also provide references. One reference must be the student's instructor for their public speaking course. Appendix B is a sample of the Speech Lab peer consultant employment application.

INTERVIEWS

Initially, the student and faculty directors of the lab review applications. The directors collaborate to select a pool of worthy candidates for in-person interviews and presentations. Applicants who are invited for this stage of the hiring process are asked to prepare a short speech about the power of successful speaking in their personal life, their desired profession, and in society. All current consultants have the opportunity to meet with the applicant, ask interview questions, and be audience members for the applicant's speech presentation.

Criteria/Requirements

Qualified applicants are students who have at least one year of college coursework and a cumulative 3.0 GPA. These applicants have also completed Grand Valley's public speaking course or an equivalent course at another college or university. A faculty recommendation that indicates the applicant is both knowledgeable about speech pedagogy and has the personal qualities needed to be a successful peer tutor is also a requirement. Feedback from current consultants helps the student and faculty director consider whether or not an applicant is serious about the position, has empathy for others, and can work well in the team environment necessary for the lab to operate successfully.

TRAINING AND ASSESSMENT

All individuals who work in the Speech Lab are expected to participate in professional training. Faculty directors, for example, attend workshops related to supervising student employees and working with at-risk students on campus. Likewise, Speech Lab office assistants have required training so that they clearly understand university policy and procedures related to topics such as student confidentiality. The following sections focus specifically on the training process for peer consultants who are responsible for working with individual students or groups of students who are developing oral presentations.

Training Philosophy

Consistent with the Speech Lab's mission, at the heart of all peer consultant training is an appreciation and understanding of the empowering role that communication plays in a society. All training events and activities include discussions of how communication is at the core of shaping, changing, or creating any and all elements of our personal, social, and professional lives. Consultant training is also attuned to a growing recognition of the empowering role communication centers can play as a site of learning outside the traditional classroom. Sandra Pensoneau-Conway and Nick Romerhasen, for example, explore the ways that communication centers overcome traditional education's barriers to empowerment.[5] Peer consulting in the center gives students the freedom to learn without the limitations of large class sizes, assignment of grades, and the power differentials between instructors and students. Altering the dynamic of a typical classroom is especially valuable for oral communication since so many students struggle to overcome communication apprehension. Through peer interactions, communication centers are well-positioned to provide a comfortable approach to alleviating communication anxiety.[6] The Speech Lab is committed to this belief:

> If students are afraid to speak—to use their physical voice—then it will be extremely challenging for them to critically engage the world around them—to use their philosophical and theoretical voice. Empowerment is inherently tied to issues of voice, and communication centers are uniquely positioned to directly impact students' conception and use of voice.[7]

Therefore, consultants are also expected to explore their own empowerment as they grow to recognize how their personal voice is shaped and activated when they engage in peer tutoring. Peer consultants need the tools to use their voices effectively, which is why the second tenet of the lab's philosophy is "rounding the learning cycle,"[8] both in training and in consultations. This approach recognizes that individuals often prefer learning in different modes and that by working through different learning styles consultants (and students) can achieve deeper learning. David A. Kolb details four modes of learning: concrete experience, reflective observation, abstract conceptualization, and active experimentation.[9] Each mode is engaged through the training process.

In each category of training described below, consultants are first provided information that will enable them to do effective consulting. Then they observe consultants and speakers in action before engaging in their own consulting experience. New consultants receive feedback on their successes and areas for improvement. Throughout training, consultants reflect on what they have learned through their experiences. This five-step model (telling, showing, inviting, encouraging, and correcting) is considered best practice for training, especially because it is the model consultants use when helping peers learn in consultations.[10]

Training Schedule

The Speech Lab is committed to continuous training for all peer consultants. At the beginning of fall and winter semesters, all consultants meet for a single-day training seminar with the faculty director of the lab. In addition, all consultants attend a joint training session with peer consultants from the lab's partnership programs in the university Knowledge Market. At the mid-point of each semester, the consultants attend a half-day seminar.

At this event, consultants and the director take up advanced training topics and discuss issues that have arisen during lab operations. Additional training opportunities are scheduled throughout the academic year and are described later in this section.

Lab Handbook

Prior to the start of training, all consultants receive a copy of the Speech Lab handbook. The manual provides consultants with detailed instructions for managing lab activities, lab procedures, and training expectations. The handbook's table of contents is provided in Appendix C. The handbook serves as the official policy guide for the Speech Lab. It lays out clear courses of actions for consultants who seek promotion or violate lab rules. It also includes important information for consultants to use in the event of an emergency. Consultants are expected to have their handbook throughout the training process. Two of the most important sections of the handbook are the lab's code of ethics (Appendix D) and a tear-out checklist to be used to document the completion of required training activities (Appendix E).

Code of Ethics

The Speech Lab's code of ethics is a product of consultant empowerment. The original code was developed by the lab's founding staff and is revisited each fall at the start of the academic year. During training, the lab's staff (including faculty and students) discuss the code and its meaning for lab operations. Experienced consultants reflect on how the code of ethics has shaped their past decisions and practices in working with other staff and during consultations. Then, all consultants are invited to brainstorm about possible revisions to the code before a final draft receives consensus from all lab staff. The code is referred to throughout training as consultants grapple with decision-making moments that arise during consultations.

Praxis Training

A key part of training for consultants is learning to apply theories about effective oral communication and oral communication pedagogy to interactions with student speakers. Put simply, consultants need to be empowered to empower student speakers. Because all consultants have very successfully completed a college-level public speaking course, they are expected to be prepared to utilize their knowledge of basic speech and presentation organizational formats, standard criteria for the effective use of evidence, and techniques for audience analysis. After a review of this foundational knowledge, consultants then delve into more depth using selected readings, lectures, speech videos, discussions, and role-playing to develop expertise in topics such as

- working with communication anxiety;

- advanced theories of persuasion;
- disciplinary speaking styles;
- designing visual presentation aids;
- presentation rehearsal strategies;
- oral presentations for non-native speakers; and
- presenting in groups.

Collectively, such topics form the basis of knowledge and techniques needed to engage in what the Speech Lab calls "speech crafting."

Turner and Sheckels' 2015 text offers three chapters that clearly summarize the pedagogical goals and approaches that should be employed by communication center consultants as they engage the topics of speech crafting. Turner and Sheckels describe the speech development process in three stages: invention, disposition, and style, delivery, and memory.[11] New Speech Lab consultants are assigned this reading, for example, as a learning tool for their first training session. During the same session, experienced tutors give sample speeches using visual aids in order to facilitate a discussion about best practices for using visuals to enhance presentations. Another example of praxis training calls for new consultants to use different rehearsal strategies before giving an extemporaneous presentation to their colleagues in the lab. This exercise emphasizes how doing the work that they may ask of student speakers can illuminate which strategy might be the best fit given what a tutor learns about a student and the student's assignment during a consulting session.

> The inclusion of videos during training was beneficial because it allowed me to see the types of speeches I should expect, to practice hypothetical feedback scenarios, and to evaluate specific elements of speech delivery. Overall, it's nice to get a preview of the work we will be doing.
>
> *Sam Showerman, consultant, Grand Valley State University*

Vocational Training

Extraordinary amounts of knowledge about oral communication are of very little value if consultants are unable to effectively engage students when they come to the Speech Lab. Wendy Atkins-Sayre and Eunkyong L. Yook explain that this feature of all peer-learning services necessitates a call for emphasis on the centrality of communication to the tutoring process. The authors explain that without effective communication, a tutoring session can turn out to be a monologue of content knowledge, as opposed to an engaged dialogue with the goal of learning. If tutoring is conducted ineffectively, students may very well be turned off by the tutor's lack of communication skills and even resist returning for more assistance when needed.[12]

For the Speech Lab, this means that we place a great deal of emphasis on helping consultants understand their role as a peer tutor and what their role means for effectively interacting with students.

Students begin by reading articles and chapters which explore what it means to be "in the middle" between instructors and students.[13] In order to communicate with peers in a peer-learning situation, consultants must navigate the middle space that emerges from their expert knowledge on speech-making intersecting with their situational position as students. This translates to training, for example, through role-playing experiences in simulated consultations. New consultants are challenged to practice, out loud, the phrases they can use with peers in order to guide rather than take over a student's speech development process. In training, consultants also discuss the negative effects on a student's learning if a consultant uses language during a session that ultimately undermines a faculty member's credibility.

These types of communication issues are embedded throughout a new consultant's vocational training, which also includes topics such as beginning/ending a consultation session, managing time during consultations, professionalism, difficult situations, collaboration with groups, and other peer-consulting techniques that apply to all content areas. During vocational training, consultants learn to round the learning by talking, doing, modeling, and evaluating during the consultation session. Consultants are trained to use communication techniques such as using critical-thinking questions to move a consultation forward, providing clear explanations of concepts, modeling effective delivery techniques, and providing useful and appropriate critical feedback for students.

Vocational training also involves efforts to help consultants communicate effectively with others in the Speech Lab's collaborative peer-learning programs. Speech Lab consultants must work side-by-side with students from the University Libraries' Peer Consulting program and the Writing Center. Therefore, training attends to the dynamics of group interaction, strategies for collaboration, managing conversations in the workplace, and even approaches for introducing oneself to a new colleague.

Administrative Training

As in any workplace, consultants in the Speech Lab must also be trained to effectively manage lab operations, such as office procedures, online scheduling and documentation software, technology, payroll, student privacy, and confidentiality. These administrative topics are very important, especially given the timing of appointments in our lab. For example, our consultants work in the Knowledge Market at night when no faculty director may be available if assistance is needed.

Diversity and Cultural Awareness

Consultants in the Speech Lab are expected to show respect for others at all times. To facilitate tolerance, understanding, and awareness, consultants attend training events sponsored by on-campus offices such as the Kaufman Interfaith Institute, the Women's Center, the Milton E. Ford LGBT Resource Center, and the Office of Multicultural Affairs. Consultants also receive training to better understand and communicate with on-campus populations, such as international students, ESL students, veterans, and first-generation students. In addition to completing required programming, consultants are made aware of other training opportunities sponsored by relevant on-campus offices throughout the academic year.

Learning Objectives

Learning objectives for the Speech Lab training program include the following:

Consultants will be able to

1. articulate the mission of the Speech Lab;
2. describe the Speech Lab's code of ethics and apply it to lab operations;
3. describe the policy related to student confidentiality;
4. express understanding of inclusion and diversity commitment for clients and university partners;
5. navigate sessions focused on collaborative brainstorming, organizing, outlining, editing, style, rehearsing, dealing with communication apprehension, and the creation of visual aids;
6. identify strategies for managing difficult interactions in consultations;
7. manage Speech Lab administrative functions; and
8. lead consultant training sessions.

Checklist

In addition to attending training seminars, consultants-in-training are required to complete multiple and various forms of training during their first semester at the lab in order to become active consultants. The training checklist allows trainees and director to track and document this process. Trainees are partnered with experienced consultants. The pairs watch recorded speeches with the dual goals of familiarizing themselves with speech content and delivery styles as well as to develop their own feedback style. Additionally, trainees observe experienced consultants during consultations, experience a debriefing meeting after each session, eventually partner with experienced consultants, and repeat the debriefing process. Once both the trainee and experienced partner feel comfortable and confident with the trainee's ability to tutor, the trainee meets with the director for a final approval meeting to become an active consultant.

Ongoing Training Opportunities

Speech Lab consultants are encouraged to actively participate in additional training opportunities. For example, our Knowledge Market partners often host training sessions relevant to all peer tutors, and Speech Lab consultants are invited to attend. Other on-campus opportunities include a bi-annual conference on peer consulting, guest lectures, and the university's student leadership institute. Consultants may also elect to complete independent study credits with faculty in the School of Communications by taking on a research project that will increase their knowledge about peer consulting, public speaking, or oral communication pedagogy.

The primary opportunity for consultant development off campus is the annual meeting of the National Association of Communication Centers. This conference event includes speaker presentations and workshops designed to develop peer consulting skills. Speech Lab consultants can also present original research at the event.

Opportunities for Promotion

Student consultants advance through three stages of titles. When students are first hired, they are known as "consultants-in-training." Once these consultants finish their checklist, they become an official consultant of the lab. This means that students are then able to lead one-on-one sessions. Consultants who make the effort to attend additional training are rewarded with the possibility of applying for a lead consultant position. In addition to getting paid extra money, these students are expected to lead training and observe and mentor new consultants. Finally, the most advanced consultants can apply for the position of student director. The student director(s) collaborate with the faculty director on training schedules, employment reviews, and lab programming.

Training Program Certification

The National Association of Communication Centers (NACC) is the organization responsible for overseeing the development and progress of programs like Grand Valley's Speech Lab. The organization offers certification and assessment of communication center training programs.[14] Key criteria for certification include attention to all three areas of training described in this section (praxis, vocational, and administrative) and the involvement of qualified communication scholars and instructors in the training process. In 2015, Grand Valley's Speech Lab became one of fifteen colleges and universities to be recognized with NACC certification for its training procedures.

ASSESSMENT

We believe that assessment should be ongoing, purposeful, and polyvalent. Therefore, assessment of the Speech Lab happens throughout the year, using a variety of measures, including appointment reports, faculty feedback, and follow-up with on-campus partners. The assessment of peer consultants and the consultant training process primarily involves the use of self-assessments, student/faculty reviews, a training quiz, and a faculty director evaluation of all consultants. The following sections these assessment processes.

Self-Assessment

At the end of each academic year, all consultants are asked to write a reflection of their experiences and work. This reflection requires a self-assessment of their performance on three levels. First, consultants assess their performance in tutoring sessions. Second, they assess their performance as a Speech Lab team member. Finally, they assess their contribution to the lab in terms of partnership collaborations with the university Knowledge Market or special programming projects, such as our on-campus speech competition or events hosted with our ESL institute. This self-assessment is reviewed by the faculty director and contributes to the faculty director's evaluation of the consultant.

Client/Faculty Reviews

Each student who visits the lab completes a consultant evaluation at the end of each session. These evaluations ask questions about the student's level of satisfaction with their appointment and about how well the consultants contribute to their development of speech-crafting skills. The faculty director compiles and reviews these evaluations as one element of the consultants' overall evaluations. Additionally, faculty members frequently email the director to comment on the services received by their students. These evaluations are invaluable in the decision-making process related to training and the future directions of the lab.

Training Quiz

A consultant-training quiz is used as a pre- and post-test to each semester's training sessions. Consultants are asked to complete the quiz prior to training in order for the director to identify strengths and weaknesses that should be the focal points of training. Following training, the quiz is repeated in order to measure training effectiveness and the comprehension concepts included in the training. A version of the training quiz is included in Appendix F.

Director Evaluation of Consultants

At the end of each semester, each consultant is required to meet with the faculty director for a performance evaluation. Prior to this meeting, the faculty director meets with the lab's student director in order to get a more well-rounded picture of a consultant's ongoing ability to follow through on the learning that takes place during training. These meetings allow the director to provide feedback to the consultant, the consultant to provide feedback to the director, and for specific, individual learning to take place in an effort to continually improve each consultant's performance. At the conclusion of the meeting, the faculty director and peer consultant come to a consensus on how to maintain success and strengthen areas of improvement during the next semester.

Communicating Assessment Findings

In order to sustain university-wide support for communication centers and their activities, it is essential that the outcome of thoughtfully planned and completed assessment efforts be shared with all stakeholders.[15] Results of Grand Valley's peer consulting assessment (including details, such as the average score from student evaluations, scores on the training quiz, etc.) are compiled with other assessment data into a yearly executive report. This report is distributed to on-campus representatives, including the university president and provost, the dean of the College of Liberal Arts and Sciences, and the director of the School of Communications. These findings are also shared with the Speech Lab's on-campus partners, and with the lab's faculty and student staff.

REFLECTION

One of the greatest challenges in working with peer consultants is that it requires a fine balance between attention to both parts of the consultant's role as employees and as students. As employees, consultants must be held accountable for their performance. In our role as supervisors then, we strive to maintain high standards and model the behaviors we hope to see in our consultants. Yet as teachers, we are motivated to help consultants learn about themselves, about working with others, and about oral communication. Clear information and expectations can accomplish many of the goals we have for consultants, but at some point, consultant learning will require opportunities to try, fail, and succeed. By keeping our attention on empowering peer consultants and the students we work with, we believe that the Speech Lab training approach is on the right path to accomplishing the experiential learning needed to be successful as both student and employee.

APPENDIX A

SPEECH LAB PROMOTIONAL AD

GVSU Speech Lab

WORDS ARE POWERFUL. USE THEM WELL.

LOCATION
Lake Michigan Hall 154
PHONE
616-331-8115
WEBSITE
www.gvsu.edu/speechlab

OFFICE HOURS
Call or schedule an appointment online.
Appointments are available on Allendale
Campus or Pew Campus.

*Drop-ins welcome

GRAND VALLEY
STATE UNIVERSITY.

APPENDIX B

GVSU—SPEECH LAB CONSULTANT APPLICATION

Section 1: Applicant Information

Name _____

Current phone _____Current email_____

Local Address _____
Include city, state & zip

Your **current** class standing (mark one): ☐ Freshman ☐ Sophomore ☐ Junior ☐ Senior
☐ Graduate

Your major(s)_____ Your minor(s)_____

Current GPA _____ (*At least a 3.0 cumulative GPA is preferred*)

Have you taken COM 201 at GVSU? _____ Yes   _____No

Section 2: Experience and Qualifications (Please attach in a separate document).

A. What previous experiences do you have with public speaking and speech crafting?

B. What previous experiences do you have with tutoring/mentoring?

C. We seek to have confident and competent consultants from a broad range of disciplines. Extra-curricular involvement and leadership experience are highly preferred. Please list any clubs and extra-curricular activities you are currently a part of

D. What leadership roles have you held in the past? How do you feel they have shaped who you are?

E. What do you think are the qualities every peer tutor must have to be successful? Why?

Section 3: Essay Response (Please attach in a separate document).

Please answer the following question: *What is the value of speech and public speaking in a contemporary society?* Write as much as you feel necessary.

Section 4: Prepared Speech

After your application has been reviewed, you may be contacted for an interview. Part of the interview process will be giving a three-minute speech that creatively addresses the following points:

1. The significance of speech for you personally.
2. The significance of speech here at Grand Valley.
3. The significance of speech for the world at large.

Note: You will be notified in advance when your interview will be held. The advanced notice will allow for proper preparation to deliver a professional presentation.

Section 5: Employment History (Please attach in a separate document).

A. Include the name, location, and contact information of your current and past employers (if applicable).
B. Indicate if we can contact your place(s) of current/previous employment.
C. Provide a short explanation of why previous employment ended.
D. If you plan to hold employment outside of the Speech Lab, how many hours do you plan on working at that other position?

Section 7: References

Please list below the names and contact information for three professional references. One of these references must be your instructor for your college-level public speaking course.

Section 8: Pre-Employment Information

Please type your name and date at the bottom of the page in acknowledgment of the following:

To confirm that the information you've provided is accurate and complete.

- If hired, I am required to attend an all-day pre-employment training session; the employment is contingent on my attendance at this training. Date TBA (usually the week before fall and spring semesters).
- Consultants can expect to work only a few hours each week with the potential for extra hours for special speech-related assignments and tasks outside of regular consultation.

Signature_____ Date_____

APPENDIX C

STAFF HANDBOOK

Table of Contents

APPENDIX D

GVSU SPEECH LAB CODE OF ETHICS

- **We are respectful.**
  - We are honest and truthful with our clients, coworkers, and selves.
  - We are understanding and willing to listen to clients and coworkers.
  - We are thankful for the opportunity to work with students and practice our communication skills.
- **We are responsible.**
  - We are engaged in learning the best practices of communication consultation.
  - We are dedicated to achieving the best possible outcomes in all of our consultations and Speech Lab projects.
  - We take pride in supporting students and advancing the Speech Lab.
- **We are welcoming, approachable, and positive.**
  - We are accepting of and open to all people and ideas.
  - We are supportive of our clients and coworkers.
  - We value diversity of individuals and thoughts.
- **We are professional.**
  - We are patient and willing to take the necessary time required to be successful.
  - We are punctual for all shifts, consultations, and projects.
  - We are tactful in the ways in which we behave, provide feedback, and communicate with clients.
- **We are self-reflective.**
  - We are committed to continual improvement as individuals and as a group.
  - We are aware that we always represent the Speech Lab.
  - We thoughtfully seek the best in all we do for our clients, coworkers, and the Speech Lab.

APPENDIX E

GVSU SPEECH LAB TRAINING CHECKLIST

1. Introduction to the Speech Lab

Training consultants will receive a complete tour of the Speech Lab's main office (and other Knowledge Market spaces as applicable) from the Director or an experienced staff member. Training consultants should review and will discuss the staff handbook with the Director or experienced staff member. Additionally, training consultants should be introduced to:

- Payroll procedures
- Online scheduling system
- Guide sheets
- LAKERS program binders
- Blackboard resources
- Technology (laptops, iPad, Sony camcorders, copier/printer/scanner, phone, email)
- Center protocol (space management, welcoming, beginning/ending sessions, what to do if…)

Date of Tour/Discussion: _____

Tour/Discussion Leader: _____

2. Videos & Critiques

Training consultants should partner with experienced consultants to watch recorded student speeches. Act as though the student is in the room as the training consultant critiques them. When watching and critiquing, be sure to pay attention to the following issues:

- High/low order needs
- Taking notes during the session
- Nonverbal control
- Organizing thoughts before launching into a critique
- Sandwich method for feedback
- Being specific with feedback and providing examples
- Offering specific advice

Each new training consultant should watch ***at least*** three videos, but watching as many videos as possible during the first semester in the Speech Lab is ideal.

After this step is completed, the experienced consultant should contact the Director with a training update. Provide specifics of the new consultant's strengths and weaknesses.

Training Consultant/Date: _____

Trainer/Date: _____

3. Shadowing Sessions

New consultants should shadow experienced consultants prior to taking their own appointments. After each shadowing, the two consultants should discuss the session and ask questions of each other. Ideally, ***training consultants should shadow at least three sessions.***

Session One, Who/When: _____

Session Two, Who/When: _____

Session Three, Who/When: _____

4. Partnered Sessions

New consultants should take the lead in at least three sessions while an experienced consultant observes them. After each partnered session, the two consultants should discuss the session and ask questions of each other.

Session One: Who/When: _____

Session Two: Who/When: _____

Session Three: Who/When: _____

5. Consultant Quiz

New consultants must pass the training quiz available on Blackboard.

Quiz completion date: _____

6. Director Meeting

New consultants will meet with the Director after training steps are complete. The meeting will be to determine the consultant's preparedness to be added to the schedule. Upon completion of the meeting, the consultant will either be added to the schedule or scheduled for further training.

Meeting Date/Outcome: _____

Consultant Signature: _____

Director Signature: _____

APPENDIX F
GVSU SPEECH LAB TRAINING QUIZ

Section I: Speech Lab Protocol

1. Before starting a typical session, list FIVE questions that a consultant should ask a client in order to best assist the client.

2. If a client asks a consultant what numeric or letter grade they are likely to earn as a result of their practice-run presentation, how should the consultant respond?

3. If a consultant feels he or she is unable to satisfy a client's needs due to the choice of speech topic (e.g., their position goes strongly against your religious beliefs), what should/can the consultant do?

4. If a client attempts to persuade a consultant to include false details in the session notes (e.g., they were required to practice, did not want to practice, but ask you to say they practiced), what should/can the consultant do?

5. In an attempt to better serve clients and increase Lab appointment numbers, what should all consultants do at the end of each session?

6. If a professor or non-Lab employee asks about a client's performance or attendance at the Lab, how should consultants respond?

7. If two consultants are scheduled to work the same shift and your partner is more than 10 minutes late for work, what should you do?

8. Scenario: You are working in the Knowledge Market, have a client who needs to practice their presentation, but both practice rooms are in use by non-Lab students. What should you do?

Section II: Running a Session

1. What are some examples of guiding questions you can ask a client to maintain the smooth flow of a session?

2. When providing feedback to a client after a practice-run of a speech, how should a consultant structure feedback/balance positive and negative feedback?

3. If a client does not have a topic and needs to brainstorm for topic ideas, what are FIVE questions the consultant can ask to start this process?

4. If a client has a complete, high-quality speech prepared, what are some areas the consultant can focus on to provide useful feedback?

5. As a consultant, what are some ways in which your approach to a session might change if a client's speech is due in two hours or two days or two weeks?

6. Scenario: A client comes in and is required to have a speech and PowerPoint (due in five days). The client wants to begin working on the PowerPoint but has not yet

begun working on their speech. What should you do? What is your strategy for helping create an effective PowerPoint in fewer than 30 minutes.

Section III: Interacting with Clients

1. If a client is exhibiting signs of anxiety and/or states that speech anxiety is a problem for them, what are some tips the consultant might give the client?
2. If a client has no goals for a session and seems to only be in the Lab for class credit, what are some steps the consultant might take to engage the client and make the session useful?
3. If you are working with a group or individual client who is either getting off topic or not taking the session seriously, what are three approaches you might take to change the situation?
4. If you are working with a client who speaks English as a second language and are having difficulty understanding them, how might you address the issue?
5. If a client is working on an informative speech but clearly has too many persuasive elements in the text, how can you correct them without making them feel "stupid?"
6. Scenario: A client comes in for a session and only gives one-word answers to all of your questions. What should you do?

Section IV: Content & Delivery of Speeches

1. List five general items all consultants should check for in an informative speech.
2. List five general items all consultants should check for in a persuasive speech.
3. List five general items all consultants should check for concerning delivery.
4. List five general items all consultants should check for when collaborating on an outline.
5. What are three organizational structures for persuasive speeches?
6. What are the elements of Monroe's Motivated Sequence? Provide an example.

NOTES

1. Kathleen J. Turner and Theodore F. Sheckels, *Communication Centers: A Theory-Based Guide to Training and Management* (Lanham, MD: Lexington Books, 2015), 3–10.
2. Grand Valley State University Speech Lab, https://www.gvsu.edu/speechlab/.
3. Kyle Anne Barnett Love, "Successful Marketing of Communication Centers," in *Communication Centers: A Theory-Based Approach to Training and Management*, eds. Kathleen J. Turner and Theodore F. Sheckels (Lanham, MD: Lexington Books, 2015), 27–43.
4. Michael L. King and Wendy Atkins-Sayre, "If You Build It They 'Might' Come: Empirically Identifying Motivations Surrounding the Use of Communication Centers" (paper presented at the annual meeting for the National Communication Association, San Francisco, CA, November 14–17, 2010). See also Danielle R. Leek, "Incentives for Participation in New Communication Centers" (paper presented at the annual conference for the National Association of Communication Centers, Glendale, AZ, April 10–12, 2014).
5. Sandra L. Pensoneau-Conway and Nick J. Romerhausen, "The Communication Center: A Critical Site of Intervention for Student Empowerment," in *Communication Centers and Oral Communication*

Programs in Higher Education: Advantages, Challenges, and New Directions, eds. Eunkyong Lee Yook and Wendy Atkins-Sayre (Lanham, MD: Lexington Books, 2012), 39–53.

6. Stephen K. Hunt and Cheri J. Simonds, "Extending Learning Opportunities in the Basic Communication Course: Exploring the Pedagogical Benefits of Speech Laboratories," *Basic Communication Course Annual* 14 (2002): 60–86.

7. Pensoneau-Conway and Romerhausen, "The Communication Center," 49.

8. Carl J. Brown, Michael L. King, and Steven J. Venette, "Learning Styles: Rounding the Cycle of Learning in the Context of Peer Tutoring," in *Communicating Advice: Peer Tutoring and Communication Practice*, eds. Wendy Atkins-Sayre and Eunkyong L. Yook (New York: Peter Lang, 2015), 123–37.

9. David A. Kolb, *Experiential Learning: Experience as the Source of Learning and Development* (Englewood Cliffs, NJ: Prentice-Hall, Inc., 1984).

10. Steven A. Beebe, Timothy. P. Mottet, and K. David Roach, *Training and Development: Enhancing Communication and Leadership Skills* (Boston: Pearson Education, Inc., 2004). See also Rhonda Troillett and Kristen A. McIntyre, "Best Practices in Communication Training and Training Assessment" in *Communication Centers and Oral Communication Programs in Higher Education: Advantages, Challenges, and New Directions*, eds. Eunkyong Lee Yook and Wendy Atkins-Sayre (Lanham, MD: Lexington Books, 2012), 257–72.

11. Turner and Sheckels, *Communication Centers*, 69–127.

12. Wendy Atkins-Sayre and Eunkyong Lee Yook, "Training the Trainers: Improving Peer Tutoring through Communication Education," in *Communicating Advice: Peer Tutoring and Communication Practice*, eds. Wendy Atkins-Sayre and Eunkyong L. Yook (New York: Peter Lang, 2015), 4.

13. Muriel Harris, "Talking in the Middle: Why Writers Need Writing Tutors," *College English* 57 (1995): 27–42.

14. Information about the National Association of Communication Centers (NACC) is available online at: http://commcenters.org/resources/certification-and-assessment.

15. Danielle Leek, Russell Carpenter, Kimberly M. Cuny, and P. Anand Rao, "Strategies for Assessment in Communication Centers," *The Communication Center Journal* 1 (2015): in press.

BIBLIOGRAPHY

Atkins-Sayre, Wendy, and Eunkyong Lee Yook. "Training the Trainers: Improving Peer Tutoring through Communication Education." In *Communicating Advice: Peer Tutoring and Communication Practice*, edited by Wendy Atkins-Sayre and Eunkyong L. Yook, 3–14. New York: Peter Lang, 2015.

Beebe, Steven. A., Timothy. P. Mottet, and K. David Roach. *Training and Development: Enhancing Communication and Leadership Skills*. Boston: Pearson Education, Inc., 2004.

Brown, Carl J., Michael L. King, and Steven J. Venette. "Learning Styles: Rounding the Cycle of Learning in the Context of Peer Tutoring." In *Communicating Advice: Peer Tutoring and Communication Practice*, edited by Wendy Atkins-Sayre and Eunkyong L. Yook, 123–37. New York: Peter Lang, 2015.

Harris, Muriel. "Talking in the Middle: Why Writers Need Writing Tutors." *College English* 57 (1995): 27–42.

Hunt, Stephen. K., and Cheri. J. Simonds. "Extending Learning Opportunities in the Basic Communication Course: Exploring the Pedagogical Benefits of Speech Laboratories." *Basic Communication Course Annual* 14 (2002): 60–86.

King, Michael, and Wendy Atkins-Sayre. "If You Build It They 'Might' Come: Empirically Identifying Motivations Surrounding the Use of Communication Centers." Paper presented at the annual meeting for the National Communication Association, San Francisco, CA, November 14–17, 2010.

Kolb, David. A. *Experiential Learning: Experience as the Source of Learning and Development*. Englewood Cliffs, NJ: Prentice-Hall, Inc., 1984.

Leek, Danielle, Russell Carpenter, Kimberly M. Cuny, and P. Anand Rao. "Strategies for Assessment in Communication Centers." *The Communication Center Journal* 1 (2015): in press.

Leek, Danielle R. "Incentives for Student Participation in New Communication Centers." Paper presented at the annual conference for the National Association of Communication Centers, Glendale, AZ, April 10–12, 2014.

Love, Kyle Anne Barnett. "Successful Marketing of Communication Centers." In *Communication Centers: A Theory-Based Guide to Training and Management*, edited by Kathleen J. Turner and Theodore Sheckels, 27–43. Lanham, MD: Lexington Books, 2015.

Pensoneau-Conway, Sandra L., and Nick J. Romerhausen. "The Communication Center: A Critical Site of Intervention for Student Empowerment." In *Communication Centers and Oral Communication Programs in Higher Education: Advantages, Challenges, and New Directions*, edited by Eunkyong Lee Yook and Wendy Atkins-Sayre, 39–53. Lanham, MD: Lexington Books, 2012.

Troillett, Rhonda, and Kristen A. McIntyre. "Best Practices in Communication Training and Training Assessment." In *Communication Centers and Oral Communication Programs in Higher Education: Advantages, Challenges, and New Directions*, edited by Eunkyong Lee Yook and Wendy Atkins-Sayre, 257–72. Lanham, MD: Lexington Books, 2012.

Turner, Kathleen J., and Theodore F. Sheckels. *Communication Centers: A Theory-Based Guide to Training and Management*. Lanham, MD: Lexington Books, 2015.

USER EXPERIENCE AT GRAND VALLEY STATE UNIVERSITY:

Training Students Who Take the Lead in Staffing the Library's Single Service Point

Kristin Meyer, Maya Hobscheid, Kristin Kerbavaz, and Kiersten Quilliams

OVERVIEW

First, a story…

Several summers ago, our user experience (UX) librarian placed a sign on the outside of her office door highlighting a common definition of UX: User experience characterizes how a person feels about using a product, system, or service.[1] The sign ended with the following blurb: "Let's make people feel…" She put out sticky notes and markers and encouraged staff and UX student assistants to share their thoughts on how we want people to feel when they visit the library. After a few weeks, the following sticky notes covered the space:

- Comfortable
- Supported
- Valued
- Heard
- Connected
- Impressed
- Delighted
- Enthusiastic
- Awesome

- Happy
- Relieved
- Inspired
- Compelled
- Appreciated
- Energized
- Gnarly
- Understood
- Well-accommodated

- Special
- Welcomed like it's their home
- Pleasantly surprised
- Kewl ("Cool," according to one of our especially hip students)

We used these sticky notes during our UX student orientation that year. While discussing the purpose and importance of UX, the UX librarian held up the sign and slowly read each sticky note. She finished by saying, "And that's why we're all here. We want every student who comes into the library to feel like this. You have the opportunity to truly make an impact here. You have the chance to shape how your fellow classmates experience the library." At that moment, every student in the room was captivated. There was an almost palpable energy. After a few seconds of letting the power of their role sink in, she said, "So, you know—no pressure or anything." Everyone laughed and, considering it was 8:15 on a Friday morning, we were off to a great start.

Our UX team values storytelling. In *Made to Stick*, Chip and Dan Heath make the case that using a compelling narrative is one of the most effective ways to ensure that an idea survives rather than dies.[2] Telling intentional stories can be an effective training technique; stories capture students' attention and increase the likelihood that certain information will "stick" with them. When we develop training activities for our UX students, we try to incorporate the power of story.

As demonstrated by the responses our UX team left on the sticky notes, we also value inclusion. We want library users to not only feel supported, but also comfortable, understood, and welcomed "like it's their home." At a historically majority white institution, we also know that inclusion has to be intentional, so we have worked to increasingly incorporate training activities that support inclusion and accessibility. This effort is ongoing and aligned with a library-wide goal to "identify and eliminate barriers to ensure that all members of the library community are able to fully participate in library spaces and services."[3] Incorporating inclusion into our storytelling allows for the sharing of more diverse perspectives and further encourages critical thinking.

User Experience Student Assistants

Grand Valley State University Libraries has a team of approximately twenty-five user experience (UX) student assistants who take the lead in staffing the single service desk at the Mary Idema Pew Library Learning and Information Commons in Allendale, MI. The primary responsibilities of these students include the following:

- greeting and welcoming library users;
- answering a variety of directional, circulation, abbreviated reference, and technology questions;
- providing library tours;
- roaming the library to assist users at the point of need, support library operations, and collect user-related data;
- assisting with a variety of user experience-related projects, primarily involving the student experience of the physical library space; and
- providing feedback on various library policies, services, programs, initiatives, and ideas.

This group of student colleagues was formed in 2012 in preparation for the move into the Mary Idema Pew Library in 2013, and this service model was created intentionally to capture the benefits of peer learning and to support one of the guiding principles of the new building—student empowerment.[4] This is high-level student work that requires a deliberate, comprehensive, and collaborative training plan that extends throughout a student's employment.[5]

> Activities that are engaging, diverse, and sometimes competitive are key when developing a training program that is motivating for student colleagues to want to grow in their jobs.
>
> *Heather Allen, Library Specialist & UX Student Supervisor*
> *Grand Valley State University*

Collaboration

The single service desk at the Mary Idema Pew Library was designed for student workers to take the lead but includes an area in the background—coined "The Perch"—for a professional support staff member to oversee desk activity, answer phone calls, respond to chat and text messaging, and troubleshoot or answer questions. Staff members also use this time to assist with student training initiatives. Involving multiple support staff in training is one of many ways that the UX student training plan includes collaboration.

Although liaison librarians do not typically work shifts at the service desk, they work collaboratively with the UX team in several ways. In addition to providing instructional sessions and supporting faculty in their areas of responsibility, liaison librarians also provide one-on-one consultations with students by appointment and on a drop-in basis. While UX students can explain how to get started searching and answer basic reference questions, they frequently refer users who have more complex questions. Liaisons also assist with training by conducting reference-related workshops and participating in the reference training portion of our student orientation.

As described in the previous chapter, our library also employs student research consultants. Our UX students are a separate group of students that serve as an entry point to the more comprehensive research services provided by our research consultants and liaison librarians. Collaboration between the services is critical for this model to be successful.

The UX team also engages in project-based collaboration with other library faculty and staff. Two specific collaborative projects highlighted in this chapter include the development of reference learning guides as well as modules on inclusive customer service.

> Training can provide opportunities for students to connect and truly become a team. Some of these connections can last a lifetime.
>
> *Deb Maddox, Circulation Coordinator*
> *Grand Valley State University*

UX Student Employment at-a-Glance

The UX student employment program starts with strategic hiring practices. The training plan includes multiple components, including:[6]

- an orientation that happens at the beginning of the fall semester;
- on-the-ground training that occurs within the first few weeks of the semester;
- workshops that are offered throughout the semester and often facilitated by liaison librarians, other library faculty or staff, or returning students; and
- a variety of "anytime" training activities, including reference learning guides, customer service modules, and other forms of asynchronous learning that students complete when it is slow at the service desk.

ADMINISTRATION

The UX team is a functional team within our operations and user services department. The UX team collaborates across multiple library locations to provide excellent customer service; evaluate services provided in our service desk environments; develop training for service desk employees; implement UX techniques to understand user needs; communicate with users through social media, digital displays, and signage; and develop user engagement activities.

The UX students at the Mary Idema Pew Library report directly to our user experience student supervisor. This staff member oversees student hiring, scheduling, and evaluations. Our UX librarian is a faculty member who is a manager in the operations and user services department and is responsible for leading the UX team and guiding the UX student employment program at a high level. The UX librarian and UX student supervisor work together with other student supervisors in the department to create hiring and training plans.

Access and delivery (A&D) student assistants are a separate group of student colleagues within the operations and user services department at the Mary Idema Pew Library. They perform many traditional access services tasks, including checking in materials, pulling holds, and shelving. Dividing this work was an intentional effort to support our service philosophy:[7] We do not want our students who work at the service desk to be deeply engaged in tasks that would reduce their approachability.

Communication

UX students work a variety of shifts between 7:00 a.m. and 2:00 a.m. and are responsible for keeping up with ever-changing information; communication can be a challenge. In 2014, we created a UX student Blackboard organization that houses procedural information and training documents and includes a discussion board for updates. The discussion board has been a useful tool because students can respond and ask questions about our posts and can utilize the search function to locate older posts. At the end of each posted update, we ask a question to ensure all UX students have read the message. Sometimes the question relates to the post, but more often the question is fun and encourages team building. For example, "If you could have one super power, what would it be?" This has been a great way to help us get to know the personalities of our students. It also encourages students to interact with their student colleagues and builds a sense of community.

Budgets

Our total student budget has increased as a result of splitting UX and A&D students. However, we review scheduling needs each year in an effort to be as fiscally responsible as possible.

Student Wages

Our UX students start at the statewide minimum wage and follow our campus-wide tier for wage increases, consistent with most student jobs on campus. We have not found that we need to advertise a higher wage to encourage students to apply; the library is an appealing place to work on campus, and the UX position is highly visible in the library. While we do not focus exclusively on hiring work-study students and, in fact, only a small portion of our existing UX students have work-study awards, work-study students are preferred when all other qualifications between students are equal.

HIRING

The UX student colleague program has a strategic hiring plan that includes elements of peer hiring.[8] Current students review applications and participate in the interview process. Involving current students provides us with valuable feedback and also gives students the opportunity to experience the hiring process from the perspective of an employer. Students have indicated that these opportunities were helpful when it was time for them to apply for jobs in their chosen fields.

The majority of UX students are hired in preparation for the fall semester. We have adjusted our hiring timeline so that hiring occurs in May through July, during Grand Valley's spring semester. Although significantly fewer students are on campus during the spring semester, this timing creates enough space for us to implement peer hiring elements, gives students an opportunity to find out whether or not they have received a work-study award, and allows first-year students to apply.

Job Description

We have intentionally crafted the UX student job description to explain the scope of the position and to set high expectations for students (see Appendix A). We want students to understand that they will have the opportunity to learn professional skills, they will be treated professionally, and we expect that they will, in turn, take pride in performing this work in a professional manner. A professional job description and a somewhat elevated application process help signify this. The job description contains several sections, including the following:

- position summary;
- job duties;
- required qualifications;
- preferred qualifications;
- employment outcomes; and
- standard hours for this position.

Employment outcomes were added to help reinforce our commitment to making student employment a high-impact learning experience. While making money may be students' primary motivation, we also want them to know that they will be gaining much more throughout their employment.

> Working as a UX student has arguably been the best thing to happen to me since coming to Grand Valley. Being part of the front-line at the library has allowed me to interact with a variety of different people and has given me social and communication skills I wouldn't have gotten otherwise. I've also learned about the many different resources the library has to offer which has helped me tremendously in school.
>
> *UX Student, Grand Valley State University*

Application

The UX student application includes standard application content as well as some short-answer questions and scenarios that help us identify students who have the potential for success in this position (see Appendix B). Specifically, we look for students who are personable and will be able to provide friendly, efficient customer service. We look for students who are enthusiastic about our libraries and are interested in helping others. Additionally, we implement inclusive hiring practices aimed at hiring students who come from diverse backgrounds and are committed to helping all students, regardless of their backgrounds and identities. Existing UX students help review applications by using a rubric; the purpose of the rubric is to help reduce unconscious bias.

Interviews

The UX student supervisor and at least one current UX student conduct interviews. Selected applicants are asked questions aimed at discovering whether or not they have the specific skills and qualities that we are looking for in this position. At the end of the interview, the candidate is asked to give the interviewers a tour of the office suite. While specific tour content is not evaluated, the interviewers look for students who display the ability to "think on their feet," are friendly, poised, and have the ability to make a personal connection with others. Students are typically surprised by this activity and end up conducting the tours in a variety of styles. Interviewees have made up stories about the objects decorating the space, pretended that they were in a shopping mall, and recited fake facts about the library. Some of them do a marvelous job, and, anecdotally, this activity seems to be predictive of future job success.

TRAINING

The UX student training plan includes multiple components, and training happens all throughout a student's employment with us.[9] UX students need to have an understanding of the big picture—what user experience is, what great customer service looks like, what the library values, and where they fit into the organization. To provide excellent customer service, they also need to understand numerous policies, procedures, searching strategies, building information, and how other library services work. We need new students to understand the basics, and we need students who have worked multiple semesters to continue to expand their knowledge and understanding so that they can, in turn, help mentor new students. The training plan involves elements that help meet these varying needs.

> Taking time to orient students to our organization, environment, and how their role fits into the bigger picture enhances their motivation and ability to deliver effective library services. This approach has been very beneficial.
>
> *Brian Merry, Head of Operations and User Services*
> *Grand Valley State University*

Orientation

The foundation of the UX training plan includes a day-long orientation (or, as we implemented in 2019, two half-days) held prior to the start of the fall semester. The orientation is mandatory for both new and returning students and students are paid for their time. Objectives include giving students a broad overview of what user experience is, what good customer service looks like, what their work will entail, what the library values, and where they fit into the organization. Policies, procedures, and task-specific training are purposely not part of orientation. During orientation, we engage in intentional storytelling, facilitate group discussions, use a variety of engaging activities, encourage both new and returning students to act out various customer service and reference scenarios, and involve numerous colleagues to promote ongoing connection and collaboration between our UX students and others in the library.

One example of purposeful storytelling that we use during orientation is the "Measuring Cup Story," which one of the authors first heard from Paul-Jervis Heath at the *UX in Libraries* conference.[10] She tells it like this:

> There were these product engineers who wanted to design a better measuring cup. They could have just asked consumers for their suggestions and feedback, but instead, they set up a test kitchen. They watched as people used measuring cups as they naturally went about baking something. It didn't take long for them to notice a pattern—almost everyone would pour something into their measuring cup and then either lift it to eye-level or they would bend down so that their eyes were level with the counter. Over and over again, they saw "pour, lift, pour, bend." The people were doing this, of course, to make sure that their ingredients were measured precisely. Well, those product engineers ended up designing an angled measuring cup that can be read from any height or direction. No bending needed! Now, if those product engineers would have just asked their test subjects for their feedback and suggestions, it's unlikely that they would have been able to point out that bending and lifting was a wasted motion. They probably wouldn't have been able to imagine a measuring cup that could be different. And that's why observation is so important. That's why we ask students for their feedback, but we also collect data and implement user experience techniques to find out what students actually do in the library. These things can often help us identify pain points for our users that we wouldn't be able to determine any other way.

This story helps illustrate the "why" behind user experience and is told intentionally to help students understand and buy-in to work that can be tedious.

Various library colleagues and building partners attend and participate in specific elements of orientation. For example, liaison librarians and our instructional design librarian participate in the reference training portion.

The reference training portion has included modified content each year. One year we divided students into groups with each group having a mix of new students and returning students. Each group was assigned a reference-related question that had been asked at the service desk. Questions varied in difficulty and were chosen to highlight multiple library resources. The groups developed skits in which new students had to play the part of a UX student, and one or more of the returning students played the part of the user. To create the skit, returning students had to act as a mentor to new students by showing them how to answer the question. The two liaison librarians were available to consult with the groups and were willing to play a part in the skit if the groups wanted. The groups each presented their skits to the full group. This gave new students the opportunity to practice answering reference questions and provided exposure to a variety of resources. After each skit, we facilitated a group discussion that included feedback on what the student did well and what they could have done differently or more efficiently in the future. In 2019 we took a different approach. Students first watched a short video on basic search strategies. The students then divided into groups and played a few rounds of Search & Destroy,[11] a multi-player card game in which players build searches to compete for the highest number of database results.

Overall our orientations have been well-received, and we continue to use student feedback to make them better each year. Evaluations indicate that students especially value the interactive components and having the opportunity to meet with others in the organization. They also really like the free lunch and coffee!

On-the-Ground Training

Although orientation does not focus on task-specific processes, we recognize that new UX students need to have thorough knowledge of a variety of procedures and policies to be able to provide excellent customer service. To gain this knowledge, new UX students work with returning students and staff to complete a job-specific checklist over the first several weeks of their employment. Including returning students in this process adds an element of peer-learning and gives returning students mentoring experience, while at the same time deepening their own understanding of library procedures and policy. Returning students also help us update and improve the checklist each year.

Another successful component of on-the-ground training has been implementing weekly "training quick checks." Each week, we select a topic for our staff at the Perch to go over with UX students. Topics are typically selected if staff have noticed that we have been getting a specific question repeatedly asked at the desk, if we anticipate a certain question will be asked because of the time of year, or if we see from our chat transcripts or service desk transactional data that students struggle answering a particular question. The topic usually includes questions for staff to ask students as well as a training script that describes how the questions should be answered. We have received positive feedback about this initiative from both staff—who indicate that this is also often a useful refresher for them—as well as students.

Workshops

Our UX student training plan also includes skill development workshops. We typically offer four to six of these workshops per semester, and students are required to attend at least two of them. These workshops are often conducted by liaison librarians, although other library faculty and staff or other campus partners, such as the Division of Inclusion and Equity, also facilitate some workshops. Some of our returning students have also developed and facilitated workshops. Content has included topics such as the following:

- using primary sources;
- researching government documents;

- working with international students;
- copyright and scholarly communication;
- accessible customer service practices; and
- emergency training.

Library research consultants, other library student employees, and other library faculty and staff are also invited to attend, encouraging interaction between library employees at all levels. Some workshops are repeated from semester to semester while some content is designed fresh. This ensures that UX students who have worked several semesters continue to learn and expand their knowledge throughout their employment.

Anytime Activities

Although the service desk is very busy during peak library hours, students have occasional pockets of downtime. We want our UX students to be as approachable as possible, so they do not work on library tasks (such as checking in carts of books) or homework. However, we recognize that students need something productive to work on during slow times and have designed a variety of asynchronous training activities that are easy to complete at the service desk.

Among these activities are a series of learning guides, self-paced training modules designed to teach UX students key concepts related to their work at the service desk. We used two pedagogical frameworks to design the guides: Universal Design for Learning and backward design. Universal Design for Learning (UDL) is a framework for developing flexible learning environments and materials to accommodate diverse learners.[12] UDL supplies three overarching guidelines to support the implementation of the UDL framework: multiple means of engagement, the why of learning; multiple means of representation, the what of learning; and multiple means of action and expression, the how of learning.[13] The guides follow these guidelines by including different types of check-ins and reflective components, embedding a variety of media such as videos and library guides, and by providing transparent instructions. The backward design model is a method of designing curriculum in which the learning goals are chosen before the assessment and instructional activities.[14] By beginning with the learning objectives when designing the guides, we could structure the guides to best support and measure student learning.

We developed a series of three reference learning guides to provide UX students with an understanding of the scope of reference questions they could expect to encounter at the service desk, prepare them to address these types of questions, and to know when and how to make referrals for more complex reference questions. We divided these guides into three sections: two guides on reference basics, and one on advanced reference topics. Each guide begins with a short introduction and learning objectives. The first reference basics guide covers navigating our discovery layer using basic limiters; identifying the differences between articles, journals, and databases; and performing a journal title search (see

Appendix C). The second reference basics guide examines recognizing a peer reviewed article, performing a basic database search, and describing the uses of a library subject guide. The advanced reference guide covers distinguishing between primary and secondary sources, locating empirical studies in the databases, using different citation styles, and searching for known items in the catalog.

Each guide is divided into sections that correspond to the learning objectives and contain a variety of types of content and interactive components. Chunking the content into manageable pieces allows students to tackle bits and pieces as the ebb and flow of the service desk allows. The guides include videos created both in-house at Grand Valley and at other institutions, library guides created by liaison librarians and Knowledge Market consultants, and quick tips for answering relevant reference questions. The guides also provide reference scenarios, interactive modules, and pre- and post-reflective questions. The reflective pieces encourage UX students to connect the content to their own experiences as students and to their role in supporting students at the service desk.

> My favorite part about being a UX student is gaining connections to the awesome people here! I've also been able to improve my customer service skills, especially with talking to professionals interested in our library. As a non-profit major and hospitality minor, the latter-mentioned skill will be most useful in my career.
>
> *UX Student, Grand Valley State University*

We have also recently developed three new learning guides that focus on customer service (see Appendix D). The guides complement and build upon customer service training provided during orientation and follow the same structure developed for the reference learning guides, including internal and external content as well as interactive elements and opportunities for reflection. The first customer service learning guide asks students to reflect on the idea of customer experience. Students read library policies around customer service, compare our guidelines to materials produced by other libraries, and brainstorm how to apply active listening skills in the service desk environment. Themes throughout the module include listening closely to user needs and making user experience as effortless as possible.

The second and third guides in this series focus on inclusive and accessible customer service practices, and expand on the content covered during orientation and in some of our in-person workshops. These topics align with our library's stated values: "We are committed to removing barriers to full access and participation for our whole community."[15]

Building off the first customer service learning guide, the inclusive customer service learning guide aims to help students think critically about prejudice, implicit bias, stereotype threat, and ways that these concepts affect customer service. Reflection questions, such as "How might stereotype threat impact a user's experience of asking for help at the desk?," encourage UX students to think about and understand the lived experiences of others. Specific approaches, such as using gender inclusive language, are then discussed as ways to provide a more inclusive customer service experience.

The third learning guide in this series, accessible customer service, further expands on these concepts and is rooted in asking ourselves how we can ensure our tools, services, and spaces are available to and usable by as many people as possible. Core to this idea is to avoid making assumptions, to empower our users, and to be aware of the language and terminology we use at our service desk. Our UX students read through an accessible customer service practices[16] document we had previously created, reflect on their own experiences of feeling supported or not supported, and reflect on how people-first language emphasizes the individual and aims to provide a great experience.

These three customer service learning guides aim to empower our student employees to improve user experience. They are encouraged to take this information and think about additional ways we can assist users, and bring forward barriers they may encounter or ideas for further support we could provide. This learning is also potentially translatable to their academics and to their future professions.

ASSESSMENT

Assessment of our UX student employee program includes individual employee assessment, holistic service assessment, and the assessment of specific components of the training plan.[17]

Individual Employee Assessment

Each of our UX student employees has a formal evaluation once per academic year. The UX Student Supervisor solicits feedback from multiple staff and incorporates that feedback into each evaluation. While evaluating students is a form of performance management, the main purpose of the evaluation process is to give students the experience of having a formal evaluation, which can be useful for overall professional growth.

Holistic Service Assessment

We also assess services by recording questions asked at the service desk and their corresponding answers. The question data that we collect through LibInsight gives us a broad understanding of what types of questions are being asked, interaction duration, referrals, and user comments and feedback. Reviewing the answers also helps us identify training successes and opportunities. If there is a question that students have trouble answering, we often include it in a weekly training quick check.

Similarly, chat, text, and email to our generic library account are also typically answered at the Perch. While staff answer the majority of these questions, UX students also occasionally answer them. Reviewing the transcripts and tracking service metrics, such as user ratings for our chat responses, provides opportunities to highlight excellent responses and to identify opportunities for improvement.

Assessment of Training Plan Components

We try to capture student feedback anytime we consider adding new training components and throughout the development process. For example, we ask students to fill out surveys at the end of each orientation. We then use that feedback to improve subsequent orientations. Additionally, we send graduating students an exit survey. The purpose of this survey is to evaluate their employment experience as a whole, but we also specifically ask for their feedback on how we can improve student training.

We have also recently implemented pre- and post-testing to measure student learning over time. UX students complete a pre-test at the beginning of their employment before any of our training. The plan is that they will complete the same test after their first year of employment and again before they graduate. By using the same pre-test and post-test, we can measure how much and what the student learned.

We initially created this pre-test assessment in conjunction with the reference learning guides and later incorporated it in the development of the customer service learning guides (see Appendix E). The decision to expand this part of the assessment program grew out of an increasing campus interest in assessing student learning outcomes, as well as campus initiatives supporting experiential learning through student employment.[18] In 2019, the library's assessment plan was updated to include new emphasis on assessing the knowledge and skills that student employees learn during their employment at the library. The customer service learning guides were developed alongside the assessment instrument, and the guides as well as their assessments will be made available to student supervisors in other departments so we can begin to gather data about the impact of student employment throughout the library.

REFLECTION

Training is Never Done

Our UX student program has existed for eight years. In those years, our training plan has evolved significantly. We have adapted our training to align with the values of the library and the mission of the university, and we have improved training methods through collaboration, assessment, and ongoing student feedback. Just as students continue to learn throughout their employment with us, we continue to enhance training efforts.

Remember those powerful stories we love to tell our UX students? We will always be on the lookout for more stories because training, learning, and empathy-building is never finished.

Collaboration is Key

Including multiple perspectives, strengths, and areas of expertise improves the content of our training and can help student employees feel supported by multiple staff and departments. Creating opportunities for separate student employee groups to learn and interact with each other and with other library professionals will encourage a shared understanding of library services.

The Future of UX Student Training

As we look ahead, continuing to embed inclusion, diversity, equity, and accessibility into our student training plan is our most important goal. When we think about the ways that we can impact student learning outside the classroom, we have the opportunity to strengthen professional skills but also to enhance critical thinking skills and empower students to be change-makers in their own communities. Through our training and storytelling, we have the opportunity to encourage our student employees to tell their own stories, to think about and consider others, and to go out and develop alternatives, inspire hope, and take action in their perspective fields.

APPENDIX A

USER EXPERIENCE (UX) STUDENT ASSISTANT POSITION DESCRIPTION

Position Summary:

Join a team designed to create a better experience for library patrons in the new Mary Idema Pew Library Learning and Information Commons! Become a User Experience Student Assistant and help staff the fast-paced library Service Desk. Excellent customer service skills, enthusiasm for the library, and the ability to work collaboratively with other students and staff are required. Primary responsibilities include assisting patrons with reference and circulation needs, providing building information and tours, and assisting with emergency and safety procedures. A variety of shifts are available; all applicants are expected to be able to work flexible hours, including some evenings, weekends, and extra hours during Exam Cram and for training purposes.

Job Duties:

- Assist patrons at the library Service Desk and throughout the building with abbreviated reference assistance, circulation tasks, and general building information.
- Roam the library to collect data, answer questions, and help with facilities and security-related issues.
- Provide tours of the library.
- Assist with opening and closing the library.
- Assist with building emergency and safety procedures.
- Promote library initiatives.
- Conduct patron interviews and other user experience research as needed.
- Other duties as assigned.

Required Qualifications:

- Excellent customer service and interpersonal skills
- The ability to prioritize multiple demands in a fast-paced work environment
- Enthusiasm for University Libraries and commitment to becoming an exemplary ambassador of the libraries
- The ability to work collaboratively with other staff and students

Preferred Qualifications:

- One year of customer service experience
- Work-study preferred

Employment Outcomes:

What you can expect to learn in this position

- Customer service skills
- Experience in promoting/marketing an organization
- Knowledge of user experience research techniques
- Basic emergency response training
- Communication skills: ability to professionally communicate with persons verbally, written, and online
- Teamwork: ability to positively work and engage in a team structure
- Problem-solving and analyzing: ability to make decisions and solve problems using creativity and reasoning
- Flexibility and adaptability: ability to manage and adapt to changing work conditions and assignments
- Administrative skills: ability to plan, organize, and prioritize work
- Cultural sensitivity and awareness: ability to demonstrate respect and awareness to other people and cultures
- Technology and computer literacy: ability to use current technology and computer software

Standard Hours for this Position:

Shifts are available from 6:30 a.m.–2:30 a.m.; you may be required to work any combination of shifts and must have transportation during these hours. Typically, UX students work between eight and fifteen hours per week during the fall and winter semesters.

APPENDIX B

STUDENT WORKER APPLICATION

Name: _____

Local Address: _____Phone: _____

Home Address: _____ Phone: _____

Email Address: _____

Major: _____ Minor:_____

Year in School: _____Work Study? ☐ Yes ☐ No

Why do you want to work for the University Libraries?

Please explain what you think excellent customer service includes.

Please explain how you would handle the following scenario: *A prospective student and her family visit the library and stop at the Service Desk. They mention that the student is interested in coming to Grand Valley. How would you respond?*

Please describe any experiences you have had interacting with people in a workplace, volunteering, or in a club or extracurricular activity.

References: Please list two (faculty or previous employers) and include one letter of reference with your application materials.

Name: _____ Position:_____Phone:_____

Name: _____ Position:_____Phone:_____

Previous Employment: Please include employer, supervisor, address, position, responsibility, length of employment, and reason for leaving. Use additional pages if necessary.

UX students work shifts between the hours of 6:30 a.m.–2:30 a.m. You will be required to be available to work early morning, late night, and weekends. You will need to have transportation for all possible hours. Are you able to make this commitment?
☐ Yes   ☐ No

You will be required to attend a mandatory all-day orientation each year in August. Are you able to make this commitment? ☐ Yes   ☐ No

You will be required to work at least one overnight shift when the library holds extended hours for Exam Cram. Are you able to make this commitment? ☐ Yes   ☐ No

Please return your completed applications to the Mary Idema Pew Library Service Desk by _____.

APPENDIX C

EXCERPT FROM "REFERENCE LEARNING GUIDE: THE BASICS PT. 1"

Reference

When assisting students at the service desk, you will often answer basic reference questions. In libraries, reference is a category of questions that requires identifying and finding the needed information for research and/or an assignment. Student employees at the service desk can assist students with basic reference questions by using the preexisting tools available through the University Libraries website and by referring more complex questions to liaison librarians or research consultants.

The key objectives of this module:

As a result of this training, student employees will:
1. Navigate Summon using basic limiters
2. Identify the differences between articles, journals, and databases
3. Perform a journal title search

This Learner's Guide will guide you through resources, activities, and reflections related to each objective. The learning is self-paced and you are encouraged to go at your own speed, allowing time to apply the learning through various activities, then returning to the guide to reflect on what you learned through application.

Pre-Learning Reflection

Think about a time you needed to find information and/or do research for a school assignment, where did you begin?

Section 1: Summon and Basic Limiters
When answering reference questions, one of the best tools at your disposal is the Library Search, Summon.

This section includes the following tips:
- **Tip 1:** Find information using the Library Search, Summon.

Tip 1: Finding Information with Summon
Summon, often referred to as the Library Search or Find It bar, is a discovery tool that searches everything in the library's collection including articles, books, ebooks, films, newspapers, magazines, and more. Students can search Summon from the search bar on the Library homepage.

Note: Though the official name of this tool is Summon, when showing it to students, we always call it the "Library Search" or "Find It!" box.

Learn

Watch the **Library Search: Refine Your Search**

In this short video, a UX student employee performs a search in Summon and uses the basic limiters to narrow the results.

Scenario: A student comes to the desk looking for help on a research paper. Their topic is how stress impacts the mental health of college students.

1. Open a browser, go to the Libraries homepage, and search for "stress, mental health, and college students."
    a. How many results did you get?
    b. What is the first result?
2. Select either "full text online" or "scholarly & peer review".
    a. How many results do you have now?
    b. How did it change the results?
3. Select and apply a content type.
    a. Which one did you choose?
    b. How many results do you have now?
    c. How did it change the results?
4. Select and apply a discipline.
    a. Which one did you choose?
    b. How many results do you have now?
    c. How did it change the results?

Reflection

How will you use Summon to support students at the service desk? What are the benefits of using Summon? What are the limitations?

APPENDIX D

SELECTIONS FROM CUSTOMER SERVICE LEARNING GUIDES

The three customer service learning guides include:

- Written explanations of content
- Links to preexisting internal documents and external content
- Questions for learner engagement

For the purposes of this Appendix, we have selected portions of the guides that are representative of the guides' style and approach. We have also included the learning objectives of each module.

Customer Service Learning Guide: Part 1
Customer Service

The key objectives of this module:

As a result of this training, student employees will:

1. Identify University Libraries' Steps to Giving Great Service
2. Give examples of strategies that they can use to improve interactions with customers
3. Use the Apology Framework when necessary

This Learner's Guide will guide you through resources, activities, and reflections related to each objective. The learning is self-paced and you are encouraged to go at your own speed, allowing time to apply the learning through various activities, then returning to the guide to reflect on what you learned through application.

Pre-Learning Reflection:

Think about a time when you received really excellent customer service. How did you feel? What did that person do to make that experience so good?

The Steps to Giving Great Service
Read

University Libraries' Steps to Giving Great Service [**we provide a link**]

Apply

Think about the excellent customer service experience you reflected on earlier in this learning guide. How did that person's actions fit the University Libraries Steps to Giving Great Service?

Customer Service Learning Guide: Part 2
Inclusive Customer Service

The key objectives of this module:

As a result of this training, student employees will:
1. Identify the ways in which prejudice can lead to implicit bias
2. Recognize the ways in which implicit biases and stereotype threat can impact customer service interactions
3. Utilize gender-neutral language

Pre-Learning Reflection:
What does it mean to be included? How does the idea of inclusion relate to the University Libraries Steps to Giving Great Service?

Take a short implicit bias test [we provide a link]

Apply
Are you surprised by the results of the test? Why or why not?

How might implicit biases affect customer service? How can using the University Libraries Steps to Giving Great Service help minimize the impact of implicit biases?

Customer Service Learning Guide: Part 3
Accessible Customer Service

The key objectives of this module:

As a result of this training, student employees will:
1. Expand upon the University Libraries Steps to Giving Great Service to understand and utilize information about select disabilities to provide accessible customer service
2. Utilize person-first language
3. Empathize with the difficulties experienced by students with disabilities

This Learner's Guide will guide you through resources, activities, and reflections related to each objective. The learning is self-paced and you are encouraged to go at your own speed, allowing time to apply the learning through various activities, then returning to the guide to reflect on what you learned through application.

Pre-Learning Reflection:

Think about a time when you had to use a system, tool, or process that wasn't designed with you in mind. How did you end up resolving the problem? How could someone have made that easier?

or

Think about a time you used a system/tool that seemed perfectly designed for you. What made it so effortless? Would that same system/tool work as well for everyone?

Libraries are for Everyone

Our University Libraries Steps to Giving Great Service guide us on how to deliver customer service across our libraries. Given the varied student population that we serve, we must expand upon this and ask ourselves how can we ensure that our tools, devices, services, and environments are available to and usable by as many people as possible.

Read Accessible Customer Service Practices

1. **Don't Make Assumptions**

    Many disabilities are invisible. We cannot make assumptions about how our patrons learn, communicate, or need assistance. As discussed in the University Libraries Steps to Giving Great Service, asking and listening to our users is the best way to support them.

    An example of this at our Service Desk could be writing down a call number on a sheet of paper and handing it to the user, assuming they will be able to read it, know what call numbers are and how they work, find its location, etc. Instead, we can ask further questions like, "would you like me to explain how call numbers work?" and after listening, go from there.

2. **Language and Terminology**

    There are many ways in which we can better support our users through the language we use at our service desks and while communicating with others. Thinking back to the Inclusivity module, this also works to ensure our spaces are inclusive and welcoming to all.

    Remember to use terms such as "accessible parking" instead of "handicap parking" and use person-first language (see more below).

3. **Empowerment**

    We want our users to feel empowered in our spaces and do as much as they can independently. When possible, we don't want to make our users feel like they do not belong or that they have to "out" themselves as having a disability to get the same level of service as everyone else.

    For example, we wouldn't want to give someone directions to the second floor and say "just take the stairs right there and it'll be to your left." Instead we could mention how to get there from both the stairs and elevator, or even better, offer to take them there and either ask if they'd prefer the stairs or elevator or just take the elevator since it is more accessible to all.

Apply

Imagine someone comes to the Service Desk and says they've been looking for a book, but can't find it on the shelf. When you look it up it's in the ASRS. You explain that the book is in the ASRS and that you can request it for them, but they don't seem to understand. How might you rephrase what you said to avoid jargon and give a clear and simple answer?

APPENDIX E

UX STUDENT ASSISTANT PRE-ASSESSMENT: ANSWERS & RUBRIC

For questions 1-8:

2 points = the student's answer touches on most of the points outlined in the answer key

1 point = the student's answer is partially accurate

0 points = the student selected "I'm not sure" or include an answer that is not at all partially correct.

1. **What is the difference between an article, journal, and database?**

   Articles are individual papers that are published in journals. Journals are serial publications that contain many articles. Databases are organized collections of journals and articles.

2. **What is a peer-reviewed article?**

   A peer-reviewed article is a scholarly article that has gone through a formal review process from other experts in the field.

3. **What is a subject guide and when would you recommend that a student use one?**

   Subject guides are created by our liaison librarians to organize resources on a particular subject or discipline. They usually include recommended journals and databases for that particular subject. They're great to recommend when helping students get started on research for a particular class or topic.

4. **When you're searching for a particular topic, and you get thousands of results, what are some common ways you could limit your results?**

   o Full text

   o Scholarly & Peer Review

   o Content type (book, newspaper, etc.)

   o Publication date

   o By subject or discipline

5. **When using the main search bar on the library homepage, what kinds of materials can be found?**

   Everything in the library's collection: journal articles, books, ebooks, book chapters, videos, book reviews, newspaper articles, microfilm, article citations

6. **True or false. Some articles can be found in multiple library databases.**
   True

7. **What's the difference between a primary and secondary source?**

   Primary sources are the "raw materials" or original documents used by each discipline. They provide first-hand testimony or direct evidence from that time or that event. Some examples might be: letters, diaries, autobiographies, memoirs, maps, photographs, speeches, interviews, official records, and oral histories. A secondary source is typically a book or article that interprets or analyzes primary sources (it's *about* the thing instead of *being directly from* the thing).

8.   **What is a call number and what call number classification system does the GVSU Libraries use?**

A call number is the number that tells you where you can find a particular book or material in our collection. We use the Library of Congress Classification System. (LC Classification)

9.   **Scenario:**

A student is asking you for help in locating two library resources. Their professor gave them citations for each of the resources, but they aren't sure what kind of resources they are. Please take each of the citations below and label each of their parts (for example, "Author," "title," etc.) Also, please explain what type of resources they are (ex/ journal article, newspaper, eBook, book chapter, etc.).

Score one point for each accurately labeled part:

Resource #1:

O'Neil, J. M., & Egan, J. (1992). Men's and women's gender role journeys: A metaphor for healing, transition, and transformation. In B. R. Wainrib (Ed.), *Gender issues across the life cycle* (pp. 107-123). New York, NY: Springer.

Resource #2:

Bernstein, M. (2002). 10 tips on writing the living web. *A List Apart: For People Who Make Websites, 149*. Retrieved from https://www.alistapart.com/articles/writeliving

For questions 10-15:

2 points = the student's answer touches on most of the points outlined in the answer key

1 point = the student's answer is partially accurate

0 points = the student selected "I'm not sure" or the student's answer is not even partially correct

1.   **What are two resources students can utilize to safely walk to and from the library during late nights?**

o Safe walk

o Laker Guardian app (or Rave Guardian app)

2.   **If the library doesn't own a resource, what are two ways students can acquire those resources?**

o Mel

o ILL/Document Delivery

3.   **What is the role of liaison librarians and how do they help students?**

Liaison librarians work with particular disciplines within the University, so every course has a specific librarian who might work with that course. Liaison librarians facilitate instruction sessions on topics that relate to information literacy. They also provide one-on-one consultations with students who need help with research. Liaisons also develop the collection (purchase materials) for their subject areas.

4.   **What service does the library offer to provide students access to materials for specific courses?**

Course Reserve

5.   **Why does the library offer some peer-led services?**

To help student users feel more comfortable asking questions and to provide meaningful learning opportunities for student employees.

6.   **What are the Steps To Giving Great Service?**

o Be Approachable

o Understand

o Get It For Them

o Go The Extra Mile

7.   **What are some things you can do to provide an excellent customer service experience?**

(A "2" score could be given if they wrote 2-3 ways that relate to anything like the following)

o Focus on the user (don't multitask)

o Ask open-ended followup questions

o Listen carefully

o Walk users to their destination

o Refer users to the people that can help them

o Read the user's body language

8.   **What is implicit bias and how can it affect interactions at the desk?**

o Attitudes, assumptions, or stereotypes that we unconsciously hold about people or groups of people

o Can cause us to:

   ▪ Make assumptions about what a patron wants or needs

   ▪ Treat some patrons differently than others

   ▪ Give better services to some patrons than others

9.   **What are some ways you can provide inclusive customer service?**

(A "2" score could be given if they wrote 2-3 ways that relate to anything like the following)

o Not making assumptions

o Using gender-inclusive language

    ○ Any of the **Accessible Service Practices**

10. **What are some ways you can provide accessible customer service?**

    (A "2" score could be given if they wrote 2-3 ways that relate to anything like the following)

    ○ Any of the **Accessible Service Practices**

11. **Give two examples of person-first language you can use at the desk.**

    (A "2" score could be given if they wrote 2-3 ways that relate to anything like the following)

    ○ Person with a disability

    ○ Person who uses a wheelchair

    ○ Person with dyslexia

    ○ Person with autism

12. **Give two examples of gender inclusive language you can use at the desk.**

    (A "2" score could be given if they wrote 2-3 ways that relate to anything like the following)

    ○ "The patron with the green sweater", etc.

    ○ They/them pronouns

NOTES

1. Aaron Schmidt and Amanda Etches, *User Experience (UX) Design for Libraries* (New York: Neal-Schuman Publishers, Incorporated, 2012), 1.
2. Chip Heath and Dan Heath, *Made to Stick* (New York: Random House, 2007).
3. Grand Valley State University Libraries, "About the University Libraries." Accessed August 28, 2020. https://www.gvsu.edu/library/about-the-university-libraries-3.htm.
4. Kristin Meyer and Jennifer Torreano, "The Front Face of Library Services: How Student Employees Lead the Library at Grand Valley State University," in *Students Lead the Library: The Importance of Student Contributions to the Academic Library*, eds. Sara Arnold-Garza and Carissa Tomlinson (Chicago, IL: Association of College and Research Libraries, 2017), 40-42.
5. Kristin Meyer and Jennifer Torreano, "The Front Face of Library Services," 46.
6. Brian Merry and Kristin Meyer, "Student Employment Virtual Forum," ACRL Access Services Interest Group, webcast, February, 9, 2017, https://www.youtube.com/watch?time_continue=4&v=6y8TQgcKa9k.
7. Carlos Rodriguez, et al., "Understand, Identify, and Respond: The New Focus of Access Services," *portal: Libraries and the Academy* 17, no. 2 (2017), https://muse.jhu.edu/article/653207.
8. Kristin Meyer and Jennifer Torreano, "The Front Face of Library Services," 46.
9. Brian Merry and Kristin Meyer, "Student Employment Virtual Forum."
10. Paul-Jervis Heath, "Transforming Insights into Services" (presented at the conference UX Libs, Cambridge, UK, March 17–19, 2015), https://speakerdeck.com/pauljervisheath/transforming-insights-into-services.
11. Mari Kermit-Canfield, *Search & Destroy*, card game (Wunderkind, 2017).
12. Anne Meyer, David Howard Rose, and David Gordon, *Universal Design for Learning: Theory and Practice* (Wakefield, MA: CAST Professional Publishing, 2014), 9-11.
13. "Universal Design for Learning Guidelines version 2.2," CAST, last modified 2020. http://udlguidelines.cast.org/.
14. Grant P. Wiggins and Jay McTighe, *Understanding by Design*, 2nd ed. (Alexandria, VA: Association for Supervision and Curriculum Development, 2005,) 17-29.

15.   Grand Valley State University Libraries. *University Libraries Mission, Vision, and Values 2016-2021*, PDF file, 2016, https://www.gvsu.edu/cms4/asset/0862059E-9024-5893-1B5AAAC2F83BDDD8/library_mission_vision__values_2016_march_22.pdf.
16.   Kristin Meyer, Samantha Minnis, Kiersten Quilliams, "Accessible Customer Service Practices," policy document, 2019, https://scholarworks.gvsu.edu/cgi/viewcontent.cgi?article=1003&context=library_reports.
17.   Brian Merry and Kristin Meyer, "Student Employment Virtual Forum."
18.   Grand Valley State University, "Student Employment+." Accessed August 27, 2020. https://www.gvsu.edu/studentjobs/student-employment-45.htm.

BIBLIOGRAPHY

Grand Valley State University. "Student Employment+." Accessed August 27, 2020. https://www.gvsu.edu/studentjobs/student-employment-45.htm.

Grand Valley State University Libraries. "About the University Libraries." Accessed August 28, 2020. https://www.gvsu.edu/library/about-the-university-libraries-3.htm.

Grand Valley State University Libraries. *University Libraries Mission, Vision, and Values 2016-2021*. PDF file. 2016. https://www.gvsu.edu/cms4/asset/0862059E-9024-5893-1B5AAAC2F83BDDD8/library_mission_vision__values_2016_march_22.pdf.

Heath, Chip, and Dan Heath. *Made to Stick*. New York: Random House, 2007.

Heath, Paul-Jervis. "Transforming Insights into Services." Presented at the conference UX Libs, Cambridge, UK, March 17–19, 2015. https://speakerdeck.com/pauljervisheath/transforming-insights-into-services.

Kermit-Canfield, Mari. *Search & Destroy*. Card Game, Wunderkind, 2017.

Merry, Brian and Kristin Meyer. "Student Employment Virtual Forum." ACRL Access Services Interest Group. Webcast. February, 9, 2017. https://www.youtube.com/watch?time_continue=4&v=6y8TQgcKa9k.

Meyer, Anne, David Howard Rose, and David Gordon. *Universal Design for Learning: Theory and Practice*. Wakefield, MA: CAST Professional Publishing, 2014.

Meyer, Kristin and Erin Silva Fisher. "Designed to Meet our Institutional Mission." In *Assessing Library Spaces for Learning*. 73-82. Edited by Susan Montgomery. Landham, MD: Rowman & Littlefield, 2017.

Meyer, Kristin and Jennifer Torreano. "The Front Face of Library Services: How Student Employees Lead the Library at Grand Valley State University." In *Students Lead the Library: The Importance of Student Contributions to the Academic Library*. 39-56. Edited by Sara Arnold-Garza and Carissa Tomlinson. Chicago, IL: Association of College and Research Libraries, 2017.

Meyer, Kristin, Samantha Minnis, and Kiersten Quilliams. "Accessible Customer Service Practices." Policy Document. 2019. https://scholarworks.gvsu.edu/cgi/viewcontent.cgi?article=1003&context=library_reports.

Rodriguez, Carlos, Kristin Meyer, and Brian Merry. "Understand, Identify, and Respond: The New Focus of Access Services." *portal: Libraries and the Academy* 17, no. 2 (2017). https://muse.jhu.edu/article/653207.

Schmidt, Aaron, and Amanda Etches. *User Experience (UX) Design for Libraries*. New York: Neal-Schuman Publishers, Incorporated, 2012.

"Universal Design for Learning Guidelines version 2.2." CAST, last modified 2020. http://udlguidelines.cast.org/.

Wiggins, Grant P. and Jay McTighe. *Understanding by Design*, 2nd ed. Alexandria, VA: Association for Supervision and Curriculum Development, 2005.

Part IV

PERSPECTIVES FROM THE CONSULTANTS

YOU TRUST US WITH THIS?!

Susannah Kopecky

If someone had told me six years ago that I would be leading information literacy sessions, I would have laughed.

I would have laughed at such a prediction because, before 2010, only academic librarians led information literacy sessions at my university library. The structure was roughly thus: instructors (from a variety of disciplines) would contact their liaison librarian to set up a library orientation or information literacy session. Next, the librarian would schedule a day and time for the session (or series of sessions) and start planning. In 2010, I was a student assistant at the reference desk. Student employees of the library had little to do with information literacy sessions. My role as a reference desk student assistant was to assist students, faculty, and other patrons with their specific research inquiries. As specialized research assistants, we were able to tackle most queries, either by searching the library catalog for books (print and electronic), by searching for relevant articles on the article databases, or through some combination thereof. The closest I got to an information literacy session was waving at the students as they filed into the library classroom.

This all changed in the 2010–2011 school year. I had always enjoyed challenges and was eager to take on new projects and responsibilities at work. One day at the start of my shift, my immediate supervisor, a tenured academic librarian, called me to her office. As I settled into the soft upholstery, she asked me to take on a new challenge. Would I be interested in leading information literacy sessions and being one of the first students to do so at the university?

There was a sense of urgency in her request. She was planning to take a leave of absence. It was not clear when she would be coming back and she wanted to avoid significant disruptions in service to the students and faculty. These services included designing and executing custom sessions in academic-level research and library usage for courses in departments such as Communication and Education. Instructors had already lined up upcoming sessions and she did not want those sessions to be lost. In response, one other student worker and I took on the exciting (and frightening!) task of preparing ourselves to be information experts.

We were not entirely in the dark, however. We had received plenty of hands-on search time and we had demonstrated our abilities to assist patrons in a thoughtful and strategic manner. We were familiar with the article databases and how to narrow down broad topic queries into manageable and specific search terms. We knew the basic organizational structure of the library. We knew how to direct visitors to popular services and areas such as the print and copy center, the interlibrary loan pick-up desk, how to understand and decipher call numbers, how to request materials in storage, and so forth. We had quite a bit of experience working one-on-one with students and faculty to assist them in their school-related research. As students ourselves, my fellow student worker and I began discussing our knowledge of information-seeking behavior and information literacy. It was time to put those research skills to use!

What does it mean to be information literate? I started reading about the best practices of academic libraries and information science professionals. One still-cited source of a guiding definition of "information literacy" is the final report of the Presidential Committee on Information Literacy. This report defines information literacy as "be[ing] able to recognize when information is needed and hav[ing] the ability to locate, evaluate, and use effectively the needed information." Furthermore, the report also points out the long-lasting positive ramifications of an information-literate populace:

> Within America's information society, there also exists the potential of addressing many long–standing social and economic inequities. To reap such benefits, people—as individuals and as a nation—must be information literate…. Ultimately, information literate people are those who have learned how to learn. They know how to learn because they know how knowledge is organized, how to find information, and how to use information in such a way that others can learn from them. They are people prepared for lifelong learning, because they can always find the information needed for any task or decision at hand.

The Presidential Committee's report certainly put into words some of the observations we had already made about those who were information literate and how their behaviors had positive ramifications. However, we still had the dual challenge of conveying to our peers the value of being information literate while simultaneously convincing visiting professors that we were well-versed enough in the field of library science to be able to effectively convey that value to their students. As student workers in the library, we observed the importance of information literacy and heard it reinforced on a daily basis. I observed the impressive skills of the academic librarians who determined source credibility by asking probing questions of sources, questions I might not have considered, such as when an article was published, whether bias was present, and whether or not sources were cited. I helped the literate students who wanted scholarly articles on a topic so they could better understand a phenomenon and retain knowledge. I saw the professors who used high-quality research sources and were subsequently invited to publish their findings in academic journals. I spoke with instructors and community members who clearly stated a need for future employees or research assistants whose judgment could be relied on and who could demonstrate information literacy.

WHAT DID WE ALREADY KNOW AND HOW WOULD WE PREPARE?

The library is a gathering point, an inspiration incubator, and an intellectual hub of university life. As an employee of the library, I had already taken that fact to heart, having carefully selected the library as an employer precisely because of my own interest in the dynamic space of a library and its great potential. Though I was not a librarian, I began to think deeply about the responsibilities and expectations of a college librarian. What would the students and professors be expecting of me during our sessions? What roles does the librarian play in the lives of students? For example, one of the many tasks of a librarian is to follow trends in knowledge creation and information sharing. Understanding these trends requires the librarian to have a strong sense of what patrons need and want at any given time, to have a finger on the pulse of the community. This also requires a strong understanding of social trends and of sound judgment because the librarian, as master of limited resources, must determine exactly which information is most valuable for their particular patrons at that particular moment. The librarian is counted on to decide what information will be readily available for knowledge and learning.

As Donald Leu points out in "Toward a Theory of New Literacies Emerging from the Internet and Other Information and Communication Technologies," simply becoming literate and familiar with some text is a transformative experience: "Teaching a student to read is also a transforming experience. It opens new windows to the world and creates a lifetime of opportunities. Change defines our work as both literacy educators and researchers—by teaching a student to read, we change the world."

Would I be able to teach students how to be information literate in a veritable (and at times overwhelming) world of ideas?

Luckily, I had help. My supervising librarian had me observe her during multiple research presentations. We were to observe, take notes, and then meet together afterward to debrief, discuss our impressions, and ask questions. She also offered tips and teaching strategies, such as providing visuals to illustrate key concepts. With my fellow reference desk student assistant, we began to lead sessions together soon afterward. We would meet beforehand

and write up an outline of the topics we wanted to make sure to cover for that particular class. The content would include how to access the library's web page, how to access and search the library catalog, how to understand the Library of Congress call number system, and how to differentiate peer-reviewed journals from popular magazines. We also prepared to cover such professor-beloved topics as plagiarism and how and why to avoid it and how properly to cite sources. Typically, one of us would lead for the first half of the session and the second would then take over.

The sessions took place in different classrooms in the library. The rooms differed in size and shape, but all classrooms had desktop computers and a master computer at the front which was connected to a projector and a large screen. Thus, anything on the master computer could be projected on the large whiteboard for all the audience to see. We devised two models. The first model involved us alternating as speakers roughly every fifteen minutes. Ideally, in our allotted times, we would have covered basic key concepts, such as the Library of Congress call number system or the difference between a keyword search and a subject search. The second model we employed involved splitting the session in two, with one of us speaking for the first twenty to thirty minutes and the second speaking for the next twenty to thirty minutes. (The times differed, as some sessions were as short as forty-five or fifty minutes and others were nearly two hours.) We experimented with how much we would collaborate during our allotted times. Sometimes we would assist one another with the computer demonstrations and speak up during the other's allotted time, and other times, we would stand by silently, ready to assist if needed.

FLYING SOLO

After a few tag-team sessions, we began to lead sessions independently.

As a student myself, an early source of anxiety was over how to command the full attention of a classroom of individuals who were basically my peers. The best remedy to overcome this (plus feelings of "stage fright") was experience, experience, and more experience. Another strategy that paid off was implementing humor in my presentations. I cracked jokes with the class, picked surprising topics for searches (such as zombies or amusement parks), and was not afraid to embrace self-effacing humor when I ran into search roadblocks.

The peer-led sessions were so successful that soon we were invited to lead other librarians' instruction sessions.

After my original supervisor left, the new supervising librarian began observing our sessions. He became a terrific mentor to me. One of the characteristics I prized most about him was that he wanted to challenge me and to give me the tools to best help others. He would visit me at the reference desk and would talk about topics that would inevitably find their way into my later sessions. He focused on Boolean operators such as "and," "not," and "or," explaining in detail how each operator functioned and affected search results. He taught me about truncating terms and how that could broaden results. He would quiz us to make sure we understood relevant terms and topics in library science. He encouraged me to actively participate in the online library chat program. He also provided feedback on our library sessions and feedback on instructional methods. He keenly observed my style of delivery (giving an overview of the topic and circling between sub-topics) and encouraged me to further clarify my in-class goals and to consistently remind students of the steps needed to achieve those goals.

THE RESULTS

After a number of student-led library sessions, my supervisor began to hear highly positive feedback from instructors. Sensing the myriad of possibilities that this peer-to-peer instruction system presented, he devised a survey that students in our sessions would fill out at the conclusion of each session. The students were led to a survey link on the library web page, filled out the surveys, and submitted them within a matter of minutes. The survey was a way to determine student feelings about the peer-led orientation and to measure success in terms of information delivery, whether students were recognizing the utility of the sessions, and what information the students were taking away and favoring post-session. These post-session surveys were straightforward and asked students to provide their thoughts on the value of the sessions. The survey asked students to rate their general satisfaction regarding the following, by ranking responses 1 to 5, with 1 being lowest and 5 being highest: whether the session gave the student a solid understanding of the material presented; whether the resources described were relevant to the student's assignment or research topic; whether the session leader presented information in a way that was easily understandable; and whether the leader encouraged and responded to questions.

As our supervising librarian would later report back to us enthusiastically, the results spoke for themselves. In one example, in the early fall of 2011, the vast majority of students (nearly all) in my sessions gave me scores of 4 and 5, the two highest scores possible. The final question of the survey asked whether the students would recommend their fellow students attend a library orientation session like the one they just had. All students surveyed responded in an overwhelmingly positive way, with over 98 percent of those students responding "yes" to this final question. Throughout the years, students would often cite my energy and excitement as highly positive factors in their session experiences.

Anecdotally and through word of mouth, I was seeing the positive inroads I was making with my peers and with the instructors who were scheduling the information literacy sessions. One instructor of a freshman level-English course wrote the following in response to a session I led for her class: "…[Susie], who presented the session to my class last term, was outstanding. Some of my students mentioned that their time in the library with [Susie] was among the most valuable sessions of the term…. What that says about my [first] term as a teacher—I dare not conjecture; however, my students were very well-prepared to embark on their research after that library session. So, thanks again for offering this service." (This same glowing review and other similar ones would also be used when my wonderful supervisor nominated me as Outstanding Student Employee of the Year. University officials must have recognized the value of this peer-learning program, as I was selected as the second runner-up and was also the first library student assistant to be selected for this honor.)

The more at-ease I felt leading these sessions, the easier it was for students to see how passionate I was about libraries and information literacy, and they, too, realized that there was quite a lot for them to be excited about! Students began to visit me during my shifts at the reference desk, explaining how their friends had recommended me to them for research help. The success of this peer-learning program was really driven home to me one evening when a student recognized me at the school gym. She came over and introduced herself, telling me that her friend recommended coming to me for help on a research project.

Objectively, I could also see the same positive responses reflected in the surveys administered at the completion of the library sessions. The survey results for both my classes and the classes being led by my fellow student library workers showed a strong rate of satisfaction. As my inspiring supervisor pointed out, at one point, out of a possible score of 5, my average score (as rated by students in my sessions) was between a 4.5 and a 4.8. Other student assistants and I began to score even higher than the librarians, a fact which our wonderful and encouraging supervisor delighted in sharing with us.

I could do as many library instruction sessions per week as I liked, as long as I did not log more than twenty hours (the hourly part-time employee limit). After performing regularly, I had requests for repeat visits by the same instructors over multiple quarters. At the opening of each new academic quarter, I could regularly expect to visit the same instructors as last quarter. Each new quarter also brought new instructors and new challenges in the form of new assignments. No matter the assignment or its level of complexity or nuance, I always looked forward to showing the students how, with a little tenacity and a little patience, and the awareness of how to search intelligently, they could be successful researchers.

HOW THIS AFFECTED ME

Today, I am an academic librarian. I still lead information literacy/library orientation sessions, though this time I do so with the additional knowledge and professional responsibilities of a librarian. My experiences leading the peer-learning sessions had a lasting impact on my life. Those experiences informed me as a teacher. Today, I still employ the instructional strategies my supervisors suggested and I still use humor to put students at ease. The experience of leading those sessions gave me a clear view of the information-seeking behavior of students. Most importantly, those classes helped to clarify for me just how much I loved the library and its infinite possibilities and how I wanted to remain active and engaged in the field of information literacy.

None of this exploration would have been possible without the encouragement and trust the librarians had in me. They had faith that, given the tools and support, I could be an effective conduit of knowledge and link between the library and students. I was heartily encouraged by my supervising librarian, who was a positive, thoughtful, and caring mentor; his faith in me (and in my fellow student workers) made me excited to take on the challenge of teaching, and his encouragement and helpful feedback showed me that I could succeed! Such active and positive mentorship played a vital role in my experience.

In the end, both the students and the student leaders benefitted from this peer-learning experiment of sorts. Tellingly, three of the members of my cohort of peer leaders are now librarians. That fact alone speaks volumes about the excitement and possibility of allowing students to lead information literacy sessions and library orientations.

BIBLIOGRAPHY

American Library Association's Presidential Committee on Information Literacy. *Presidential Committee on Information Literacy: Final Report.* Washington, DC: American Library Association, 1989.

Leu, Jr., Donald J., Charles K. Kinzer, Julie L. Coiro, and Dana W. Cammack. "Toward a Theory of New Literacies Emerging From the Internet and Other Information and Communication Technologies." *Theoretical Models and Processes of Reading* 5, no 1 (2004): 1570–613.

A REFLECTION ON BEING A CONSULTANT

Caitlin Lewis

"Hi! Welcome to the Knowledge Market! My name is Caitlin and I'll be your consultant today." I brightly greeted my first-ever consultee. My smile—I hoped—masked the storm of butterflies that threatened to overwhelm me. As we walked to an open table, I reviewed everything I learned in training, and the butterflies relented. Slightly. We sat down and the rest is a happy blur because my training kicked in and we fell into easy conversation. The thing I remember most clearly is my consultee's comment after our session: "Thank you. I actually feel like I can complete my assignment now!" That's common in our consulting practice. In fact, 98 percent of the students who visit the research consultants at Grand Valley State University report feeling more confident in their abilities to complete their assignment.[1] I attribute this success to the training program I experienced, and there are many components of this program I think other schools should emulate to establish a successful research consultant service.

First, my program coordinators adhered to effective teaching practices when training new and returning consultants. For example, as noted by educational scholar George Hillocks, teachers who excel possess "specialized knowledge of students, of particular content and tasks, and how to represent and teach this knowledge."[2] Through a rigorous application and interview process, our coordinators gain this "specialized knowledge." They then use this knowledge of each consultant's strengths and weaknesses to format the initial training program to best fit each of our needs. Similarly, each semester, we have engaging training sessions that our coordinators plan based on our feedback and interests.

They also demonstrate effective teaching practices by following a Vygotskian notion of teaching and learning. As our initial training program progresses in difficulty, our coordinators deliberately guide us through our zones of proximal development until we can successfully complete a consultation independently.[3] The first experience we have is observing our coordinator conduct a mock-consultation. We then discuss scholarship on effective peer tutoring techniques which we then use to critique mock-consultations. After a cycle of observing and critiquing mock-consultations, we practice consulting with our peers to receive feedback. We then conduct an authentic and unannounced thirty-minute consultation with volunteer librarians. By going through this process, we are able to hone our abilities as consultants prior to our first consultation with a student. This structure greatly enhanced my sense of self-efficacy as a research consultant which, in turn, enabled me to enhance the confidence of the students with whom I work.

Another component that makes this training program effective is the time we spend reflecting on our practice. For example, according to Lana Danielson, chair of education at the University of Nebraska, reflection is a vital skill because it enables one "to identify and replicate best practice, refine serendipitous practice, and avoid inferior practice."[4] During training, our coordinators explicitly request us to reflect on our expectations for the training program, questions we have, and how we can use the new information and skills we have learned. Through this practice, I learned to reflect on my own consulting practice, which allowed me to adapt my consultation style to best accommodate each unique student.

The most important component of our training is the incorporating of effective collaboration among peers. Our coordinators empower us to become adept peer tutors by enabling ongoing peer support via our mentor groups. Our mentor groups operate without a coordinator present and are similar to William Glasser's "Learning Communities" in which learning is fostered through peer collaboration.[5] Professor and scholar Kenneth Bruffee states that collaborative learning such as this promotes the overall growth of an individual academically, socially, and personally, as agents of change.[6] Hence, mentor groups are quintessential for a successful service. Within these mentor groups, we discuss a variety of topics, such as providing feedback for difficult consultations, best practices for students who are English-language learners or who have a learning disability, the pros and cons of non-directive versus directive tutoring, etc. Additionally, our mentor groups allow us to explore and discuss any new ideas we have to better our service that we then can relate to our coordinators. Most importantly, our mentor groups allow us to learn from one another's experiences.

Ultimately, to establish a successful training program and, thus, a successful research consultant service, one must (1) have expert coordinators who follow effective teaching practices, (2) continuously practice and reflect upon the skills and abilities one has, (3) surround oneself in a support system of peers and expert mentors, and most importantly, (4) learn from one's mistakes to continuously improve the overall service.

NOTES

1. Mary O'Kelly et al., "Building a Peer-Learning Service for Students in an Academic Library," *portal: Libraries and the Academy* (2015): 174.
2. J. D. Wilhelm, *Strategic Reading: Guiding Students to Lifelong Literacy* (Portsmouth, NH: Boynton Publishers, Heinemann, 2001), 13.
3. Wilhelm, *Strategic Reading*, 10. According to Russian psychologist Lev Vygotsky, learners learn best when they are guided through their zones of proximal development via appropriate scaffolding and mentorship from the teacher.
4. Lana Danielson, "Fostering Reflection," in *Kaleidoscope: Contemporary and Classic Readings in Education*, eds. Kevin Ryan and James M. Cooper (Belmont, CA: Wadsworth, Cengage Learning, 2013), 26.
5. William Glasser, *Choice Theory in the Classroom* (New York: Harper Perennial, 1998), 81–85.
6. Kenneth A. Bruffee, "Collaborative Learning and the 'Conversation of Mankind,'" *College English* (1984): 649.

BIBLIOGRAPHY

Bruffee, Kenneth A. "Collaborative Learning and the 'Conversation of Mankind.'" *College English* 46 (7) (1984): 635–52.

Danielson, Lana. "Fostering Reflection." In *Kaleidoscope: Contemporary and Classic Readings in Education*, edited by Kevin Ryan and James M. Cooper, 26–31. Belmont, CA: Wadsworth, Cengage Learning, 2013.

Glasser, William. *Choice Theory in the Classroom*. New York: Harper Perennial, 1998.

O'Kelly, Mary, Julie Garrison, Brian Merry, and Jennifer Torreano. "Building a Peer-Learning Service for Students in an Academic Library." *portal: Libraries and the Academy* 15 (1) (2015): 163–82.

Wilhelm, Jeffery. *Strategic Reading: Guiding Students to Lifelong Literacy*. Portsmouth, NH: Boynton Publishers, Heinemann, 2001.

AUTHOR BIOGRAPHIES

Amanda Starkel. Amanda Starkel graduated with an MLS from Indiana University-Bloomington in 2009. She served as the Information Commons and eLearning Librarian at Butler University in Indianapolis, IN from 2013 to 2018. In this role, Amanda collaborated with the Center for Academic Technology to lead the Information Commons program. Her responsibilities included ongoing training and management of the student employees and two library staff members who provided circulation and reference at the library's single service point. Before joining Butler, Amanda served as the Instruction Librarian and Interim Library Director at Defiance College in Ohio.

Amy Benton. Dr. Benton is an associate professor of Educational Leadership at Samford University. She received a doctorate in Research Methodology from Loyola University of Chicago. Her research methodological expertise ranges from qualitative analysis to advanced statistical techniques. Dr. Benton works extensively with students in their continuing education to become teachers and administrators, as well as adult learners. She focuses on how learning occurs in the classroom as well as informal settings such as mentoring. She has presented both nationally and regionally and serves on several journals as a consulting editor.

Amy Wainwright. Amy Wainwright is the Head of Research, Learning, and Outreach at John Carroll University, just outside of Cleveland, OH. Amy's research focus is on cross-campus collaboration to support the whole student. In her spare time, Amy teaches Intro to Gender and Sexuality, spends a ton of time in the garden, is terrible at running, and reads without even getting paid for it.

Andrew Palahniuk. Andrew Palahniuk is the Lead of the Peer Research Consultant Program at the University of Minnesota Libraries. He also does instructional design work and information literacy instruction for the Libraries. Andrew earned a B.A. in anthropology and a B.A. in Spanish from the University of Minnesota.

Annie Donahue. Annie Donahue is an Associate Professor Emeritus and served as the Director of the UNH Manchester Library until her retirement in 2020. After completing a B.A. in Humanities from UNH Manchester and a MLS in Library Science from Southern Connecticut State University, she joined the faculty of UNH Manchester in 1998. In the ensuing years, she completed an ALM in Liberal Arts from Harvard University and an Ed.D. in Learning, Leadership, and Community from Plymouth State University. During her time at UNH Manchester, Dr. Donahue taught several undergraduate courses, including a Humanities Inquiry course entitled Everlasting Fame: The Hero in Literature, Film, & Popular Culture. She was also a member of the graduate faculty and regularly taught a graduate course entitled Classroom Research and Assessment Methods. Dr. Donahue also served the College and University in a variety of administrative appointments, such as Faculty Chair, Humanities Division; Interim Dean of the UNH Library; Executive Director for Experiential Learning; and Interim Assistant Dean for Student Engagement. Her scholarship focused on the collaborations between teaching and library faculty, assessing student learning, and integrating information literacy within the curriculum. She has shared her research nationally and internationally, and is published in several academic journals, including *Reference Services Review, Evidence Based Library and Information Practice, The Nordic Journal of Information Literacy in Higher Education*, and *Advances in Physiology Education*. Additionally, she is a co-author for several book chapters.

Brett B. Bodemer. Brett Bodemer is the College of Liberal Arts Librarian, Coordinator of Reference, and Coordinator of the Digital Projects Lab at the Robert E. Kennedy Library at Cal Poly, San Luis Obispo. After arriving at Cal Poly in 2009, he co-founded the LibRAT program, a peer-to-peer learning initiative in which undergraduates provide library research assistance and lead information literacy workshops. This model not only benefits the students, but has allowed Kennedy library to deliver hundreds of workshops annually to lower division courses. As coordinator of the Digital Projects Lab, he is teaming with Kennedy Library and Cal Poly colleagues to apply this same innovative approach in getting students in all disciplines to engage with key components of quantitative and visual literacy.

Caitlin Lewis. Caitlin Lewis graduated from Grand Valley State University with her degree in Secondary English Education and is currently an English Teacher at West Michigan Aviation Academy. At Grand Valley, she served as a peer research consultant for the Grand Valley State University Libraries for two years.

Carl Brown, PhD. Carl Brown in the Executive Director of the Grand Valley State University Speech Lab and an Assistant Professor of Communications. He has won multiple awards from the National Association of Communication Centers for both research and service. Brown primarily uses quantitative methods to study language and social interactions at the communication center.

Carolyn White Gamtso. Carolyn White Gamtso is an Associate Professor and the Director of the University of New Hampshire at Manchester Library. She is interested in creative information literacy initiatives, and enjoys working with faculty to design interactive, experiential student workshops. She collaborates with UNH Manchester's Center for Academic Enrichment to train writing tutors in information literacy skills as part of the college's Research Mentor Program. Carolyn's research interests include faculty/librarian classroom collaborations, and peer tutoring in the library. She has shared her scholarship in the area of library instruction at local, regional, national, and international conferences, and has co-authored articles and book chapters that discuss information literacy projects and practices. Carolyn earned a BA in English from the College of the Holy Cross, an MA in English from Indiana University, and an MLIS from the University of Rhode Island. She is an alumna of the ACRL Immersion Program (Teaching Track 2003 and Program Track 2017), and she is currently a student in the Doctorate of Education (EdD) Program at Plymouth State University.

Christopher Jones. Christopher Jones is the Special Collections Librarian and Archivist of the College at Grinnell College in Grinnell, Iowa. He earned a Bachelor's Degree in French from the University of Northern Iowa and a Master's Degree in Information and Library Science from the University of Illinois at Urbana-Champaign. Prior to his current position, Chris worked as a Library Assistant in Special Collections at Grinnell, a scanning center supervisor for the Internet Archive, and as an assistant to the Curator of Special Collections at the University of Illinois Urbana-Champaign.

Clinton Baugess. Clinton K. Baugess is a Research & Instruction Librarian and instruction coordinator at Gettysburg College's Musselman Library. He has been part of Musselman Library's peer research mentor program since its inception in 2014.

Dan Kelley. Dan Kelley worked at Lewis & Clark College for twenty years as a Research Librarian, the Information Literacy Coordinator and the Faculty Outreach Librarian. While there he directed semester-abroad programs to East Africa, Ecuador and Australia, served on the curriculum committee, and worked closely with the humanities and social sciences departments. After spending time as Director of Library Services at the Oregon College of Art and Craft he currently serves as Head Librarian at the International School in Portland, Oregon. He is an advocate of international education and the value of reading and of critical inquiry. Dan studied in Cologne Germany as a Fulbright Exchange student before attending university. He studied history and political science at Indiana University and received his MLIS from the University of Maryland. He can be reached at danklibrarian@gmail.com.

Danielle Leek. Danielle Leek, Ph.D, is the Dean of Online Learning at Reynolds Community College in Richmond, VA where she oversees the Center for Excellence in Teaching & Learning. As an Associate Professor of Communications at Grand Valley State University she founded the Speech Lab. Professor Leek was recognized with the 2014 National Association of Communication Centers Von Till Award for excellence.

Donald Welsh. Don was formerly the Head of the Research Department at Swem Library at the College of William and Mary where he has also served as the Acting Associate Dean for Research and Public Services and as Head of the Reference Department. Previously, he was Philosophy and Religion Bibliographer at Mugar Library at Boston University. Don has a B.A. from the University of South Carolina, an M.S.L.S from the University of North Carolina, and an M.L.A. from Boston University. He is now retired and living in New York City.

Elise Silva. Elise Silva is the former Writing Programs Librarian and Freshman Programs Librarian at Brigham Young University. She is currently pursuing her PhD in English composition at the University of Pittsburgh where she studies student information habits in writing contexts. She holds Master's degrees in Information Science and English.

Emily Mann. Emily Mann is currently an assistant librarian at University of South Florida Libraries St. Petersburg Campus where she focuses on undergraduate student success including data literacy and diversity and inclusion. Previously, she served as the Research Services and Information librarian at Florida State University Libraries where she created, implemented and supervised the reference associate program. She has left the program in the capable hands of Elizabeth Dunn, the current Instruction and Reference librarian and a former reference associate.

Heidi Gauder. Heidi Gauder is professor and coordinator of research & instruction at the University of Dayton. She chairs the Instruction and Research Teams of Roesch Library, coordinating and scheduling the work of the team members. She is the subject liaison to the History and Political Science Departments, and the Honors Program.

Janelle Wertzberger. Janelle Wertzberger is Assistant Dean and Director of Scholarly Communications at Gettysburg College's Musselman Library. Previously she served as Director of Reference & Instruction, where she helped design and launch the peer research mentor program.

Jennifer Torreano. Jennifer Torreano is the Knowledge Market Manager for the Grand Valley State University Libraries. She earned her Master's degree in higher education at GVSU. Jennifer is responsible for the Library Research Center and the coordination of the Knowledge Market, a collaborative partnership between the Library Research Center, Speech Lab, and Writing Center. Her research interests include peer learning, student development, and the intersections of cognitive bias and information literacy.

Jill Markgraf. Jill Markgraf, professor, is Director of Libraries at the University of Wisconsin-Eau Claire. She is co-author of the book, *Maximizing the One-Shot: Connecting Library Instruction with the Curriculum.*

Jody Gray. Jody Gray (she/hers) is currently the Director of the Office for Diversity and Inclusion (ODI) in the College of Food, Agricultural and Natural Resource Sciences

(CFANS) at the University of Minnesota. Jody has worked in the arena of equity, diversity, and inclusion for over 15 years. Previously, she held the position of Diversity Outreach Librarian for the University of Minnesota Libraries from 2005-2015. She has also been the Director of the Office for Diversity, Literacy and Outreach Services at the American Library Association in Chicago, IL from 2015-2019. Jody has a Master of Information Science from the University of Wisconsin, Milwaukee, and a Bachelor of Arts from the University of Minnesota, Morris. Jody is an enrolled member of the Cheyenne River Sioux Tribe of South Dakota.

Jonathan R. Paulo. Jonathan is an Online Learning and Reference Librarian at Harvard University in Cambridge, Massachusetts. Before joining Harvard in 2015, from 2010-2015 he was the Education Librarian at James Madison University in Harrisonburg, Virginia. Jonathan received his MLIS from San Jose State University and his BA from James Madison University.

Kaila Bussert. Kaila Bussert is the Foundational Experiences Librarian at the Robert E. Kennedy Library at Cal Poly, San Luis Obispo where she leads a foundational information literacy program. Her research and teaching interests center on the role of visual literacy across the disciplines of science, technology, engineering, arts, and mathematics. She is a co-author of the book *Visual Literacy for Libraries: A Practical, Standards-Based Guide* published by ALA Editions in 2016. She holds an MA in Near Eastern Studies and an MLIS from the University of Arizona.

Kate Peterson. Kate Peterson is the Undergraduate Services Librarian at the University of Minnesota-Twin Cities. She joined the University in 2008 and is the librarian for Writing Studies, First Year Writing, the University Honors Program and supports Orientation and First-Year Experience courses. Her MLIS is from the University of Wisconsin-Madison and her previous institutions include the California State University, Long Beach, St. Cloud State University and Capella University.

Katherine Baker. Katherine Baker worked as a Graduate Assistant for the John Carroll University Library Learning Commons. She is now working as a School Psychologist in the Cleveland Metropolitan School District. In her free time, Katherine enjoys walking her dogs, reading, and spending time outdoors.

Kate Hinnant. Kate Hinnant, associate professor, is the Head of Instruction and Communication at McIntyre Library at the University of Wisconsin-Eau Claire. She is the co-author of Making Surveys Work For Your Library.

Kelly Miller-Martin. Kelly is Director of Facilities Operations for the James Madison University Libraries where she has held a number of positions including Access Services Manager for JMU's Rose Library.

Kiersten Quilliams. Kiersten Quilliams' (she/her) love for learning new things led her to libraries, where she solves new puzzles every day. Kiersten is currently a Library Specialist for Grand Valley State University Libraries, where she is a part of the User Experience (UX) team and is passionate about graphic design, accessibility, and how libraries can support non-traditional/adult students.

Kim Donovan. Kim Donovan is the Director of the Center for Academic Enrichment at the University of New Hampshire at Manchester. Previously, she was an assistant professor of English at Southern New Hampshire University. She has taught college composition and coordinated writing tutoring since 2000, following a thirteen-year career in secondary English teaching that included serving as department chair and district K-12 Language Arts coordinator. A previous doctoral candidate in Composition and TESOL at Indiana University of Pennsylvania, and current doctoral student in Educational Leadership at Plymouth State University, she is interested in writing and learning center pedagogy, first-year writing, writing across the curriculum, and access in higher education.

Kristin Kerbavaz. Kristin Kerbavaz is the Strategic Assessment Librarian at Grand Valley State University. Her current research focuses on library assessment and the student employee experience, with particular emphasis on professional development and mentorship for LIS graduate students.

Kristin Meyer. Kristin Meyer is the User Experience Librarian at Grand Valley State University and a Certified Customer Experience Professional. Kristin has worked in libraries for nineteen years and is passionate about design thinking, creating user-centered library spaces and services, and training and development.

Lauren Manninen. Lauren was formerly the Science Librarian at William & Mary Libraries where she worked to develop a program for a triaged Research service point. She has a B.S. in Wildlife Management and a M.S. in Biology from Eastern Kentucky University and a M.S. in Library Science from the University of Kentucky. She currently lives in Hawaii with her family where she runs a small business and plays Dungeons & Dragons regularly.

Mallory Jallas. Mallory Jallas is the Student Success Librarian at Illinois State University. Her work centers on connecting students with the library's services and collections to support their academic and personal success. Previously she served as Research & Instruction Librarian at Musselman Library at Gettysburg College, where she co-coordinated the peer research mentor program.

Mary Kathleen O'Kelly. Mary is the Associate Dean for Education and User Services at Western Michigan University. Previously she served as the head of instructional services at Grand Valley State University, where she was responsible for developing and evaluating a training program for student peer research consultants in the GVSU Knowledge Market. Her work at both institutions has been deeply involved with student-focused academic programming, professional development for faculty and staff, embedding information literacy into the curriculum, online and hybrid learning, and assessment. Mary has published and presented nationally on peer research consulting programs in academic libraries and has a deep interest in the relationship between library services and student success.

Maya Hobscheid. Maya Hobscheid is the Instructional Design Librarian at Grand Valley State University. Her research and professional interests include pedagogical approaches to learning and teaching, with a focus on Universal Design for Learning and Trauma Informed pedagogies, and student learning assessment.

Meggan Smith. Meggan Smith is a Research & Instruction Librarian and reference services coordinator at Gettysburg College's Musselman Library. She has co-coordinated the Musselman Library's peer research mentor program since its inception in 2014.

Melanie Rabine. Melanie Rabine is the Digital Student Experience Specialist for Grand Valley State University Libraries. She investigates the ways in which the Knowledge Market is best supporting the virtual needs of students while they learn and of student library colleagues while they work. She also manages the digital consulting service. Melanie earned her M.Ed in Literacy and TESOL from GVSU. Her scholarly interests include learning and teaching with technology, client privacy, service transparency, and linguistic diversity.

Michelle Millet. Michelle Millet is the Director of the Grasselli Library & Breen Learning Center. She works to ensure that the library is an engaging and enriching atmosphere for all students. In her spare time, she moms, walks dogs, feeds cats, and loves tacos.

Patrick Johnson. Patrick Johnson is the full-time Director of the Fred Meijer Center for Writing and Michigan Authors. He earned his Master's degree in Rhetoric and Composition from Washington State University, followed by several years of work as a writing tutor, teacher, and Writing Center Coordinator. His scholarship and presentations have focused on small-group tutoring, program assessment, teaching, and tutor training. He enjoys movies, books, and games from any medium or genre, hates pickles, and has an inexplicable love of rain.

Phil Jones. Phil Jones [jonesphi@grinnell.edu] is Humanities Librarian and Coordinator of Research Services for Grinnell College Libraries. Phil holds BA degrees in Psychology from Purdue and in Spanish from Adams State University, an MA in English from the University of Kentucky, and an MLIS from the University of Arizona.

Stefanie E. Warlick. Stefanie is an Interim Associate Dean of Libraries and Professor at James Madison University. She received her Master of Science, Library Science at the University of North Carolina at Chapel Hill, School of Information and Library Science.

Susannah Kopecky. Susie Kopecky is a librarian and associate professor in sunny California. She loves libraries, information literacy, teaching research skills, and eating delicious food. She is often found reading a book, and she once set a goal of reading 100 books in a year. (She ended up reading 102.)

Suzanne Julian. Suzanne Julian is the Library Instruction Coordinator at Brigham Young University. Her responsibilities include administrative oversight for the Research and Writing Center and assessment of information literacy instruction. She has Master's degrees in Library Science and Education.